"Focusing on the Hakkas in northwest Taiwan, Christofferson finds the traditional 'people group' lens insufficient to understand the tensions of being Hakka and being Christian. Through interviews with thirty-six cultural informants, Christofferson identifies the fixity and fluidity of the way Hakkas think and act. This study effectively moves beyond a static understanding of ethnicity to, in the conclusion, providing insights and recommendations for ministry in a globalizing world of hybrid ethnic identities."

—RICHARD R. COOK,
Associate Professor of Church History and Missions, Logos Evangelical Seminary

Negotiating Identity

American Society of Missiology
Monograph Series

THE ASM MONOGRAPH SERIES provides a forum for publishing quality dissertations and studies in the field of missiology. Collaborating with Pickwick Publications—a division of Wipf and Stock Publishers of Eugene, Oregon—the American Society of Missiology selects high quality dissertations and other monographic studies that offer research materials in mission studies for scholars, mission and church leaders, and the academic community at large. The ASM seeks scholarly work for publication in the Series that throws light on issues confronting Christian world mission in its cultural, social, historical, biblical, and theological dimensions.

Missiology is an academic field that brings together scholars whose professional training ranges from doctoral-level preparation in areas such as scripture, history and sociology of religions, anthropology, theology, international relations, interreligious interchange, mission history, inculturation, and church law. The American Society of Missiology, which sponsors this series, is an ecumenical body drawing members from Independent and Ecumenical Protestant, Catholic, Orthodox, and other traditions. Members of the ASM are united by their commitment to reflect on and do scholarly work relating to both mission history and the present-day mission of the church. The ASM Monograph Series aims to publish works of exceptional merit on specialized topics, with particular attention given to work by younger scholars, the dissemination and publication of which is difficult under the economic pressures of standard publishing models.

Persons seeking information about the ASM or the guidelines for having their dissertations considered for publication in the ASM Monograph Series should consult the Society's website—www.asmweb.org.

Members of the ASM Monograph Committee who approved this book are:

Michael A. Rynkiewich, Asbury Theological Seminary
Paul V. Kollman, CSC, University of Notre Dame
Roger Schroeder, SVD, Catholic Theological Union

PREVIOUSLY PUBLISHED IN THE ASM MONOGRAPH SERIES

David J. Endres, *American Crusade: Catholic Youth in the World Mission Movement from World War l through Vatican ll*

W. Jay Moon, *African Proverbs Reveal Christianity in Culture: A Narrative Portrayal of Builsa Proverbs Contextualizing Christianity in Ghana*

E. Paul Balisky, *Wolaitta Evangelists: A Study of Religious Innovation in Southern Ethiopia, 1937–1975*

Auli Vähäkangas, *Christian Couples Coping with Childlessness: Narratives from Machame, Kilimanjaro*

Negotiating Identity

Exploring Tensions between Being Hakka and Being Christian in Northwestern Taiwan

ETHAN J. CHRISTOFFERSON

American Society of Missiology
Monograph Series

VOL. 13

⌘PICKWICK Publications · Eugene, Oregon

NEGOTIATING IDENTITY
Exploring Tensions between Being Hakka and Being Christian in Northwestern Taiwan

American Society of Missiology Monograph Series #13

Copyright © 2012 Ethan J. Christofferson. All rights reserved. Except for brief quotations in critical publications or reviews, no part of this book may be reproduced in any manner without prior written permission from the publisher. Write: Permissions, Wipf and Stock Publishers, 199 W. 8th Ave., Suite 3, Eugene, OR 97401.

Pickwick Publications
An Imprint of Wipf and Stock Publishers
199 W. 8th Ave., Suite 3
Eugene, OR 97401

www.wipfandstock.com

ISBN 13: 978-1-61097-503-2

Cataloging-in-Publication data:

Christofferson, Ethan J.

   Negotiating identity : exploring tensions between being Hakka and being Christian in northwestern Taiwan / Ethan J. Christofferson.

   xvi + 316 p. ; cm. — Includes bibliographical references and index(es).

   American Society of Missiology Monograph Series #13

   ISBN 13: 978-1-61097-503-2

   1. Taiwan—Religion and Culture. 2. Missions—Taiwan. 3. Hakka (Chinese people)—Ethnic identity. 4. Hakka (Chinese people)—Missions. I. Title. II. Series.

BR1298 C33 2012

Manufactured in the U.S.A.

All scripture quotations, unless otherwise indicated, are taken from the Holy Bible, International Version®, NIV®. Copyright ©1973, 1978, 1984, 2011 by Biblica, Inc.™ Used by permission of Zondervan. All rights reserved worldwide. www.zondervan.com.

*Dedicated to my wife, Sandy,
and to our children, Caleb and Hannah*

Contents

List of Tables / ix
Acknowledgments / xi
List of Abbreviations / xii
Introduction / xiii

1 Research Problem / 1
2 Precedent Literature / 13
3 Research Methodology / 96
4 Being Hakka in Northwestern Taiwan / 110
5 Non-Christian Hakkas in Northwestern Taiwan and Being Christian / 179
6 Christian Hakkas in Northwestern Taiwan in the Context of Negative Categorizations of Being Christian / 214
7 Summary, Implications, and Recommendations / 265

Appendix 1: Interview Questions / 287
Appendix 2: Three-Memorials Ceremony / 291

Bibliography / 293
Index / 303

Tables

Table 1: Taiwan Social Change Survey Respondents Who Identified Themselves as Christian—According to Year and Ethnic Identity / 86

Table 2: Profile of Interview Sample / 101

Table 3: Detailed Information about Interview Sample / 103

Acknowledgments

I AM INDEBTED TO the many people who have contributed to making this book possible. I am grateful to Robert J. Priest, Tite Tiénou, and Richard Cook, for their wisdom, encouragement, guidance, and suggestions that helped shape and mature the ethnographic research project detailed here. I am thankful for the enthusiastic support of Matthew Rogness and my other colleagues at Lutheran Brethren International Mission (LBIM). I am indebted to the many Hakkas who have welcomed and embraced me and my family, taught us so much about life in Taiwan, and helped me in this study.

I am thankful to my parents, Arve and Marilyn Christofferson, for their prayers and encouragement and for instilling in me a desire to share the gospel with the unreached. I am especially grateful to my wife, Sandy, for her endless sacrificial love. Without her support and continuous help, this book would not have been possible. Caleb and Hannah have also been a great encouragement to me.

Most of all, I am thankful to God for His tenacious love for me, for the opportunity that He provided for me to pursue this study, and for the wisdom, endurance, and strength to be able to complete it. I am blessed!

Abbreviations

CHEA Christian Hakka Evangelical Association

DPP   Democratic Progressive Party

HMS   Hakka Mission Seminary

HUP   Homogeneous Unit Principle

KMT   Nationalist Party, Chinese Nationalists

PCT   Presbyterian Church in Taiwan

TSCS Taiwan Social Change Survey

Introduction

THE ETHNOGRAPHIC RESEARCH PROJECT detailed in this book addresses the question of why the Hakka Chinese Christian community in Taiwan is known to be very small despite evangelistic efforts on this island for more than 140 years. This project proceeds by exploring the tensions between being Hakka and being Christian in northwestern Taiwan and what both Hakka non-Christians and Christians are doing and saying in the context of these tensions. In doing so, this study provides insights that can help Christian workers ministering in Taiwan to better understand Hakka ministry settings there. This study looks at being Hakka and being Christian through the lens of social constructionism (especially as it is worked out in the context of discussing ethnicity and ethnic groups) and consequently also offers an example of how the social science scholarship in this area can help Christian workers in a variety of contexts to understand and more effectively interact with those around them.

This study was stimulated by the author's experience that the people group lens, one commonly used by Christians to talk about and seek to understand people in cross-cultural missionary and other ministry settings, was inadequate to explain the complexities he encountered in ministry among Hakkas in Taiwan. In the first chapter, the author's experience of using the people group lens to conceptualize his ministry to Hakkas in northwestern Taiwan is shared with the desire to help the reader understand the context in which this study emerged. This chapter also details the important aspects of this study: the research concern, the significance of this study, some definitions of key terms, a note on translation, the research context, some important assumptions, a statement of the problem this study is seeking to address, the research questions that provide direction for this study, and some key delimitations.

The second chapter acquaints the reader with what scholars are saying in four areas that are important for this research project. First, a brief look at the literature on the Homogeneous Unit Principle (HUP), an understanding of society from which the emphasis on people groups that is commonly used in mission circles initially emerged, helps the reader better understand this concept, reveals some concerns with the HUP, and highlights the need to engage the social science scholarship in the area of ethnicity and ethnic groups. Second, a major section detailing the scholarly conversations about ethnic identification among social scientists serves to set a theoretical framework for this study. This section is of particular interest for readers seeking a deeper understanding of the social constructionist lens on ethnicity and ethnic groups. A third area of scholarly writings discussed in this chapter details important aspects of being Hakka in Taiwan and provides insight into the cultural "stuff" shaping those who are being Hakka in northwestern Taiwan and serving as a reservoir of symbols and habits for them as they relate to being Christian. Finally, a review of the writings about Christian ministry to those who are being Hakka in Taiwan supplies essential information about the cultural "stuff" that is influencing and providing a repertoire of symbols and habits for Christians who are engaged in Hakka ministries to use as they respond in the context of tensions that surface as those who are being Hakka relate to being Christian.

Chapter 3 details the research methodology used in the face-to-face interviews conducted in the course of this study. Basic interpretive qualitative research is explained to help the reader understand the principles guiding the researcher throughout these interviews and the analysis of the procured data. The subjective nature of this research is discussed as well as efforts that were made to control this subjectivity. Finally, the data-gathering and analysis procedures are summarized. Details about the interview sample—the thirty-six informants who were interviewed for this project—are included to help readers understand the diversity of this sample as well as some factors that may be influencing each informant. The nature of the actual interviews and the way the researcher developed and revised the questions that were used are discussed. Also described is the six-step procedure used to process and analyze the data procured in these interviews.

In the fourth through sixth chapters, the responses of informants are discussed according to themes and topics that emerged as interview data was analyzed. The fourth chapter elaborates how Hakkas talk about being Hakka—the meanings and boundaries they associate with this ethnic identity—providing a description of the responses of informants to interview questions in this area. The symbols that most frequently surfaced as informants talked about being Hakka in Taiwan, especially those related to being Christian, are grouped into five themes. The responses informants gave as they were queried about the boundary markers of being Hakka are mapped out and discussed. Also enumerated is the variety of feelings that informants reported emerge when Hakkas think about being Hakka. The fixity and fluidity present in the way Hakkas think and act is highlighted throughout the discussion.

Chapter 5 focuses on the way Hakkas perceive and respond to being Christian. The negative categorizations of being Christian that surfaced as informants answered questions about the thoughts and actions of Hakkas in this area are reported and discussed. These negative categorizations are organized according to the same five themes that surfaced in chapter 4. The close connection between these categorizations and the cultural "stuff" of being Hakka is detailed and underscored. The fixity and fluidity evidenced in these categorizations are also recounted and reflected upon.

The topic of the sixth chapter is the way Hakka Christians are responding in the context of the negative categorizations of Hakka non-Christians. In this topic area, informants discussed the way Hakka Christian leaders emphasize the Hakka dimension of their ministries to differing extents. Also detailed are some of the narratives and actions that Hakka Christians use to contest these negative categorizations. How Hakka Christians construct Hakka in order to justify prioritizing ministry to Hakkas is also related. The chapter ends with a discussion of how these three kinds of responses reveal that Hakka Christians, too, are involved in the process of ethnic identification.

The final chapter summarizes the findings of this ethnographic research project and then details three categories of implications and recommendations for ministry. First, general thoughts applying to Christian workers living and working in various contexts are articulated. Next, implications and recommendations that are related to the use of the people group perspective to view ministry settings are offered. In this topic area, some reasons why the people group lens is so widely used as well as some of its weaknesses are discussed. An alternative lens of negotiating identity is described, and the helpfulness of using this lens in ministry settings is explained. The third category of implications and recommendations is those that specifically relate to Christian workers working among the

Hakkas of northwestern Taiwan. The chapter closes with some recommendations for further research.

I

Research Problem

THIS CHAPTER RECOUNTS THE author's experience of looking at a ministry setting through the lens of people groups (see chapter 7 for a further discussion of this perspective) and introduces some important aspects of the ethnographic research project which this book entails—the research concern, the significance of this study, some definitions of key terms, an important note about translation, a short description of the research context, some important assumptions, a statement of the problem that this study is seeking to address, the research questions that provide direction for this study, and some key delimitations.

An Experience of Looking at a Ministry Setting Through the Lens of People Groups

It was during my undergraduate years in college in the early 1980s that I first learned about the Hakka Chinese of Taiwan. The group of churches to which I belong had recently begun a church-planting ministry among these Hakkas, and Christians around me often spoke of the great spiritual need among this group of people. I had also recently learned about the concept of an unreached people group (defined as "an ethnolinguistic people among whom there is no viable indigenous community of believing Christians with adequate numbers and resources to evangelize their own people without outside [cross-cultural] assistance."[1]) in a course called "Perspectives on the World Christian Movement." I possessed a strong desire to invest my life in a location in the world where the spiritual need was great—to spend my life working to "reach" an unreached people group.

1. Mandryk, *Operation World*, 962.

I began praying for the Hakkas of Taiwan, reading everything I could about them, and seeking God's will about the possibility of becoming a missionary among them. When I read in a book by David C. E. Liao[2] that only three out of every one thousand Hakkas were Christians, a significantly lower percentage than that of the other ethnic groups in Taiwan, my interest was particularly piqued. I wanted to be a part of a team of people working to provide opportunities for Hakkas to hear the gospel. The doors opened for me to go, and, in 1990, I embarked on a career as a missionary working among Hakkas of Taiwan.

Upon my arrival in Taiwan, I began diligently working to understand the language and culture of Hakkas around me. Influenced by Liao and his Homogeneous Unit Principle (HUP) thinking (see chapter 2), I strove to learn Hakka ways so that I could make it possible for Hakkas to hear the gospel without requiring them to cross group and cultural boundaries. I strongly believed that developing an evangelistic and church-planting approach that was truly Hakka was a strategic and responsible way to work as a missionary among them. I went through a "bonding" period, living with a Hakka family and deliberately distancing myself from non-Hakkas for the first six weeks of my time in Taiwan. I understood that this sort of arrangement would enable me to develop deeper relationships with Hakkas and a better understanding of their culture. Even though Mandarin Chinese is the national language in Taiwan and fluency in this language is exceedingly beneficial, I intentionally chose not to learn Mandarin (at that point), focusing all of my efforts on learning the Hakka language.

During my first year in Taiwan, I progressed at an exhilarating pace. Wherever I went, Hakkas seemed excited and curious that a Westerner would want to learn to speak Hakka. One middle-aged Hakka man was so moved by my desire that he volunteered to help me in my endeavors, and he came to my home almost daily to serve as my primary language and culture teacher. We were both encouraged and proud when someone would occasionally say to us, "This foreigner is more Hakka than we are."

The perspective of the other missionaries on our Hakka church-planting team was also in harmony with Liao's point of view. We were unified in the belief that if we focused our ministry on Hakkas and used the Hakka language in our church-planting efforts, Hakkas would be more likely to respond positively to the gospel. We understood that Hakkas had certain characteristics, and we tried to develop ministries that would

2. Liao, *Unresponsive*.

engage and honor people with these characteristics. For example, believing that Hakkas highly value the Hakka language, we strongly insisted on using this language in our ministry, even when it was exceedingly inconvenient. We rejoiced when the "Today's Taiwan Hakka Version" of the New Testament and Psalms[3] was published, and we used it prodigiously to share God's Word in public and private settings. We were overjoyed when someone wrote a new Hakka Christian song, and we used Hakka music as much as possible in our ministries. Several of us even learned to play some Chinese musical instruments so that, when we sang these new songs in meetings, a real Hakka flavor emerged.

Yet it was not long before I started noticing that Hakkas did not always act in ways I expected. Non-Christian Hakkas were not noticeably more responsive to our efforts to engage them than they were to those ministries that were not using our strategies. While many were fascinated with foreigners who spoke Hakka and who valued Hakka things, these non-Christians still had significant obstacles keeping them from really hearing and considering the gospel. Many Hakka Christians also were not interested in focusing so strongly on being Hakka. For example, I once tried to give a gift of recently published Hakka language New Testaments to our church in the name of a Hakka couple as a way of honoring and thanking them for their kindness to us. In a very uncharacteristically direct response, this couple strongly opposed my intended gift and rejected having their name associated with such a gift. As I explored their response further, I found that they did not want to have to use the Hakka language scriptures in our Hakka church and preferred to continue using the Mandarin Bible. I remember being flabbergasted and thinking to myself, "Aren't they Hakka?" I was even more baffled when many of the other Hakkas in our Hakka church seemed to resonate with their negative response.

I was also puzzled by the many Hakkas who were not using the Hakka language—the language that many would refer to as their "heart language" or the language used to discuss matters close to their hearts. For example, I noticed that Hakka pastors in a group of churches known for their burden for and emphasis on Hakka were rarely using the Hakka language in their worship services. I observed that many young Hakkas I encountered could not speak the Hakka language, and I met several Hakka adults living in Hakka areas who preferred to speak Mandarin Chinese rather than Hakka.

3. Zhonghuaminguo Shengjing Gonghui, *New Testament and Psalms*.

For example, a Hakka woman in one of our ministry groups quit attending, saying she did not want to come anymore because she did not like to speak and sing songs in Hakka whenever our group met.

The response of our missionary team to attitudes like these was to assure the Hakkas around us that their Hakka identity and language was not something to hide, but rather something of which to be proud. We gently chided our Hakka Christian brothers and sisters for not caring enough about their own people to be willing to change their own habits and be as Hakka as possible in order to reach them. We tried to show these Hakka Christians that if Hakkas were going to come into the church, the church needed to be a place where Hakkas could feel at home. We talked about speaking to Hakkas about the things of God in their "heart language" rather than in Mandarin Chinese, the language usually used in schools and government offices. We also encouraged them to use the portions of the Hakka-language Bible that were available and to learn to sing the Hakka songs written by Christians.

The conflict between what I expected Hakkas to do and the attitudes I observed in my Hakka friends climaxed six months after I transitioned out of the Hakka church in which I had served as a pastor and moved back to America to begin my doctoral studies. I received a telephone call from the new pastor, my good friend and long-time colleague in that church, informing me of the decision that the church board had made to end the more than twenty-year old practice of having the sermon preached in the Hakka language (with a simultaneous translation into Mandarin Chinese). The Christians in this church had had constant and deep contact with members of our Hakka church-planting missionary team for more than twenty years; they had heard us frequently talk about the importance of being as Hakka as possible to reach Hakkas. I remember thinking, "If any church were to embrace this principle, this church should have been the one." As I pondered this new development, several questions came to my mind: "Why do Hakkas often not act like Hakkas?" "Is there a Hakka way and if so, what exactly is it?" "If the Hakkas in Taiwan are not just a group of people who have certain characteristics or a common way, how can I think about them in ways that will better facilitate my ministry as a missionary among them?" "Is there something about being Hakka that makes Hakkas less responsive to the gospel?" Motivated to find answers to these questions and others like them, I embarked on a study of related scholarly literature and then designed and implemented an ethnographic research project, all of which is detailed in this book.

Research Concern

This study is concerned with the small size of the Hakka Christian church in Taiwan despite evangelistic efforts by expatriate missionaries and local Christians on this island for more than 140 years. According to Jason Mandryk in *Operation World*, 2.8 percent of the total population of Taiwan but only 0.35 percent of Hakkas identified themselves to be evangelical Christians in 2010.[4] This study assumes that the small size of the Hakka Christian community is a problem and that there are things that can be done to better facilitate the growth of the Hakka church. A better understanding of tensions between being Hakka and being Christian is thought to be helpful for missionaries and local Christians seeking to become more effective in engaging and evangelizing Hakkas in Taiwan.

Significance of Research

This research is significant because an increased understanding of the dynamics of the relationship between those who are being Hakka and their perceptions of Christians and Christianity will help expatriate missionaries and local Christians to more effectively share the gospel with their non-Christian relatives, friends, colleagues, and neighbors who are Hakka. Like a medical doctor who deepens his/her understanding of the workings of the human body in order to better treat a patient, a better understanding of the situation at hand can help missionaries and national Christians determine the most appropriate things to say and do as they relate in evangelism and other ministry contexts with those who are being Hakka. This study is unique; no scholar has looked at the problem of the small size of the Hakka Christian community in Taiwan through the social constructionist lens on ethnicity and ethnic groups. In fact, only a few scholars have applied the wealth of social science scholarship regarding ethnicity and ethnic groups to other specific mission endeavors in the world. This research provides missionaries and other Christians working in varied contexts throughout the world with an example of how an understanding from the social science literature of the process of ethnic identification in a particular context can inform mission endeavors there.

4. Mandryk, *Operation World*, 259, 261.

Definitions

There are several important terms that appear often in this study that need to be carefully defined for the sake of clarity. For the purposes of this study, an "ethnic group" is a self-conscious "collectivity within a larger society having real or putative common ancestry, memories of a shared historical past, and a cultural focus on one or more symbolic elements defined as the epitome of their peoplehood."[5] These "groups" are not "substantial entities" but rather are "collective cultural representations . . . widely shared ways of seeing, thinking, parsing social experience, and interpreting the social world."[6] "Identity" refers to "the ways in which individual and collectivities are distinguished in their relations with other individuals and collectivities."[7] "Negotiating identity" denotes the ongoing interactive process of identification that takes place between an individual or collection of individuals and others concerning their own identity and the identity of these others in regard to one or more symbols (e.g., ethnic labels, social roles, ideas, habits, values, religious practices, truth statements, etc.). This process includes interactions about the meanings attached to these symbols and how those involved are located in regard to these symbols. In the context of this interactive process, identity is understood, not as something that remains constant in each and every environment, but as something that exhibits both fixity and fluidity as it is influenced by things like: primary socialization and habit; deep needs for belonging, continuity, and stability; the active nature of individuals and groups in constructing how they want to be viewed by others; the availability (or unavailability) of resources; the often changing dynamics of the situations and environments in which interaction takes place, etc. "Ethnicity" or "ethnic identification" is the process of "collective identification that is socially constructed with reference to putative 'cultural' similarity and difference."[8] "Cultures" are "differentiation based in variation of language, religion, cosmology, symbolism, morality, ideology, and so on."[9] The following admonition from Jenkins is critical: "Neither ethnicity nor culture is 'something' that people 'have,' or, indeed, to which they 'belong.' They are, rather, complex repertoires which people experience, use, learn and 'do' in their daily lives,

---

5. Schermerhorn, *Comparative Ethnic Relations*, 12.
6. Brubaker, *Ethnicity without Groups*, 79.
7. Jenkins, *Social Identity*. 3rd edition, 18.
8. Jenkins, *Rethinking Ethnicity*, 15, 78.
9. Ibid., 14.

within which they construct an ongoing sense of themselves and an understanding of their fellows."[10] A "tension" is a state or condition where two individuals, groups of people, and/or phenomena are different in a way that makes it difficult for them to naturally fit together with and/or embrace the other. "Being Christian" is anything (e.g., behavior, thinking, history, symbols) that an individual or a group of people associates with "Christians" and/or "Christianity." In the same vein, "being Hakka" is anything (e.g., behavior, thinking, history, symbols) that an individual or a group of people associates with the Hakka ethnic identity. It is essential to note that, rather than being something that is static, unchanging, and innate, "Hakka" refers to a diversity of meanings that can resist change but also can and do change. "Hakka" is best understood to be something that people "do" and not something that "is."

Note on Translations

Some key words used in this study do not translate easily between Chinese and English or between English and Chinese. A brief discussion of the way these words are being used in this book is necessary to help the reader avoid any confusion. The meanings associated with "ancestor worship," an important English expression used in this study, vary to some extent with a number of scholars arguing that the ancestor practices referred to are religious, motivated by a desire to appease or gain help from the ancestors, while others argue that these practices can also be or are only ethical, motivated by a desire to show respect, honor, and affection for the ancestors. Some scholars indicate that they use this expression broadly, wanting to avoid making a judgment as to the motivation behind these practices.[11] Others use this expression without specifying their intended meaning.[12] Seeking to be descriptive rather than make judgments about motivations, this study uses general expressions such as "ancestor practices," "ancestor rituals," and "ancestor veneration" to render words in the Chinese literature like *jizu* and *bai zuxian*, words that have often been translated "ancestor worship." It retains "ancestor worship" when this expression is used in English by authors being cited.

In a similar vein, translating the Chinese word *bai* when this word is used by informants to refer to ceremonial actions in the context of ancestor

10. Ibid., 15.
11. E.g., Thompson, *Chinese Religion*, 40.
12. E.g., Chuang, "Settlement Patterns," 169.

practices can be problematic. The question that arises is whether this word should be rendered as "to venerate" or as "to worship." The expression "to venerate," used in the context of discussing ancestor practices in this book, refers to the socially-accepted ceremonial acts for expressing respect, honor, and affection for the ancestors. The expression "to worship," used in this same context, refers to the ceremonial acts that most Christians consider to be idolatrous because these acts are thought to involve communication with ancestors and are designed to meet the needs of these departed and/or to gain their favor. Translated in this way, "to worship" is understood to be one possible form of the broader expression "to venerate." Cecil Kwei-heng Wang explains, "The scope of ancestral veneration includes the practical expression of ancestral worship, yet ancestral worship might not necessarily share the philosophical and social background of ancestral veneration."[13] Translating *bai* in connection with ancestors often requires that a judgment be made about the motivations behind the behavior being described. In some cases, motivations are fairly obvious (e.g., in the statement, "Christians need to find a way to participate in ancestor rituals without 'worshiping.'"), but in other cases, underlying motivations are not as clear. Making a determination as to motivations is complicated by the reality that, "It is not uncommon for people practicing these rites to assume more than one attitude . . . to have several complex and often overlapping attitudinal responses."[14] Also complicating the issue, informants were not only reporting and discussing their own behavior, but also the behavior of a group of people whose individual motivations could differ widely. Additionally, since *bai* is also used to describe attitudes and behavior relating to God or the gods (e.g., "worshiping" God), the use of the English word "worship" to render *bai* in conjunction with ancestor practices can easily lead to the misunderstanding that the acts being described are "worship" in the same way that "worship" of God is "worship." Seeking to avoid these complications and to avoid saying more than what informants have said, the term *bai* will be translated broadly in this study as "to venerate." Translating *bai* in this way does not suggest that the ritual acts being described are definitely not "worship" or even that they are less likely to be "worship." Only when it is fairly obvious from the context that the narrower translation "to worship" is the sole meaning possible will *bai* be translated as "to worship."

13. Wang, "Ancestor Veneration Practices," 92.
14. Ibid., 90.

Research Context

The aspects of the research context significant for this study include the present situation in Taiwan, the primary ethnic distinctions used in Taiwan, and the relationship between the ethnic distinctions Hakka and Chinese. Historical aspects of the research context are also significant and are discussed in the next chapter under the headings, "Being Hakka in Taiwan" and "Being Hakka in Taiwan and being Christian."

The Present Situation in Taiwan

This research takes place in an environment of change. The residents of Taiwan live in an economy that is export-oriented and tied to significant financial investments in mainland China. Politically, the Taiwan people live in a democracy, and one frequent topic of discussion is the question of whether or not Taiwan is an independent nation or a province of China. The residents of Taiwan encounter influences from outside Taiwan in many avenues—for example, in business contacts with outsiders, in the media (internet, television, movies, music, etc.), in their education, in their own travels overseas, and in contacts with relatives living overseas.

Primary Ethnic Distinctions in Taiwan

The approximately twenty-three million people living in Taiwan can be divided into four main ethnic groups: the Hoklo, the Hakka, the Mainlanders, and the Aborigines. Dividing Taiwan residents into these four categories does not in any way suggest that these groupings are neatly bounded or consist of people who are homogeneous and significantly different in culture and physical appearance from those in other categories. With the exception of the Aborigines, all of these groups perceive themselves to be Han Chinese and can be viewed as sub-ethnic groups of this broader category.

The largest ethnic group in Taiwan is often referred to as the Hoklo. Some other labels used for this group include: Holo, Taiwanese, Taiwanren, Heluoren, Fukienese of Taiwan, Minnanren, Hokkienese, and Fujianren. Approximately 70 percent of the people in Taiwan are Hoklo.[15] For the most part, the ancestors of the Hoklo immigrated to Taiwan from Fujian Province in the seventeenth and eighteenth centuries.[16]

---

15. Government Information Office, *Yearbook*, 32.
16. Vermeer, "Expansion in Late Ming," 66; Shepherd, "Frontier of Ch'ing," 124–25.

Hakkas (*kejiaren*) comprise about 20 percent of the Han Chinese population in Taiwan.[17] This percentage can vary depending on how Hakka is defined. The National Hakka Population Basic Data Survey in 2004 included eleven different possible definitions and found that when Hakka is defined most narrowly as those who choose Hakka as their ethnic identity in exclusion of any other ethnic identity, the percentage was only 12.6 percent of the population of Taiwan, whereas when Hakka is defined most broadly as someone with either a Hakka ancestor or who in some way identifies themselves as Hakka, the percentage swells to 26.9 percent.[18] The ancestors of these Hakkas migrated to Taiwan from Guangdong and Fujian Provinces in China between the late seventeenth century and the early nineteenth century with the majority most likely making the transition somewhere between 1725 and 1800.[19] There are several areas of Taiwan that are considered Hakka areas because of the high concentration of Hakkas living there.

The next largest ethnic group is known as the Mainlanders (*waishengren*). This group consists primarily of political refugees who fled to Taiwan between 1945 and 1950 and their descendants. Until recently, these Mainlanders have maintained a disproportionate amount of power, dominating in high-level government, military, and academic positions in Taiwan. The Mainlanders primarily live in urban areas and make up around 10 percent of the total population.[20]

The Aborigines (*yuanzhumin*) are the smallest grouping of people in Taiwan and are actually comprised of fourteen different groups of indigenous people.[21] "Their languages belong to the Austronesian linguistic family, whose over 200 million speakers inhabit an area of the globe that stretches from Madagascar in the west to Easter Island in the east and from Taiwan in the north to New Zealand in the south."[22] They comprise about 2 percent of the total population of Taiwan and live, for the most part, in concentrations located in the hills and mountains which are in the middle of the island of Taiwan.[23]

17. Government Information Office, *Yearbook*, 32.
18. Yang, "Preface," sec. 1, 14.
19. Leong, "Hakka Migrations," 54.
20. Yang, "Preface," ii.
21. Government Information Office, *Yearbook*, 33.
22. Ibid.
23. Ibid.

Both Hakka and Chinese

The Hakka ethnic category emerged out of and is maintained by differences within the broader Chinese (or Han Chinese) ethnic category.[24] Consequently, those who identify themselves as Hakka also identify themselves as Chinese. This relationship between the narrower and broader ethnic categories means that Hakkas and other Chinese in Taiwan, both as individuals and as groups, have been shaped by much of the same cultural heritage and, consequently, have access to and use many of the same cultural symbols as they seek to construct their identities.[25]

Assumptions

The meaning that a phenomenon like ethnicity has for individuals is understood to be socially constructed by their interactions with their world. Constructions and interpretations of different phenomenon are also understood to change, depending on context and the passage of time. Individuals are understood to be externalizing or projecting their subjective experiences in their interactions with other members of their society. The "products" of this externalization process (e.g., their ethnic identity) attain a reality that is objectified in the mind of the individual and a "facticity" that is outside of and independent of the individual. This reality is then "reappropriated" from the objective dimension back into the individual's subjective experience and shapes that experience.[26] Regular and continued interaction with significant others is understood to be important in order for the individual's conceptual world to be continually recharged and maintained.[27]

Problem Statement

This research is focused on the following problem: What tensions exist between being Hakka in northwestern Taiwan and being Christian? There are three aspects to this problem. The first aspect is to explore the way Hakkas in northwestern Taiwan construct their Hakka ethnic identity, focusing on areas that relate to their perceptions of being Christian. The second aspect is to investigate the negative categorizations that non-Christian

24. Constable, "What Does It Mean?," 29–30.
25. Pang, "Being Hui."
26. Berger, *Sacred Canopy*, 4.
27. Berger and Kellner, "Marriage and Reality," 4–5.

Hakkas in northwestern Taiwan have of being Christian. The final aspect is to explore the way Christian Hakkas in northwestern Taiwan respond in the context of these categorizations of being Christian.

Research Questions

This research will seek to answer the following questions:

RQ1. What does it mean to be Hakka in northwestern Taiwan?

    A. How are Hakkas different from other Han Chinese in Taiwan?

    B. What are the boundary markers of the Hakka ethnic identity?

    C. What factors are contributing to the maintenance and persistence of being Hakka?

    D. How are Hakkas relating to the Hakka ethnic identity?

RQ2. What tensions exist between being Hakka in northwestern Taiwan and being Christian?

RQ3. How are Hakka Christians in northwestern Taiwan responding in the context of tensions between being Hakka and being Christian?

Delimitations

This study is limited to Hakkas who live in northwestern Taiwan, specifically in Taipei City, New Taipei City, Hsinchu City and County, and Taoyuan and Miaoli Counties. While large differences in the topic area of this research among Hakkas in other areas of Taiwan are not expected, it is important to note that the interview sample did not include Hakkas from central, southern, and eastern areas of Taiwan.

While this research inquires about perceived differences between being Hakka and other ethnic groups, it does not seek to compare Hakkas and other ethnic groups in any area. In other words, this research will not be exploring questions such as, "Are Hakkas less responsive to Christianity than other ethnic groups in Taiwan?"

This study does not seek to explore tensions between being Hakka and being Christian from a spiritual or biblical perspective. For example, the Bible says that the message of the gospel is foolishness to non-Christians (1 Cor 1:18, 23; 2:14), revealing that Christians should expect there to be aspects about Christian teachings and practices that any non-Christian would find difficult to fully or even partially embrace.

2

Precedent Literature

THERE ARE FOUR BODIES of literature that are relevant to an exploration of tensions between being Hakka in northwestern Taiwan and being Christian. A brief look at the literature on the Homogeneous Unit Principle, an understanding of society from which the emphasis in mission circles on people groups initially emerged, locates this study with regard to this missiological concept. The social science literature on ethnic identification serves to set a theoretical framework for this study. The literature detailing important aspects of being Hakka in Taiwan provides insight into the cultural "stuff" that shapes those who are being Hakka in northwestern Taiwan and that serves as a reservoir of symbols and habits for them as they relate to being Christian. The literature on Christian ministry to those who are being Hakka in Taiwan supplies essential information about the cultural "stuff" that is influencing and providing a repertoire of symbols and habits for Christians who are engaged in Hakka ministries to use as they respond in the context of tensions that surface as those who are being Hakka relate to being Christian.

Homogeneous Unit Principle

This section briefly reviews the literature on the Homogeneous Unit Principle (HUP) with the goal of locating this study within discussions in this area. This review describes the concept of the HUP, outlines the primary critiques in missiology of the HUP, and details one critique of these responses of missiologists to the HUP.

The Homogeneous Unit Principle Described

Donald A. McGavran, the originator of the Homogeneous Unit Principle, argues, "The greatest obstacles to conversion are social and not theological."[1] McGavran sees society as made up of "homogeneous units," or "section[s] of society in which all the members have some characteristic in common."[2] He explains that these homogeneous units may include any of the following: a culture, a language group, a people, a caste, a tribe, a lineage, a clan, a political unit, or a geographical unit.[3] People within these homogeneous units are understood to have a "people consciousness," an understanding that they are a separate people. When their "people consciousness" is strong, they actively resist any influence from the outside. Based on this understanding of society, McGavran articulates what he calls the Homogeneous Unit Principle, saying, "People like to become Christians without crossing racial, linguistic, or class barriers."[4] Consequently, he argues that the gospel spreads more easily within these barriers and in expressions that respect the people consciousness of those within the barriers. His assertion that "intense racial consciousness" or racial prejudice encountered in a tribe "should be made an aid to Christianization," is one of the more controversial remarks he made in this area.[5] McGavran challenges missionaries to take the HUP seriously, arguing, "by ignoring social stratification and disregarding homogeneous units and webs of relationships, [Western churches, missions, and those nationals trained by them] constantly diminish the effectiveness of their presentation of Christ."[6]

McGavran appeals to the Bible for support of this HUP and argues that the words *panta ta ethnē* found in the Great Commission in Matt 28:18–20 and in other passages should be translated "all peoples" rather than "all nations" (as it is in many English translations) because Paul had in mind "cultural groupings—tongues, tribes, castes, and lineages."[7] McGavran postulates that since "peoples" or homogeneous units are so prominent in the Great Commission, the use of HUP strategies in evangelism and church planting is logical.

1. McGavran, *Understanding Church Growth*, 156.
2. Ibid., 69.
3. Ibid., 69–70.
4. Ibid., 163.
5. McGavran, *Bridges of God*, 10.
6. McGavran, "Homogeneous Populations," 78.
7. McGavran, *Understanding Church Growth*, 40.

McGavran also raises examples from the New Testament where he sees this principle being used in church planting. For example, he argues, "As the common people among the Jews came flooding into the Church in the years following Pentecost, they came as Jews. They continued going to the temple; they continued circumcising boy babies, banning pig meat, and observing Saturday as the Sabbath. To it they added a gathering on Sunday, the day the Lord rose from the dead. And they evangelized only Jews (Acts 11:19). Thus one-race congregations arose by the dozens, perhaps by the hundreds."[8] The conversion of Lydia in Acts 16:14–15 is one of the many examples McGavran raises as evidence of this principle working in church planting efforts in the New Testament. He argues that Lydia's quick response could have been because she was "overcome by the spiritual power which manifested itself through Paul," but he considers a more reasonable alternative to be either that Paul was known to Lydia or that "what he said about his friends made it clear to these women that they were dealing with genuine Jews—members of the family, so to speak."[9] In other words, one possible reason Lydia responded so quickly to Paul's witness is that Paul was a member of the same homogeneous unit. Significantly, McGavran adds this comment about his assertion that the HUP is evident in the New Testament, "I do not argue that this notable beginning into a one-race church is biblical validation for the fact that much church growth does still take place that way. I do plead, however, that it be recognized as a way in which God did bless and has blessed amazingly. The church had to grow strong within one people before it could break over into other peoples, other ethnic and linguistic groups."[10]

While McGavran's HUP has been very controversial in missiological circles, the concept has also been very influential. C. Peter Wagner points out that "the people approach to evangelism" is a more contemporary way to talk about the HUP.[11] The terms "hidden peoples" and "unreached people groups" are rooted in the homogeneous unit perspective.

The Homogeneous Unit Principle Critiqued

Several missiology scholars problematize the theological dimensions of McGavran's HUP. David Smith challenges McGavran's translation of the

8. McGavran, *Christianity and Cultures*, 23.
9. McGavran, *Bridges of God*, 29.
10. McGavran, "Priority of Ethnicity," 15.
11. Wagner, "Homogeneous Unit Principle," 455.

panta ta ethnē as "all peoples" and asserts that most likely these words were used for "a general sociological category" like "a collective designation for the Gentiles" and "virtually synonymous in the gospels with *holē hē oikoumenē* (the whole inhabited world)."[12]

Also discussing the theological dimensions of the HUP, René Padilla argues first that there is no evidence in the New Testament that church planting specifically targeted homogeneous units (racial or social groups). He states, "More often than not . . . Jews and Gentiles heard the gospel together."[13] Padilla secondly asserts that "the breaking down of barriers that separate people in the world was regarded as an essential part of the gospel, not merely a result of it."[14] Thirdly, Padilla highlights the way New Testament churches grew across cultural barriers and argues, "The New Testament contains no example of a local church whose membership had been taken by the apostles from a single homogeneous unit, unless that expression is used to mean no more than a group of people with a common language."[15] Next, Padilla points out that the strategy of planting churches in separate homogeneous units which would then express their unity through inter-church relationships was never considered in the New Testament period.[16] Padilla's final critique is that there is no evidence that the New Testament church made any changes to counter the criticism of some that believers were "traitorously abandoning their own culture in order to join another culture," arguing, "They regarded Christian community across cultural barriers, not as an optional blessing to be enjoyed whenever circumstances were favorable to it or as an addendum that could be left out if deemed necessary to make the gospel more palatable, but as *essential to Christian commitment*."[17]

Other missiology scholars critique the HUP from the perspective of the social sciences. Sociologist Wayne McClintock compares McGavran's thinking to many of the assumptions of the structural-functional school of anthropology and argues that, by focusing on the separateness and discrete nature of these homogeneous units, McGavran neglects the way these units are interacting both socially and economically with other groups in

---

12. Smith, "Church Growth Principles," 26.
13. Padilla, "Unity of the Church," 29.
14. Ibid.
15. Ibid.
16. Ibid.
17. Ibid.

society.¹⁸ McClintock argues that, consequently, McGavran will "at best only obtain a partial understanding of the complex social realities in the homogeneous unit."¹⁹

McClintock's second critique is that McGavran has "a lack of concern with the processes of social change."²⁰ He notes that McGavran does not account for the change happening within these units and the way people in a unit are responding differently to changes initiated from the outside. McClintock points out that if McGavran's goal is to penetrate homogeneous units with the gospel, an understanding of those who are most likely to respond to ideas from the outside would be helpful.²¹

A third critique offered by McClintock is that McGavran has "a view of social boundaries as rigid barriers to inter-ethnic relations."²² In viewing boundaries so rigidly, McGavran accounts neither for the way people pass over boundaries nor for the way people maintain relationships across boundaries. McClintock argues that this passing and interacting across boundaries makes it likely that, at least in some cases where the interaction is highly developed, church planting and evangelism across social boundaries would be quite effective.²³

Anthropologist Robert J. Priest focuses his critique of McGavran on the way McGavran's school of missiology has ignored the revolution that has taken place in the field of anthropology regarding ethnicity and ethnic boundaries. Priest argues that, rather than grappling with the complex nature of social identities and the boundaries associated with them and isolating the identities and boundaries that surface in any given context as anthropologists are seeking to do, "[McGavran's school of missiology] treated 'boundaries' as natural and automatic by-products of difference (which could include differences of phenotype, language, culture, wealth), with assumed homogeneity within any given unit. . . . Boundaries of hatred and prejudice were treated as equivalent to boundaries of language and culture."²⁴

---

18. McClintock, "Sociological Critique," 111.
19. Ibid., 112.
20. Ibid.
21. Ibid.
22. Ibid., 114.
23. Ibid.
24. Priest, "Missiological Reflection," 186.

A Critique of the Response of Missiologists to the Homogeneous Unit Principle

The response of missiologists to the HUP controversy has also been critiqued. Priest points out that in problematizing the HUP from different perspectives and increasingly abandoning this concept, missiologists have "stopped attending to certain social realities that the [the HUP] called attention to."[25] In doing so, missiologists "moved people even further away from the anthropology of race, ethnicity, and social class than McGavran had been."[26] Priest highlights the absence of a response that one might expect upon the discovery of a flawed understanding in this area, that of working to develop "new and more sophisticated understandings of race, ethnicity, and social class in the context of global patterns."[27] Priest is also concerned that there has been no call among missiologists for "new efforts to understand how such identities are historically constructed and sustained or contested" or for "nuanced and open-ended efforts to explore all sorts of implications of [these new understandings] for the churches formed in such settings."[28] Essentially this critique is a call to missiologists to seriously engage anthropological scholarship in this area.

Closing Remarks

This section has discussed the Homogeneous Unit Principle, the primary critiques of this principle that are found in missiology, and a critique of that missiological response. This study is positioned as an effort to engage the anthropological scholarship on ethnicity and ethnic groups and to use this perspective to better understand and minister in the context of those who are being Hakka in northwestern Taiwan.

Ethnic Identification

This section reviews and critiques the scholarly literature regarding the phenomenon of ethnicity and ethnic groups. Scholars participating in this conversation can be thought of in groups of those who either (1) primarily emphasize the fixity of ethnic groups, (2) primarily emphasize the fluidity

---

25. Ibid.
26. Ibid., 187.
27. Ibid., 186.
28. Ibid.

of ethnic groups, or (3) envision a double-sided discourse of both fluidity and fixity in ethnic groups.

Locating the Conversation

The current conversation about ethnicity and ethnic groups can be traced back to the mid-twentieth century and the failure of old paradigms (e.g., assimilationist assumptions and an essentialist view of groups) to explain the social behavior that scholars were observing in many different contexts in the world. For example, some immigrants entering the United States, rather than being gradually assimilated into the "melting pot" of American culture as Robert Park's race-relations cycle had taught scholars to expect, continued to maintain separate cultures and identities many years later.[29] Also, anthropologists doing ethnographic studies of groups of people began to discover that these entities were not as bounded, simple, and discrete as their existing paradigms had led them to imagine. A growing dissonance between ethnic realities and the traditional understandings of social interactions beginning in the mid-twentieth century stimulated much scholarly interest, study, and writing in the area of ethnicity and ethnic groups.

Emphasizing the Fixity of Ethnic Groups

Some scholars in this resulting wave of scholarly activity have focused on the fixity of ethnic groups and argue that this fixity is the most important factor in explaining ethnic behavior. These scholars are often called primordialists.

PRIMORDIALISM

The term "primordialism" is widely used in the literature and, in its narrowest sense, refers to a fixity which is extremely rigid. Stephen Cornell and Douglas Hartmann define primordialism narrowly as "the idea that ethnic . . . identities are fixed, fundamental, and rooted in the unchangeable circumstances of birth."[30] Gil-White problematizes this definition, "Primordialists supposedly believe that [ethnic groups] are natural and eternal historical entities, with hermetically impermeable social boundaries."[31]

---

29. Park and Burgess, *Science of Sociology*, 735.
30. Cornell and Hartmann, *Ethnicity and Race*, 51.
31. Gil-White, "Ethnic Groups," 516.

Believing that there are no scholars who actually hold to the extreme fixity of this understanding of primordialism, he offers the following alternative as a summary of this tradition:

> [Primordialism] claims that certain kinds of attachments, 'primordial' attachments, are felt towards co-ethnics because of who they are *categorically* (usually, co-biological descendants from a primary group), and not necessarily as a result of interaction with them. . . . Ascription here is not really a matter of choice, much less rational choice, but of tradition and the emotions evoked by perceptions of common ancestry. Thus, what motivates the behavior of ethnic actors is not some calculation of their interests, but rather the history that binds them, as they themselves perceive this history.[32] Resonating with this summary, Steve Fenton comments that "primordiality" implies "'first order'. . . sentiments, ties, and obligations, and an unquestioned sense of identity which are embedded in the individual from an early age and remain a fixed point of reference."[33]

Primordialism has roots in the thinking of Edward Shils. He disagreed with the assessment of scholars like Émile Durkheim[34] and Ferdinand Tönnies[35] that as modernity advanced in the world, social cohesion would be reduced to utilitarian interests and cohesion. Shils argued instead that society is held together by, among other factors, "primordial affinities" or "'significant relational' qualities, which can only be described as primordial."[36] He especially highlighted the "certain ineffable significance [that] is attributed to the tie of blood."[37] We are not tied to our kin because we "like" them, but because of the unique and special nature of the kinship bond. Shils believed that these "first order" connections generate strong feelings of loyalty and obligation in individuals.

Three other scholars are typically associated with primordialism. Pierre van den Berghe articulates a socio-biological perspective, arguing that ethnicity is solely an extension of kinship.[38] The primary ties of the individual are formed at birth where the ascription of connections to a

---

32. Gil-White, "Thick Blood," 802.
33. Fenton, *Ethnicity*, 9.
34. Durkheim, *Division of Labor*.
35. Tönnies, *Community and Society*.
36. Shils, "Primordial Ties," 131, 142.
37. Ibid., 142.
38. van den Berghe, *Ethnic Phenomenon*, xi.

nuclear family also brings ties to larger groups (e.g., kin and ethnic group) within which that family is set. For him, ethnic groups are fixed and will always persist because people will always have kinship ties.

Clifford Geertz talks about primordial attachments and suggests that these "assumed 'givens'" are primarily "immediate contiguity and kin connection" but also include things like religion, language, and social practices.[39] He argues that these "congruities of blood, speech, custom and so on are seen to have an ineffable, and at times overpowering, coerciveness in and of themselves."[40] For Geertz, these ties are not only the result of "personal affection, practical necessity, common interest, or incurred obligation"; people just naturally take them for granted to be of great importance in their lives.[41]

Harold Isaacs is another scholar who is often thought of as a primordialist. He raises the idea of a "basic group identity"—something that is derived from "belonging to what is generally and loosely called an 'ethnic group'."[42] This basic identity is powerful because it meets the deep human needs to belong and to have self-esteem.[43] Isaacs lists eight factors that assist in building this identity: (1) one's body and all of its observable characteristics, (2) one's names—personal and family, (3) the group into which one was born—its history and origins, (4) one's nationality or connections to other groups of people, (5) one's mother tongue, (6) one's natal religion, (7) one's natal culture, and (8) one's birthplace—its geography and topography.[44] He postulates that these aspects of our lives gain their power, resilience, and meaning because they shape us first, before we are conscious of their influence and of the other available alternatives.

PRIMORDIALISM CRITIQUED

Primordialism offers a helpful explanation for why ethnic identities are so resilient and powerful. However, this approach also has several limitations. Philip Yang argues that while primordialism has some valid points, there is an abundance of social behavior for which this approach cannot account. For example, this approach cannot explain why the substance and salience

---

39. Geertz, *Interpretation of Cultures*, 259.
40. Ibid.
41. Ibid.
42. Isaacs, "Basic Group Identity," 30.
43. Ibid., 34–6.
44. Isaacs, *Idols of the Tribe*; Cornell and Hartmann, *Ethnicity and Race*, 51.

of ethnic identities change and why new ethnicities emerge while others wane and die out. Yang further argues that this approach ignores the impact that the context—particularly the historical, political, economic, and structural dimensions of life—has on ethnic loyalties and actions.[45] James McKay also adds that where primordialists see ethnic emotions running high because of primordial attachments, there are many other factors that might produce those emotions.[46]

Jack Eller and Reed Coughlan have the most scathing critique of primordialism, arguing that "there are logically no circumstances in which ethnicity can be described as primordial."[47] For these scholars, "primordiality" has a strong sense of "primeval" and is "deeply rooted in the natural order of things." Reacting to the extreme fixity they perceive in this word, they suggest that primordialism is "unsociological, unanalytical, and vacuous" and should not be used again.[48] They argue that the problem with this concept is that it "offers no mechanism for the genesis of its phenomena, nor does it recognize or explicate any significant relationship between ethnic attachments and the ongoing social experiences of ethnic members."[49] Eller and Coughlan ridicule van den Berghe for saying, "Ethnicity, then, is both primordial and highly changeable," arguing that something cannot be both primordial and changeable at the same time.[50]

The problem with van den Berghe and other primordialists is not one of logic but one of definition. The fact is that, for some primordialists, the meaning of "primordiality" can include some fluidity. For example, when Geertz talks about the primordial "givens of social existence," he also emphasizes that these givens are often only "assumed."[51] While primordialism, in its narrow sense, cannot function as the sole explanation for ethnicity and ethnic behavior, when defined broadly to include some fluidity, primordialism is very helpful in explaining some important aspects of ethnic behavior.

---

45. Yang, *Ethnic Studies*, 43.
46. McKay, "Primordial Approaches," 398–99.
47. Eller and Coughlan, "Poverty of Primordialism," 184.
48. Ibid., 183.
49. Ibid., 186, 194.
50. van den Berghe, "Ethnic Pluralism," 243; Eller and Coughlan, "Poverty of Primordialism," 196.
51. Geertz, *Interpretation of Cultures*, 259.

Emphasizing the Fluidity of Ethnic Groups

Some scholars, in the wave of scholarly activity seeking to explore why some ethnic groups do not assimilate as expected and are not as bounded as is anticipated, have focused on the fluidity of these groups. These scholars (including both the circumstantialists and Fredrik Barth) argue that fluidity is the most important factor in explaining ethnic behavior.

CIRCUMSTANTIALISM

Circumstantialists focus on the ever-changing circumstances and contexts that surround ethnic groups to explain why people behave so diversely. Ethnic groups are seen as "largely the products of concrete social and historical situations that—for a variety of reasons—heighten or reduce the salience and/or the utility of such identities in the lives of individuals and groups."[52]

Key for circumstantialists is the assumption that individuals and groups primarily operate as interest groups which are actively pursuing the collective interests that arise as they compete on socio-economic and political planes with others in their particular contexts. Sometimes these actors choose to unite around "ethnic" rather than other commonalities. These "ethnic" identities are understood to be instruments that can be asserted in settings where drawing a boundary between "self" and "others" is perceived to be advantageous to "self." For example, when people feel threatened socially or economically, they often pick out the easily identifiable characteristics which those who are particularly threatening to them have in common—characteristics such as "race, language, religion, local or social origin, descent, residence, etc."—and then use these characteristics as a rallying point in efforts to exclude these others from access to scarce or limited resources.[53] When circumstances change and no threat is perceived, these differences will often go unnoticed.

One of the distinctions that some circumstantialists make is between a cultural group and an ethnic group. Orlando Patterson argues that a cultural group "is simply any group of people who consciously or unconsciously share an identifiable complex of meanings, symbols, values, and norms."[54] He maintains that an ethnic group forms out of a cultural group when, in situations of socio-economic competition with others, members

---

52. Cornell and Hartmann, *Ethnicity and Race*, 63.
53. Weber, *Economy and Society*, 342.
54. Patterson, "Context and Choice," 309.

mobilize and unite together in solidarity around shared culture. Patterson explains that aspects of the cultural group are only important in "the ways in which they are used to maintain group cohesiveness, sustain and enhance identity, and to establish social networks and communicative patterns that are important for the group's optimization of its socio-economic position in society."[55] Another critical part of an ethnic group for Patterson is "a conscious sense of belonging."[56] Ethnic group members consciously choose to join together.

Circumstantialism Critiqued

There are two main critiques of circumstantialism in the literature. First, critics note that people are not as utilitarian in the way they assert their ethnicity as circumstantialists suggest. Often people assert an ethnic identity even when it is not in their best interest to do so. For example, Cornell and Hartmann point to several groups of native Americans that have maintained their separate identity even when it was not politically and economically advantageous to do so.[57] Jenkins argues, "We cannot deny the longevity and stubbornness, in certain circumstances, of ethnic attachments."[58] He gives the example from a study by John Rex of how ethnic minorities in Britain resisted strong pressure to form interest groups and clung instead to those "with whom they had ties of ethnic sameness."[59] Evidently, there is more to ethnic identities than individuals or groups acting in their own best interests in the various circumstances they encounter.

Second, some critics argue that, if an ethnic identity is an instrument that emerges in the face of competition or opposition from others, then in the absence of these threatening situations, there would be nothing left to keep these identities viable.[60] These critics argue that, in fact, this is not the case. Often, once threats have passed and the circumstances change, many ethnic groups and identities continue to persist. Several scholars contend that ethnic identities do not need the context of competition or opposition to exist as circumstantialists suggest. For example, Eugene Roosens claims that an ethnic identity can simply be a natural social distinction

---

55. Ibid., 306.
56. Ibid., 309.
57. Cornell and Hartmann, *Ethnicity and Race*, 69.
58. Jenkins, *Rethinking Ethnicity*, 48.
59. Ibid.
60. e.g., Cornell and Hartmann, *Ethnicity and Race*, 69.

that people make and all that is needed for such a distinction to be made is a reference to a common origin and a "vague 'non-we.'"[61]

Barth

Fredrik Barth's approach to ethnicity emphasizes the boundaries between ethnic groups. He argues, "The critical focus of investigation from this point of view becomes the ethnic boundary that defines the group, not the cultural stuff that it encloses."[62] Barth writes in opposition to those who say that cultural diversity in the world is the result of groups of people living in isolation from one another. Rather, he points out, "Categorical ethnic distinctions do not depend on an absence of mobility, contact and information, but do entail social processes of exclusion and incorporation whereby discrete categories are maintained despite changing participation and membership in the course of individual life histories."[63]

Barth draws attention to the fact that people agree to make certain symbols, "overt signals or signs" and/or "basic value orientations" the distinguishing markers or boundaries that separate them as an ethnic group from people who are different from them in some way.[64] Differences between groups are the raw material out of which boundary markers are chosen. Barth asserts, "ethnic groups only persist as significant units if they imply marked difference in behaviour, i.e., persisting cultural differences."[65]

Barth understands that the makeup of these boundary markers can change over time and can vary from place to place and from circumstance to circumstance. He maintains that as long as two individuals are "playing the same game" in their interactions with others—displaying the agreed upon markers—even if they are completely different from each other in every other way, they can still consider themselves and be considered by others to be members of the same ethnic group.[66]

Barth also asserts that ethnicity entails "stable, persisting, and often vitally important social relations" with others across ethnic boundaries.[67] He argues that ongoing negotiations across these boundaries, namely

---

61. Roosens, "Primordial Origins," 101.
62. Barth, "Introduction," 15.
63. Ibid., 9.
64. Ibid., 14.
65. Ibid., 15–16.
66. Ibid., 15.
67. Ibid., 10.

"self-ascription and ascription by others," are crucial to generating and maintaining these boundaries.[68]

Barth Critiqued

Since Barth's ideas have been so influential in the study of ethnicity, he has been critiqued from a myriad of different perspectives. Four important and helpful critiques are mentioned here. First, some scholars argue that Barth treated ethnic groups as "fixed ascriptive categories, with borders permanently guarded by linguistic and cultural symbols (such as dress, food, and architecture)."[69] Jenkins contends that in Barth's usage of terminology like "boundaries" and "maintenance," he unintentionally "contributed to the further reification of the ethnic group as a perduring corporate entity."[70] "Boundaries" imply boundedness. "Maintenance" infers some "thing" that is maintained in its original state. In raising this critique, Jenkins also reminds his fellow anthropologists not to forget that "'groups' are not distinct 'entities' or 'things' in any sense."[71] Some scholars suggest that we should talk about "groupness" rather than of "groups."[72] Jenkins concurs, "Human society is best seen as an ongoing and overlapping kaleidoscope of 'group-ness,' rather than a 'plural' system of separate groups."[73] This critique is helpful as it reminds scholars to keep the fluidity of ethnic "groups" in the forefront of their thinking.

Second, other scholars suggest that Barth, in his emphasis on ethnic boundaries in opposition to the cultural "stuff" they enclose, failed to appreciate the inter-relatedness of these boundaries and the cultural elements associated with them. Making this point, Don Handelman argues, "'Cultural stuff' . . . and ethnic boundar[ies] mutually modify but support one another. The [cultural 'stuff'] establishes and legitimizes the contrast of the boundary; while the [ethnic group], often in response to external conditions, modifies or alters the relevance to the boundary of aspects of the [cultural 'stuff']."[74] Joane Nagel expands further, "[Culture] animates and authenticates ethnic boundaries by providing a history, ideology, symbolic

---

68. Ibid., 13.
69. Hutchinson and Smith, *Ethnicity*, 33.
70. Jenkins, *Rethinking Ethnicity*, 21.
71. Ibid., 52.
72. Brubaker, "Ethnicity without Groups."
73. Jenkins, *Rethinking Ethnicity*, 52.
74. Handelman, "Organization of Ethnicity," 200.

universe, and system of meaning."[75] As a result of this important critique, scholars studying ethnicity are sensitized to view the assertion of ethnic boundaries more holistically than before—to analyze these assertions in a way that sees ethnic identification embedded in the context of the cultural "stuff" that the boundaries enclose.

Third, some scholars argue that Barth's approach focuses too much on people acting together and fails to see the primacy of the cultural "stuff" within those boundaries. This critique raises the question of which comes first, the boundaries or the culture within them. Shaye J. D. Cohen says, "It is not the boundary that makes the group; it is the group that makes the boundary."[76] Anthony D. Smith maintains that the reason we perceive others to be different from us is because we have "an already existing sense of shared experiences and values, a feeling of community, or 'us-ness' and group belonging" that is derived from our upbringing.[77] He argues, "The sense of ethnic identity emanates from a commitment and attachment to the shared elements which unite the members of a group, rather than from the differences which debar outsiders."[78] In this view then, boundaries are not something primary that members of ethnic groups assert, but secondary and passive markers of the edges of "us-ness." Roosens agrees, "What is found inside the boundary, namely, what one is and what one possesses as a specific social category, cannot be reduced to being the product of boundary formation. One could say that the feeling of continuity, or identity, comes logically first, and that this identity originates from genealogy 'before' it has anything to do with boundaries."[79] This critique highlights the important role that the elements one shares with others have in the construction of one's ethnic identity.

Fourth, Barth's influence has also been criticized for stimulating so much interest in the active role of the ethnic actor in maintaining ethnic boundaries that the negative influence from others outside the boundaries has been overlooked. Richard Jenkins argues that scholars have "concentrated upon the internal process of group identification, at the expense of categorization."[80] Jenkins maintains that the labels or categories that are

---

75. Nagel, "Constructing Ethnicity," 9.
76. Cohen, *Beginnings of Jewishness*, 6.
77. Smith, *Ethnic Origins*, 49.
78. Ibid.
79. Roosens, "Primordial Origins," 87.
80. Jenkins, "Identity and Power," 197.

assigned or ascribed by others, especially when they originate from others who have significant power or authority, can dominate and even be forced on the ethnic actors.[81] He argues that some scholars, while acknowledging that ethnic boundary work entails transactions between ego and others, do not realize that these transactions are not always "rooted in reciprocation, exchange and relatively equitable negotiation," as many scholars have assumed. While ethnicity can be a "social resource," it can also be a "social liability or stigma."[82] Joane Nagel agrees with Jenkins, "We do not always choose to be who we are; we simply are who we are as a result of a set of social definitions, categorization schemes, and external ascriptions that reside in the taken-for-granted realm of social life."[83] Nagel maintains that "while an individual can choose from among a set of ethnic identities, that set is generally limited to socially and politically defined ethnic categories with varying degrees of stigma or advantage attached to them."[84] Clearly, the influence of categorization needs to be included when scholars are analyzing the way that individuals choose their ethnic identities.

The Double-Sided Discourse of Fixity and Fluidity in Ethnic Identification

More recently, most scholars writing in the area of ethnicity, recognizing the weaknesses of a sole emphasis on primordialism on the one hand and circumstantialism or Barth's theory on the other, argue that both fixity and fluidity are important in explaining ethnic behavior. In doing so, they develop a helpful synthesis of key concepts taken from primordialism, circumstantialism, and Barth. These scholars are often referred to broadly as "constructionists" because of the way they emphasize that ethnicity, ethnic groups, and categories are socially constructed.

Richard Jenkins helpfully summarizes four elements of what he calls the "basic social constructionist anthropological model of ethnicity":

- ethnicity is a matter of cultural differentiation—although . . . identification always involves a dialectic interplay between similarity and difference;

---

81. Ibid., 199.
82. Ibid., 201.
83. Nagel, *Ethnic Renewal*, 26.
84. Nagel, "Constructing Ethnicity," 155.

- ethnicity is centrally a matter of shared meanings—what we conventionally call 'culture'—but is also produced and reproduced during interaction;
- ethnicity is no more fixed and unchanging than the way of life of which it is an aspect or the situations in which it is produced and reproduced;
- ethnicity, as an identification, is collective and individual, externalized in social interaction and the categorization of others and internalized in personal self-identification.[85]

This summary succinctly captures much of the flavor of constructionism's discourse about fluidity and fixity in ethnic identification. The details of each side of this discourse will be discussed in separate sections below.

FLUIDITY IN ETHNIC IDENTIFICATION

The use of the word "fluidity" in this section is metaphorical and is intended to capture the way that ethnic identification is variable and changing. Four aspects of this fluidity will be discussed in this subsection: (1) fluidity as a result of the interactive nature of ethnic identification, (2) fluidity in the salience of ethnic identification, (3) fluidity as a result of the context surrounding ethnic identification, and (4) fluidity from the nature of symbols.

Fluidity as a Result of the Interactive Nature of Ethnic Identification

Much of the fluidity of ethnic identification can be traced to the interaction between what Jenkins calls the processes of "internal definition" and "external definition."[86] Individuals and groups are seen as actors involved in both of these processes. In internal definition, these actors define their own identity. Cornell and Hartmann refer to this process of internal definition as "assertion," and Jenkins calls it "identification" or "self-identification."[87] In external definition, on the other hand, these actors define the identity of others. This process of external definition requires the presence, in one way or another, of others and "is a meaningful intervention in

---

85. Jenkins, *Rethinking Ethnicity*, 14.
86. Jenkins, *Social Identity*, 15–26.
87. Cornell and Hartmann, *Ethnicity and Race*, 83; Jenkins, *Rethinking Ethnicity*, 54–76.

their lives, an acting upon [these others]."[88] Cornell and Hartmann refer to this process of external definition as "assignment," and Jenkins calls it "categorization."[89] Jenkins points out that external definition "is a basic dimension of internal definition."[90] In other words, in defining "I" or "us," we also separate out "other" and vice versa. Additionally, Jenkins argues that it is highly likely that external definition will be "pejorative, negative, or stigmatizing."[91]

The processes of internal and external definition interact in a dialectic relationship with each other. The identifications that individuals and groups make about themselves are shaped by the categorizations that others make regarding them and vice versa. The give-and-take nature which characterizes this internal-external interaction introduces potential for a great deal of fluidity in ethnic identification. Constructionists argue that ethnic boundaries and the meanings associated with them are constructed in this ongoing interaction between internal and external definitions of actors on both sides of these boundaries.

Constructionists also emphasize the active, strategizing role that individuals and groups have in the internal-external interaction that takes place during ethnic identification. These scholars build on Erving Goffman's concept that people present themselves (or perform) in social encounters in ways that they think will achieve a desired response from others.[92] Cornell and Hartmann point out that individuals and groups, "guided by their own perceptions, dispositions, and agendas" and using "the raw materials of history, cultural practice, and preexisting identities," say and do things in strategic attempts to cultivate an image that they perceive will be the most beneficial for them.[93] Stella Ting-Toomey argues, "[H]uman beings in all cultures desire both positive group-based and positive person-based identities in any type of communicative situation."[94] In pursuit of this positive identity, individuals and groups actively "accept, resist, choose, specify, invent, redefine, reject, actively defend, and so forth"

---

88. Jenkins, *Rethinking Ethnicity*, 55.

89. Cornell and Hartmann, *Ethnicity and Race*, 83; Jenkins, *Rethinking Ethnicity*, 54–76.

90. Jenkins, *Rethinking Ethnicity*, 59.

91. Ibid., 65.

92. Goffman, *Presentation of Self*; Goffman, *Strategic Interaction*.

93. Cornell and Hartmann, *Ethnicity and Race*, 81.

94. Ting-Toomey, "Identity Negotiation Theory," 217.

the labels (and everything that goes with them) that the circumstances ascribe to them.[95]

The active, strategizing character of actors can also be seen in the response of these actors to the categorization of others. Jenkins notes that categorization by others, when it is similar to self-identification, will reinforce and strengthen that identification. When there are significant differences between categorization by others and self-identification, actors may respond in one of at least three different ways. Some individuals or groups may accept and internalize the categorization of others, especially when those others are in positions of power where they can force their categorizations on the categorized. Other individuals or groups may adjust their self-identification somewhat to the categorization of others, internalizing a synthesis of elements of both. Some individuals or groups may respond to the categorization of others by rejecting it totally, and consequently a significant part of their self-identification becomes a denial of that categorization.[96] The way the categorization of others is internalized differently by different individuals and groups introduces another dimension to the fluidity of ethnic identification.

Jenkins notes that self-identification and categorization interact differently in three different orders of observable reality (all overlapping and implicated in each other).[97] First, the "individual order" refers to the human world that includes "embodied individuals and 'what-goes-on-in-their-heads'."[98] This order is worked out by individuals internally during interaction between their "I" and their "me." The "I" refers to the part of the individual that responds to others. The "me" refers to the internalized opinions and expectations that others have of the individual. In this order, the categorization by significant others during the largely one-sided interactions of primary socialization creates and shapes both "me" and "I." Experience and further socialization continue this shaping process throughout life. Second, the "interaction order" describes the human world that is generated "in the relationships between embodied individuals" or "what-goes-on-between-people."[99] Categorization in this order is

---

95. Cornell and Hartmann, *Ethnicity and Race*, 81.

96. Jenkins, *Rethinking Ethnicity*, 74–76; Yang, "Responses to Modernization," 78–79.

97. Jenkins, *Rethinking Ethnicity*, 58–64.

98. Ibid., 59.

99. Ibid.

characterized by what Jenkins calls the public image—how others view one—and is contrasted with one's self-image and the way one presents oneself to others. This order is constituted during the interaction between public image and self-image. Third, the "institutional order" is the human world as seen through the lens of "pattern and organization" or "established ways-of-doing-things."[100] This order is constituted in and by embodied individuals in the context of negotiations between claims a group makes about itself and the social categorization of one's group by a group of others.

Fluidity in the Salience of Ethnic Identification

Constructionists also note the way ethnic identities vary in salience. An important distinction they make is that of ethnicity being "thick" or "thin." Cornell and Hartmann use this distinction to highlight the way that ethnic identities vary or are fluid in the degree to which they organize the lives of a particular person or group.[101] When ethnic identities are "thick" or salient, they affect and order every aspect of life. When they are "thin," they have little relevance to the way social life is organized and lived. One version of thin ethnicity is called "symbolic ethnicity"—something that is characterized by "a nostalgic allegiance" to one or more ethnic symbols.[102] Fenton refers to this lack of salience as "ethnicity with the cultural difference stripped out."[103]

Constructionists explain the variability that exists in the thickness of ethnic identities in at least three ways. First, George De Vos points out that ethnicity is only one of the many different social identity options that people, stimulated by "the human need to belong and survive," can assert.[104] De Vos explains that in addition to a past-oriented identity like ethnicity, individuals and groups constructing their continually changing self-identifications can assert a present-oriented identity (e.g., centered around a profession) and/or a future-oriented identity (e.g., centered around a political cause).[105] For De Vos, ethnic identities are thin when other social identities are primary.

    100. Ibid.
    101. Cornell and Hartmann, *Ethnicity and Race*, 76.
    102. Gans, "Symbolic Ethnicity," 9.
    103. Fenton, *Ethnicity*, 98.
    104. De Vos, "Ethnic Pluralism," 12.
    105. Ibid., 13–15.

Second, Brubaker explains the variable thickness of ethnicity by noting the way that the ethnic perspective is often activated by a certain stimulus or cue. Brubaker explains, "Activation depends on proximate, situationally specific cues and triggers, not directly on large-scale structural or cultural contexts."[106] He also notes the way actors can play an active role in this triggering—for example, triggering "groupness" by framing a particular conflict in ethnic terms.[107] Hence, a "thin" ethnic identification can become instantly "thick" to the point where certain cultural differences suddenly not only matter but "really matter." In the absence of these triggering factors, cultural differences (and similarities) are not seen as significant and ethnicity becomes thinner.

Third, some scholars also explain the variability that exists in the salience of ethnic identities by focusing, at least in part, on the characteristics and assets of groups. Cornell asserts that the degree of shared bonds in things like interests, institutions, and culture affects the thickness and persistence of an ethnic identity.[108] Cornell and Hartmann, speaking more specifically, highlight the way the following six areas of group characteristics/assets (explained below) contribute to variability in ethnic identities: preexisting identities, population size, internal differentiation, social capital, human capital, and symbolic repertoires:[109]

1. When individuals involve themselves in ethnic identification, they bring with them other *preexisting identities* and all that is associated with them. Cornell and Hartmann argue that all human beings interacting in the ethnic-identification process "[already] see themselves as members of groups, as occupiers of categories, as variously similar to and different from other people."[110] Ethnic identification then is a process of rethinking or reconstructing these preexisting identities. The salience of ethnic identities varies to the extent with which "preexisting ethnic identity is embedded in social relations."[111]

---

106. Brubaker, *Ethnicity without Groups*, 76.
107. Ibid., 16–17.
108. Cornell, "Variable Ties," 268.
109. Cornell and Hartmann, *Ethnicity and Race*, 212–43.
110. Ibid., 212.
111. Ibid., 245.

2. The *numerical size* of a minority ethnic group in a particular context can influence the salience of their ethnic identity.[112] The larger the group, the less likely its members will find it necessary to interact across boundaries to meet needs (e.g., for marriage partners) and to solve problems. The larger the ethnic group relative to the size of the dominant population, the stronger this group will be in situations of competition with these others for limited resources, and hence, the more threatening they can become to others. Larger ethnic minority populations often have increased ethnic salience.

3. Cornell and Hartmann discuss how three kinds of *internal differentiation* in groups can result in varying degrees of ethnic saliency within these groups. First, they note how sex ratios affect the saliency of ethnic identities. When males greatly outnumber females, as is the case in many immigrant communities, there are at least two possible scenarios: intermarriage with "others," which undermines ethnic salience, and laws prohibiting marriage with "others," which have the opposite effect.[113]

The second kind of internal differentiation that accounts for some variation among group members in the saliency of their ethnic identity is differences between generations of people. With each successive generation, ethnic group members become more and more removed from "the society of origin and all that is associated with it," and the ethnic identity of their parents becomes less and less important for them.[114] In the context of immigrant societies, contacts with the society of origin in the form of new immigrants can recharge these ethnic identities. These contacts can also result in intra-group boundaries as some members are perceived by new arrivals (and other older members) to have integrated themselves too much into the culture of the new society.[115]

The third kind of internal differentiation that can lead to differences in ethnic salience is difference in class. Cornell and

---

112. Ibid., 215–18.
113. Ibid., 219–21.
114. Ibid., 225.
115. Ibid., 222–24.

Hartmann argue that lower classes of people in immigrant situations tend to live and interact socially together, thereby increasing the saliency of their ethnic identities. Higher classes of immigrants, on the other hand, often choose to live and work outside of the areas where their ethnic compatriots who have less economic resources and/or need the ethnic connection live. These higher class group members have the resources to be more independent and to locate in neighborhoods and businesses more in line with their class status. In other words, their class status becomes thicker than their ethnic identity. This dispersion increases their contact across ethnic boundaries and often reduces the salience of their ethnic identities.[116] Hence, the ethnic salience of ethnic immigrant populations comprised primarily of higher class members tends to be thinner than that of populations comprised primarily of lower class members. While Cornell and Hartmann use examples of class differentiation from first-generation immigrant situations, the effect of these class differences on ethnic salience does not need to be limited to these settings.

4. The amount of *social capital* that a group possesses can also affect the salience of their group identity. Cornell and Hartmann argue, "Groups that have high social capital—that are characterized by substantial or dense networks of relationships characterized by trust or obligation—are capable of doing things that groups with low social capital have difficulty doing."[117] Often, when "others" are not needed and the ethnic community has adequate ways and sufficient resources to meet the needs of their members, group identity is reinforced and salience is heightened. The opposite is also true.

5. The varying amounts and kinds of *human capital* (e.g., knowledge, skills, experience) that individuals within the group, and hence the group, have earned can influence the salience of their ethnic identities. Cornell and Hartmann point out that when immigrants of a particular ethnic group, by virtue of common human capital or lack of it, cluster together in occupational

---

116. Ibid., 226.
117. Ibid., 228.

concentrations, their group identity tends to be stronger. When ethnic groups have higher human capital, ethnic group members have more employment opportunities from which to choose. As a result, they are often somewhat dispersed and socially separated from each other, and this broader dispersal undermines ethnic salience.[118]

6. The size of the *symbolic repertoire* of ethnic groups can also affect the salience of their group identity. Cornell and Hartmann discuss the importance of having symbols that can be conscripted to communicate and revitalize the value, uniqueness, essence, meaning, and so forth of the group to members and others. These scholars elaborate, "Symbolic resources [can be] transformed into such things as solidarity, emotional attachment, pride, commitment, and mobilization."[119] Collective representations can include stories, festivals, and cultural practices (e.g., language, religious rites) that are chosen to be significant in ethnic identification. Slogans can also serve as effective symbols.[120] Groups can and do expand and transform their repertoires. When symbols are plentiful and are used effectively in ethnic identification, saliency increases.

Fluidity as a Result of the Context Surrounding Ethnic Identification

Scholars explain the variability that exists in ethnic identities by highlighting the contexts where ethnic identity construction takes place and the categorization forces they see at work in these contexts. Since these contexts are often inter-related and overlapping and their conceptual boundaries are somewhat arbitrary, constructionist scholars use somewhat different frameworks to organize their discussions about them. For example, Cornell and Hartmann structure their comments around the following contexts: politics, labor markets, residential space, social institutions, culture, and daily experience.[121] This section will use a significant portion of

---

118. Ibid., 234–36.
119. Ibid., 239.
120. Liu, "Persuasion in China," 128–29.
121. Cornell and Hartmann, *Ethnicity and Race*, 169–209.

Jenkins' framework and ideas to structure a summary of some of the contexts and contextual factors that are relevant for this study.[122]

1. The context of "primary socialization"—the way that the adults who surround a child during its early years significantly influence the internal and external definitions of that child.[123] The verbal and non-verbal interactions that happen during this early socialization become the tools that are used to pass on to the child the ethnic perspective of these adults (as well as the cultural "stuff" that undergirds that perspective). Jenkins puts it bluntly, "Socialization is categorization."[124] When ethnic identity is salient in childhood settings, that saliency and meanings associated with it are often passed on to children.

2. The context of "routine public interaction"—the daily experience of face-to-face public encounters with others.[125] Important tools in this context are the subtle (cues and small signals) and the sometimes not-so-subtle ways that are used to communicate, enforce, or, in some cases, even compel self-identity claims or categorization. The extent to which ethnic categorizations are embedded in these routine interactions also affects the degree to which they influence the ethnic-identification process for actors participating in them.

3. The context of "sexual relationships"—the sensitivity that individuals and groups have toward male-female relationships across ethnic boundaries.[126] Prohibitions of inter-ethnic marriage, either normative or legal, are important tools for and evidence of ethnic categorization. When inter-ethnic sexual relationships are restricted, the salience of ethnic boundaries usually increases. Marriage across group boundaries, on the other hand, tends to decrease the salience of those boundaries.

4. The context of "communal relationships"—the networks of connections that can gradually develop because actors share what

---

122. Jenkins, *Rethinking Ethnicity*, 65–73.
123. Ibid., 65–66.
124. Ibid., 170.
125. Ibid., 66–67.
126. Ibid., 67.

Cornell and Hartmann call "residential space."[127] These relationships provide fertile ground for ethnic identification because of the way that actors in these networks are known to mutually influence each other. When ethnic distinctions are important in these networks, ethnic identity is naturally more salient. In communities that are relatively homogeneous ethnically, the internal and external definitions of that one group also gain strength in numbers through these networks. Jenkins suggests that gossip is one of the tools employed in this context to challenge deviance to the locally sanctioned articulations of identification and categorization.[128]

5. The context of "life-course transitions"—important junctures in the life of the individual.[129] These transitions can include "the acceptance/recognition of the new infant, puberty, the transition to adulthood, parenthood, significant stages of midlife, withdrawal from economic activity, transitions to the category of the aged, and death."[130] Jenkins argues that, in the rituals of passage commonly used at these times, "[the categorization that is] manifest in recognition or consecration by others, whether ritual specialists or audience, is fundamental."[131] The power inherent in others to determine the appropriateness of the rituals used can heighten awareness of differences between ethnic groups and thus increase the strength of the group identity. The desire to have one's actions affirmed by powerful others at these important times can also result in the downplaying of differences, and consequently, decrease the salience of ethnic identification.

6. The context of "healing and medicine"—the arena of diagnosing physical problems and providing solutions.[132] In this context, certain persons (not only medical doctors) are given the authority to make decisions about who fits into categories such as "sick," "insane," "incurable," "unsafe," and "dead," as well as if

127. Cornell and Hartmann, *Ethnicity and Race*, 182; Jenkins, *Rethinking Ethnicity*, 67.
128. Jenkins, *Rethinking Ethnicity*, 67.
129. Ibid., 68.
130. Ibid.
131. Ibid.
132. Ibid.

and how people in these categories should be treated. Jenkins urges his readers not to underestimate the extent to which ethnic categorization influences these judgments.[133] When ethnic distinctions influence decisions in this context, the value and meanings ascribed to ethnic identities gain power and have significant consequences for those who identify with them.

7. The context of "secondary socialization"—the formal and informal learning that continues throughout life.[134] Some examples of tools used in the formalized dimension of this context include the categorization contained in the textbooks, curriculum, and language policies of educational institutions. Actors also learn informally in social settings, so family members, community members, peer group members, and work colleagues, both in what they say and what they model, can also be tools that informally influence the ethnic attitudes of these actors.[135] Consequently, when the categorization voices of the "teachers" who surround actors during secondary socialization vary, ethnic identities and their thickness can also vary.

8. The context of "market relationships"—interaction that involves buying and selling.[136] Access to suppliers, buyers, and opportunities as well as the price one has to pay for goods is often structured by ethnic categorization. When ethnic categorization affects market relationships, the salience of ethnic identities is usually heightened.

9. The context of "marketing."[137] In the process of marketing their products, professional marketers often engage (or seek to shape) the ethnic self-identification of potential consumers in ways that connect these consumers with their products. The use of ethnic symbols (e.g., language, stories) in advertisements is evidence of this engagement. Marketers may also join the categorization voices in a particular context. For example, their advertisements may subtly mirror the ethnic perspective of a dominant group

---

133. Ibid.
134. Ibid., 68–69.
135. Bandura, *Social Foundations*.
136. Jenkins, *Rethinking Ethnicity*, 69.
137. Ibid.

or limit access to their "high-status" products for members of low-status ethnic groups. Consequently, when ethnic distinctions are invoked in advertising, the salience of ethnic identities often increases.

10. The context of "employment"—the acts of hiring and promotion in the labor market.[138] Employers and supervisors are gatekeepers who have the power to determine who gets access to which opportunities to earn money and contribute to society. Actors can be excluded from certain jobs or channeled into certain fields simply because they belong to a particular ethnic category. Actors often feel that they have a vested interest in aligning themselves, as much as possible, with the ethnic attitudes of those guarding the gate for job opportunities they desire. When ethnic categorization affects hiring and promotions, ethnic identities can also become very thick.

11. The context of "administrative allocation"—those placed in charge of making decisions about the distribution of public or private resources.[139] These decisions carry authority and legitimacy and have significant consequences for those being categorized. For example, the disadvantage of an ethnic minority can be reinforced as resources flow in ways that benefit a dominant group. Access to higher education, public housing, loans, and the like are included here. When decisions in this context are based on ethnic categorization, ethnic identity is thrust into the forefront.

12. The context of "social control"—the desire of individuals and groups to facilitate and protect social order.[140] The institutions established in societies to keep control (e.g., police, courts, military) are often tools that express and enforce the categorization of a dominant ethnic group. The extent to which an ethnic identity in this context gets associated with social deviance has a great deal of effect on the thickness of that identity for those connected to it.

13. The context of "organized politics"—the political system, the means used to make the laws and regulations that govern a

---

138. Ibid.
139. Ibid., 70.
140. Ibid., 70–71.

society.¹⁴¹ In this context, political parties and politicians often channel the power and resources at their disposal in ways that promote a certain ethnic categorization. Sometimes, they may even deny the existence of certain ethnic groups. Ethnic actors can also join together to support parties and elect politicians who are sympathetic to their own ethnic perspective. The degree to which ethnic categorizations direct the use of political power also influences the salience of and the meanings one associates with one's ethnic identity.

14. The context of "social policy"—the approaches that governments or other groups develop to help segments of their society that are perceived to have problems and be in need of help.¹⁴² The judgments of what constitutes a legitimate problem and which persons are worthy of being helped often reflect and further ethnic categorization. When ethnic categorization is the basis for social policy, the ethnic identities that are implicated become thicker.

15. The context of "official classification"—the way that governments group, classify, and label segments of their population during census taking and other settings where statistics are gathered.¹⁴³ Government officials have the power to highlight certain differences between people and to use these differences to categorize people into groups. These categories gain credibility and become "powerfully constitutive of social reality through public rhetoric, the formulation of policy, the targeting of resources, and social control measures."¹⁴⁴ They can also become symbols that are conscripted by actors for use in ethnic self-identification and categorization. The use of an ethnic identity in this way increases its salience.

---

141. Ibid., 71.
142. Ibid.
143. Ibid., 71–72.
144. Ibid., 72.

Fluidity from the Nature of Symbols Used in Ethnic Identification

Social constructionist scholars also highlight the fluidity of the cultural symbols that are marked as significant in ethnic identification. For example, these scholars point out that ethnic labels and the meanings associated with them have fluidity in that they both can change and do so independent of each other. Jenkins helpfully refers to this relationship as the nominal-virtual distinction. "Nominal" refers to the ethnic label, while "virtual" refers to the meanings associated with the label or the "consequences for those who bear it."[145] Consequently, even though the ethnic label remains consistent over time, meanings associated with that label can and most likely will be changing. Similarly, different ethnic labels may be used to refer to the same set of associated meanings.

Constructionists also note the fluidity in the nature of symbols. While members of an ethnic group may rally around the same symbols, they may also be attaching totally different meanings to them. Symbols, by their very nature, have the capacity to "encompass and condense a range of not necessarily harmonious or congruent meanings."[146] As a result, Jenkins notes that people, to some degree, "can say and do the 'same' things without saying or doing the same things at all."[147] This possible variance also means that while two "groups" of people may reach consensus on the symbols that mark boundaries between their "groups," the meanings each associates with these symbols can vary considerably.

Constructionists also point out that the symbols that are understood to be fixed by many ethnic actors are actually quite fluid or "imagined." For example, ethnic categories, contrary to the assertions of many who use them, have not always existed. Rather, these categories are understood to have emerged at some point in the past when individuals and groups of people began to band together around shared ethnic symbols in response to their circumstances. Nagata gives another example showing how genealogies, the tools that members of ethnic groups often use to "irrefutably" show common origins, are known to mysteriously change under certain circumstances.[148] Hsien Rin gives an example of the leader of a small Aboriginal group in Taiwan who constructed a myth that linked the

---

145. Ibid., 76.
146. Jenkins, *Social Identity*, 112.
147. Ibid.
148. Nagata, "Ethnic Boundaries," 94.

origin of his group, traditionally understood to be culturally and linguistically "Malayo-Polynesian," to the "prestigious and dominant" Chinese.[149]

Fixity in Ethnic Identification

Social constructionists also acknowledge that there is a fixed or primordial dimension to ethnic identities. It is important to emphasize that the terms "fixed" and "primordial" are used here metaphorically and do not imply anything that is essential. Rather, both of these words refer to something that is constructed. "Fixity" is used here to capture the way constructionists see people "experiencing" their identities and to explain how ethnic identities can be extremely durable and the deep feelings that these identities often evoke. In this regard, Cornell and Hartmann argue, "A constructionism that does not take the primordial metaphor into account loses touch not only with how ordinary human beings in many cases experience their own identities but also with much of what is most potent, distinctive, and revealing about ethnic . . . phenomena."[150]

The seeming incongruity of something being both "fixed" and "fluid" at the same time has led many scholars to address the question of why people construct fixity—why they attach such significance to primordial attachments. At least three common and interrelated themes have emerged in constructionist writing on the fixity of ethnic identification. First, fixity is the result of primary socialization and habit. Second, fixity is valued because fixity satisfies deep needs. Third, fixity is the natural result of cognitive classification.

Fixity from Primary Socialization and Habit

The first theme found in the literature discussing fixity in ethnic identification highlights early experiences and habit. A sense of self is constituted in what Jenkins calls, "the early verbal and non-verbal dialogue—a complex interaction of separation *from* and identification *with*—between the child and significant others."[151] These significant others not only tell children who they are (the internal dimension) but also what they should do (the external dimension, the social expectations they face). It is during the interaction between the internal and external that begins initially in early

---

149. Rin, "Synthesizing Mind," 152.
150. Cornell and Hartmann, *Ethnicity and Race*, 95.
151. Jenkins, *Rethinking Ethnicity*, 60.

socialization and continues throughout life that the individual's sense of self is constituted.

While Cornell and Hartmann do not put the focus on "early" experiences and socialization, they, too, note the influence of experience and socialization in the constitution of self.[152] They point to the way this influence "leads individuals to see themselves as connected to other people—and, more important, as connected to categories of people."[153] Cornell and Hartmann also note that when these self-concepts and collective identities are embedded in "established relationships, institutions, cultural practices, or ways of seeing the world, they gain considerable inertial force."[154] These scholars see individuals participating in the process of ethnic identification with "well-established . . . interpretive windows on the world and potential bases for action."[155]

Jenkins highlights the important role that habitualization plays in human life.[156] Social constructionists argue that "all human activity is subject to habitualization."[157] Habitualization benefits the ethnic actor by relieving him or her of the burden of rethinking and reanalyzing anew each situation detail-by-detail every time it is encountered. Consequently, mental energy is conserved for handling new situations where precedents have not already been established in habit. When certain individual habits become used by a group of people over a period of time, they become institutionalized—seen unthinkingly as the way to do things in a particular situation. Those who first initiated the habit retain the meanings and rationale behind the original decision, but as this habit is passed on, future generations comprehend these habits simply as an objective reality and may even attach other explanations of the origin of these habits. Language and tradition are examples of institutionalized habit.[158] Giddens affirms this perspective, calling tradition "established habit."[159]

Several constructionist scholars find Bourdieu's concept of habitus helpful in explaining the effect of early experiences and habit on

---

152. Cornell and Hartmann, *Ethnicity and Race*, 103.
153. Ibid.
154. Ibid.
155. Ibid.
156. Jenkins, *Social Identity*, 70.
157. Berger and Luckmann, *Social Construction of Reality*, 70.
158. Ibid., 70ff.
159. Giddens, *Modernity and Self-Identity.*, 80

individuals.[160] According to Bourdieu, the habitus is "an acquired system of generative schemes objectively adjusted to the particular conditions in which it is constituted."[161] It is "a system of dispositions common to all products of the same conditionings."[162] When the objective "conditions of existence" vary between groups (e.g., different generations in the same society or different cultures), the habitus of these groups also varies.[163]

The constitution of the habitus begins in primary socialization, and once internalized, is somewhat resistant to change. Bourdieu explains, "Early experiences have particular weight because the habitus tends to ensure its own constancy and its defense against change through the selection it makes within new information by rejecting information capable of calling into question its accumulated information, if exposed to it accidentally or by force, and especially by avoiding exposure to such information."[164] This resistance does not mean the habitus is unchanging; rather Bourdieu argues that it is "endlessly transformed" in the face of changing circumstances.[165] In each new situation, the habitus generates a range of possible actions or strategic practices for the individual that fit with and replicate the objective conditions that constituted this habitus. As a result, these actions or practices are experienced as "reasonable" and "commonsense" and are contrasted with other actions or practices which are "unthinkable or scandalous" and "not for the likes of us."[166] The dispositions of the habitus have tremendous power and efficacy because they function "below the level of consciousness and language, beyond the reach of introspective scrutiny or control by the will."[167] Jenkins notes that habitus' inability to explain how "actors or collectivities can intervene in their own history in any substantial fashion" is a weakness.[168]

Relating habit and the phenomena Bourdieu labels "habitus" to ethnicity, Jenkins argues, "Nothing could be more basic and nothing more

---

160. E.g., Jenkins, *Rethinking Ethnicity*; Bentley, "Ethnicity and Practice"; May, *Language and Minority Rights*.

161. Bourdieu, *Theory of Practice*, 95.

162. Bourdieu, *Logic of Practice*, 59.

163. Bourdieu, *Theory of Practice*, 78.

164. Bourdieu, *Logic of Practice*, 60–1.

165. Bourdieu, *In Other Words*, 116.

166. Bourdieu, *Logic of Practice*, 55–56; Bourdieu, *Theory of Practice*, 78.

167. Bourdieu, *Distinction*, 466.

168. Jenkins, *Pierre Bourdieu*, 83.

inextricably implicated in ethnicity."[169] He argues that the cultural "stuff" of ethnicity is located in the habitus, describing the habitus as "the embodied and unreflexive everyday practical mastery of culture: unsystematic, the empire of habit, neither conscious nor unconscious."[170] This location of the cultural "stuff" in the habitus is significant because it means that much of the repertoire of ethnic identification is experienced by individuals and groups as surprisingly resistant to change and as unthinkingly commonsensical.

Jenkins' use of Barth's cultural "stuff" term as he talks about habit and the habitus needs an explanation. Jenkins, in contrast to Barth, views this cultural "stuff" to be closely related to the process of ethnic identification. In making this point, Jenkins is not suggesting that "cultural content" comprises or constitutes ethnic identity. Jenkins reasons first that "cultural content" is closely connected to ethnic identification because it, "even if only in part, reflect[s] our interactions with [others]" across ethnic boundaries.[171] He points out that this "stuff" includes things like the meanings associated with ethnic categories, the routines engaged by "us" to respond to the categorization by "them" and vice versa, and the balances achieved between the self-ascription of "us" and the categorization of "them."[172] Another way Jenkins describes this content is "the common sense, common knowledge and patterns of behavior shared by the people inside the boundaries."[173]

Secondly, Jenkins asserts that cultural "stuff" is implicated in ethnic identification because it provides the raw materials—the differences between "us" and "them" as well as the similarities evident in "us"—that can be highlighted and made significant in the ethnic-identification process.[174] While these differences or commonalities can be minor, they cannot be arbitrary. Jenkins argues, "Even in the context of categorization, the criteria of identification have to possess at least some social relevance: they have to be differences [and commonalities] that make a difference to someone."[175]

---

169. Jenkins, *Rethinking Ethnicity*, 79.
170. Ibid.
171. Ibid., 171.
172. Ibid.
173. Jenkins, *Social Identity*, 115.
174. Jenkins, *Rethinking Ethnicity*, 172.
175. Ibid.

A third close connection between the cultural "stuff" and ethnic identification for Jenkins is the way this "stuff" affects the interaction at the border between "us" and "them." There are at least two aspects to this influence for Jenkins. First, the cultural "stuff" can affect the intensity of the feelings that are expressed at the boundaries. At times, certain ethnic boundaries "really matter."[176] For example, when members of an ethnic group encounter categorization that threatens the symbols that represent or support their whole culture, they can be extremely resistant. Cornell and Hartmann explain, "It is one thing to take up a new set of interests or to turn to different institutions to solve life's problems, but it is quite another to turn your back on an interpretive scheme on which you have come to depend for an understanding of the world around you and your place within it."[177] Second, the cultural "stuff" can also affect the character of interactions between "us" and "them" at the ethnic border. Jenkins gives the example of how "the 'cultural' acceptability of violence as a means for the pursuit of ends" could affect these interactions significantly.[178]

Stephen Cornell makes another helpful point about cultural "stuff." He argues that the cultural content produced by interactions at the border can shape circumstances. He points out that ethnic identity "is both a prism and a tool through which people interpret and conceptually construct the world."[179] He elaborates, "Our self-concepts shape our perceptions of the world around us and, therefore, our perception of our interests. This, in turn, shapes action, often with transformative consequences for circumstance. While circumstances construct identities, identities, via the actions they set in motion, are also capable of reconstructing circumstances."[180]

Fixity Because Fixity Meets Deep Needs

The second common theme found in the literature that relates to fixity in ethnic identification is a highlighting of the way that ethnic fixity meets deep needs. Scholars note that ethnic identification satisfies the desire of individuals to be connected with others in deep and lasting ways. Eugeen Roosens explains that people attach special significance to ethnic elements because an ethnic identity can bring "psychological security in

---

176. Ibid.
177. Cornell and Hartmann, *Ethnicity and Race*, 91.
178. Jenkins, *Rethinking Ethnicity*, 172.
179. Cornell, "Variable Ties," 267.
180. Ibid.

this identification, a feeling of belonging, a certainty that one knows one's origin, that one can live on in the younger generations of one's people who will carry on the struggle, and so on."[181] DeVos and Romanucci-Ross affirm, "To know one's *origin* is to have not only a sense of provenience, but perhaps more importantly, a sense of *continuity* in which one finds the personal and social *meaning* of human existence to some degree. It is to know *why* one behaves and acts in accordance with custom. To be without a sense of continuity is to be faced with one's own death."[182] Psychologist Jean S. Phinney also affirms, "The evidence indicates that an ethnic identity, although dynamic and influenced by the historical and social contexts, can provide for ethnic group members, to varying degrees, a stable 'core' sense of belonging that is a central aspect of the self."[183]

Social constructionists also note that this fixity is important for the ontological security of individuals. Elaborating on this point, Giddens notes that people want to have confidence "in the continuity of their self-identity and in the constancy of the surrounding social and material environments of action."[184] Continuity in self-identity comes from being able to "keep a particular narrative going . . . to be able to integrate events which occur in the external world, and sort them into the ongoing 'story' about self."[185] Habit and routine support a sense of constancy and predictability in life.[186] Hence, ethnic actors often find fixity expressed in continuity and constancy in ethnic identification, as well as other aspects of their worlds, very important.

Some scholars argue that people engage in categorization in an attempt to reduce uncertainty in their world. Henry E. Hale notes people naturally divide themselves and others into categories and groupings in order to reduce uncertainty and to map out some personal "reference points" for navigating their social world.[187] People are also understood to naturally join with others in groupings when there is a mutual perception of a common fate.[188] Hale argues that "some ethnic identifications are in

---

181. Roosens, *Creating Ethnicity*, 16.
182. De Vos and Romanucci-Ross, "Ethnic Identity," 375–76.
183. Phinney, "Ethnic Identity," 193.
184. Giddens, *Consequences of Modernity*, 92.
185. Giddens, *Modernity and Self-Identity*, 54.
186. Jenkins, *Social Identity*, 63.
187. Hale, "Explaining Ethnicity," 464.
188. Ibid., 465.

fact quite 'old,' thick, and/or stable" and that these characteristics make these precedents more appealing to those seeking to reduce uncertainty in their social world.[189] He writes, "Ethnic symbols can gain such powerful connotation via reference to shared histories, blood relationships, and past commonalities of fate because all of these lend credibility to suggestions of future commonalities of fate for those who have a certain relationship to these symbols."[190]

Some scholars add that the fixity in ethnic identification is especially appealing because it provides individuals with a sense of security and stability in an increasingly complex and disconcerting world.[191] Cornell and Hartmann agree, "Ethnicity, with its sense of historical continuity and its claims to deep—even primordial—interpersonal ties, holds out the prospect of communion and connection, of a mediating community between the individual and large, impersonal processes and institutions."[192] Ting-Toomey adds, "In an unfamiliar cultural environment, it is inevitable that most individuals would fall back on their familiar ethnocentric nets or habits and put on their stereotypic lens to help them to adapt more efficiently to an unfamiliar cultural environment."[193]

The way ethnic identification meets deep needs makes the fixity of ethnic identities important to people. Some constructionist scholars highlight the fact that many people are troubled when confronted with the idea that their ethnic identity is constructed rather than fixed. They see it as an attack on the very foundations of their culture and feel their culture is being accused of being "inauthentic."[194] Cushman elaborates:

> There is something in the very nature of being human that makes it extremely difficult to differentiate what we are from what we construct. . . . We construct the social world in such a way so that we can consider it, experience it, as reality itself—the one, true, concrete truth. To do otherwise would be to open up the existential abyss for us, to force us to confront our own lacks, absences, and emptiness, to challenge the taken-for-granted power relations, economic privileges, and status hierarchy of our era, to acknowledge the relational rules, alliances, and secrets of our fam-

189. Ibid., 481.
190. Ibid., 477.
191. Zelinsky, *Enigma of Ethnicity*, 215.
192. Cornell and Hartmann, *Ethnicity and Race*, 102.
193. Ting-Toomey, "Identity Negotiation Theory," 220.
194. Cornell and Hartmann, *Ethnicity and Race*, 95–96.

ily of origin. For various reasons, an awareness of the constructed nature of our world appears to be too difficult to acknowledge and too frightening to live with.[195]

Judith Butler postulates that distancing ourselves from the norms that have shaped us and on which we are dependent is not easy because doing so means "undoing" the "I" that I am. In the undoing, this "I" becomes, "to a certain extent unknowable, threatened with unviability, with becoming undone altogether."[196]

Fixity from the Cognitive Dimensions of Ethnic Identification

A third theme found in the constructionist literature that relates to fixity in ethnic identification focuses on the cognitive dimensions of this process. An emphasis on the influence of cognition, as opposed to social and cultural influences, yields at least two important insights that deepen our understanding of the fixity of ethnic identification. First, cognitive categorization reifies groups, and second, ethnic symbols are cognitively very accessible and plausible and therefore seem especially appropriate to use in differentiating people. It is important to note that scholars discussing cognition in this subsection use the term "categorization" differently than the way this term is used in the remainder of this study. Rather than being the action of a person or group to identify an "other" (e.g., a Hoklo saying that Hakkas are stingy), in this subsection "categorization" will mean "the process of dividing the world up into classes of phenomena on the basis of criteria of similarity or difference."[197]

The first insight from the cognitive dimensions of ethnic identification is that the nature of cognitive categorization brings fixity to ethnic identification by reifying ethnic groups. Important to this argument is the ubiquity of categorization and categories. George Lakoff argues, "There is nothing more basic than categorization to our thought, perception, action, and speech."[198] He goes on to explain, "Every time we see something as a *kind* of thing . . . [or think about, or treat or talk about something as *kinds* of things], we are categorizing."[199] Rogers Brubaker explains, "[Categories]

---

195. Cushman, *Constructing the Self*, 309.
196. Butler, *Undoing Gender*.
197. Jenkins, *Rethinking Ethnicity*, 57.
198. Lakoff, *What Categories Reveal*, 5.
199. Ibid., 5–6.

allow us to see different things—and treat different cases—as the same."²⁰⁰ Eleanor Rosch notes that categories "provide maximum information with the least cognitive effort."²⁰¹ Brubaker accents the importance of categorization, "Without categories, the world would be a 'blooming, buzzing confusion'; experience and action as we know them would be impossible."²⁰²

When categorization is observed in the realm of ethnic identification, scholars note the reifying effects. More is going on than just sorting. Ethnic groups become discrete and bounded, "substantial entities to which interests and agency can be attributed."²⁰³ The people categorized to be in them are "depersonalized, transmuted from unique persons to exemplars of named groups."²⁰⁴ In other words, even when we do not know a person, the category in which we place them can lead us to have expectations of and "knowledge" about them, which in turn influences our judgments of them and the way we treat them. This reifying in categorization often results in dual accentuation; homogeneity among group members tends to be emphasized and differences between groups tend to be magnified.²⁰⁵ In-group bias can also be the result of the reifying of groups that happens in categorization. Tajfel and Turner argue, "The mere awareness of the presence of an out-group is sufficient to provoke intergroup competitive or discriminatory responses on the part of the in-group."²⁰⁶ Hence, the reifying of groups that happens in categorization can lead people to experience their ethnic group as something essential and natural, bringing fixity to what is more accurately seen as "something that happens."²⁰⁷

The second insight from the cognitive dimensions of ethnic identification is that the way "ethnic" symbols seem appropriate to distinguish kinds of people also contributes to fixity in this process. Hale maintains that "there tends to be intrinsic value to those markers we call 'ethnic' in constituting boundaries distinguishing these groupings."²⁰⁸ "Ethnic" reference points—like "perceptions of common descent, history, fate, and

200. Brubaker, *Ethnicity without Groups*, 71.
201. Rosch, "Principles of Categorization," 28.
202. Brubaker, *Ethnicity without Groups*, 71.
203. Ibid., 8.
204. Levine, "Reconstructing Ethnicity," 169.
205. Hogg and Abrams, *Social Identifications*, 19.
206. Tajfel and Turner, *Intergroup Conflict*, 56.
207. Brubaker, *Ethnicity without Groups*, 9, 12.
208. Hale, "Explaining Ethnicity," 481.

culture, which usually indicate some mix of language, physical appearance, and the ritual regulation of life, especially religion"—are often very important in social categorization because they are usually very accessible and plausible.[209] Brubaker calls ethnic categories "easy to think" in comparison to other categories (e.g., class).[210] He argues, "Representations that are easy to think will be more easily communicated, transmitted, and remembered, and as a result more widely shared, than others."[211] One example Hale gives is of how these "ethnic" markers are so accessible and appear appropriate because they are often closely tied to communication barriers. Since communication is so important in the social world, when language, culture, or other differences impede that interaction, these differences become immediately relevant and accessible as reference points for categorization. Brubaker argues that the fact that ethnic categories are easy to think "would help explain in part why they tend to be widely shared and powerfully entrenched cultural representations."[212]

Concluding Remarks

Primordialism, circumstantialism, and Barth provide key insights for understanding ethnic behavior in the world today, but if looked to separately cannot explain all aspects of the ethnic phenomenon. The constructionist approach of combining the discourses of fixity and fluidity is helpful as it draws important concepts from each of the three approaches. The constructionist approach to understanding ethnicity and ethnic groups offers much hope for explaining the diversity of ethnic behavior in the world today.

As what informants share about their perspectives on the way Hakka non-Christians categorize being Christian and the way Hakka Christians respond in the context of these categorizations is examined, keeping the following insights from this literature in mind will open the door to a deeper understanding of what is being said and done. First, everything informants say about an aspect of being Hakka is only one perspective on this phenomenon. Different perspectives on the same aspect often exist and can be found both inside and outside the ethnic boundary. Second, the responses constructed by informants and those they talk about can be

---

209. Ibid., 473.
210. Brubaker, *Ethnicity without Groups*, 80.
211. Ibid.
212. Ibid.

expected to provide evidence that they have a desire to cultivate a positive public image of themselves. Third, what is said can be expected to provide evidence that informants and those they talk about use different strategies as they define themselves and categorize others. Fourth, it can be expected that the responses of informants and Hakkas they discuss will be influenced by the varying degree of salience that being Hakka has for them. Fifth, variability in the salience and meanings in being Hakka for informants and other Hakkas often can be traced to contextual factors. Sixth, the responses of informants and those they talk about may also vary as a result of group factors, the corporate characteristics and assets of those who are being Hakka. Seventh, it can be expected that the symbols informants and those they discuss use in their responses will have a variety of different meanings attached to them. Eighth, it can be expected that informants will give evidence that early experiences were influential in shaping the Hakka perspective on the world and in establishing the habits Hakkas practice. There should also be evidence of the taken-for-grantedness of this perspective and these habits. Ninth, the responses of informants should also reveal that Hakkas place importance on ethnic attachments because they meet deep needs for belonging, continuity, and stability. There should also be evidence of resistance to the idea that their ethnic attachments are constructed. Tenth, the responses of informants should provide evidence that ethnic distinctions are easy to think and that when Hakkas classify someone as "other," doing so affects the way they see them (e.g., individuals are seen as a representative of a group; homogeneity between insiders and differences between insiders and outsiders is accentuated).

Being Hakka in Taiwan

This section will review the literature related to important aspects of being Hakka in Taiwan and, in doing so, will detail the important aspects of the cultural "stuff" that is shaping the thoughts and actions of those who are being Hakka in Taiwan as well as serving as a reservoir of symbols and habits on which they draw to construct their identity in relation to being Christian in the midst of a world that is rapidly changing around them. Important aspects of this literature include: (1) the historical development of being Hakka for Taiwan Hakkas, (2) modernization, and (3) the recent developments for being Hakka in Taiwan.

The Historical Development of Being Hakka for Taiwan Hakkas

History has shaped Hakkas and provides symbols for Hakkas to use in the process of ethnic identification. Anthropologist Nicole Constable writes, "The key to the Hakka identity . . . is not exclusively language, shared political interests, shared cultural practices, religion, or native place; it is the way in which these and other elements are invariably tied to Hakka history."[213] This subsection will discuss the historical perspective of Luo Xianglin, the genesis of the Hakka ethnic identity, Hakka ethnicity in Taiwan during the Qing Dynasty, and being Hakka under the Japanese and the Chinese Nationalists.

Luo Xianglin's Perspective

Historian Luo Xianglin, a scholar whose writings have significantly shaped the present day understanding of Hakka history, dates the origin of the term "Hakka" to the end of the Tang Dynasty, the Five Dynasties, and the early Song Dynasty (874–1276).[214] Basing his view of Hakka history primarily on the genealogies of Hakka families, Luo asserts that the bloodlines of those who came to be known as Hakka can be traced back to brave and important Han Chinese patriots at various points in Chinese history. He argues that, as these patriots and their descendants, fleeing political strife, migrated from the north of China to the south and to Taiwan and other places in the world in five distinct migrations, they preserved the language and culture of the Central Plain of China, their original homeland (the cradle of Han Chinese civilization), and in doing so, they and their descendants came to be seen by themselves and others as Hakka, as different from other Han Chinese they encountered in the south.

Historian Sow-theng Leong points out that Luo's book *Kejia yanjiu daolun* (An Introduction to the Study of the Hakkas) "is cited as the authority by everyone whose research touches on the Hakkas . . . [and is] a veritable Bible for the Hakkas themselves."[215] Leong critiques this book as "part scholarship and part ethnic rhetoric."[216] He points out, "Luo came at the end of a long line of ethnically awakened scholars stretching back to the turn of the nineteenth century." He continues, "[These scholars] identified and codified Hakka cultural values and forms, propagated a Hakka

---

213. Constable, "Construction of Hakka Identity," 76.
214. Luo, *Study of Hakkas*, 71.
215. Leong, "Origins of the Hakkas," 28.
216. Ibid., 29.

cultural past with a view to enhancing the depressed social status of a despised people."[217] In Leong's mind, Luo's historical analysis was colored with the desire that Hakka be seen quite positively.

Several scholars have challenged Luo's assertion that the migrants who became Hakkas completely preserved the language and culture of the Central Plain. For example, Fang Xuejia argues that the Hakkas were a mixture of a minority of Han migrants and a much larger majority of the original inhabitants (*guyuezu*) of what many scholars refer to as the Hakka heartland (*kejia dabenying diqu*), the highland area that is at the conjuncture of modern-day Fujian, Guangdong, and Jiangxi Provinces in southern China. He postulates that this mixture of people gradually developed into a distinct cultural grouping between the time of the Qin Dynasty and the Southern Dynasty. Fang continues that, during the period between Sui-Tang Dynasties and the Five Dynasties, after a distinct language and culture emerged, this Hakka grouping was influenced by Han culture from the Central Plain and, as a result, became more Han Chinese. While some scholars have disputed Fang's conclusions, his views have led to calls that the influence of the original inhabitants of the Hakka heartland on the Han Chinese migrants be studied in more detail.[218]

Others challenge Luo's method of working upstream through the genealogies of Hakka families to determine the unique migration patterns of the Hakkas. Chen Yundong points out that a look at the larger context of what was happening in other groups reveals that the migrations to the south of those who became Hakka are hard to distinguish from the migrations to the south of other Han Chinese migrants and that, as a result, all these migrants were bound to be intertwined and intermixed together.[219] Chen Zhiping agrees that Luo's five migrations were not limited to Hakkas. He adds that the Hakka language was not brought with the Han Chinese who moved into the Hakka heartland. Chen cites his own study of both Hakka and non-Hakka genealogies and postulates that as migrants from the same northern lineages moved to different locations in southern China, they learned the language prevalent in their new homes. As a result, descendants of the same northern lineages could be found in different

---

217. Ibid., 30.
218. E.g., Wang, *Introduction to Hakkaology*, 81.
219. Chen, "Origins," 22.

ethnic groups in different locations throughout southern China at different points in history.[220]

Other scholars argue that genealogies, Luo's primary source of data, are problematic. For example, Andrew Char argues that since genealogies did not take their present form until sometime during the Song Dynasty (AD 960–1279), genealogical data must be viewed as suspect before that time. He further asserts that the desirability of certain geographical origins (e.g., the Central Plain) also opens the possibility that, when genealogies were put on paper, stylistic conventions were taken to include ancestors from these prestigious origins. He also points out that genealogical records only represent those clans wealthy enough to compile them and therefore only present part of the whole picture of what was happening.[221] Leong adds that Luo's sample was "disappointingly small."[222]

The Genesis of the Hakka Ethnic Identity

Sow-theng Leong, following Patterson's distinction between a cultural group and an ethnic group, argues that Han Chinese migrants first developed into a distinct Hakka cultural group and did not act together ethnically as Hakkas until later. He explains that it was during an extended incubation period of living in the mountain areas of the Hakka heartland and being involved in prolonged ethnic conflicts with the non-Han Chinese She group also living there that these migrants evolved into a cultural group. While they were still proud of their Han Chinese roots, they developed unique cultural markers and a separate dialect that distinguished them from other Han Chinese.[223] Leong argues that it was not until the late sixteenth century that the Hakka ethnic identity began to emerge when people from this Hakka cultural group migrated from the Hakka heartland into contiguous areas in southern China where earlier migrants, often called Punti (*bendiren*, literally "locals"), already lived.[224]

These new arrivals in Punti areas were often called Hakka (literally "guest families"), a label that clearly distinguished them as newcomers. Anthropologist Myron L. Cohen, writing specifically about the situation in the area in what is now known as Guangdong Province and the

220. Chen, *Hakka Origins*.
221. Char, "Origins of Ethnicity," 75.
222. Leong, "Origins of the Hakkas," 29.
223. Leong, "Hakka Migrations," 39.
224. Leong, "Origins of the Hakkas," 26.

adjoining areas of Guangxi Province, argues that initially, the Hakka-speaking migrants and the Cantonese-speaking Punti had a symbiotic relationship—the Punti had extra land and needed tenant farmers, and the migrants needed a way to make a living.[225] However, the reciprocal relations that existed did not mean the new migrants were welcomed as equals and assimilated with the Punti. Instead, the migrants lived scattered in pockets that were in close proximity to but separate from the linguistically exclusive Punti villages.[226] Char highlights the localism that characterized the Punti areas, pointing out that in both single and multiple surname Punti villages, outsiders were seen as potential threats to village control of the physical space or territory they claimed and would only be allowed to remain if they could be kept in situations where they could not accumulate enough wealth and power to pose a threat.[227]

Early on, the Punti noticed that the culture of these newly arrived migrants was strikingly different from their own. For example, their women worked in the fields and had unbound feet, while the Punti women had bound feet and stayed at home. Knowing that the new arrivals had most recently come from an area originally inhabited by the non-Han Chinese She people, the Punti saw these differences as evidence that these migrants were descendants of the She, an affront to any Chinese. David Liao explains the seriousness of this Punti conclusion: "To be called non-Chinese or mongrel is to a Chinese a grave insult."[228]

The response of the Hakkas to the prejudice of the Puntis was threefold. First, they continued to take advantage of whatever opportunities were offered to them and worked diligently. Wherever they went, the Hakkas worked hard and frequently found ways to make marginal and often unused land yield good profits. Quoting the Yongfu County gazetteer records in 1612, Leong gives an example of the way Hakkas operated: "[They] were willing to become tenants on land inaccessible to irrigation, and managed to derive more income by raising cash crops than the lowlanders did from their rice crop, exciting much native envy."[229]

The Hakka habit of taking advantage of opportunities and working hard was not limited to farming. Once they were allowed to participate in

225. Cohen, "Hakka or 'Guest People'," 54.
226. Ibid.
227. Char, "Origins of Ethnicity," 69–70.
228. Liao, *Unresponsive*, 86.
229. Leong, "Hakka Migrations," 45.

government examinations, Hakka test takers were quite successful. Leong gives one example, "Late in the eighteenth century, in a series of examinations for the *juren* degree in Guangzhou, four Hakka candidates . . . performed the consciousness-raising feat of successively carrying off first prize, to the discomfort of their Cantonese [another name used for the Puntis in Guangdong province] rivals."[230]

Secondly, in the face of Punti prejudice, Leong states that the Hakka chose a response that made them an ethnic group. While they could have chosen to accept the Punti negative ascriptions, they instead asserted a claim that their differences, rather than being an indicator of their barbarian roots, were really an indicator that they possessed "a Chineseness that was equal, if not superior, to that of other Chinese."[231]

Leong argues that the speech of a Hakka scholar named Xu Xuzeng in the early 1800s was the first time the Hakka ethnic identity was articulated in a way that brought the pockets of Hakka-speaking migrants scattered around southern China together in solidarity. Xu traced the roots of the Hakka back to the central plain of China, the cradle of the Han Chinese civilization. He described the Hakka as patriotic loyalists who immigrated south to serve and support the Song dynasty rulers against invasions of the Mongols. Xu explained how the Hakka had chosen to live in the mountains along the Guangdong-Fujian-Jiangxi border rather than be ruled by Mongol barbarians during the Yuan dynasty (1271–1368). Xu's manuscript continues, "They felt they should reside together [and] preserve their customs and speech . . . so that their patriotic spirit would not diminish."[232] Thus, in the isolated setting of the mountains, the ancient language and culture of the Han Chinese could be preserved in the Hakka language and culture.

Xu's speech further articulated the Hakka identity by reporting that the Hakka had obeyed the early Qing dynasty (1684–1895) decrees prohibiting footbinding for women. Consequently, Hakka women were able not only to manage their households and raise their children but also to help their husbands work in the fields. Rather than being uncivilized and low class as the Punti around them had taunted, Xu suggested that Hakka women modeled the loyalty and hard work of the true Chinese woman.[233]

230. Leong, "Hakka Ethos," 76.
231. Ibid.
232. Ibid., 77.
233. Ibid., 79.

Xu's manuscript continued to describe the people whom the Punti looked down upon with disdain. "In essence, the Hakka are diligent by habit, thrifty and unostentatious in customs, courteous, modest, elegant, and polished by disposition."[234] Quoting the Hakka historian Luo Xianglin, Leong adds, "[The Hakka displayed] all the prized virtues believed to inhere in the uncorrupted people of the Golden Age of great antiquity."[235] Clearly, in the minds of Hakka, they were true Han Chinese, and the Punti were grossly mistaken when they questioned this fact.

Thirdly, Leong maintains that the Hakka mobilized in solidarity around this ethnic identity. Leong quotes a Xunzhou fu zhi (Gazetteer of Xunzhou prefecture) from 1874 as saying, "Although [the Hakka] dwell in solitary huts within the fields, without neighbors, their sentiment of ethnic solidarity . . . is very strong. In an emergency, a hundred will respond to a call, arriving with spears and spades on their shoulders, fearless of death."[236] The God Worshippers Society, one of the key forces in the Taiping Rebellion, provides an example of this phenomenon. Franz Michael writes, "[This society] was formed among Hakka by Hakka leaders. Once the society was established and its many branches were functioning, the Hakka found it an organizational protection in their fight against the Punti. Large groups of Hakka, already in conflict with their non-Hakka neighbors, joined the rapidly growing society."[237]

HAKKA ETHNICITY IN TAIWAN DURING THE QING DYNASTY

Another important aspect of the development of being Hakka for Taiwan Hakka is the experiences of their Hakka ancestors who migrated from China to Taiwan between the late seventeenth and early nineteenth centuries. Overpopulation in southern China drove many Hakkas to migrate, while the promise of good opportunities drew them to Taiwan.[238] There has been some discussion among scholars as to the reasons why Hakkas settled in the areas of Taiwan that are currently known as Hakka areas. The traditional position is that the Hakkas arrived later than the Hoklos, those Chinese who immigrated to Taiwan from Fujian province, and therefore had to settle in the less favorable areas because the better land was no

234. Ibid.
235. Ibid.
236. Leong, "Hakka Migrations," 67.
237. Michael, *Taiping Rebellion*, 30.
238. Leong, "Hakka Migrations," 54–55.

longer available.[239] Supporting this view is the fact that, during its early days, the Qing dynasty officials prohibited immigration from two Hakka areas of China to Taiwan, allowing only residents of Fujian Province to move to Taiwan. This island was considered a part of Fujian Province, and immigrants from other parts of this province were treated as if they were migrating internally. In contrast, Hakkas came to Taiwan primarily from Guangdong Province and were classified as outsiders attempting to immigrate, often facing discrimination from Fujian Province officials who controlled the borders.[240] Leong asserts that the majority of Hakkas came to Taiwan between 1725 and 1800 when these restrictions were relaxed somewhat.[241] More recently, scholars have given other possible reasons for why Hakka immigrants concentrated primarily in the hilly areas of Taiwan.[242] Two possibilities are commonly raised. First, the Hakkas chose the hilly areas, which had similar topography with the places where they originated in China, because they already possessed the skills necessary for work there. Second, the Hakkas initially settled on the plains but later were driven into the hills after they lost bitter conflicts with Hoklos.

Harry J. Lamley contributes to a further understanding of being Hakka in Taiwan by looking through the lens of what he calls "sub-ethnic" rivalry in Taiwan during the Qing dynasty (1684–1895).[243] John R. Shepherd also contributes details from the earlier portion of this period (1684–1780).[244] The rivalry these scholars detail occurred between the Hakkas and two groups of Hoklos (those from Zhangzhou and those from Quanzhou) who immigrated to Taiwan from different areas of southern China. Shepherd argues that the immigrants tended to settle together with people from their home communities and were suspicious of those from other locales, those who often spoke a different language or worshiped different deities.[245] The Hoklos and Hakkas were extremely prejudiced toward each other, and between 1683 and 1895, fifty-one significant Hakka-Hoklo conflicts took place.[246]

239. E.g., Li, "Ethnic Relations," 108.
240. Yang, "Ethnic Relationships," 393–94.
241. Leong, "Hakka Migrations," 54.
242. Ibid., 56; Knapp, "Taiwan's Landscapes," 17; Lamley, "Subethnic Rivalry," 300; Wu, "Settling and Developing."
243. Lamley, "Subethnic Rivalry."
244. Shepherd, "Frontier of Ch'ing."
245. Ibid., 128.
246. Xu, "Conflict," 153, 165.

Adding volatility to the situation was the nature of the frontier society. Many of the migrants were unattached males with "traditions of violence and self-defense."[247] Lamley explains that conflicts often developed over property boundaries and water rights and frequently mushroomed into large-scale organized feuds.[248] He describes how the minority Hakka banded together in solidarity against the Hoklo by settling together in communities, forming religious societies, and building community temples rather than ancestral halls.[249] These temples and the structure of religious societies were used to organize and facilitate Hakka opposition to the Hoklo.

Lamley argues that this sub-ethnic conflict occurred not only in the early pioneer stage of the Han development of Taiwan, but also in the middle stage when local economies were already established and growing and in the advanced stage when everything had already been developed to the same level as the areas of China from which the immigrants came.[250] The strife was especially severe between 1782 and 1862. Since the Qing government's response to the conflicts was weak, the settlers were largely left to resolve them on their own. This epidemic of sub-ethnic conflict finally came to an end in the late 1860s.[251] Lamley notes that the prejudice toward Hakka still present among the Taiwanese in Taiwan at the time he wrote was largely the result of these conflicts.[252]

Ying-chang Chuang raises some other aspects of the settlement patterns of Hakka immigrants in Taiwan during the Qing Dynasty. He reviews several studies showing that during the earlier part of this period, Hakka immigrants settled together with others from their hometowns in China.[253] In his own study, he determined that in the latter part of this period, Hakka settlement patterns switched to ones in which they would join with others who had the same surname, not only to facilitate ancestor worship, but also to pool their capital and labor to purchase and cultivate land.[254]

247. Shepherd, "Frontier of Ch'ing," 128.
248. Lamley, "Subethnic Rivalry," 289–90.
249. Ibid., 293–95.
250. Ibid., 302.
251. Ibid., 305.
252. Ibid., 317.
253. Chuang, "Settlement Patterns," 171.
254. Ibid., 169.

Being Hakka Under the Japanese and the Chinese Nationalists

In 1895, the Qing dynasty rulers ceded Taiwan to Japan, and Japan subsequently ruled the island for fifty years. After Japan was defeated in the Second World War, Taiwan was returned to the Chinese. The Chinese Nationalists (KMT), in the midst of fighting a civil war with the communists at that time, quickly sent troops and official representatives to ensure their control over Taiwan. In 1949, the Nationalists were forced to retreat to Taiwan and began to occupy most of the senior posts in the government, schools, and state-owned businesses. Martial law was established and continued to be in effect until 1987.

The Japanese and the Chinese Nationalists had much in common in the way they treated the Hakkas and other residents of Taiwan. Both governments heavily restricted the public use of Hoklo, Hakka, or Aboriginal languages. These languages were relegated to a second-class status, even though, in the case of Hoklo, it was spoken by a majority (more than 70 percent) of the population. For example, the KMT government referred to these languages as "dialects." Use of the national language (Japanese or Mandarin respectively) was required in public places such as government offices, educational institutions, and by the media. During their rule, the Japanese restricted the use of Chinese characters, while the Nationalists later restricted the use of romanization or anything that would encourage people to use local languages. These national-language policies were intended to shape the loyalties and culture of the Taiwan population in certain ways. The Japanese hoped to break the Taiwan people's ties with China and to make them Japanese. The Nationalists, on the other hand, wanted to encourage ties with China and Chinese culture, intending to, at some future point, return and retake mainland China by defeating the communist government there.

One of the significant results of these government policies supporting a national language was that Hoklo, Hakka, and other local languages came to be used primarily in more informal settings and were stigmatized to a degree. Simpson explains that, during Japanese rule, people often used Japanese to talk about more formal topics, things like "politics, education, and other intellectual matters";[255] they had never learned or had already forgotten native language vocabulary in these topic areas. Gates reports that there was a stigma associated with non-Mandarin languages (in this case Hoklo) under KMT rule, "[Hoklos and Mainlanders typically agree

---

255. Simpson, "Taiwan," 239.

that the Hoklo language] is hopelessly scatological, impossible to reduce to writing, and perhaps . . . not a real language with form and order at all."[256]

Another result was that, during the period under Nationalist control, there was a substantial shift in the ability of the younger generations of Hakkas to speak Hakka.[257] Fan Zhengan explains that Hakkas, in order to survive in the changing economy of Taiwan, often had to leave Hakka areas to live and work isolated and "hidden" among Hoklos or Mainlanders in the cities. Consequently, they often faced pressure to assimilate into the dominant culture and had little help from other Hakkas in resisting these pressures. He details how this situation affected the passing on of the Hakka language to the younger generation: (1) overworked parents had little time to spend with their children and speak Hakka with them; (2) parents routinely spoke Mandarin or Hoklo at work, and so, even when spending time with their children, they often did not speak Hakka; (3) many parents assumed that if their children spoke Hakka at home, they would speak Mandarin with a Hakka accent once they started school (something they wanted to avoid); (4) many Hakkas married non-Hakka speakers, and these couples often chose to speak Mandarin between themselves and with their children, further decreasing opportunities for their children to learn Hakka.[258]

Fan also points out to what extent the lives of children were immersed in non-Hakka-language environments—public schools, after-school tutoring, and the media all used Mandarin.[259] The pressure to learn English and other international languages, supported by government policies and school curriculums designed to help Taiwan citizens be more competitive in the international community, often made learning Hakka even less of a priority.[260] Loss of native language ability also meant that younger Hakkas were distanced from and unable to develop strong emotional ties with certain aspects of being Hakka (e.g., history, customs, music, and drama) where language was important.[261] When younger people cannot speak the primary language used by senior members of their family, this inability can easily create distance and misunderstandings between them.

256. Gates, "Ethnicity and Class," 253.
257. Huang, "Language and Conflict," 145.
258. Fan, "Social Movements," 423–24.
259. Ibid., 422–23.
260. Ibid., 424; Tsao, "Language Planning," 352.
261. Fan, "Social Movements," 422.

Another effect of the Nationalist control over Taiwan society can be found in the makeup of social classes. Being Mainlander was perceived, both by Mainlanders and by Hakkas and Hoklos, as being of a higher social class.[262] The second-class status of Hakkas and Hoklos was difficult to totally overcome, even when they were able to remove most evidence of their ethnic roots in their behavior and speech. Ancestral home was usually accentuated by Mainlanders in social settings and on government-issued identity cards.[263] Gates explains that "elite government and military" positions were generally filled by Mainlanders, while upper-class Hoklos and Hakkas were generally "big industrial and commercial entrepreneurs."[264] He argues that Hoklos and Hakkas seeking upward social mobility had two potential paths. First, they could pursue positions in government service, positions considered to be more reputable and stable. Since access to these positions was often controlled by Mainlanders, this path involved distancing oneself from one's ethnic roots and cultivating connections with Mainlanders. Success in education was especially important for those pursuing this path. Second, these Hoklos and Hakkas could pursue positions in commerce, often considered to be the "crooked road." Since business interactions often required the ability to draw on local roots and manipulate community connections, ethnic roots and language often were more important for success in this arena.[265]

A significant result of the forced shaping by the Japanese and Nationalists is that the Taiwan population began to develop "a clear sense . . . that they formed a collectivity with common interests linked to a specific territory."[266] Simpson, describing this phenomenon in the 1980s, writes, "Years of frustration caused by heavy-handed KMT attempts to instill a Chinese national identity led to negative feelings towards such an idealized 'foreign' identity centered on culture, history, and geography from the mainland rather than Taiwan, and many on the island began to explore instead how the pre-1945 inhabitants of Taiwan and their offspring might be *different* from mainland Chinese and have their own collective identity."[267] Martin argues that consequently, many

262. Gates, "Ethnicity and Class," 253–55.
263. Ibid., 254–55.
264. Ibid., 274.
265. Ibid., 276–78.
266. Simpson, "Taiwan," 240.
267. Ibid., 246.

scholars writing in the 1980s[268] grouped Hoklo and Hakka together as native Taiwanese (*benshengren*) and contrasted them with the mainland immigrants (*waishengren*), reflecting the "ethnic consciousness" at that time.[269] Wang Fuchang argues that the distinction between Hakka and Hoklo gradually weakened in the face of the emergence of a salient distinction between native Taiwanese and mainlanders.[270]

Modernization

During the twentieth century, especially during the period between the late 1940s and mid-1980s, Taiwan society underwent dramatic change. Taiwan changed from being a rural, agricultural society to being a highly urbanized, industrial one, and from being a society largely isolated from outside contacts to being one highly influenced by a flood of global input and connections. One area where these dramatic changes have had a significant impact which is relevant to this study is family relationships. According to a group of scholars studying social change and the family in Taiwan, the aspects of this societal change that have had the most impact on the family include: (1) an increase in formal education, (2) new kinds of employment opportunities, (3) changes in residence patterns, (4) new wealth, (5) influence of the mass media, and (6) secularization.[271] Because the family is such an crucial part of being Hakka, a brief summary of these aspects affecting the family is important for this study.

Increase in Formal Education

One important aspect of societal change affecting the family in Taiwan has been the increase in the amount of formal education that the younger generations receive.[272] When the society of Taiwan was more rural and agriculturally based, parents were primarily responsible for the education of their children. Since the growth of compulsory schooling and higher education opportunities in Taiwan in the latter half of the twentieth century, children spend more and more of their time away from their parents and under the influence and authority of teachers. Public and private school

268. E.g., Gates, "Ethnicity and Class."
269. Martin, "Hakka Ethnic Movement," 178.
270. Wang, *Ethnic Imagination*, 130.
271. Thornton and Lin, "Continuity and Change."; Thornton et al., "Family Change."
272. Thornton et al., "Family Change," 90–94.

education exposes children to many new ideas and is an important factor affecting their attitudes, behavior, and values.[273] In addition, many children are now more well-educated than their parents and, as a result, are often more capable and equipped than their parents to meet the challenges and opportunities of a modernizing Taiwan. This differential reduces the authority and confidence of the older generation.[274] With increased education, children often are able to secure better-paying jobs and to contribute more financially to their parents. The successes of children in the academic arena also bring honor and prestige to the family.

New Kinds of Employment Opportunities

Changes in employment opportunities have facilitated changes in the family.[275] Traditionally, Chinese families labored together on the family farm or in the family business. Any income earned from these labors was collected by the head of the family and was spent only at their discretion. This practice gave family leaders a tremendous amount of authority and control over the younger generations. With industrialization, opportunities for working outside of the family have increased. When they have outside sources of income, individual family members have the opportunity to earn their own money, and some separate their financial dealings from the family rather than contributing these wages to the joint family funds controlled by their parents. With the reduced economic importance of the farmland that was passed down from ancestors, the ties between the living and these dead have also been weakened.[276] Outside jobs lessen the time family members spend together and increase the possibility of exposure to and acceptance of ideas that might conflict with the standards and practices of the family.

New Residential Patterns

Another significant factor facilitating familial change has been the shift in residence patterns that came with industrialization.[277] Many young people move away from their homes to live in factory dormitories or in cities where they are closer to job opportunities. Rather than living together

---

273. Chiu, "Education and Change," 193.
274. Thornton et al., "Family Change," 91.
275. Ibid., 96–98.
276. Ibid., 97.
277. Ibid., 99–103.

with parents and extended family, as was the traditional pattern in Taiwan, these family members live among others. This change in living arrangements exposes these migrants to new ideas and significantly reduces the time they spend with and are influenced by their families and the communal relationship network of their home communities. The influence of home is not entirely cut off though, as they usually live close enough so that frequent trips home are possible. When these migrants visit their parents and relatives, they also bring with them the new ideas they are learning, providing an effective conduit for new ideas to penetrate rural areas.

Urban living has also changed the depth and intimacy of many of the relationships Hakkas maintain with others. Rather than interacting with others as complete individuals, as is usually the case in rural areas, people now interact with others more in specialized relationships. Thornton and others write, "As specialized relationships become predominant over general ones, individuals are less dependent upon particular persons and less constrained by the personal and emotional controls of intimate groups."[278]

New Wealth

Another important factor facilitating changes in families in Taiwan during the twentieth century has been the rapid growth in income and standard of living.[279] This increase in expendable income makes the option of increased independence available to a growing number of people. For example, young couples can rent or buy their own house or apartment, or parents who accumulate enough money do not need to depend financially on their children during old age.

Influence of the Mass Media

The mass media has also played a key role in facilitating familial change in Taiwan.[280] In the past, family and local community norms largely shaped the values and attitudes of children. As magazines, newspapers, radio, television, and movie consumption increase, these media join in as important vehicles shaping young people and adults throughout Taiwan. While the mass media continues to portray traditional Chinese values and practices, readers and viewers are also exposed to alternative values and practices from the West. These alternative Western symbols are embraced by many

---

278. Ibid., 103.
279. Ibid., 103–4.
280. Ibid., 104–10; Thornton and Lin, "Continuity and Change," 398.

Chinese and transform many different aspects of Chinese society. One example of a symbol being embraced is the increasing acceptance of the Western emphasis on the nuclear family and individual choice in marriage and childbearing.

SECULARIZATION

Thornton and others also refer to the influence of secularization as an important factor facilitating change in the family in Taiwan.[281] Lee Fong-mao points out that while people in Taiwan still turn to religious specialists for help in funeral rituals and ancestral worship, attitudes are changing.[282] Lee reports that, in the past, families leaned heavily on religious specialists to alleviate "the anxieties and insecurities associated with pregnancy, childbirth, and the gender of the newborn" but now turn to medical doctors and medical science for these things.[283] Sometimes, the religious dimension of a practice disappears while the practice remains.[284] For example, Yang, Thornton, and Fricke found that the same women in Taiwan whose belief that participation in ancestral rituals would influence the future of the family was decreasing were also increasing in their involvement in those ancestor rituals.[285]

Recent Developments for Being Hakka in Taiwan

In 1987, Chiang Ching-kuo, president and chairman of the KMT party, discontinued repression of the growing opposition to his government and lifted martial law. The results of this significant development for being Hakka in Taiwan were many. Most important for this study include: (1) the flourishing of a Taiwan consciousness with a strong Hoklo focus, (2) the development of a Hakka ethnic movement in response to this Hoklo focus, and (3) a subsequent emphasis on a multicultural Taiwan.

A FOCUS ON TAIWAN RATHER THAN MAINLAND CHINA

With the lifting of martial law in 1987, voices opposing KMT hegemony were officially allowed. The various restrictions on the use of Hakka, Hoklo, and Aborigine languages were gradually lifted. Hoklos quickly

---

281. Thornton et al., "Family Change," 110–11.
282. Lee, "Daoist Priesthood," 136.
283. Ibid.
284. Yang, "Responses to Modernization."
285. Yang et al., "Religion and Family," 142.

moved to oppose Mainlander domination and to improve their standing in Taiwan society and politics. Much of the focus of the opposition party, the Democratic Progressive Party (DPP), was placed on Taiwan in contrast to the KMT's China focus. Members of the DPP used the Hoklo language "as a symbol of defiance against the establishment, as an expression of democratization, as a sign of localism, and as an assertion of ethnolinguistic identity."[286] For example, Hoklo was used in DPP meetings, in massive political rallies, in protests, and in shaming non-Hoklo-speaking Mainlander officials. Many promoted Hoklo as the new national language.[287]

Enthusiasm for speaking Hoklo spread rapidly through the population, composed primarily of Hoklo speakers. Speaking Mandarin was viewed, especially in parts of Taiwan with dense Hoklo populations, as un-Taiwanese. Some of this animosity toward Mandarin was directed at Hakkas who in many cases could not speak Hoklo and used Mandarin in their interactions with Hoklos.[288]

The Taiwan focus also clashed with another aspect of being Hakka, namely their ethnic emphasis on their roots in China. In an environment where Taiwan connections were important and China connections were suspect, Hakkas, whose identity traditionally emphasized the noble origins of their ancestors in China, were naturally open to accusations of not identifying with Taiwan.

The Hakka Ethnic Movement

This strong Hoklo language emphasis had two different results for Hakkas. Many Hakkas responded, often out of fear, by learning Hoklo, by hiding their Hakka identity, and/or by assimilating with the Hoklo.[289] Other Hakkas responded more defensively. They became concerned that they and their language would again be pushed to the margins of Taiwan society. Their perception was that, when demanding equality of languages in Taiwan, Hoklos were thinking only of equality between Hoklo and Mandarin, not of equality for Hakka.[290] Hakkas began to mobilize to ensure that their interests would not be excluded from debates about Taiwan's

---

286. Tse, "Language and Identity," 161.
287. Simpson, "Taiwan," 250.
288. Ibid., 251; Liao, "Changing Language Use," 170.
289. Martin, "Hakka Ethnic Movement," 178; Simpson, "Taiwan," 251; Liao, "Changing Language Use," 170.
290. Liao, "Changing Language Use," 173.

political future.[291] The establishment of the magazine Hakka Storm (*kejia fengyun*) in 1987 was pivotal. Also significant was the staging of a protest on December 28, 1988, to demand that the Hakka language be returned to its rightful place in society. On September 18, 1994, a private Hakka-language television station was established. Hakkas also opposed referring to the Hoklo language and literature as "Taiwanese," which inferred that the Hakka counterparts were less "Taiwanese."[292]

This Hakka ethnic movement was not monolithic, and, outside of a desire to preserve and promote the Hakka language, common goals did not exist.[293] Fan gives two factors that impeded Hakkas from forming a unified group. First, individuals and groups of Hakkas were geographically dispersed throughout the island. Consequently, they often had somewhat different histories and collective memories from which to draw. They often had more in common with others in their communities than with other Hakkas. Second, these Hakkas spoke at least five different dialects of the Hakka language.[294]

Martin (1996) maintains that the diversity of meaning surrounding the word "Hakka" in this movement reflects three different views in the national political debate regarding the relationship between Taiwan and China. He labels these positions as those of traditionalists, moderates, and radicals. "Traditionalists" are those who support reunification of Taiwan with China. This group of Hakkas values their ties with a common past in China and emphasizes their belief that it is they who best retain the true Chinese culture and language of northern China. For traditionalists, being Chinese is a big part of what it means to be Hakka. Martin describes "moderates" as those who believe that "neither independence nor unification is desirable given Hakka strength on Taiwan."[295] These Hakka understand the meaning of Hakka in Taiwan to include being a weak and manipulated minority group—a tool which is being used by political groups in Taiwan to pursue their own selfish, non-Hakka interests. "Radicals," according to Martin, are those who largely support Taiwan independence, and they are the most articulate and organized of any of the three groups. Many of these radicals argue that the Hakka identity should reject the

291. Martin, "Hakka Ethnic Movement," 178.
292. Hsiau, *Taiwanese Cultural Nationalism*, 143.
293. Martin, "Hakka Ethnic Movement," 194.
294. Fan, "Social Movements," 427–28.
295. Martin, "Hakka Ethnic Movement," 184.

idea of common origins in China. They argue that Taiwan Hakkas should see themselves as "new Hakkas" and focus on their common history in Taiwan. Martin argues, "Migration from China, suffering, shedding sweat and blood, pioneering, and establishing roots in Taiwan are important images" in what it means to be Hakka in Taiwan.[296]

Martin highlights two symbols that he observed being used by people within this Hakka ethnic movement. First, history is a symbol that plays an important role in the Hakka identity. Images of a "pioneering spirit," "able to withstand deprivation and denial," and "fidelity" and "loyalty," all traits which are seen in the Hakka of the past, are used heavily.[297] In this regard, Fan argues that *yiminye* worship is a symbol that was successfully activated as a part of this movement to bring Hakkas together and raise their profile in Taiwan society.[298] The *yiminye* temple located in Fangliao (in Xinpu Township, Hsinchu County), where the bodies of the *yiminye*—those who sacrificed their lives fighting against Hoklo rebels (in support of the Qing dynasty during the Lin Shuangwen Rebellion of 1786–87)—are buried, was and still is an important focal point in this worship. Many in the Hakka ethnic movement held the *yiminye* up as models, emphasizing their willingness to sacrifice their lives and how their sacrifice made it possible for the Hakka language and Hakka culture to continue.[299]

Second, Martin argues that the Hakka language was a symbol that "unites all elements in the Hakka movement."[300] He continues, "Language, not common origin or shared blood, is elevated as the primordial characteristic Hakka use to identify themselves."[301] Fan argues that this symbol of the Hakka language was primary. These Hakkas felt their language was vital because it had been passed on to them by their ancestors and was the most important way of distinguishing themselves from those around them who are so similar to them in many other respects.[302] Martin agrees, "the primary public expression of ethnicity in Taiwan is how well—or how poorly—one speaks Hakka, [Hoklo], or Mandarin."[303]

296. Ibid., 186.
297. Ibid., 190.
298. Fan, "Social Movements," 424–27, 439–43.
299. Ibid., 440.
300. Martin, "Hakka Ethnic Movement," 191.
301. Ibid., 192.
302. Fan, "Social Movements," 420.
303. Martin, "Hakka Ethnic Movement," 178.

Politically, the Hakkas became a block of voters to be wooed.[304] The strong Hoklo emphasis of the DPP drove many Hakkas to support the KMT party.[305] As a result, politicians of both parties began to work to win the Hakka vote. They emphasized their connections to Hakka (e.g., Hakka ancestry) and voiced their commitment to rescuing the Hakka language and nurturing Hakka culture. There was a sense that the Hakkas needed to be compensated for the years during which their culture and language had been undermined by repressive government policies.[306]

Multicultural Taiwan

As the conversation about Taiwan's future has moved forward, the idea of pursuing a multicultural Taiwan has emerged, become widely accepted, and begun to shape government policy. The multicultural Taiwan that politicians and those who support them have come to envision include the following five elements: (1) that four major ethnic groups (Hoklos, Hakkas, Mainlanders, and Aborigines) are included, (2) that each ethnic group should have a voice in building the future Taiwan, (3) that the language and culture of each ethnic group should be valued and given the space and resources to grow and develop, (4) that ethnic groups should pursue harmonious relationships with each other and not degrade each other to increase their own status, and (5) that all groups should work together toward developing a strong nation.[307]

One of the most influential results of this pursuit of a multicultural Taiwan has been the establishment of the Council for Hakka Affairs of the Executive Yuan on June 14, 2001. This high-level government organization is a focal point for strategizing, organizing, and managing efforts to revitalize the Hakka language and culture. Other results include: the increased use of Hakka in public settings; the inclusion of two hours per week of required mother-tongue language classes in elementary school; the establishment of a Hakka public-television station in July of 2003; the opening of Hakka studies programs in several major universities; the establishment of various Hakka culture and food festivals, organized

---

304. Tse, "Language and Identity," 161.
305. Liao, "Changing Language Use," 167–68.
306. Simpson, "Taiwan," 254.
307. Qiu, "Policy," 551; Wang, "Multiculturalism in Taiwan," 304–5.

activities, and museums; and the cultivation of contemporary expressions of Hakka culture.[308]

One of the questions that the multicultural emphasis raises is "How should we define Hakka?" Li-jung Wang argues that government policies treated Hakka and the other ethnic labels as if they were "homogeneous, unified ethnic cultures." She points out that, in reality, these ethnic labels refer to "shifting, hybrid, unstable, multiple" identities.[309] She notes that mixed bloodlines, the varying thicknesses of Hakkas in their connections with hometowns as well as diversity between these localities, the inability of many Hakkas to speak Hakka, and the mixing of culture among the various groups in Taiwan make it difficult to have a clear "Pan-Hakka" definition of the Hakka identity.[310]

There are also differing thoughts, often falling along generational lines, of what is important to emphasize in this multicultural Taiwan. Robert Wilson, in his anthropological study of Hakka culture workers in Taiwan, tells how these younger workers are often frustrated because those who hire them only want them to be representatives of "colorful minorities" rather than to do anything "overtly political."[311] Hence, these workers are expected to provide opportunities for the older generations of Hakkas to "perform for themselves in public spaces" by sponsoring parades, costumes, dances, karaoke-style singing of folk songs (*shan-ge*), and pig-raising competitions.[312] Wilson discovered that these young workers would rather focus their efforts on mobilizing people to work for specific Hakka causes.[313] For example, something that one of these workers opposed was the building of a new dam in an area upriver from the Hakka village of Meinong—a project that was perceived by many to threaten this important Hakka cultural site.[314]

The government policy emphasis on multicultural Taiwan shapes the Hakka identity of many Hakkas. Many of these policies, and the working out of them, provide Hakkas with an increasing amount of raw materials that can be used to draw boundaries between themselves and other groups

308. Qiu, "Policy," 548–57; Wang, "Multicultural Taiwan," 881–83.
309. Wang, "Multiculturalism in Taiwan," 313.
310. Wang, "Multicultural Taiwan," 885–88.
311. Wilson, "Invisible Ones," 94.
312. Ibid., 101.
313. Ibid., 94.
314. Ibid., 92.

in Taiwan. Wang provides the following example: "Hakka cultural activities help the younger Hakka generation to understand their cultural heritage and identify material that can be used to further define their unique ethnic identity in the real world."[315] The surfacing of many traditional aspects of Hakka culture that have been hidden and/or ignored for many years, as well as the inclusion of many newer, contemporary expressions of Hakka culture, can strengthen the Hakka identity of many Hakkas.

The emphasis on multiculturalism has shaped Hakkas in another way—differences with others are, in some ways, becoming less important, and commonalities are becoming more evident. Initially after martial law was lifted, it appeared that differences in language would divide the people of Taiwan. As time has passed, however, threats from China and other factors have created a sense among the different ethnic groups that their future is "inextricably bound together on this island."[316] This sense of unity is further encouraged as each group has learned about their common past in Taiwan. School textbooks have been written to tell the history, culture, and religion of each aspect of multicultural Taiwan.[317] As Mainlander immigrants increasingly identify with Taiwan and intermarry with members of other ethnic groups, the language associated with them (Mandarin) has lost much of its negative connections with the repressive years of martial law and nationalist focus on mainland China.[318] This language continues to function as the national language and continues to be widely used in education, at formal public occasions, and in printed publications throughout Taiwan. The general population of Taiwan increasingly embraces Mandarin as a "useful, *neutral* language no longer tied to a particular dominant group on Taiwan," a common language that all can use.[319] The widespread practice of mixing the Mandarin and Hoklo languages is pointed to as evidence that much of the animosity between ethnic groups in Taiwan is disappearing.[320]

There are differing understandings of the importance of Hakka culture in this multicultural Taiwan. Some envision multiculturalism in Taiwan to be hierarchical with Chinese culture as the most important, the

315. Wang, "Multicultural Taiwan," 883.
316. Tse, "Language and Identity," 161.
317. Simpson, "Taiwan," 252.
318. Ibid., 256.
319. Ibid.
320. Huang, "Language and Conflict," 144.

Hoklo culture as next in importance, and the Hakka and Aborigine cultures as least important, with government resources allocated to support these cultures according to their relative value.[321] Others envision multiculturalism in Taiwan to be like a "symphony," with each culture supported to maintain its core elements or to produce its own sound so that, when added together, they create a beautiful song.[322]

Christian Ministry and Being Hakka in Taiwan

This section will review the literature related to Christian ministry to those who are being Hakka in Taiwan and, in doing so, will detail the important aspects of the cultural "stuff" that is shaping the thoughts and actions of Hakka Christians and others involved in ministry to Hakkas and serving as a reservoir of symbols and habits on which these Christians draw to construct their identity in order to achieve positive results in the midst of a rapidly changing world. This review is organized around the following six themes: (1) language use in Christian churches in Taiwan, (2) perceived difficulties of doing Hakka ministry, (3) counting Hakka churches, (4) counting Hakka Christians, (5) isolating the problem(s), and (6) recent increase in Hakka-focused ministries.

Language Use in Christian Churches in Taiwan

For more than thirty years prior to the Japanese takeover of Taiwan in 1895, when two groups of Presbyterian missionaries (from Canada and England) began ministries in Taiwan, they learned and used Hoklo, the language being used by the majority of people in Taiwan. Until 1925, no other Protestant denominations were present in Taiwan, and so, early on, most church services throughout Taiwan were conducted in Hoklo, using Hoklo hymns and the romanized Hoklo Bible.

During the period when Taiwan was under Japanese rule (especially toward the end of that period), the church, because it was using Hoklo, came into conflict with the desire of the Japanese to make the population of Taiwan, in the words of missionary Thomas Barclay, "body, soul, and spirit—Japanese."[323] Initially, the Japanese tolerated the use of the romanized Hoklo Bible and the use of Hoklo in preaching. However, after 1931,

---

321. Wang, "Multiculturalism in Taiwan," 305.
322. Ibid.
323. Tong, *Christianity in Taiwan*, 54.

the use of Hoklo came to be seen as hindering the spread of the Japanese language, and so the Japanese began to insist that the Japanese language be used in mission schools and in sermons.[324] Eventually, in the early 1940s, the Japanese took control over the Christian churches because of perceptions that these churches were loyal to foreign elements and opposed to things important to Japan.[325]

When the Nationalists (KMT) took over power in Taiwan in 1945, their emphasis on mainland China and the Mandarin language once again conflicted with the Hoklo-language habits of the Presbyterians. A-Chin Hsiau reports, "In the postwar years, the KMT issued regulations several times to forbid the Presbyterian Church from using romanized native languages, lest romanization might encourage people to use local languages and hence blunt their interest in learning Mandarin. The publication of the Bible, hymn books, and bulletins in romanized local languages was banned."[326] In response to the hostile attitudes of the KMT government toward local languages (Hoklo, Hakka, and Aborigine tongues), Rubinstein reports, "Presbyterians saw themselves as activists and saw the need to bear witness against oppression."[327] The strong opposition of the Presbyterians to KMT hegemony became something that shaped much of their ministry and efforts over the ensuing years.

Post-World War II Taiwan saw rapid changes in missionary activity. While up to that point the Presbyterian mission had primarily used the Hoklo language, the influx of approximately one million mainland Chinese refugees provided fertile ground for the gospel. With the Communists in power in mainland China, many Protestant missionaries fled from China to Taiwan to continue their ministries to the Chinese people. These "old China hands" and the churches they formed ministered primarily to Mandarin-speaking Mainlanders.[328] Rather than learning Hoklo or Hakka, they located themselves in areas where there were great concentrations of Mainlanders and worked among them. Between 1950 and 1960, thirty-nine missions began works in Taiwan, most of them choosing to work with this most receptive group. Allen Swanson states, "In 1955 about two-thirds of all missionaries in Taiwan were working among

---

324. Ibid., 71–83.
325. Rubinstein, "Taiwanese Protestantism," 257.
326. Hsiau, *Taiwanese Cultural Nationalism*, 136.
327. Rubinstein, "Taiwanese Protestantism," 258.
328. Ibid., 268–69.

the [Mainlanders], a group representing 13 percent of the population."[329] Hollington Tong reports that in 1954, there were only three missionaries in Taiwan working with the Hakka. This compares with 117 working with the Mainlanders, 46 with the Hoklo, and 10 with the Aborigines.[330]

Wen Yongsheng compiled a chart of all of the missionaries who have learned to speak Hakka or worked among Hakkas in Taiwan.[331] Included in his chart are two periods of time (1865–1900 and 1901–1950) that are each labeled "Neglected Period." He argues, "Between 1865 and 1950, not one missionary who came to Taiwan learned to speak Hakka."[332] Liao offers conflicting information, reporting that Hugh Ritchie learned to speak Hakka.[333] Wen also mentions this missionary but says, "He wanted to do ministry among Hakkas but died of sickness before he could learn Hakka."[334] In addition to Ritchie, Liao reports several other early missionaries who worked among Hakkas prior to 1950 but did not learn to speak Hakka.[335] Another time period included in Wen's chart is that of 1951–1975 in which he lists fifteen missionaries who learned Hakka but adds the comment, "[They composed] a small number in each denomination or mission and [Hakka] was only a secondary priority [to these organizations]."[336] As he lists the forty-six missionaries for the period 1976–2008, Wen adds, "Currently only fifteen are still working in Hakka areas."[337]

Perceived Difficulties of Doing Hakka Ministry

One of the strong themes in the literature about Christian ministry to Hakkas in Taiwan is that the task of evangelizing Hakkas is difficult. Several famous stories illustrate this point. When discussing the early Hakka response to the gospel, one of the most well-known incidents is that of Thomas Barclay's 1885 encounter in southern Taiwan with Hakkas in the village of Jilun who were opposed to missionary attempts to establish a church there. Fellow missionary Edward Band reported that, in

329. Swanson, *Church in Taiwan*, 25.
330. Tong, *Christianity in Taiwan*, 88.
331. Wen, "Double in Ten," 168–70.
332. Ibid., 163.
333. Liao, *Unresponsive*, 40.
334. Wen, "Double in Ten," 168.
335. Liao, *Unresponsive*, 50–54.
336. Wen, "Double in Ten," 168.
337. Ibid., 169–70.

response to reports of violence against Christians there, Barclay visited and met with leaders of the village, after which he and the Christians there decided to proceed with their plans to hold a service the following Sunday. During that service, local Hakkas arrived, dumped human waste in the place where the Christians were meeting and on Thomas Barclay, and beat several local Christians. Later that evening, after being informed of a threat on his life, Barclay fled.[338] A monument commemorating this incident was erected at a church in southern Taiwan in 1981.

Another example revealing the perception that ministry to Hakkas is difficult is the categorization of Hakkas found in "A Centennial History of the Presbyterian Church in Formosa."[339] Zheng Lianming, writing in this book about how encountering the Hakkas had affected late nineteenth-century pioneer missionary George L. Mackay's ministries, says, "Originally, the evangelism efforts of [Mackay] in northern Taiwan were going smoothly and had expanded among the Han Chinese and Plains Aborigines as far [south] as Hsinchu, but when he encountered a different language and deep superstition in Hakka areas, the strength of the southern advance of his evangelism efforts stopped temporarily in Hsinchu."[340]

Xia Zhongjian reports that prior to doing his research on Hakkas, his own impression of Hakkas was that "they are stubborn and resistant to the gospel" and that "the Hakka community in Taiwan is a piece of hard ground."[341] He explains that his perception was quite common, saying, "Most people think that Hakkas are a stingy, selfish, stubborn, and exclusive group. Even church people have these misconceptions and consider Hakka areas to be hard ground for the gospel."[342] Swanson also comments that the Hakkas are the "so-called 'resistant' people."[343] Zeng, Qiu, Wen, and Wu write, "Almost every Christian church and Christian in Taiwan unconsciously views Hakkas as hard ground for the gospel."[344]

As a part of his research, Liao surveyed the perceptions of 105 pastors (twenty-six from Hakka churches in the Presbyterian Church in Taiwan [PCT], thirty-one from other Hakka churches, and forty-eight

338. Band, *Barclay of Formosa*, 61–66.
339. Zheng, *Centennial History*.
340. Zheng, "From Self-Governance," 155.
341. Xia, *Hidden Group*, i.
342. Ibid., 12.
343. Swanson, *Church in Taiwan*, 41.
344. Zeng et al., *Day for Doubling*, 55.

from non-Hakka churches). He reports that these pastors "were asked to write down their own analysis and opinions as to why the growth of [the] Hakka church has been so slow and hesitant. Each pastor could list as many reasons as he felt necessary."[345] Liao divided their responses into two categories: "those having to do with inadequacies of church and mission" and "those having to do with the Hakkas."[346] For example, those having to do with inadequacies of church and mission included "lack of Hakka-speaking church workers, lack of specialized efforts for evangelizing Hakkas, and financial weakness (because Hakkas are poor and stingy)" and those having to do with Hakkas included "conservatism, idol worship, ancestor worship, tight control by lineage groups, stubbornness, self-assertion, exclusiveness, and emphasis on material gain only."[347] Liao reports that the pastors who participated in his survey blamed the difficulties on Hakkas three times more than they blamed outreach ministries of the church, revealing that "the 'resistance' of the people is in the foreground of the thinking of most churchmen."[348]

Counting Hakka Churches

Scholars who have studied the Hakka Christian community in Taiwan classify certain churches as "Hakka" churches. For example, Liao reports that existing Hakka churches in the PCT were planted in three different periods of time. In the 1890s, five PCT churches were established in Hakka areas—one in southern Taiwan and four in the north.[349] Liao points out that four of these five churches were Hakka and the fifth was only "partly Hakka." In the period between 1910 and 1926, six more Hakka PCT churches were planted by disciples of Mackay. Between 1952 and 1958, "three Hakka churches and seven Hakka chapels came into existence [in the PCT]."[350] Writing in 1972, Liao adds, "Since 1958, none has been added."[351] Liao also relates that one of the PCT churches described had since been closed, and there were other PCT church plants mentioned by early missionaries and nationals that he

---

345. Liao, *Unresponsive*, 22.
346. Ibid.
347. Ibid., 23.
348. Ibid., 22.
349. Ibid., 43–46.
350. Ibid., 47.
351. Ibid.

did not include because they no longer existed.³⁵² Based on his field survey in 1968, Liao reported that an additional forty-one other Hakka congregations were planted by non-PCT organizations, most of which only began ministry in Taiwan in "the early 1950s."³⁵³

It is challenging to accurately determine the number of churches at any given point in history that could be considered Hakka. A discrepancy in Liao's statistics on Hakka churches reflects this difficulty. He reports that twenty Hakka churches (twenty-one minus one that closed) were planted in the PCT up to the time of his writing (see above), but at the same time he also points out that his field survey found that there were thirty Hakka PCT churches in existence at that time.³⁵⁴ In general, a combination of factors is taken into consideration to determine which churches count as Hakka churches. One factor used was the perceived ethnic makeup of the church. For example, Liao revealed that he used this factor when he talked about "predominantly Hakka congregations" but also included, at one point, a church that was "partly Hakka as Hakka."³⁵⁵ A second factor that was used to determine whether or not a church was Hakka was the location of the church. For example, Xia revealed that he included churches in "areas that are generally recognized as Hakka areas."³⁵⁶ The language used in church services was also used to determine whether a church was Hakka or not. For example, Xia talked about the possibility that a church in a Hakka area could be a "Mandarin-speaking church," something that he did not consider Hakka.³⁵⁷ The self-identity of the church was also a factor that was used. For example, the literature for CHEA's "Double the Hakka Church in Ten Years Movement" talks about churches that "identify themselves as a Hakka church."³⁵⁸ A fifth factor used to determine whether a church was Hakka or not was ascription by knowledgeable pastors. For example, Xia enlisted the help of two knowledgeable pastors to help him select which churches to count as Hakka.³⁵⁹

---

352. Ibid., 47, 50–54.
353. Ibid., 48–49.
354. Ibid., 49.
355. Ibid., 46, 48.
356. Xia, *Hidden Group*, 7.
357. Ibid., 89.
358. Zeng et al., *Day for Doubling*, 207.
359. Xia, *Hidden Group*, 89.

Counting Hakka Christians

There are several sources available to Hakka Christians and others as they seek to determine the size of the Hakka Christian community in Taiwan. This review focuses on four sources: (1) David C. E. Liao, (2) Allen J. Swanson, (3) Xia Zhongjian, and (4) the Taiwan Social Change Survey.

David C. E. Liao

Much of the literature that references Christian ministries to Hakkas in Taiwan reports and/or builds on the statistic that only three out of every thousand Hakkas are Christian.[360] This figure originated with missiologist David C. E. Liao and for many years has been the most widely recognized statistic used to talk about the size of the Hakka church in Taiwan.[361] This figure is often contrasted with the percentage of Christians in other groups or in the total population of Taiwan. For example, Liao also reported that in 1967, 1.4 percent of Hoklos, 10.1 percent of Mainlanders, 33.3 percent of Aborigines, and 2.9 percent of the total population of Taiwan were Christian.[362] Prior to mid-2010 and during the time that the research for this book was taking place, the 0.3 percent statistic was being widely used on the web pages, in the newsletters, and in other literature published by the Christian Hakka Evangelical Association (CHEA), the Hakka Mission Seminary (HMS), and the "Double the Hakka Church in Ten Years Movement."

Liao's figure is an estimate based on data obtained from his own field survey of churches in 1967 and several other publicly available sources. To determine the size of the Hakka Christian community in Taiwan, Liao asked "predominantly Hakka congregations located in predominantly Hakka areas" to report their "Hakka communicant membership" and then multiplied that reported number by two (2.3 in the case of churches in the PCT) to obtain the size of the Hakka Christian community.[363] Liao does not provide his rationale for this doubling, but presumably he is assuming that there are twice as many Christians connected to the church as are taking communion. The result of his calculations was a size of 4,600 which he then

---

360. E.g., Raber, *Protestantism in Taiwan*, 73; Bolton, *Treasure Island*, 120–22; Wen, "Hakka 997," 162–63; Li, *History in Taiwan*, 152; Johnstone and Mandryk, *Operation World*, 188; Zeng et al., *Day for Doubling*, 29–30.
361. Wen, "Hakka 997."
362. Liao, *Unresponsive*, 137.
363. Ibid., 49.

rounded up to 5,000.³⁶⁴ Liao added, "It must be pointed out, however that [this figure refers] *only* to the Hakka Christians in predominantly Hakka congregations located in predominantly Hakka areas. There are other Hakka Christians who live in the rural frontiers on the east coast or in the large urban centers. In such places, the population is not predominantly Hakka and no Hakka church is in existence. These Hakka Christians join [Hoklo] or Mandarin churches, and their number is not included in what is termed Hakka Christian in our present study."³⁶⁵ The absence of data from the areas not included in Liao's sample is significant because many Hakkas live outside of Hakka areas. For example, the National Hakka Population Basic Data Survey reported that, in 2004, the Hakka percentage of the population in some of the areas that Liao excluded was: Taipei City (11.7-25.7 percent) 306,000-676,000; Taipei County (New Taipei City) (8.0-24.0 percent) 296,000-882,000; Hualian County (22.1-38.8 percent) 78,000-136,000; and Taidong County (12.7-29.2 percent) 31,000-71,000.³⁶⁶

To determine the Hakka general population in Taiwan in 1967, Liao started with the figure from the Taiwan Provincial Government General Census of 1956 under the category, "Taiwanese of Kuangtung [Guangdong] Ancestry." This way of using the available data was not without precedent, but it is problematic. In his preface to the "Report on the National Hakka Population Basic Data Survey," Yang Wenshan explains that during the 1956 and 1966 censuses, the Taiwan population was divided into two groups of people; those already living in Taiwan in 1945 and those who came to Taiwan in the late 1940s as a result of the civil war in China. Pre-1945 residents were further divided into those with an ancestral home in Fujian Province, those with an ancestral home in Guangdong Province, and Aborigines.³⁶⁷ Those whose ancestral home was in Guangdong Province were considered to be Hakkas. Yang further reports that at the time of these censuses, many pre-1945 residents did not know the location of their ancestral home, so census takers categorized them according to the language (e.g., Hakka, Hoklo) they spoke in their homes. Yang writes, "Since the definition of 'ethnic groups' was not clear at that time, the figures obtained during this period can be used for reference only, and do not accurately provide data on the distribution of the Hakka population."³⁶⁸

364. Ibid., 49, 137.
365. Ibid., 48–49.
366. Yang, *Hakka Population Survey*, Appendix A, 7–8.
367. Yang, "Preface," i.
368. Ibid.

Treating "Taiwanese of Kuangtung Ancestry" as Hakka, Liao calculated that Hakkas made up 13.28 percent of the population of Taiwan at that time. Next, assuming that the ethnic ratios in the Taiwan population stayed the same between 1956 and 1967, Liao calculated the 1967 Hakka population of 1,759,000 by taking 13.28 percent of the total population of Taiwan in 1967 as reported in the China Yearbook 1968.[369] The resulting percentage (5000/1,759,000) of Hakka Christians was 0.284 percent which he rounded up to 0.3 percent. Liao's method reflects the nature of the data that was available to him at that time as well as how difficult it was to find and count all of those who were both Hakka and Christian at that time.

Recently, both the CHEA and the HMS have begun reporting that the Hakka Christian population has increased from 0.3 percent to 0.4 percent of the total Hakka population. This change was first reported without any accompanying explanation in CHEA and HMS newsletters in the fall of 2010.[370] This new figure is based on Liao's 0.3 percent statistic and was explained to this author by one key Hakka Christian leader to be a reflection of the fact that there has been an improvement on the 0.3 percent statistic—that since the beginning of the "Double the Hakka Church in Ten Years Movement" in 2005, not a few Hakkas have become Christians through the ministries of the member churches in this movement and that worship attendance at these member churches has increased.

ALLEN J. SWANSON

Allen J. Swanson published two other figures for the number of Hakka Christians: 0.55 percent in 1981 and 0.58 percent in 1986. For his 1981 study, Swanson used a "stratified random sample," and, after "an initial rejection rate of 32.4" and "up to four random selections" to replace churches who did not cooperate with the study, obtained a sample of 203 churches; they comprised 14 percent of "all plains churches that recognize and have fellowship with one another and more or less stand in the historic mainstream of Protestant Christianity."[371] Catholic, True Jesus, Assembly Hall, Adventist, and Aborigine churches were excluded. He sent a trained assistant to visit each church on a Sunday morning to administer a questionnaire immediately following the morning service to all attendees

---

369. Liao, *Unresponsive*, 138–39.
370. *Kefu Jianxun*, 14; *Keshen Jianxun*, "Greatest Opportunity," 2.
371. Swanson, *Church in Taiwan*, xix, xxi–xxiii.

fifteen years old and over. Swanson reports that 20 percent of these attendees either refused to participate or had to leave early.[372]

Swanson's formula for determining the size of the Hakka "Total Christian Membership" involves several steps. To his raw figures obtained from the returned questionnaires, he added 20 percent (to account for those in attendance who did not take the survey), multiplied this figure by 83.26 percent (since only this percentage of respondents were baptized Christians), multiplied it again by 7.35 (since the sample was only 13.26 percent of all "plains" churches in Taiwan), doubled the result (in order to account for church members who were not in attendance), and finally, added 50 percent (to account for children under fifteen years of age).[373]

In order to determine the size of the Hakka population, Swanson used government data that, like the data Liao used, did not use the Mainlander/Hoklo/Hakka/Aborigine ethnic breakdown. A significant difference from Liao's study is in the ethnic-population ratios that Swanson used. Citing the fact that soldiers, mostly Mainlanders, were not included in census data prior to 1969, he argued that the percentage of Hakkas should be reduced to 10 percent (compared to Liao's 13.28 percent) and the percentage of Mainlanders increased to 13 percent of the total population and concedes, "This change will make a considerable difference when computing the percentage of Christians from [the Hakka and Mainlander] groups."[374]

Swanson also offers the following comments about this 1981 study: "This is not a highly sophisticated survey.... No attempt is made to offer absolute, final answers. Everything is tentative," and "What is offered here is a first step, contributed by a group of volunteer missionaries and Chinese, most of whom were without any basic theoretical training in the realm of social research."[375]

The main difference between Swanson's 1981 and 1986 studies is that, for the 1986 study, he only studied 113 churches (100 churches from the 1981 study and thirteen of the 170 churches that had been planted in Taiwan since the 1981 study) and that he limited himself to those churches that could be categorized as "urban churches in northern Taiwan." This limitation means that churches in Hakka areas, usually not thought to be in urban areas of the north, were not included in his 1986 study.

    372. Ibid., xxii–xxiii.
    373. Ibid., 35, 44–45.
    374. Ibid., 19.
    375. Ibid., xxiii–xxv.

Xia Zhongjian

Based on his 1982 survey of 1,344 people, another researcher, Xia Zhongjian, argued that only 0.24 percent of Hakkas were Christian.[376] Xia reports that he mailed Swanson's 1981 questionnaire to fifty-nine churches determined by two knowledgeable Hakka pastors to be Hakka. From the thirty returned questionnaires, he found an average Sunday morning worship attendance of 37.8 in Hakka churches. To account for the children, he added one-third (12.6) of the average attendance and then doubled the resulting amount to account for non-attending members. He multiplied the resulting figure of 101 attending each Hakka church by the fifty-nine Hakka churches and arrived at a quotient of 5,959, which he rounded up to a figure of 6,000. Xia next, not revealing his sources, calculated a Hakka population figure of 2,494,00 by taking 13.75 percent (compared to Liao's figure of 13.28 percent and Swanson's of 10 percent) of a total Taiwan population of 18,130,000.[377]

Taiwan Social Change Survey

In order to triangulate these figures calculated by Liao, Swanson, and Xia with more recently available data, this researcher used the SPSS computer program to analyze data from the 1998–2010 years of the Taiwan Social Change Survey (*Taiwan shehui bianqian jiben diaocha*) to explore the number of Hakkas who identified themselves as Christian. The Taiwan Social Change Survey (TSCS) project is conducted by the Institute of Sociology, Academia Sinica, and sponsored by the National Science Council, Republic of China. These surveys studied non-institutionalized adults in Taiwan and used the "Probability Proportional to Size" method to arrive at a sample that was determined to be representative of the entire adult population of Taiwan.

Ethnic identity in this data was determined by the interviewee's response to a question regarding the ethnicity of their father such as, "What is your father's ethnic background?" This method of determining ethnicity produces slightly different results than those relying on self-identity. Yang reports, based on the National Hakka Population Basic Data Survey (2004), that 93.3 percent of those whose father is Hakka self-identify themselves as Hakka when forced to choose only one ethnic identity, and

---

376. Xia, *Hidden Group*, 92.
377. Ibid.

96 percent do so when allowed to choose more than one ethnic identity.[378] Identity as a Christian was determined by the interviewee's response to a question about religious preference like, "What is your religious belief?" The difference between self-identification as "Christian" and regular church attendance is noteworthy. Data from the Christian Resource Center (*Jidujiao ziliao zhongxin*) reveals that in 2009, only 2.77 percent of the total population of Taiwan attends church on Sundays, significantly lower than the 3.90 percent who identify themselves as "Christian" in the TSCS data for the same year.[379]

The TSCS results from the most recent year for which data is available (2010) are as follows: the percentage of Hakkas who identify themselves as Christians is 2.20 percent and can be compared with 3.26 percent of Hoklos, 7.99 percent of Mainlanders, 22.73 percent of Aborigines, and 3.95 percent of all ethnic groups combined in Taiwan. Catholics were considered in a separate TSCS category and thus are not included in these figures. The results from each of the thirteen years analyzed are displayed in table 1 below.

Year	All	Hakka	Hoklo	Mainlander	Aborigine
1998	3.62%	2.57%	3.14%	5.91%	36.36%
1999	3.92%	0.85%	2.73%	7.91%	35.56%
2000	3.74%	1.32%	2.43%	8.13%	32.93%
2001	4.26%	1.38%	2.56%	8.39%	46.09%
2002	4.03%	2.01%	2.36%	9.22%	48.24%
2003	4.32%	1.30%	3.58%	3.21%	43.86%
2004	3.33%	2.03%	2.40%	9.63%	55.00%
2005	3.61%	2.21%	2.23%	10.40%	34.62%
2006	4.07%	1.93%	2.76%	10.40%	34.38%
2007	3.96%	2.68%	3.04%	8.57%	38.46%
2008	—	—	—	—	—
2009	3.90%	3.35%	2.69%	8.24%	26.83%
2010	3.95%	2.20%	3.26%	7.99%	22.73%

Table 1: TSCS Respondents Who Identified Themselves as Christian—
According to Year and Ethnic Identity

378. Yang, "Preface," sec. 2, 15.
379. Chu, "Trends in Taiwan."

The data displayed in this table was collected from all cycles (except four) in the 1998–2010 years of the TSCS. Since no interview question about religious affiliation was included in the 1998-I, 2003-I, and both 2008 survey cycles, these cycles could not be used. The fluctuating nature of the results from year to year suggests that it is difficult to obtain a representative sample of those who are both Hakka and Christian.

Isolating the Problem(s)

Motivated by the 0.3 percent statistic, many Hakka Christians and others have sought to determine the reason(s) behind the small size of the Hakka Christian population and to determine appropriate responses to this situation. This review will present the perspectives of Liao and those of Zeng, Qiu, Wen, and Wu and offer a short critique of these perspectives.

Liao

David C. E. Liao writes about the Hakka response to Christianity in Taiwan and raises the question of whether resistance to conversion to Christianity is part of the meaning of being Hakka in Taiwan. His answer to this question is a resounding "No," arguing instead that the Hakka are "unresponsive" because they have been "neglected" by missionaries and the church in Taiwan. Liao blames the lack of growth of the Hakka church on the missionaries and the church who have ignored "the strong people-consciousness which the Hakkas have—the consciousness of belonging to a distinct group, the sense of a peoplehood."[380] He asks, "Could it be that the church has shown the worst kind of neglect over the Hakkas, the neglect of their ethnic self-image?"[381] Liao views the PCT's lack of long-term boards specifically tasked with coordinating outreach among Hakkas, the lack of Hakka-speaking missionaries, and the manpower shortages in churches in Hakka areas as evidence of this neglect.[382] He writes, "The Hakkas have never been reached as a people. Their desire to preserve their identity has been rejected and denied. Their sense of peoplehood has been continually infringed. Is this not a serious neglect on the part of the church? It is nothing short of tragedy that the people who are so conscious

---

380. Liao, *Unresponsive*, 68.
381. Ibid.
382. Ibid., 55–59.

of themselves have had that consciousness so steadily ignored in the vital matter of leading them to the Saviour of their souls."[383]

Liao also fingered what he coined the PCT's "one-language policy" and the policy of "following a course of integration" as perpetuating this neglect.[384] Desiring to cultivate unity and to keep from perpetuating tensions between ethnic groups in Taiwan, Presbyterian church leaders cited Col 3:11, "Here there is no Greek or Jew, circumcised or uncircumcised, barbarian, Scythian, slave or free, but Christ is all, and is in all," and worked to remove any ethnic distinctions from their ministries.[385] This policy involved exclusively using the Hoklo language in all meetings and literature.[386] One significant result for Hakkas was that churches in Hakka areas used only Hoklo Bibles and hymnbooks, and Hakka Christians, even if they used the Hakka language every day at home and in their businesses, used Hoklo in church on Sunday.

Liao compares the lack of a "separated approach" for Hakkas in Taiwan to the biblical example in Gal 2:11–16 of the Gentiles being forced to follow Jewish ways. Liao argues from this passage that, while there is an offense of the cross that is unavoidable in evangelistic outreach, it should stop there. He maintains, following Donald A. McGavran, that requiring Hakkas to cross ethnic boundaries and "become Christians in an alien culture" is an offense that is unnecessary and similar to Peter's wrong attitude of applying Jewish dietary restrictions in a Galatian setting.[387]

Liao also argues that, while unity without ethnic distinctions is a noble goal, prematurely forcing this kind of unity actually hinders church growth and brings spiritual division.[388] He advocates a "temporary separation" of ministries to the Hakka. Liao argues:

> This temporary separation appears to be the very way in which the unity of the church can be truly attained, because it ensures full development of the selfhood of each group so that a unity that is fair to all groups is possible. Moreover this temporary separation, in as much as it helps Christianization of each people, can contribute tremendously to the reconciliation and integration of

383. Ibid., 96.
384. Ibid., 60–68.
385. Ibid., 60–66, 106–7.
386. Ibid., 60–65.
387. Ibid., 103.
388. Ibid., 107.

the various groups, because becoming a Christian is the first step toward true brotherhood. . . . To approach the Hakkas as a people and to produce thoroughly Hakka churches into which Hakkas may come with joy, will not only bring more of God's blessings to the Hakkas, but also bless the whole church in the long run.[389]

Liao has many suggestions that he argues will "harness people-consciousness for church growth" among the Hakka.[390] For example, he suggests evangelizing groups rather than individuals and going through the proper channels—using strategies that communicate respect to community and family leaders—so that people who become Christians will not be viewed as betraying the group.[391] Liao also argues that special strategies need to be implemented to address the special challenges that the Hakka emphasis on ancestor worship creates. For example, rather than rejecting all of the Hakka funerary practices because some of them include elements of ancestor worship, Liao argues that the church must develop functional substitutes for the offending practices and seek other visible means that Christians can use to resoundingly express their love and respect for their ancestors.[392]

In summary, Liao suggests that being Hakka in Taiwan means valuing being treated as a "separate people" and working to preserve this distinction.[393] He adds that being Hakka means desiring to maintain the solidarity of the Hakka people.[394] He also asserts that being Hakka means valuing Hakka ways—treasuring things like the language, music, festivals, rituals, and social structure of Hakkas.[395] Liao ties it all together, arguing that the growth of the Hakka church has been slow primarily because past ministries did not engage these aspects of being Hakka in Taiwan.

Zeng, Qiu, Wen, and Wu

Zeng Zhengzhong, Qiu Shanxiung, Wen Yongsheng, and Wu Ruicheng, all Hakka Christian workers involved in ministry to Hakkas, argue that, since the beginning of mission outreach in Taiwan, Christians did not support ministry focused on Hakkas for three reasons: (1) Taiwan Hakkas

389. Ibid., 109.
390. Ibid., 98.
391. Ibid., 109–15.
392. Ibid., 130–34.
393. Ibid., 99.
394. Ibid., 109.
395. Ibid., 105–6, 110–11.

appeared to be facing a crisis of assimilation into other ethnic groups, (2) Taiwan Hakkas were seen as "hard ground," and (3) there was a flow of people and talent leaving Taiwan Hakka areas.[396]

Zeng and his coauthors first point to the words of George Mackay, a Presbyterian missionary whom they and others in Taiwan highly respect and who pioneered Christian missions in the north of Taiwan in the late nineteenth century, as having played a significant role in this lack of Hakka focus.[397] In the context of writing a brief summary of the different ethnic groups living in Taiwan in his book, *From Far Formosa: The Island, Its People, and Missions*, Mackay wrote a one-paragraph general description of Hakkas that finishes with the prediction, "The younger generation learn the Hoklo dialect, and in time, the Hakkas may become extinct."[398] Based on this quote, Zeng and his coauthors assert that Mackay, in his evangelism efforts, had a conscious strategy to treat Hakkas as Hoklos.[399] In addition, noting that Mackay's words were spoken at a time when there had been significant conflict between the Hakkas and the Hoklos, these four authors extrapolated, "In that societal situation, Dr. Mackay hoped that the Hakkas would be assimilated by the Hoklo and become one ethnic group in order that the fighting between them would stop."[400]

Zeng and his coauthors point out two mistakes of an evangelism strategy of treating Hakkas like Hoklos. First, every ethnic group is God's creation, and He does not want any of them to become extinct.[401] Second, this strategy violates the principle of incarnation, of becoming like someone to win them.[402] These four authors continue, describing some of the influences that Mackay's "strategy" had. The first influence was that any desire of the PCT to evangelize Hakkas was destroyed.[403] Second, PCT churches in Hakka areas did not value Hakkas enough to want to establish and/or join a Hakka presbytery.[404] Zeng and his coauthors give two reasons why many PCT churches in Hakka areas did not want to establish

---

396. Zeng et al., *Day for Doubling*, 38.
397. Ibid., 41.
398. Mackay, *From Far Formosa*, 102.
399. Zeng et al., *Day for Doubling*, 41–42, 74–75, 114.
400. Ibid., 42.
401. Ibid., 42–44.
402. Ibid., 44–45.
403. Ibid., 46–47.
404. Ibid., 47–49.

a Hakka presbytery. First, these churches wanted to emphasize harmony between ethnic groups, and second, these churches feared financial difficulties because churches in Hakka areas were often financially weak.[405]

Zeng and his coauthors assert that the second reason ministry to Hakkas has been neglected is the perception that Hakkas are "hard ground."[406] They raise and contest three common perceptions of Hakkas—that they are stiff necked, that they are cliquish, and that they are involved in ancestor practices. In response, these four authors focus attention on the positive aspects of being stiff necked, argue that rather than being cliquish, Hakkas are adaptable and adept at fitting in with the majority, and suggest that ancestor practices continue to be a stumbling block for Hakkas because churches are not using the contextualized ancestor practices that have been developed.[407] They also discuss the attack on Barclay in 1885 and argue that this response was characteristic of the societal situation at the time and was not because Hakkas are "hard ground."[408] Next, these authors highlight examples of responsiveness among Hakkas. They discuss the situation in Sabah, Malaysia, where 35 percent of Hakkas are Christian, saying, "Worldwide, the highest percentage of Han Chinese that are Christian are Hakkas," and also cite a successful ministry to older Hakkas in Zhudong.[409] They close their discussion of Hakkas as "hard ground" by arguing that, even if Hakkas are "hard ground," the Bible does not allow the church to set them aside.[410]

Zeng and his co-authors argue the third reason that Christians do not focus on Hakkas is because many younger Hakka Christians are moving out of Hakka areas.[411] While the actual population in Hakka areas has not decreased, "those who are left, mostly old people and children, are unable to effectively share the gospel with Hakkas who remain."[412] These authors highlight the way many Hakka Christians now living in urban areas do not seem to care about the people in their hometowns. They quote a non-Hakka pastor who worked in Hakka areas for many years as saying, "I keep

---

405. Ibid., 52–54.
406. Ibid., 55.
407. Wen, "Double in Ten," 165; Zeng et al., *Day for Doubling*, 55–59.
408. Zeng et al., *Day for Doubling*, 55.
409. Ibid., 69–70.
410. Ibid., 70–72.
411. Ibid., 83.
412. Ibid., 84.

thinking that the reason that outreach to Hakkas is struggling is primarily because . . . of Hakka pastors. I know more than ten famous Hakka pastors who are in important positions in the Presbyterian Church in Taiwan or who are pastoring large churches, but they do not use the vast resources at their disposal to help churches in Hakka areas."[413] Zeng and his coauthors argue that Hakka Christians' unconscious neglect of their roots is uncharacteristic of the intrinsic nature of Hakkas.[414]

Next, Zeng and his coauthors assert that the plurality of ethnic groups and languages, mutual support and respect between ethnic groups in the church, the use of multiple languages in worship of God, and the innate desire of humans to focus on their ethnic identity are all characteristics designed by God.[415] They argue that a plurality of ethnic groups and languages in the church reveals God's wisdom and glory, provides an example of the multiple persons and oneness in the Trinity, and allows the church to participate in the plurality of different voices worshiping God.[416] Zeng and his coauthors continue, suggesting that Christians should promote ethnic unity in the church by allowing every ethnic group to fill their role as parts of the same "body" and, in doing so, be a testimony of ethnic unity for the world to see.[417] They add that God not only created ethnic groups, He imprinted ethnic identities on our hearts, and so the church should diligently work to evangelize with this fact in mind by using the Hakka language.[418]

The final chapter of Zeng and his coauthors' book details possible actions to be taken in the context of past mistakes and God's desires. These authors focus on two areas—using Hakka history and culture in ministry and praying for Hakka ministry. In the first area, citing Paul's evangelism strategy as he spoke at the Areopagus in Athens (Acts 17:16–34), they suggest beginning evangelistic endeavors which meet Hakkas, both rationally and emotionally, in their situation, as well as using the importance humans place on history and culture as a tool for outreach.[419] These four authors argue that, rather than directly criticizing Hakka culture, unconditionally affirming it, or concentrating on loving people, Christians can indirectly

---

413. Ibid., 84–85.
414. Ibid., 85.
415. Ibid., 96–145.
416. Ibid., 116.
417. Ibid., 118–29.
418. Ibid., 141–43.
419. Ibid., 176–87.

challenge Hakka culture, conditionally accept it, and work to find a good balance between loving people and discoursing with them about Hakka history and culture.⁴²⁰ Zeng and his coauthors close by calling Christians to pray for guidance on how they might be involved in Hakka ministries and for Hakka ministry in general.⁴²¹

Liao and Zeng, Qiu, Wen, and Wu Critiqued

Liao's perspective reveals a heavy influence of the Homogeneous Unit Principle which was prevalent at the time of his writing. For example, as Liao talks about the history of Hakkas, he points to a period of time (AD 900–1300) when, in the seclusion of a mountain area, "the inhabitants [the progenitors of Hakkas] had ample time to consolidate into a homogeneous unit, with an intense consciousness of being a separate people, and to develop their own culture quite independently of the more rapid changes in other parts of China."⁴²² As Liao talks about a "separate approach," he clearly has this Hakka homogeneous unit in mind and wants to use Hakka ways so that Hakkas do not have to cross any barriers to become Christians. When his book was reprinted by the William Carey Library in 1979, the subtitle was changed to *The Homogeneous Unit Principle Illustrated by the Hakka Chinese in Taiwan*.⁴²³

Liao's approach helpfully highlights the cultural "stuff" that has, to one extent or another, shaped the Hakkas of Taiwan, that serves as a repertoire of symbols upon which they draw as they construct their identities, and that provides security in a world that is changing at a dizzying rate. But Liao's approach does not focus on the way that being Hakka is changing, and the active and varied ways that Hakkas, as individuals and as individuals acting together, are manipulating and transforming their Hakka identity as they seek well-being in the contexts in which they find themselves. Liao calls Christians to do their ministry in a certain Hakka way (that can easily be seen in static and essentialist ways) rather than, in line with the social constructionist perspective on ethnic identification, encouraging these Christians to learn how and why the Hakkas around them are "playing the Hakka game" and how to engage this dimension appropriately and strategically in ministry to Hakkas. For example, in the

---

420. Ibid., 188–91.
421. Ibid., 198–205.
422. Liao, *Unresponsive*, 84.
423. Liao, *Unresponsive: Homogeneous Unit*.

area of the language used in ministry, Liao suggests that "efforts must be made to design a system under which all aspects of Christian activities can be carried out entirely in the Hakka language."[424] In contrast, an approach to the use of language in ministry that takes seriously both the fixity and fluidity of being Hakka would highlight and seek to understand the diverse ways that the Hakka language is used, and language use would vary situationally, emphasized in settings where its use is determined to be strategically important and set aside at other times.

One of the primary emphases of Zeng and others is that Hakkas are different from Hoklos and that the failure of missionaries and churches in the past to take this difference seriously has resulted in the small size of the Hakka Christian community today. These authors see these different Hakkas as a group of people having a Hakka culture. For example, they discuss the intrinsic nature of the Hakkas and contend that Hakka Christians who are not acting in line with this nature, making use of their resources to help struggling Hakka churches, are behaving uncharacteristically.[425] They also ignore the differences among those who are being Hakka. For example, when these authors encourage Christians to "become Hakka in order to win Hakkas," they are wanting to relate the gospel to Hakka history and culture rather than thinking about relating the gospel to Hakkas who are engaging Hakka history and culture in a variety of different ways.[426] While the perspective of these four authors is extremely helpful in thinking about engaging the fixity of being Hakka, their failure to highlight the fluidity with which Hakka ethnic actors—those who have been shaped, to a certain extent, by the same cultural "stuff"—are individually relating to that "stuff" in a variety of ways at different times and in different contexts during the same period of time is a weakness.

Recent Increase in Hakka-Focused Ministries

In recent years, there has been a significant increase in the number of institutions or ministries that prioritize or primarily emphasize ministry to Hakkas. One of the most significant developments in this area was the establishment of the World Hakka Evangelical Association (*Quanqiu kejia fuyin xiehui*) in 1978. Six hundred representatives from Taiwan and around the world met and decided that, in order to accomplish their desire to reach Hakkas around

---

424. Liao, *Unresponsive*, 105.
425. Zeng et al., *Day for Doubling*, 85.
426. Ibid., 176.

the world with the gospel, an organization was needed to facilitate and promote this vision.⁴²⁷ In 1993, the name of this organization was changed to the Christian Hakka Evangelical Association (*Jidujiao kejia fuyin xiehui*) (CHEA). The vision of this interdenominational organization is threefold:

> 1. To communicate the need for the gospel among Hakkas and the priority of this need. (There are five million Hakkas in Taiwan and only 0.3 percent of them belong to the Lord.)
>
> 2. To coordinate the gathering of resources of churches and to advance the growth of Hakka churches.
>
> 3. To participate in the mission to evangelize the world by building Hakka churches.⁴²⁸

According to a record of the important events and activities of this organization since its inception, the CHEA has been very active in these three areas.⁴²⁹

Another noteworthy development in Hakka-focused ministries was the establishment in 1999 of the Hakka Mission School (*Kejia xuanjiao xueyuan*), an institution which has since changed its name to Hakka Mission Seminary (*Kejia xuanjiao shenxueyuan*). The HMS mission statement says that this institution exists: "(1) to equip full-time workers for Hakka mission, (2) to offer training for the grass-roots outreach of churches, and (3) to carry out research to expand outreach to Hakkas."⁴³⁰

Other significant developments in ministry to Hakkas include the establishment within the Presbyterian Church in Taiwan in 2007 of a Hakka Mission Presbytery (*Kexuan zhonghui*), the translation work on the "Today's Taiwan Version" (*Xiandai Taiwan keyu yiben*) of the Hakka Bible, the formation of a Hakka choir (*Kejia shengyue tuan*) in 2007, and the annual large-scale ancestor-memorial services (which use contextualized ancestor rituals) that are held in several different areas of Taiwan and are co-sponsored by local churches. At this writing, the CHEA is in the midst of a "Double the Hakka Church in Ten Years Movement" (*Kejia jiaohui shinian beijia yundong*) which encourages churches and individuals who are concerned about the spiritual needs among Hakkas to join together and seek to double the Hakka church in the ten-year period between 2005–2014.⁴³¹

427. Zeng, *Anniversary Publication*, 21.
428. Ibid., 32.
429. Ibid., 23–30.
430. Ibid., 47.
431. Zeng et al., *Day for Doubling*, 218–23.

3

Research Methodology

THIS CHAPTER DETAILS THE methodology used in this study to explore tensions between being Hakka in northwestern Taiwan and being Christian. It is divided into the following sections: (1) basic interpretive qualitative research, (2) impact of the researcher, (3) limitations, and (4) data-gathering and analysis procedures.

Basic Interpretive Qualitative Research

This research used the basic interpretive qualitative research perspective and methodology to explore the meaning of the Hakka ethnic identity. According to Sharran Merriam, qualitative research designs have four general characteristics:[1]

1. Qualitative researchers seek to understand the meaning that individuals are constructing and attaching to a particular phenomenon at a particular time and in a particular place. "Putting oneself in the place of the other and seeing things from the perspective of others" is considered crucial for the researcher.[2] Merriam clarifies, "Qualitative researchers are not interested in people's surface opinions as in survey research. . . . Rather, [they] want to know *how* people do things, and what meaning they give to their lives."[3]

---

1. Merriam, "Qualitative Research," 4–6.
2. Crotty, *Social Research*, 76.
3. Merriam, "Assessing and Evaluating," 19.

2. These researchers deeply embed themselves in every aspect of their study and thus are able, in the process of collecting and analyzing data, to be more responsive and adaptive to learning opportunities and challenges that arise. The exact direction and details of the research emerge in the course of the study and are continually open to revision and refining and are not bound to follow a "tightly prefigured" plan.[4]

3. Qualitative research is inductive. Rather than starting with theories, concepts, or hypotheses, the research builds toward them. John Creswell points out how the thinking process is iterative, "cycling back and forth from data collection and analysis to problem reformulation and back."[5] Merriam explains, "Typically, findings inductively derived from the data in a qualitative study are in the form of themes, categories, typologies, concepts, tentative hypotheses, and even substantive theory."[6]

4. The end result of qualitative studies is a rich, thick description of what the researcher has learned about the phenomenon being studied. Creswell adds that rich detail about individuals and context can also be an important part of qualitative reporting.[7]

Impact of the Researcher

It is assumed that informants constructed their responses to the researcher's questions based in part on their perceptions of him. For example, his skin color (white), his age (forties), his gender (male), his level of education (PhD candidate), his Hakka and Mandarin skills (able to communicate), his social skills (still learning after living in Taiwan for more than twenty years), the extent and level of his relationship with the informants (some first-time encounters, some acquaintances, and some friends), and his self-introduction as a Christian pastor all affected the perception informants had of the researcher and the subsequent way they self-identified and presented themselves in response to his questions. In addition, informants' perceptions of how the researcher was seeing them, what he already knew,

---

4. Creswell, *Research Design*, 181.
5. Ibid., 183.
6. Merriam, "Qualitative Research," 5.
7. Creswell, *Research Design*, 182.

what he needed to know, and how they wanted to be seen by him also affected their responses.

This researcher assumes that three of his attributes had a more significant effect on the responses of informants. First, informants' perceptions of him as a Westerner may have caused informants to present themselves and Hakkas in a way that gives them honor in the eyes of an "outsider." Informants may have responded differently had the interviewer been another Hakka, a Hoklo, or a Mainlander. For example, since the boundaries between Chinese and Westerners might be more salient for them during an interview with a Westerner than the boundaries they normally assert (those between Hakka and other ethnic groups in Taiwan), their self-identifications may have been somewhat atypical.

Second, knowing that the researcher is a Christian pastor most likely had an impact on the responses of both Christians and non-Christians. Christians may have felt pressure to present themselves as "good" Christians through their responses. Non-Christians may have felt somewhat uncomfortable saying anything negative about being Christian. The researcher was aware of the discomfort of non-Christian informants several times, when, during the course of an interview, the topic shifted from more general things to how Hakkas feel about Christians. This same awkwardness also surfaced when the researcher asked others for interview prospects. Many people advised that potential informants should not be informed in advance that they would be asked about the perceptions that they personally have of Christians and Christianity, a revelation that would make them likely to refuse an interview. The researcher did not hide his intent or topic but sought to avoid creating uncomfortable situations for non-Christian informants during interviews by primarily focusing his questions on their perception of the perspective of Hakkas in general toward being Christian rather than on their own personal perspective.

Third, the fact that the researcher was able to speak the Hakka language may have had a significant effect on the responses of informants. Very few Westerners in Taiwan are able to communicate using Hakka, and this ability generated some curiosity and built rapport with informants. Since this ability combined with the time the researcher has lived in Taiwan also assumes previous significant contact with Hakkas, informants may have assumed that they did not need to provide certain details due to an expectation that the researcher should already be aware of them.

Creswell argues that researchers should be continually reflecting on who they are and how their "biases, values, and interests" are shaping the study.[8] Merriam adds that the researcher's "assumptions, worldview, . . . theoretical orientation, [and] relationship to the study" should also be kept in mind.[9] As he collected, analyzed, and wrote about the data, the researcher was intentionally conscious of and cautious about the following influences affecting his work: (1) his desire to find answers to the problem of the small size of the Hakka Christian church in Taiwan, (2) his Christian worldview, (3) his Western worldview, (4) his understanding of ethnic identification, and (5) his preconceived ideas gained from his experience of living in Taiwan for more than twenty years.

Limitations

This exploratory study carries all of the limitations of any qualitative study. Since this study involved only thirty-six informants who live in northwestern Taiwan, it is not appropriate to use the findings of this study to "generalize statistically" for a large population.[10] The findings of this study should be taken as the researcher's interpretation of the meaning of being Hakka, the categorizations that non-Christian Hakkas have of being Christian, and the responses of Hakka Christians in the context of these categorizations based on the presentations of informants at a particular time and in a particular context.

Data-Gathering and Analysis Procedures

The researcher interacted with informants in semi-structured interviews around the topics raised in the research questions. Interviews were conducted over the course of one year (October 17, 2007 through October 23, 2008). This subsection discusses the sample, interview questions, and the process used to analyze the data obtained.

Sample

Thirty-six people who self-identified as Hakkas were interviewed for this study. Reputational-case selection and chain-referral selection were used to obtain a sample that is "purposive or purposeful" in that it maximized

---

8. Ibid.
9. Merriam, "Assessing and Evaluating," 31.
10. Ibid., 28.

variation.[11] Informants were sought who could represent a broad spectrum of Hakka voices speaking about the meaning of being Hakka and Hakka perspectives on being Christian. Twenty-seven of them were male and nine were female. Sixteen of these informants were non-Christians (NC) and twenty were Christians, ten of whom were Christian pastors or evangelists (CL) and ten of whom were Christians who were not in leadership roles in a church or ministry (CM). Fifteen of the Christians were also first generation Christians. Thirty informants were married (M), three were single (S), one was widowed (W), and two were divorced (D). Of these thirty-six Hakkas, two were between nineteen and twenty-nine years old, four between thirty and forty-nine, twenty-two between fifty and sixty-five, and eight were sixty-six and older. Seven of these informants had a graduate degree (G), twelve had graduated from college (C), five from junior college (JC), seven had a high school diploma (HS), two completed junior high school (JH), and three did not complete elementary school (<E). Of these informants, eleven live in Hsinchu County, thirteen in Taoyuan County, one in Miaoli County, one in New Taipei City, seven in Taipei City, and three in Hsinchu City. Twenty of these Hakkas live in Hakka areas (H) and sixteen do not (NH). (According to the National Hakka Population Basic Data Survey, a Hakka area is an area where Hakkas [those who choose Hakka when they are forced to choose one ethnicity from many] make up more than 50 percent of the population. The determination of whether informants live in a Hakka area or not was made by comparing informants' places of residence with the results of this survey).[12] See table 2 below for a profile of the interview sample.

---

11. Merriam, "Qualitative Research," 12; Schensul et al., *Essential Ethnographic Methods*, 240–41.

12. Yang, "Preface," Section 3, 1.

Gender		
Male	Female	
27	9	

Interview Category		
Non-Christian	Christian Leader	Church Member
16	10	10

Marital Status			
Married	Single	Widowed	Divorced
30	3	1	2

Age			
19-29	30-49	50-65	66+
2	4	22	8

Educational Attainment					
< Elementary	Junior High	Senior High	Junior College	College	Graduate
3	2	7	5	12	7

County or City of Residence					
Miaoli County	Hsinchu City	Hsinchu County	Taoyuan County	Taipei City	New Taipei City
1	3	11	13	7	1

Residence	
Hakka Area	Non-Hakka Area
20	16

Table 2: Profile of Interview Sample

Thirty-one of these informants were interviewed once. These interviews ranged from one hour and nineteen minutes to six hours and fifty-one minutes and averaged two hours and nineteen minutes. Five informants were interviewed multiple times with total combined times ranging from three hours and four minutes to six hours and fifty-one minutes and averaging four hours and thirty-two minutes. Thirty informants were interviewed using the Hakka language (H), and Mandarin (M) was used for the seven who were not comfortable with or unable to speak in Hakka. Interviews were conducted in the *hailu* dialect of the Hakka language whenever possible. If the informant did not speak this form of Hakka, the *si-xian* dialect was used. The primary use of Hakka was intentional with the desire to use every tool available to ensure that being Hakka was kept in focus during the interview. Interviews were conducted primarily in the homes of informants (IH) or in public places (PP) such as restaurants, churches, or offices. Six informants were interviewed in the researcher's home (RH). In addition, two speeches (S) that #19 and #24 each gave in separate settings to groups of Christians and church leaders about the situation in the Hakka Christian community in Taiwan were included as data in this study. These speeches were approximately one hour and eleven minutes and eleven minutes in duration respectively. For an overview of the details of this interview sample, see table 3 below.

Research Methodology 103

#	Cat.	Gender	Age	Educ.	Area of Residence	Interview Location(s)	Total Time	Lang
1	NC	M	50-65	C	NH	IH	3:01	M
2	NC	F	50-65	C	H	IH	3:07	M
3	NC	M	50-65	C	NH	IH	6:51	H
4	NC	M	66-80	HS	H	IH	1:51	H
5	NC	M	66-80	HS	H	IH, RH	3:04	H
6	NC	M	66-80	C	H	IH	1:19	H
7	NC	M	50-65	HS	H	IH	3:39	H
8	NC	F	50-65	C	H	IH	1:51	H
9	NC	M	50-65	JH	NH	IH	1:42	H
10	NC	F	50-65	C	H	PP	1:22	H
11	NC	M	50-65	JH	H	IH	2:43	H
12	NC	M	19-29	HS	H	IH	1:42	H
13	NC	M	50-65	<E	H	IH	2:05	H
14	NC	M	66-80	HS	H	IH	1:53	H
15	NC	F	30-49	JC	H	RH	2:18	M
16	NC	M	50-65	JC	H	IH	1:55	H
17	CL	M	66-80	C	NH	PP	1:31	H
18	CL	M	50-65	C	NH	PP	4:03	M
19	CL	M	50-65	G	H	IH, RH, PP, S	6:51 / 1:11	H, M, M
20	CL	M	50-65	G	NH	PP	2:09	H
21	CL	F	50-65	C	NH	RH	2:13	H
22	CL	M	30-49	G	NH	PP	2:23	H
23	CL	M	50-65	G	H	IH	2:32	H
24	CL	M	50-65	G	NH	PP, S	1:44 / 0:11	H, M
25	CL	M	50-65	G	NH	PP	1:47	H
26	CL	M	30-49	G	NH	PP	1:36	H
27	CM	M	19-29	C	NH	PP	1:36	M
28	CM	M	66-80	<E	H	IH	2:09	H
29	CM	F	50-65	<E	H	IH	2:36	H
30	CM	M	50-65	JC	H	IH	2:25	H
31	CM	M	50-65	HS	NH	RH	1:23	H
32	CM	M	66-80	C	NH	PP	3:42	M
33	CM	M	50-65	JC	NH	IH	1:52	M
34	CM	F	50-65	C	NH	PP	2:04	H
35	CM	F	30-49	JC	H	IH, RH	5:15	H, M
36	CM	F	66-80	HS	H	IH, PP	4:23	H

Table 3: Detailed Information about Interview Sample
(see above text for the meaning of abbreviations)

As the researcher sought out and interacted with informants, he presented himself as a learner seeking experts in being Hakka to help him understand the Hakka "lived experience" better.[13] As he began an interview, he introduced himself, clearly stated his topic, and explained the mechanics of the interview. The researcher requested permission to record the interview, and, in every case, permission was granted.

Interview Questions

The researcher used the interview questions found in appendix 1 to stimulate informants to begin to share freely in the topic areas being explored in this research project. Follow-up questions differed with each informant, dependent on their responses to initial questions, and were designed to get at deeper meanings. For example, when a person asserted that hierarchical relationships in the family are an important part of being Hakka, the researcher probed for examples of the value Hakkas place on hierarchy and explored the feelings associated with challenging and submitting to senior family members.

As the research progressed, a few initial questions were revised or replaced with better ones, and new ones were added. For example, after seeing some early informants' hesitation to share freely in response to certain questions, the researcher revised these questions to begin with something like, "Some people say . . . ," and then briefly stated what other informants had already told him and asked informants to respond to and share about things in this topic area. Another example of this change in questions posed is when early informants shared about the importance of Hakka language, the researcher added the question, "When do Hakkas use the Hakka language?" The interview questions listed in appendix 1 are the final version of the questions used.

As the researcher constructed the interview questions detailed in appendix 1 as well as the follow-up questions he used during interviews, he made choices from three kinds of questions suggested by James Spradley: descriptive, structural, and contrast questions.[14] Spradley divides descriptive questions into the following five categories: (1) grand-tour questions—questions which ask the informant to assume that the interviewer knows nothing about a broad cultural scene and to give a detailed and comprehensive introduction to that scene; (2) mini-tour questions—questions

13. Bernard, *Research Methods*, 213.
14. Spradley, *Ethnographic Interview*.

which are like grand-tour questions but are asked about a smaller, more specific activity or place; (3) example questions—questions which ask the informant for an example of something that is being talked about; (4) experience questions—questions which encourage the informant to share their experiences about something; and (5) native-language questions—questions which are used to seek to discover and use emic terminology.[15] Spradley breaks structural questions down into five categories: (1) verification questions, (2) cover-term questions, (3) included-term questions, (4) substitution questions, and (5) card-sorting structural questions.[16] These sorts of questions are helpful to explore the way the world of the informant is organized. Spradley also suggests seven different types of contrast questions to be used to explore differences. This researcher also used various kinds of probes, when appropriate, to facilitate and encourage each informant to share freely during the interview.[17]

Interview questions stimulated the following kinds of responses: (1) individual Hakkas talking about their own feelings, (2) individual Hakkas talking about their perceptions of Hakkas in general, (3) individual Hakkas telling stories about themselves, and (4) individual Hakkas telling stories about others.

Analysis

An important aspect of the data analysis involved in this research project is the way the process of analysis of data began with the initial interview data and took place simultaneously with subsequent interviews. Insights gained in earlier interviews were tested and developed further in later interviews with different informants. Some informants were interviewed several times to facilitate further development of insights after a period of analyzing earlier interview data. The researcher was continually repeating the basic process of "gathering information, analyzing it, winnowing it, and testing it."[18]

The first step in the process of analyzing the interview data, following John Creswell's six-step model, is the transcription of the recordings of the interviews.[19] A team of transcriptionists, some of them volunteers and some of them paid, helped with this process. If there was any part

15. Ibid., 86–90.
16. Ibid., 126–31.
17. Bernard, *Research Methods*, 217–22.
18. Babbie, *Social Research*, 300.
19. Creswell, *Research Design*, 191.

of an interview that needed to be kept confidential because of what had been said, the researcher transcribed this part himself. Each of these transcriptions was entered into the NVivo 8 computer program. Since most interviews were conducted in the Hakka language, the reduction of spoken Hakka into Chinese characters often involved some translation. Most of the transcribers who helped in this process of changing spoken Hakka into Chinese characters, like most people in Taiwan, habitually connected Chinese characters with Mandarin pronunciations. Hence, when they encountered a Hakka spoken word they understood but, since there was no direct Mandarin equivalent, did not know a Chinese character to use with the Hakka pronunciation, they substituted something similar. As the researcher worked through each of the transcriptions the first time, he also listened to the audio files of the interviews and looked for and noted when these kinds of substitutions were made.

Creswell's second step in the analysis of data is to read through the transcriptions "to obtain a *general sense* of the information and to reflect on its overall meaning."[20] During the interviews and afterwards, as the researcher interacted with the transcripts and thought about the tone, depth, and credibility of what had been said and noted what stood out as interesting, he was also consciously looking for domains—their cover terms, their included terms, the semantic relationship between these terms, and their boundaries.[21] He made notes of his reflections and conclusions and entered them into the NVivo 8 program.

The third step in data analysis according to Creswell is coding.[22] The researcher used NVivo 8 to code the transcripts and his own notes and reflections. The researcher sought to collect together the words of each informant that related to the various topics and domains that were emerging as significant. The codes generated in this process were continually re-evaluated and adjusted, and new ones were added as the researcher began to explore symbols and their relationships in domains at deeper levels. He primarily used descriptive codes with "low levels of inference" which were organized hierarchically in "branching tree diagrams, with sub-subcodes collapsing into subcodes, which are then subsumed into larger codes."[23] For example,

20. Ibid.
21. Seidman, *Interviewing*, 100–101; Spradley, *Ethnographic Interview*, 100–102; Creswell, *Research Design*, 191.
22. Creswell, *Research Design*, 192.
23. LeCompte and Schensul, *Analyzing and Interpreting*, 57–58.

where certain issues surfaced in interviews as something being contested or discussed by those who are being Hakka, the different voices were separated and coded according to their position on the issue and then placed under a more general code labeled with the issue in question.

While coding the transcripts, the researcher listened to the audio of the interview, checking the accuracy of the transcription. When there was a problem with the transcription (e.g., missed words or a misunderstanding of what had been said) the transcripts were corrected. Annotations were added to the transcriptions, noting issues that were particularly significant or something that needed further exploration in future interviews. In this process, Chinese characters that were new to the researcher were also learned so that they could be used in future interviews and recognized when they were encountered in the Chinese language literature.

The fourth step in Creswell's analysis process is comparing and sorting the data in ways that will generate the raw materials for a description of the context and the participants and will isolate five to seven of the most important categories or themes for further analysis.[24] The researcher used the NVivo 8 computer program to manipulate the coded data to accomplish this comparing and sorting process, organizing existing codes into larger categories and shifting some data into new codes based on themes that were emerging. The researcher developed a diagram displaying a detailed conceptual framework (or a schematic diagram) that contained important domains and themes that were emerging.[25]

In this process of sorting, comparing, and looking for domains and themes, the researcher was particularly interested in things that revealed the way informants had been shaped, the symbols that repeatedly surfaced, the way informants related to and used these symbols, and the way they talked about and interacted with their context. The researcher looked for similarities, differences, themes, categories, patterns, kinds, and relationships in the data. He also looked for frequencies, magnitudes, structures, processes, causes, and consequences.[26]

As the researcher sorted and compared, he sought to understand what informants were saying at a deeper level. From the first interview

---

24. Creswell, *Research Design*, 193.

25. LeCompte and Schensul, *Analyzing and Interpreting*, 188–89; Spradley, *Ethnographic Interview*, 197–99.

26. Babbie, *Social Research*, 370–71; Lofland and Lofland, *Analyzing Social Settings*, 127–45.

forward, the researcher was constantly reflecting and building on what he had already discovered. After an interview, he often reflected on and compared what informants had said with his own experience in Taiwan and went to the literature to try to better understand some of these topics. For example, in an interview early in the research process, an informant said Hakkas were far more concerned about "face" than others around them. The researcher reflected on his own understanding of face and researched the scholarly literature on this topic. In future interviews, when the topic of face came up, the researcher explored this symbol more and sought to map its meanings, especially those that related to his research questions.

To achieve a deeper understanding, the researcher sometimes problematized things informants stated as fact and went to the literature to explore the sources of this information. For example, when the researcher heard several informants talk about George Mackay's remarks regarding the Hakka language, he researched the writings of Mackay and found the words being quoted. This exercise helped the researcher deepen his understanding of the way Hakka Christians were using the raw materials of history to construct Hakka in ways that would help them achieve their goals.

The literature also helped the researcher as he looked for patterns and domains that would draw together some of the phenomena he was observing. For example, Kuo-shu Yang's concept of the Chinese Social Orientation and Kwang-kuo Hwang's ideas about the principles governing the allocation of resources in Chinese societies were helpful in developing themes and deepening the researcher's understanding in the area of the Hakka cultural "stuff." [27]

The researcher also accessed other kinds of data that helped him explore the meanings of what informants were saying. For example, when a particular statistic on the percentage of Hakka Christians kept surfacing in interviews, the researcher looked for other means of triangulating this statistic. He obtained the data files for ten years of the Taiwan Social Change Survey and used the SPSS computer program to analyze this data to determine the percentage of Hakka Christians among the respondents of these surveys.

Creswell suggests that the fifth step in the analysis of data is to "advance how the description and themes will be represented in the qualitative narrative."[28] The researcher chose to present the data in three large blocks:

27. Yang, "Chinese Social Orientation." Hwang, "Face and Favor."
28. Creswell, *Research Design*, 194.

(1) that related to the cultural "stuff" of being Hakka, (2) that related to the categorizations of non-Christian Hakkas, and (3) that related to the actions of Christians in the context of the categorizations. Within these blocks of data, everything was arranged in line with the themes gleaned from previous analysis of the data. In two cases, some details about situations informants discussed were changed in order to protect confidentiality.

For the final step in the process of analyzing data, Creswell recommends that the researcher interpret the data.[29] This step involves answering the question, "What were the lessons learned?" In this step, the researcher used the social constructionist theory on ethnic identification to uncover the way informants and other Hakkas were involved in the process of ethnic identification as they constructed their categorizations of being Christian or responded in the context of these categorizations. These insights were included in three different ways. First, these insights were included in the way the data was organized and presented. For example, when talking about the categorizations that non-Christian Hakkas have of being Christian, the way these Hakkas had been shaped by and were accessing their cultural "stuff" was highlighted. Second, the interpretations were also included in separate critique or reflection sections. For example, at the end of the section on the categorizations of Hakka non-Christians, a discussion of the fluidity and fixity of ethnic identification found in these categorizations is included. Third, the lessons learned are also included in the section on implications in the final chapter.

29. Ibid.

4

Being Hakka in Northwestern Taiwan

THE FIRST STEP IN understanding tensions between being Hakka in northwestern Taiwan and being Christian is to explore the way Hakkas in northwestern Taiwan construct being Hakka, focusing on areas that relate to their perceptions of being Christian. Taking this step provides a deeper understanding of the cultural "stuff" shaping the thoughts and actions of these Hakkas and serving as a reservoir of symbols and habits that they draw upon to construct their identity as it relates to being Christian. Such an understanding helps to reveal the perspective that those who are being Hakka have that causes them to notice cultural differences between being Hakka and being Christian, the reasons why differences in certain areas are important, the ways they have been shaped to act, as well as the raw materials available for non-Christian Hakkas to use in constructing their responses to being Christian and for Christian Hakkas to use as they act in the context of these categorizations.

This chapter focuses on the ways informants presented being Hakka in Taiwan. Informants' descriptions or self-identifications are arranged in three different sections. The first section recounts the symbols that most frequently surfaced when informants talked about being Hakka. In the second section, the focus is on the symbols that informants pointed to as the boundary markers of being Hakka. The final section reviews informants' perceptions of the way Hakkas are relating to being Hakka.

The data presented in this chapter is not meant to be a comprehensive or exhaustive detailing of the phenomenon of being Hakka in northwestern Taiwan. The interactive process of Hakka ethnic identification is much too complex to capture in its entirety in the space available here. Rather, the scope of the data presented and discussed in this chapter reflects an overarching desire to understand the way those who are being Hakka interact with others about being Christian. Consequently, explorations with informants on the topic of being Hakka focused on the following areas: (1) those aspects of being Hakka that appeared to be shaping the responses of informants (and those they discussed) to being Christian, and (2) those aspects of being Hakka that informants (or those they discussed) used to construct these responses. The aspects of being Hakka focused on in this chapter are those that shaped or provided resources for non-Christians who are being Hakka as they categorized being Christian and shaped and provided resources for Hakka Christians as they responded in the context of these categorizations.

Informants also affected the scope of this data as they chose how to construct being Hakka for a non-Chinese researcher. Limited by time and other constraints, informants selected what they thought was important to tell the researcher (given their perceptions of him, his questions, and their relationship) and constructed a response to his inquiries about being Hakka.[1]

What is reported and discussed in this chapter is an analysis of the constructions of these informants given in response to the questions posed in which the common themes and the way each construction fits into the bigger picture of the responses of all informants combined are noted.

Important Shared Symbols

This first section recounts and discusses the symbols that most frequently surfaced when informants talked about being Hakka and especially about being Hakka in the context of discussing their perceptions of Christians and Christianity. These symbols are grouped into the following five themes: (1) Hakka history, (2) family, (3) reciprocal relationships, (4) everyone, and (5) Christianity (the categories "family," "reciprocal relationships," and "everyone" originate with Hwang and Yang).[2] The data presented in this section comes from responses informants gave to interview questions emerging out of research question 1, "What does it mean to be Hakka in northwestern Taiwan?" and research question 2, "What tensions exist between being Hakka in northwestern Taiwan and being Christian?"

---

1. Pang, "Being Hui," 185.
2. Yang, "Chinese Social Orientation"; Hwang, "Face and Favor."

This discussion will be limited to those aspects of being Hakka that came up regularly in interviews. The fact that informants raised these symbols instead of others suggests that these symbols are the most relevant in the context of discussing being Hakka and Hakka categorizations of being Christian. Other possible reasons these symbols surfaced include: (1) these are the symbols that seemed most logical for informants to present to a person with the researcher's phenotypical and cultural characteristics; (2) these were the symbols that interview questions stimulated and other questions might have elicited other symbols; and (3) these symbols were important to these particular informants, but other informants might have valued and considered other symbols to be more relevant.

Hakka History

As informants talked about being Hakka, they often tied their comments to Hakka history. Their constructions using Hakka history usually presented Hakkas as having noble roots and as having the character and ability to prosper in the context of significant challenges and difficulties. Negative dimensions of being Hakka were shown to have their roots as a reaction to impossibly unfavorable circumstances. This positive presentation of Hakka is consistent with the argument in the ethnicity literature that actors use the raw materials of history to construct a self-image beneficial to them. The main points raised by informants in this area are also echoes of responses of Hakkas to many of the categorizations of the Puntis during the period of time when the Hakka ethnic identity emerged. This subsection is divided into three themes: (1) good roots, (2) disadvantaged guests, and (3) shaped by history.

GOOD ROOTS

Many informants raised the idea that Hakkas have extraordinary ancestors, claiming these ancestors clearly have their roots in the central plain of China. This ancestral homeland claim is significant because Chinese consider the central plain to be the center of the Han Chinese civilization. #16 described why this is significant:

> The first place that develops in a country is its capital, and a long time ago, the capitals of the Yuan, Ming, and Qing dynasties were Beijing, Nanjing, and Tianjin [all located in this central plain]. In the eyes of Han Chinese, the quality culture is located at the center, and the place where the government officials were located

was high level. The central area was more developed and was a strategic place for culture. The Hoklos were living below this central area in Fujian Province. For Chinese, the center of the country is most important and respected while every other area is considered less important. The farther one was from the center, the less [important] they were considered to be. Hakkas migrated from the central plain . . . so their blood is better. All people were originally equal, but if you compare them, the blood of the Hakkas, because they come from the central plains, is purer.

When informants talked about the ancestral roots of Hakkas originating in the center of Han civilization, some mentioned a related claim, that Hakkas are the one Chinese group who best preserved Han culture. For example, several informants pointed out that Hakka was the language of the central plains. #6 proposed that when you use the Hakka language to read poems written during the Tang Dynasty, they read much more smoothly than if you try to read them in other Chinese dialects. However, other informants disagreed with the idea that Hakkas are more Han than other Chinese groups.

Disadvantaged Guests

Informants emphasized that the ancestors of Hakkas in Taiwan today faced great challenges as they fled conflicts and sought better economic opportunities by moving southward from the central plains of China in five large migrations and then eventually to Taiwan. As these ancestors moved into new areas, they were often disadvantaged because the better opportunities had already been taken by earlier immigrants and the new arrivals were in the minority. Informants reported that while these challenges affected these Hakka ancestors negatively in some ways, they also produced many positive character traits.

Hard Life

When the Hakkas arrived in Taiwan, some informants noted that the prime land had already been occupied by earlier Hoklo immigrants. Hence, Hakkas were forced to develop the less fertile land as well as the land closer to the mountains, resulting in a poorer and harder life than that of the Hoklos who lived in the better locations. For example, #7 told how the area where he lives was considered undesirable because there was no source of water for farming. His ancestors depended primarily on rainwater for their crops, and, if it did not rain or the rain did not fall at the proper times, there would be little or nothing to harvest.

Many older informants told stories of the struggles of their own childhood as evidence of the hard life of Hakkas. For example, #29 told how she was not allowed to go to elementary school because her parents had to work and she was needed to look after her younger siblings and other household tasks. When she was a bit older, she daily carried different kinds of produce to a distant village and sold them in the marketplace to supplement in a small way the meager income of her parents. She emphasized that she was *never* given time off to rest. When she married, #29 reported that the situation was similar. Her husband's family was also very poor, so she worked day and night. She said she was responsible for *all* of the work in the family's fields, and when times were tough, she even had to sell things in the market and do manual labor for other people. In addition to all of these responsibilities, she also had to care for her children while her husband worked in construction.

Those older informants who had the privilege of going to school also suffered. #4 told how he often studied late into the night by the light of a small candle. When he advanced to junior high school, he had to walk for almost an hour and a half to get to school. He also had to cook breakfast on a wood-burning stove before he left because his mother had worked so hard the previous day and was often too tired to get up and help him. In order to save wear on his shoes, he carried them to school and put them on once he got there. He reported that the only reason he advanced past junior high school was because he was able to test into a teacher-training school where he could attend without paying tuition or room and board.

Bullied and Scorned

According to informants, the fact that those who are being Hakka have been in the minority in Taiwan has resulted in them being bullied or scorned. They reported that, when anyone is different from or weaker than the majority in any way, they stand out and are more likely to become the target of derision. Informants told stories of being bullied in school and when serving their compulsory military service. They were called derogatory names and ridiculed. They were considered by many to be lower class. For example, a professor at a prestigious university in Taiwan revealed this attitude when, in response to the question, "Do you have any Hakka students?" he replied, "No . . . the only Hakkas in our school are those who work in the cafeteria or clean the bathrooms."

Shaped by History

Informants articulated that being disadvantaged shaped Hakkas in many ways. The symbols that surfaced in this area are: stiff-necked Hakka spirit, hardworking, frugal, conservative, Hakka mountain songs, solidarity, adaptability, and able persons.

Stiff-necked Hakka Spirit

Informants pointed out that the past experiences of the Hakkas have shaped them into a group of people who have a "stiff-necked Hakka spirit." One meaning of this symbol is that Hakkas are persistent when they decide to do something. #7 said Hakkas have a stronger will or determination than others around them. When #15 was asked to talk about stiff-necked Hakkas, she said, "When we say 'stiff necked,' we mean strong; . . . How shall I say it?" Her non-Hakka husband tried to help her by providing the interpretation, "Very obstinate, very stubborn," but she continued, "No, not obstinate. It has the feeling that Hakkas are not easily defeated; they will not easily compromise . . . very resolute."

Hardworking

Informants also reported that those who are being Hakka are hardworking people. Some informants even suggested that this diligence is a part of the nature of Hakkas, and, when comparing themselves with other groups, they notice a difference. For example, #34 opined, "Hakkas say Hoklos are lazier than Hakkas." #35 gave the example of her Mainlander friends who are more likely to buy pre-cooked food rather than cook for themselves. She contrasted the attitudes of these Mainlanders with her Hakka friends who like to do things themselves, not just in the area of cooking, but in every other aspect of managing their household, even if it is time-consuming. She said that cooking is one way she can show her children she is working hard for them.

Frugal

Another aspect of being Hakka that informants raised is that of being frugal. Since their families have experienced poverty, at least in the past, informants said Hakkas have a habit of being careful money managers. #7 told how Hakkas often save half of their income so that, if there is a disaster or they encounter difficulties, they will have money to use. He compared this with Hoklos who are more willing to spend money and so must borrow money when difficulties arise. #7 said Hakkas continue to be frugal now, but their frugality has changed from that of the past. In the past, Hakkas bought cheaper clothes and shoes. Now, their frugality is evidenced in the way they avoid spending large sums of money. When traveling, even though they can afford to stay in a five-star hotel, they choose to stay in a three-star hotel instead, because they think a five-star hotel would be wasteful. #7 expressed that he thinks Hakkas are definitely more frugal than Hoklos, who are more frugal than Mainlanders, who are more frugal than Westerners.

Some informants questioned whether being frugal still distinguishes Hakkas from others. #2 said younger Hakkas are not necessarily more frugal than other ethnics and doubted whether being frugal should be considered a special characteristic of being Hakka. She suggested that being frugal in the past was actually the result of environmental factors (such as living in the mountains and being poor) rather than a distinct part of being Hakka.

Conservative

Informants also mentioned being conservative as an aspect of being Hakka. The caution with which Hakkas face their world is considered to be the result of so many years of being bullied and scorned. #23 said, "Maybe this culture or personality has been passed on from generation to generation. Hakkas have not been the masters, so they are more careful with everything. They moved a lot in the past and, as a result, feel less secure; hence, they are cautious [and] conservative." #19 echoed this sentiment and argued that this is a characteristic of any minority group, claiming that Hakkas do not want to be different but want to be like everyone else. #13 articulated that Hakkas are generally submissive and not very assertive.

Mountain Songs

Informants also connected Hakka mountain songs with being Hakka. These songs originated when Hakkas working together in the fields sang them. Informants reported that in the past, there were certain occasions where Hakkas were more likely to hear these mountain songs. Mountain song melodies were often used in different kinds of opera presentations, and one common venue was the community theater. #5 told about how his wealthy grandmother would choose a different grandchild each day to accompany her and other wealthy people in their area to watch an opera which was acted out over ten days. Another common opera venue was the temple. On special festival days two or three times a year, everyone would donate money and together hire an opera troupe to act out a particular story over three days in the square in front of the temple. Sometimes medicine sellers would act out a short opera in order to attract a crowd to buy their products. More recently, people have more opportunities to hear Hakka mountain songs, both in singing competitions and in performances by musicians, on the new Hakka television station.

Those who are being Hakka vary in the way they feel about these mountain songs. When asked if any of their own family members sang these songs or liked to listen to them, several informants reported that, in the more recent past, Hakkas were often too busy trying to survive to have time to listen to or to sing Hakka mountain songs. Most informants, regardless of age, said that, while they do not sing these songs themselves, they enjoy listening to them. For example, #2 said she is very familiar with and likes the mountain song melodies because her father enjoyed listening to mountain songs when she was small. #27 said he likes to listen to Hakka mountain songs and knows several other young people who also like them. The one informant who directly said he did not like mountain songs added that he did not really care for music in general. Three informants mentioned knowing someone who *really* likes Hakka mountain songs, and, in all three cases, the individuals who treasured these songs were well over sixty-five.

Mountain songs are not the only kind of music that those who are being Hakka enjoy. When informants said they like these songs, they often added that they also like different kinds of music. Those Hakkas who went to school during the Japanese occupation of Taiwan learned to sing Japanese songs. They have good memories of singing those songs with their teachers, and many still like Japanese songs today. #19 told about learning to sing when he was in school as well. He said he learned both foreign and local songs. #2 reported that she likes the music of Taiwan Aborigines as well because the words of their songs are more down-to-earth than those found in Hakka mountain songs and other types of music.

Some Hakkas connect Hakka mountain songs with low-class things. #2 said the words to some of the songs were in poor taste so, while she likes the melodies, she does not listen to these mountain songs very often. When #3 was a child, his grandfather, a wealthy landowner, forbid anyone in his house from singing Hakka mountain songs. His siblings and cousins could listen to this music on the radio, but they were not allowed to sing themselves. He talked about how the children in his family were taught that actors and singers were low-class people, and that, rather than learning to sing, one should work hard in school.

Solidarity

Another aspect informants tied to history when talking about being Hakka is solidarity with other Hakkas. Some felt Hakkas displayed much solidarity, while other informants did not. Those who saw solidarity among Hakkas argued that the reason for joining together was that, as a minority group, they needed more strength in order to resist being bullied and taken advantage of or cheated by other ethnics who were in the majority. For example, some informants said that, in the past, Hakkas often helped each other deal with rejection, teasing, and other challenges they encountered in school or when they were serving their compulsory military service. #24 gave an example of Hakka solidarity in the political realm, stating, "If Hakkas are not strong politically, we will not be assured of obtaining the rights and benefits that are rightly ours." Hence, many Hakkas support Hakka politicians who will enable their voice to be heard on the stage of Taiwan politics. #13 argued that if Hakkas do not fight to ensure that they are not unfairly overlooked when government resources are distributed, others will take away what should belong to Hakkas. #24 mentioned several results of recent Hakka political solidarity—the establishment of a public Hakka-language television station, the Executive Yuan's Council for Hakka Affairs, and a program teaching Hakka in elementary schools.

Other informants argue that solidarity with other Hakkas is not something that characterizes those who are being Hakka. When asked if Hakkas have areas where they join together in solidarity, #2 reported, "[Hakkas] have significant differences of opinion about things. For example, Hakka culture is becoming more and more . . . in decline . . . faint, but Hakkas are not working together to turn things around." #31 told how he used to get furious with his Hakka classmates and workers in the factory where he was employed because they downplayed their Hakka identity and spoke

Hoklo rather than fighting for Hakka. #2 pointed out that Hakkas will only join together in solidarity if they perceive they have a stake in something. #11 agreed, "Look at what happens during elections. If there are a Hoklo candidate and a Hakka candidate running for a particular position, some Hakkas do not join together with other Hakkas in solidarity. They follow their own interests, voting for the candidate whom they perceive will benefit them personally." #34 added, "Everyone is becoming more and more pragmatic and concerned only with what will bring benefit to oneself . . . It is hard for them to work together in solidarity with others."

Adaptability

Another aspect that surfaced as informants talked about being Hakka is adaptability to new situations. When Hakkas move into a non-Hakka area, they usually work to blend in with the people in that location. Rather than resisting the status quo, they seek to learn from others around them and try to integrate themselves into their new environment. They still keep some of their private customs and habits that do not conflict with others but adapt to others when in public areas. Informants continually raised the example of Hakkas learning and using the dominant language in the new area, sometimes to the extent that their children did not have opportunities to learn to speak Hakka. Informants gave several examples of locations where the people all speak Hoklo but are reported to have Hakka ancestry as evidenced by certain customs they engage in and other historical evidence.

People with Ability

While some informants accepted the fact that Hakkas were a weak minority who adjusted themselves accordingly, other informants disputed this weakness. They emphasized the strengths of Hakkas. For example, they reported that Hakkas were quite numerous worldwide. They gave examples of famous historical figures (e.g., Sun Yat-sen) who were Hakka. They pointed out that continual migration down through the years has made the Hakkas a better people. #19 reported, "Hakkas are a little arrogant. They say the reason they kept migrating was because they were a superior group of people." Elaborating on this logic, he said that rich people were more likely to migrate in the face of war because they had more to lose. Those who were weaker had to stay behind and take whatever came their way. Furthermore, it was only those who had money, or who were government officials, or who were stronger and had confidence in themselves who could migrate.

Family

As informants described being Hakka in the context of thinking about the way Hakkas respond to being Christian, the topic of family was often mentioned. By "family," Hakkas and other Chinese usually mean "the male descendants of a common ancestor, bearing the same surname, and their wives and children."[3] The discussion in this subsection focuses on four symbols that regularly surfaced as informants talked about the family aspects of being Hakka: (1) respect, (2) incense fires, (3) ancestors' language, and (4) traditions.

RESPECT

Traditionally for Hakkas and other Chinese, "duty to the family surpasses every other responsibility, be it to *tian* (heaven) or to the state."[4] Since much of what they possess (e.g., physical characteristics, wealth, and social position) came to them as a result of their membership in a particular family, each person was expected to strive for the good of that family and to fulfill his or her role in that family.[5] Duty to family was spelled out in the principle of *xiao* (filial piety). According to this principle, children were obligated to "provide for the material and mental well-being of one's aged parents, perform ceremonial duties of ancestral worship, take care to avoid harm to one's body, ensure the continuity of the family line, and in general conduct oneself so as to bring honor and avoid disgrace to the family name."[6]

One important aspect of filial piety that informants often referred to as they talked about being Hakka is evidenced in the concept of relationships within the family being hierarchical. The family system, in many respects, is organized around the understanding that junior members of the family show respect for and submit themselves to senior members. This habit of respecting senior family members makes it likely that change will occur at a slower rate, that various aspects of being Hakka that are

---

3. Thompson, *Chinese Religion*, 32.
4. Carpenter, "Familism," 503.
5. Gao et al., "Chinese Communication Processes," 283; Hsu, *Ancestors' Shadow*, 224.
6. Ho, "Filial Piety," 155.

important to senior Hakkas will persist longer than if seniors and ancestors were not held in such high regard.

As informants considered interactions within the family, the hierarchical nature of family relationships was often assumed. Senior family members expect younger members to submit to their will and not vice versa. #7 talked about a situation where a father accidentally stepped on his son's foot. He explained how Japanese and Western fathers might say, "Sorry" in this situation, but a Hakka father would not. In fact, #7 reported that he had never heard his or any other Hakka father apologize, even when it was clear that the father was at fault. #7 said, "[If a father accidentally stepped on his son's foot], that is no big deal. The son should just remove his foot. [The father would think], I am his father. . . . I am heaven (*tian*), he is earth (*di*). Why should I say I am sorry?"

The hierarchical nature of family relationships was also evident in the way informants personally talked about choosing to defer to family members who are their seniors, even when they do not necessarily agree with them. For example, #8 said that she dares not to make any changes in ancestor practices while her family elders are still alive. She said, "When the family elders are gone and we are managing our household affairs, it is possible that we will experiment with making a few changes in our ancestor practices. At this time though, we dare not make any changes." She went on to explain what happened when one of her Taipei relatives only prepared fruit to offer as a sacrifice to the ancestors. "The senior family members voiced their displeasure about his actions saying, 'He is not acting appropriately. He has not even prepared one piece of meat to sacrifice.'" #8 continued, "The thinking of the older generation is so deep-rooted that it cannot be changed." She stated that her own generation can accept those who do not burn incense and spirit money in ancestor rituals, but those who are seventy- or eighty-years-old have this habit. She continued, "The older generations definitely feel they need to burn incense and spirit money in order not to let down their ancestors." #3 said he would be reluctant to make too many changes to ancestor rituals because of his feelings of affection and devotion for his dead father and grandfather. #19 explained that other rituals are not as important as ancestor rituals to the senior members of the family, and so they do not oppose change in these areas. For example, wedding ceremonies have changed significantly over the years. However, because many senior family members care deeply about maintaining traditions at funerals, younger family members defer to their wishes.

One informant talked about the importance of outward compliance with the demands of older and senior members of the family even if one does not agree with them. #23 explained:

> Traditionally, the head of the family was like a dictator. Family members were not free to do whatever they wanted. The expectation placed upon them by their culture was that they should follow and obey . . . that compliance was important . . . the outward act of doing was important. They knew that they could not voice their opinions, they could not oppose the family leader; they could not expect to be able to raise issues and discuss them. Over time, people got in the habit of not speaking their hearts but continuing to outwardly comply with the demands of senior family members. This habit has truly become a part of our culture.

The way Hakkas relate to their ancestors also provides an example of this hierarchical thinking and willingness to submit to seniors. In general, many of those who are being Hakka assume that one should show respect to the ancestors in ancestor rituals. For example, #11 said, "When your parents demand that you participate in ancestor rituals, you cannot refuse! This is venerating your own ancestors; it is not a responsibility that you can forget and throw aside. You would be rejecting your ancestors." Some informants highlighted the point that they venerate their ancestors not to gain some benefit, but rather to show respect for ancestors and to fulfill one's filial duty. #1 stated that one of the main reasons he insists that his son attend his family's tomb-sweeping ceremony is to show respect to his father who died several years ago.

The pervasiveness of hierarchical thinking in the way Hakkas relate to their ancestors is also evidenced by the arrangement of urns filled with bones and ashes inside the common mausoleum of the clan. Inside these mausoleums, the urns of the dead are arranged in order according to well-defined principles of hierarchy (for a detailed description of Hakka mausoleums and the general principles governing the placement of urns inside them, see Martin).[7] When relatives gather for ancestor veneration at special times like Tomb Sweeping, hierarchy is evident in their procedures. Relatives often participate in the rituals in a certain order (seniors first) according to generation and, within generations, according to age.

7. Martin, "Hakka Mausoleums," 88–95.

Hierarchical thinking related to family relationships among those who are being Hakka can also be seen in the way some Hakkas relate to the gods. The gods are considered to be higher in the hierarchy than ancestors. This is evidenced by the placement of the image of the gods in the center and the ancestor tablet on the left side of the family altar. In the twice-daily rituals that take place at the family altar in many Hakka homes, the gods are worshiped in the order of their rank in the spirit world and prior to venerating ancestors.

However, the hierarchical thinking that has characterized being Hakka in the past is changing in many families. The younger members of the family do not always unquestioningly go along with their senior family members. #7 said, "Things have changed. In the past, the head of a family could control his children. If a child did not listen to him, that child would have to leave the family and would starve [because he would have no way of providing for himself]. Now, my children tell me what they have already decided to do. . . . If I do not like it, they will still do it. They tell me what they are doing only because they want to show respect to me." #16 said younger people will discuss desired changes to ancestor rituals with their elders and seek to influence them but will usually respect their decisions.

One reason for the change in the hierarchical thinking that characterized being Hakka in the past is that people are becoming more independent. Younger Hakkas no longer give all of their earnings to their parents but instead manage their finances independently. Younger Hakkas often live with their immediate family away from relatives and so do not learn from senior family members the details of certain rituals and ways of handling things. In addition, schools and the media expose them to alternatives to traditional ways. For example, #16 said the reason the family hierarchy is not so important to him is because he went to school. He said that without the influence of his schooling, he would still think that he, as the oldest (and only) son and as a man, was more important than other family members.

INCENSE FIRES

The symbol of "incense fires," usually used to refer to the burning of incense that takes place in ancestor rituals, was raised often by informants. Informants' frequent use of this symbol reflects the value Hakkas place on ancestors and ancestor veneration, the context where incense is widely used. The symbol of "incense fires" evokes the idea of continuity in the minds of those who are being Hakka. Five aspects of this continuity that regularly surfaced as informants talked about being Hakka and five dimensions of how things are changing are discussed below.

The first aspect of this continuity associated with incense fires can be seen in the way Hakkas traditionally see themselves as a part of a continuous line of people, from their earliest ancestors through themselves to their children and their children after them. Consequently, bearing a male heir who will continue the family line and burn incense to the ancestors on the family altar is considered an important filial responsibility.

The heirs' involvement in these practices is assumed. #4 reflected this assumption when he explained that even though his son is not involved in venerating ancestors now, that will change in the future, "The young will get old. Until that time, they usually do not involve themselves in these things. When I am gone, they will have no choice but to burn incense to the ancestors. While I am alive . . . they can be lazy and not burn incense, they do not need to concern themselves with these things. But, when I am old, when I am gone, they will have no choice . . . they will venerate, my son will have no choice but to venerate." Some informants said that venerating ancestors is not a habit that parents cultivate in their children or that their children learn or decide they want to do; they just venerate because that is "the way things are."

The importance placed on maintaining this continuous line of incense fires can also be seen in the flexibility that exists in marriage and adoption patterns in order for a family to be able to have male offspring.[8] For example, when a couple cannot produce an heir, the family will find an acceptable substitute by buying a boy from another family, by adopting a boy from another relative, or by designating the son of a concubine to fill this role.[9] Uxorilocal marriage (*zhaozhui*) is also practiced. #3 commented, "Those who do not have a son are often very troubled. They say, 'My incense fires will cease to burn, and I am the one who broke the line.'" #7 said that not having someone in the next generation to burn incense for the ancestors would be extremely shameful for him.

Informants provided several examples of the importance placed on having a male heir. For example, #18 told how even ethnicity and surname distinctions can fall if necessary in order to procure an heir. He said, "I

---

8. Wang et al., "Who Married How?"
9. Thompson, *Chinese Religion*, 39.

have a cousin who was originally surnamed [Ye]. My father's brother did not have a son . . . so he arranged with the [Ye] family to adopt one of their sons. . . . From the time he was little until he became my uncle's son, this cousin had told everyone that he was a Hoklo, surnamed [Ye]. . . . Now he goes around and tells everyone that he has [our] surname and is a Hakka. . . . In the future he will receive my uncle's inheritance."

The second aspect of this continuity associated with incense fires that informants raised is evidenced by how Hakkas document that continuity and their own place in it. One way Hakkas document this continuity is on their ancestor tablet. #3 reported that Hakkas put the individual names of ancestors on their ancestor tablet, whereas Hoklos do not. Displaying his ancestor tablet to me, #4 said, "Here are my ancestors. . . . Look, here is my name. . . . I am in the nineteenth generation. We arrange the names like this . . . eleven, twelve, thirteen, fourteen . . . this is me. Look, I am in the nineteenth generation. My father is here in the eighteenth generation . . . we moved to Taiwan in the eleventh generation."

Another way this continuity with the past is documented is in the ancestor record (*zupu*). These records are usually in book form and have the names and other details of their ancestors. Sometimes, these records become tools that are used to cultivate respect for the ancestors and traditional ways. For example, #8 told how she and her husband had recently edited a new ancestor record for their family. They had all of the illiterate elders in their family learn to write a few words using calligraphy. Her husband helped her mother-in-law write the phrase, "When you drink water, think of its source; you must not forget your roots (*yinshui siyuan buke wangben*)." #25 reported that, as a result of these ancestor records, Hakkas are very clear about their roots, much clearer than other ethnics in Taiwan.

The third aspect of this continuity associated with incense fires that regularly surfaced as informants talked about being Hakka is the way incense fires of ancestor veneration facilitate a connection with one's ancestors and one's roots. The incense that is burned has several practical benefits. The smell of incense is understood to communicate to the ancestors that the rituals are taking place, calling them to come and partake in the food being presented. The smoke is also understood to carry the thoughts from the hearts of the ritual participant to the ancestors in appropriate ways. For example, #4 reported how incense helps, "When I worship, I am speaking to the gods and ancestors. Even though I have brushed my teeth, I am still afraid that my mouth might not be totally clean. When my words are separated by a layer of incense, they are not so dirty.... Also, I do not have to worry about accidently spraying them with my saliva as I speak."

Informants also reported that the incense fires of ancestor veneration often become the focal point for some Hakkas who want to return to their roots. Informants told how, after spending their lives working away from the original home of their family, many Hakkas develop an interest in returning to their roots as they approach retirement age. The ancestors, the incense fires, and the places where ancestral rituals are held become the focal point of their interest. In one sense, these rituals facilitate a return to their roots. As they trace their roots, they naturally focus on their ancestors and start to diligently venerate them. #19 explained that there are very few people who are in their twenties and thirties who are diligent about venerating their ancestors. They may return home on their mother's birthday but not when the clan gathers for ancestor rituals at the time of tomb sweeping. However, when these people are in their fifties and sixties, they become more diligent in visiting the grave of their parents. They want to repay the love their deceased parents showed to them. They have no other way to express their respect and filial piety to their parents, so they spend a lot of time and money in this pursuit. They may remodel their father's home or the ancestral hall or prepare another kind of memorial.

The fourth aspect of this continuity associated with incense fires raised by informants is the way incense fires facilitate a continued relationship with living relatives. The idea of "returning" was frequently raised when informants discussed the ancestor rituals that take place on important holidays like Lunar New Year and Tomb Sweeping. Informants talked about returning to places like the original home of their family where an older relative sometimes still lives or a common mausoleum often located in the country close to the original home of the family. #19 said Hakkas are more diligent than others about returning home for ancestor ceremonies. #21 agreed and said that when a Hoklo moves to another place, they just arrange to venerate their ancestors in their new location. She said, "But Hakkas are not this way. Even when they live far away they will prepare sacrifices and return. This is a wonderful part of Hakka culture. For Hakkas, it is important to venerate ancestors together with many other relatives."

Informants also spoke about the affection and devotion that many of those who are being Hakka have for things they connect with ancestor practices. Gatherings where the veneration of ancestors takes place bring clan members together and enable them to maintain and develop affection and devotion between them. People anticipate returning to the family home to see those they love. If someone is unable to attend, everyone will ask about them. Informants reported that clan members sometimes eat together during these times, and, as they spend time together, they are able to keep abreast on what has been happening in the lives of others. #4 reported, "The times when ancestor rituals take place are times for the relatives to gather and fellowship together, to tell about what is happening in one's immediate family. This is a rare opportunity. Everyone cherishes these times."

Returning to the family home and participating in ancestor rituals with other members of one's clan for some carries more meaning than what happens in the rituals themselves. These rituals bring them into relationships that are filled with affection and devotion and a sense of belonging. For example, #3 reported:

> When I venerate my ancestors, I am not just holding up a stick of incense. There is much meaning behind this act. I am participating in a common clan activity. I am a part of this clan. Today, my clan is the one that the people whose names are on the ancestor tablet have passed down to me. It is an identity. So every time I go back to my family home, there is much noise and excitement. Everyone is happy, and we venerate our ancestors together one more time. This identity comes from the house. . . . My cousins and I grew up together there and, as a result, have common ways of saying things and common memories. These are the things behind our veneration. Today, we all have the opportunity to come and venerate the same ancestors. This identity is really the strongest motivation for doing so.

For #3, participating with the clan in ancestor veneration brings many childhood memories of times together with his cousins to mind. The older cousins led and took care of the younger ones. They invented and played games together. They worked together to catch small animals. They got in trouble together. At meal times, they often filled up their rice bowls with food at their own immediate family's table and then carried them to join the other cousins at their tables in other parts of the large house. They were welcome at any table. #3 continued, "Because all of us venerated the same ancestors, this warm affection and devotion for each other naturally developed."

Significantly, rather than using individual graves as others around them often do, Hakkas in northern Taiwan often join together with other relatives in their agnatic descent group (clan-grouping) and build mausoleums or communal graves where the remains of their loved ones can be placed together.[10] Ying-Chang Chuang found that, in contrast to Hoklos, who usually only worship their closest ancestors and set up separate ancestor tablets when the family is divided, Hakkas usually have a shared tablet and worship at and care for the graves of ancestors going back to their first Taiwan ancestor.[11] Martin highlights the significance of this joint mausoleum as a burial method when he states, "In light of the Chinese preference for dispersed burials and the underlying belief in the magical forces of the earth, an innovative practice of common burial in monumental tombs is worthy of attention."[12] He suggests that this practice reflects the desire of Hakka families to cultivate close agnatic ties.[13] He writes, "[These mausoleums] are physically imposing, demonstrable evidence of intense and complex corporate labors, and their occupants precisely define a concise group. In the absence of corporate property (ritual estates), descent groups have adopted or invented *a means to reinforce solidarity among the living* while honoring the ancestors in a most appropriate fashion."[14] Ying-chang Chuang affirms that these Hakka ancestor practices reveal that Hakkas have "a stronger spirit of solidarity and cooperation" than the Hoklos around them.[15]

The fifth aspect of this continuity associated with incense fires that regularly surfaced is the way some ceremonies involving the incense fires are a means for recently departed loved ones to transition into the corporate group of ancestors. #3 described the process in great detail. After death, the individual tablet of the deceased is placed in a basket that is hung on the wall and is venerated there for approximately three years. After three years, on Lunar New Year's Eve, this basket is placed with the main ancestor tablet, and they are venerated together. Then the basket is

10. Chuang, "Ancestor Worship," 155–56; Martin, "Hakka Mausoleums," 88.
11. Chuang, "Ancestor Worship," 156.
12. Martin, "Hakka Mausoleums," 85.
13. Ibid., 95.
14. Ibid., 98, emphasis added.
15. Chuang, "Ancestor Worship," 156.

burned and the ashes taken to a place where there is running water and allowed to float away. The incense that was burning in the basket is then placed into the incense burner in front of the corporate ancestor tablet, and the deceased person's name is written on a piece of red paper and stuck onto that tablet. This rite of passage enables a newly deceased family member to transition from being a living family member who venerated the ancestors to one of the ancestors who is venerated in an ever-continuous line of incense smoke. Thompson elaborates on the significance of this continuity:

> The ancestor cult, the carrying on of family relationship through time, provided basic psychological security just as the family organization provided social security. The ancestor cult assured that the family system in which the individual had been subordinated all of his or her life was triumphant over death itself. It was a self-fulfilling cycle of meaning from life to death and back to life. The individual did not face the endless emptiness of time alone and helpless; one was a link in the continuous chain of being that was conceived as an organismic reality.[16]

In addition to the above five aspects of the continuity associated with incense fires that regularly surfaced for informants, they also talked frequently about the way things associated with "incense fires" are changing. Five aspects of this change will be highlighted here.

First, informants discussed how people improvise when they are unable to continue participating in the ancestor rituals of their clan-grouping. Informants talked about relatives who live too far away to conveniently return for ancestor rituals and how they find alternative ways to continue their duties. #4 described how one of his relatives wrote down the names of key family members on a piece of paper, folded it up, and carried it with him when he relocated. Then, rather than returning to the place where the ancestor tablets were kept, he worshiped in his new location, using that piece of paper to represent the ancestor tablets. He burned incense, prepared offerings, and used moon blocks to determine if his ancestors had heard him and had come to accept his sacrifices. Regarding this improvisation, #4 commented, "The most important thing is that their heart returns." #5 talked about his sister, a professor in a well-known university in the United States, who has placed a picture of their mother in a hidden place in her house, and when she misses her, she lights a stick of incense

---

16. Thompson, *Chinese Religion*, 128.

in front of this picture. When #5 went to visit, his sister lit a stick to tell her mother that her brother had come for a visit. #5 also told how, when his father was going to live in another country, he arranged to have his ancestors moved to a temple that provides the service of venerating your ancestors for you.

A second kind of change that informants talked about in this area is the way people are developing a concern for the environment. This attitude change makes the burning of incense and other things in ancestor rituals unattractive. #8 talked about this change, "In a Daoist funeral, spirit money and incense are burned. My generation . . . sees the need to protect the environment. Burning so much spirit money creates pollution. We have this understanding, but the older generation does not. They feel you must burn these things. In the past, people burned clothes for the deceased to wear, creating a huge amount of pollution. Actually, it is okay if you do not burn these things."

Third, informants often mentioned the fact that changes in the eating habits of Hakkas are influencing the kinds of offerings that are presented to the ancestors. #8 talked about how traditionally, people offered three kinds of meat to the ancestors. In the past, when people were poorer and had less to eat, eating the meat that had been offered as a sacrifice during ancestor rituals was a rare treat. #8 said:

> We are adjusting ourselves to contemporary thinking and making appropriate changes. We are the ones who have to eat all of the food that is offered to the gods and ancestors. We are not thinking only of what we can offer to show our sincerity to the ancestors, we also are thinking of our own health. [In the past], around the time of each major festival during the year, we ate so much meat that it was not healthy for us anymore. Our cholesterol got too high. As a result, everyone gradually started to eat less meat. When our older family members began to notice that we never ate up all the meat in the refrigerator, we had a chance to talk to them about making changes in sacrificial offerings. They would listen and think about it. In this way, change was forced on them.

She reports that now her relatives use fruit in worship of the gods but meat in ancestor rituals. Some use fruit for the ancestors as well.

A fourth kind of change that informants talked about in this area is the way many in the younger generation are not as interested in ancestor rituals. #3 talked about his son, revealing some of the conflicting feelings that surfaced in his own mind, saying, "I grew up at a time when the clan and the family were more important than they are today, but this culture may not continue with my son and those after him." He explained:

> I know my son has his difficulties in continuing to venerate in the traditional ways . . . I can understand that. I can accept this situation but . . . my heart will still feel a bit regretful. I think of how the incense fires continued until this generation and then stopped. On the one hand, I do not mind, but on the other hand, I feel I have let down my father and grandfather. My feelings are a bit complicated. . . . My [middle-aged] generation is stuck in the middle. The worldview of the younger generation is very much new wave. They do what they want. They are very much influenced by the internet and travel freely. The difference between our two generations is great; . . . their world and thinking are very different from mine. I have to adjust my own thinking. . . . When I say I do not mind, I do not mean that I would choose to have things go this way.

Fifth, as a result of these other changes, people are becoming less concerned with the details of the rituals and are just happy that family members choose to make the effort to attend. For example, #3 said, "The older generation cannot accept if you do not use incense during ancestor practices. My generation can accept that—just so long as you return." #1 reported, "We change what we offer to the land god (fruit) but still do the traditional offerings with the ancestors. I have seen some people bring fruit to offer to the ancestors. That does not matter—what is most important is that they return."

Informants often added that one's heart attitude is what is most important. For example, #8 put the focus on the heart rather than on rigidly following traditional practices: "Actually, it is okay if you do not burn incense and spirit money. My opinion is that these things only seem to be efficacious because they are sincerely believed. . . . Our feeling is that when you participate, if your heart is there and communicating with the ancestors, that is good enough. But in the mind of the older generation, you definitely must burn incense and spirit money. Otherwise, they feel they would let their ancestors down." #13 provided another example of this attitude. He attends the ancestor rituals of his clan-grouping but does not burn incense. He abstains because he feels burning incense creates pollution but, more importantly, because he, as a professional photographer, wants to take pictures. When asked if his clan members ever talked about his unwillingness to burn incense as rejecting the ancestors, he said, "They do not have any reason to say that. I am not rejecting my ancestors. Having a sincere heart is most important." He continued, "I reply that I am using another method to [show my filial piety to my ancestors].... I [take pictures of what is happening] and prepare exhibitions of pictures." He elaborated that he feels that people who burn incense, believing that doing so will enable them to communicate with the gods and ancestors, are close-minded, and ... that those who burn spirit money do so without really considering the meaning behind these actions.

Ancestors' Language

As informants talked about being Hakka, they frequently raised the symbol of "the Hakka language" or "the language of the ancestors." This discussion will focus first on informants' comments about the Hakka-language habits of those who are being Hakka and then discuss five points which informants raised as they talked about the importance those who are being Hakka place on the Hakka language, four reasons they suggested for the decline in Hakka-language use among those who are being Hakka, and the effect that government programs are having in this area.

In describing the language habits of those who are being Hakka, informants revealed a pattern. Roughly dividing the Hakka population into three generations—young, middle-aged, and old—informants generalized that each generation has its own language habits. Informants used these categories loosely, usually thinking of those thirty years and under as "young," those sixty-five to seventy and older as "old," and those in between as "middle-aged." Examples of the looseness of these categories include an informant in his seventies thinking of "old" as referring to those older than he and a fifty-something informant including himself in "young" when talking about the "old." Informants generalized that the older generation primarily speaks Hakka. The younger generation primarily speaks Mandarin and is generally quite weak in Hakka-speaking and -listening abilities. The middle-aged generation speaks both Hakka and Mandarin, speaking primarily Hakka with the older generation, Mandarin with the younger generation, and Mandarin and some Hakka with others of their own generation.

The influence of education also was raised by informants as they discussed the language habits of those who are being Hakka. The wife of #19, who has taught extracurricular subjects in a junior high school in an area with a high concentration of Hakkas, noticed that the students in that school who were better students used Mandarin to speak to each other, while the students who did not do as well in school spoke Hakka with each other. She reported that speaking Hakka was a marker that the poorer students used to distinguish themselves from the other group. She linked this phenomenon with another observation that she had made about the grass-roots people in their church: "The grass-roots people all use Hakka more. This includes the younger people and the teenagers. If they go to school through college, even though they are Hakka, they probably will not speak Hakka with you. They probably can speak Hakka, but they will not speak with you. I do not know if this is an unconscious thing or if they just feel differently, that Mandarin is better or what. I do not know." #19 affirmed these comments and added, "Especially during the time when students were only allowed to speak Mandarin in school, there were those who thought speaking Mandarin was more high class. Consequently, the more obedient students—the ones who did better in school, the ones who the teachers liked more because they got better grades—spoke Mandarin more naturally."

When those in the young generation are stronger in their Hakka-language abilities, informants attributed this strength to close involvement with other Hakkas who can speak only Hakka or who insist on speaking only Hakka with them and/or living in an area where there is a high concentration of Hakkas. For example, the grandson of #29 lives with her, and she only speaks Hakka with him, so consequently, his Hakka-language ability is remarkably strong. Another young informant, #12, reported that he gradually picked up his self-declared "mediocre" Hakka-language ability when his family moved to a location with a high concentration of Hakkas and he started spending time with a group of friends who spoke Hakka. When #26 saw how his older child struggled to speak Hakka, he and his wife decided to only speak Hakka with their newborn child. This plan was so successful that the older child became motivated to improve his Hakka-language ability so that he could communicate with his little brother. #16 reported that because he and his wife lived with his Hakka-speaking mother, his wife, a Hoklo, was able to learn Hakka well. When asked whether or not grass-roots people were more likely to speak Hakka, #23 suggested that grass-roots children were more likely to be tended by family members from the old generation who were more likely to only be able to speak Hakka with them.

Informants raised five different reasons that the Hakka language was important to those who are being Hakka. First, there are good feelings connected with the use of the Hakka language. Most informants reported that when they hear strangers speaking Hakka, they felt closer to them than to other strangers. #23 gave an example of how he felt when he heard people speaking Hakka, saying, "One day, I was sitting outside, and I overheard my neighbors talking to each other. Because they were speaking . . . Hakka, things felt very friendly and familiar, and I had a sense that this environment was very safe." He explained that the language was a marker that these people were a part of a world he knew well, that these were people he could easily understand and who, because they had things in common with him, would help him if he was in need. #7 told a story about how, on a trip to mainland China, he encountered someone who could speak Hakka and felt close to that person, even though they were both far from home.

Several informants pointed out that this good feeling connected with speaking Hakka is often useful in obtaining other benefits. The most common example is that Hakka vendors in an open market often lower their prices for those who speak Hakka with them. For example, #26 said about the market in Taipei, "If one of the Hakka sellers hears you speak Hakka, he or she will point out all of the other Hakkas in the market, and you will get your vegetables cheaper." Interestingly, #28, who is retired from a career of selling his products wholesale in the market, denied lowering his prices when he heard someone speak Hakka but added, "I usually talked with them a little more than usual."

Informants also noted that the good feelings that emerge when one hears the Hakka language do not necessarily translate into a deeper relationship; they do not always result in more than just a fleeting connection. #27 said that even though he would feel an initial connection with a classmate who could speak Hakka, that commonality would not guarantee that they would end up being close friends. He said, "Whether or not a closer relationship would develop would depend on that person's personality." He continued, "[The ethnic connection] is not the most important factor." #2 agreed that an initial feeling of some friendliness and familiarity with someone because they can speak Hakka does not necessarily lead to a meaningful relationship.

In addition, good feelings toward the Hakka language do not automatically translate into an interest in attending Hakka-language events or watching Hakka-language programming on television. Some informants were very much interested in attending Hakka-language events like drama presentations, but others showed little interest. For example, #1 reported, "A Hakka-language event will not have a special draw for me, even though I am happy these kinds of events are being planned to help expand the influence of the Hakka language." When asked if those who are being Hakka watch the Hakka television station, there were a variety of responses. #30 enjoyed a particular program so much so that he turned it on during the interview for this research. Most informants reported that they rarely watch this station, but several often spoke of an older family member who enjoys the programs.

Good feelings towards languages for those who are being Hakka are not limited to the Hakka language. #4 admitted that he mixes in a lot of Mandarin words when he speaks Hakka and said, "Speaking Mandarin is easy and I like the sound of it." #19 reported that while he likes singing Hakka songs, singing certain songs in Hoklo is also enjoyable and can really move him. #2 said she really enjoys using the Hoklo language with older Hoklos and the feeling of affection and devotion this use creates between her and them. She said that when she was little, she liked to watch Hoklo-language drama, and consequently also liked to listen to the Hoklo language. #19 raised the example of older Hakkas who enjoy reminiscing about the Japanese language from the time that they were learning Japanese songs in elementary school. #23 reported that he prefers to use Mandarin rather than Hakka because of two problems with using Hakka: "First, there is no way to use characters to write everything out [using Hakka]. Second, there are some words that Hakka probably originally had, but since I am not skillful, there are some things I want to talk about, but I do not know the Hakka words for them and need to use Mandarin instead. I cannot express 100 percent of what I want to say using Hakka and need to switch to Mandarin. This creates a feeling in my mind that this language is not very easy to use."

Second, those who are being Hakka often feel it is their responsibility to speak and pass on the Hakka language. Some informants talked about how those who are being Hakka feel responsible to speak Hakka simply because they are Hakka. For example, #2 said, "Hakkas should learn to speak their own language." #24 said many Hakkas who cannot speak Hakka are very embarrassed about this. #25 said, "My father had a very strong Hakka consciousness, so he required all of us children to speak only Hakka in our home." #13 said, "[If I do not use my talents to support Hakka culture], I feel I have let myself down. If I do not do these things, I will have a hard time explaining my actions in the future."

In other cases, informants talked about how those who are being Hakka felt responsible to their ancestors to speak and pass on the Hakka language. #13 talked about a common saying: "Sell your ancestors' fields if you have to, but do not give up your ancestors' language (*ningke mai zuzong tian, bu mai zuzong yan*)." He explained, "If you give up your language, you will not have any culture. You will not be able to communicate. A grandchild will not be able to communicate with his grandfather."#34 said, "[Speaking Hakka] is very important to the old generation. They feel it is not acceptable if the children cannot speak Hakka. [When they scold them for not speaking Hakka,] they say things like, 'You are turning your back on and denying your ancestors' to threaten you." She continued, "My father could speak Japanese. He spoke it with my mother, but he would not teach it to us children. He told us the ancestors taught him to speak Hakka, so we children will speak Hakka." #22 said, "If we throw out our language, we offend our ancestors."

Third, the Hakka language is sometimes important to those who are being Hakka because it is the language the senior members of their families are most comfortable using. #2 said, "When my brother was younger, about ten to twenty years ago, he insisted on speaking Hakka. . . . He said, 'When mom [who speaks only Hakka] goes out in our community, and no one is able to speak Hakka with her, what will you think then?' . . . When my brother said this, I began to see the importance of speaking Hakka." #22 said, "We currently have my mother-in-law living with us, so we speak Hakka with her. If we did not have her living with us . . . my wife and I would only speak Mandarin. That is our habit. We have been using Mandarin to speak to each other ever since we first met." Some informants talked about those women who originally could not speak Hakka but married into a Hakka family with a father-in-law or a mother-in-law who could not speak Mandarin. They gave examples of women who, in this case, learned to speak Hakka in order to communicate with the older family members. #16 said, "My wife had no choice but to learn to speak Hakka."

Fourth, the Hakka language is often important to those who are being Hakka because they are concerned the Hakka language may become extinct. #8 told about how her husband and she, as teachers, followed government policies and used Mandarin to teach their students. She said, "My husband suddenly realized that something is not right; when we go out, there are very few people who can speak Hakka. We started treasuring our Hakka language, realizing that there were a lot of things we could say in Hakka that could not be expressed well if we tried to use Mandarin to say them." #8 told how at one point she realized that all of the younger members of her own extended family, living together in the same large house, were in the habit of speaking Mandarin together. She said:

> I suddenly realized that something was wrong. . . . How could a Hakka family all be speaking Mandarin? We became vigilant. This situation was very serious. We did not want it to continue. My husband said we needed to be more proactive. When the children were downstairs speaking Mandarin, we yelled down, "Speak Hakka!" They would speak a couple sentences of Hakka, and then they would go back to speaking Mandarin. I did not know what to do to stop Hakka culture from being wiped out. In the end, I decided to go downstairs and slap their faces and ask them why they were not speaking Hakka. Of course, I only slapped my own children. I did not dare to slap the other children but scolded them harshly saying, "Your parents are Hakka, why do you not speak Hakka? Why are you teaching my kids to be like this?" After that happened a few times, my kids started to speak Hakka when they were at home. They were afraid of me slapping them again.

#8 also told how, before her son got married, her husband told him that he needed to find a Hakka wife. She described the situation:

> My husband told him that he only had one requirement. He said, "Hakkas are diminishing, and soon there will not be any left. When you get married, you must marry a Hakka girl." But every girl my son liked was a Hoklo. Each time, my husband told him, "We do not want her." My son was very obedient and listened. But at one point he said, "In my work environment, it is very hard to meet a Hakka girl." He works in an area where there are mostly Hoklo people living. He asked if it was possible to marry a Hoklo girl. My husband thought about how many times he had asked my son to keep looking and how hard it was for my son to find a girl he wanted to marry. . . . He told my son he could marry a Hoklo . . . as long as she was willing to learn Hakka. The Hoklo girl my son had in mind was willing . . . so they got married. When they had a son, we told our daughter-in-law she had to teach the child Hakka and not speak Mandarin to him. Our grandson will natu-

rally learn Mandarin from society around him, but if he is going to speak Hakka, he needs to learn it from his family.

Some informants stated that Hakkas have traditionally felt strongly about preserving their culture and language, even when it was not easy to do so. For example, #22 said some Hakkas insist on speaking Hakka at home even when they dare not let outsiders know they are Hakka. He said it is like they have a sense of mission about this. When it was suggested that this was the way it was in the past, he agreed and said now most young people cannot speak Hakka. He said this is in some ways good because then the ethnic divisions will not be as important as they were in the past.

Informants suggested that if the Hakka language became extinct, much of Hakka culture would also become extinct. They pointed to the culture contained in the Hakka language. #16 stated it strongly, "Hakka language is important. If there is no Hakka language, there will be no Hakka culture." For example, there are Hakka words or sayings that cannot be translated into Mandarin, or, if they can, they do not maintain the thickness of their meaning. #36 said, "There are some things that must be expressed in Hakka in order to understand what they are. If you try to use Mandarin, you do not know how to talk about them. My grandfather's generation used many of these kinds of words and sayings. Gradually, these sayings have fallen out of use and are not being passed down. In those days, if you said them, everyone would be very clear about your meaning." #6 said, "The Hakka language is a root thing. If you do not have any language, then you do not have any culture." Also regarding this close connection between culture and language, #23 had this to say:

> The Hakka I speak has a lot of Mandarin grammar in it. When [two older Hakkas I know] speak Hakka, when they give [speeches in Hakka], the more traditional Hakkas feel a sense of friendliness and familiarity in what they say because they use the "words of the aged (*laorenyan*)" Hakka proverbs. These are the kinds of things I am unable to use, so . . . when I speak Hakka, there is no Hakka culture in what I say, because I do not use the "sayings of masters (*shifuhua*)" or the illustrations from life that people once used. . . . I cannot use these illustrations because I have not had these kinds of life experiences. Consequently . . . I think my Hakka does not have this kind of culture in it.

In a similar vein, some informants highlighted the way the Hakka language is a tool necessary to learn about Hakka culture. For example, #2 said, "The only way children can learn more about Hakka things is if they have the Hakka language."

Fifth, those who are being Hakka value the Hakka language, but not to the point of excluding other languages. There is a sense that an emphasis on ethnic distinctions and languages was the problem that caused war and discrimination in the past, and it needed to be overcome. #18 expressed this point well when he said, "We do not want to overemphasize our own ethnic consciousness. There is an appropriate amount of restraint. Every ethnic group is like one part of a body. . . . We want to fulfill our role in the body. . . . We want to grow in what we do but also join together with the rest of the body. So we encourage the use of the Hakka language, but we also need to have a common language [like Mandarin]. . . . We do not want to cut ourselves off from others, but we also do not want to give up . . . our unique characteristics." #27 also raised the point that a common language is necessary. He reported that the lack of a common language would really complicate things when you travel or move from one area to another since each area has distinct dialects or languages.

Informants raised four reasons why the use of the Hakka language is declining among those who are being Hakka. First, informants reported that Hakka-language use is declining because speaking Hakka can put one at a disadvantage or make one the target of discrimination. #22 described this situation:

> In the past, the Hakkas and the Hoklos in Taiwan fought and the Hakkas lost. Consequently, the Hakkas now try to fit into Hoklo society. They are afraid. They often do not reveal their real identity. They do not admit they are Hakka. In order to fit in, they work hard to learn the Hoklo language. Otherwise, when everyone else is speaking Hoklo, they do not understand and feel a sense of isolation. That is what happened to me. When I went to work, the others were all speaking Hoklo. Even though I could understand and speak a little Hoklo, when I was with them, they sometimes spoke Mandarin with me. It did not feel very friendly and familiar. I came to the realization that if I wanted to succeed, if I wanted to survive, I probably needed to learn Hoklo. In this situation, can I insist on speaking Hakka well? Consequently, I tell my children they probably need to also learn Hoklo for everyday life. It is like the way people are currently learning English and setting their mother tongue aside. The way things are forces me to do this.

#16 added, "Hakkas are in the minority. When there are two or three Hakkas together, they often speak Hakka. The Hoklos cannot understand or speak it, so they think the Hakkas are saying things behind their backs and dislike Hakkas even more. Because of this, there are some people who do not admit they are Hakka because they are afraid of being bullied by people from the dominant Hoklo group."

Second, use of the Hakka language is declining because there are few practical reasons for young Hakkas to learn or maintain this language. #23 explained that since Mandarin is the language used in school, diligent students' time is most often spent working in Mandarin, and little time is spent using Hakka. #10 pointed out that today's children are studying too many subjects. She said, "Most people think learning English is more useful than learning Hakka. Why learn Hakka? There needs to be a reason." She continued, "Parents keep on telling their children they must definitely not forget that they are Hakka . . . but these parents do not provide a strong reason why children should not forget. The children think, 'It is not like, if I am not a Hakka, something bad will happen to me.'" #10 suggested that, rather than trying to teach children to speak Hakka in school, the government should make the ability to speak Hakka a valuable commodity. For example, she suggested adding bonus points to the scores of those who are testing to get government jobs if they can provide evidence that they can speak Hakka fluently.

One phenomenon that frustrated #30 is Hakka parents who, rather than availing their children of the Hakka-mother-tongue classes taught in elementary school, enrolled them in the Hoklo-mother-tongue classes instead. Their logic was that many more opportunities to use Hoklo exist, whether speaking or viewing television, and so they wanted their children to learn Hoklo rather than Hakka.

Third, in the context of talking about being Hakka, informants revealed that Hakka-language use is declining because Mandarin Chinese is the language used most widely in education and by the media. For example, #34 said when she went to school and was not able to speak Hakka there, her Hakka-language skills declined. #1 said:

> I can only say that Hakka is my mother tongue. I do not dare to say that it is the language I speak most fluently. That is because when I went to school, I was taught that Mandarin is the official language. I studied in Mandarin for several decades; in the schooling process, I responded in Mandarin. If you are talking about conversations

about everyday things, then my Hakka is very fluent. If you asked me to get up in front and be a host or give a speech using Hakka, I will not be able to do as well as I would using Mandarin.

#6 added, "Adults can speak Hakka, but their children in school do not have the environment necessary to learn Hakka. Our media all uses Mandarin, even the advertising." #2 reported that even when one of her brothers prioritized and intentionally cultivated his children's Hakka-language ability when they were small, this was not enough to keep them in the habit of speaking Hakka at home after they went to elementary school.

Even in areas with higher concentrations of Hakkas where one would expect to find the strongest Hakka-language abilities, the influence of the use of Mandarin in education and in the media was still reported to have a significant weakening influence on Hakka-language abilities. Several informants, those who themselves live in these areas, reported that the younger generation primarily speaks Mandarin and cannot speak Hakka well. For example, #4, a retired elementary school teacher, reported, "Almost all of the elementary school children [in this area], even though they are Hakka, are able to speak very little of the Hakka language." #16 reported that, sooner or later, the Hakka language will disappear because young people are not speaking it, and the media is using other languages. However, this assessment was not universal. Other informants, speaking about the same areas as #11 and #4 above, reported that the young people in these areas can speak Hakka. For example, the grandson of #29 said, "All of my elementary and junior high school classmates spoke Hakka." Perhaps the difference between these assessments is the subjective nature of the standard of what it means to be "able to speak Hakka." The language level one person considers to be "able to speak Hakka" may not be the same as what another person considers to be sufficient to qualify. For some, being able to understand and speak some basic phrases is sufficient. Others suggest that one should be able to communicate in Hakka about everyday life things with ease in order to qualify. For still others, the standard might be speaking as well as an older Hakka.

Informants pointed out that the habit of speaking Mandarin is hard to change even when people decide they want to speak more Hakka. For example, #15 reported, "Sometimes when my brothers, sisters, and I are talking together, I will say something like, 'Let us try not speaking Mandarin for a while; let us speak Hakka together instead.' Even though everyone agrees to my suggestion, it is not long before we forget and are speaking Mandarin again. This is because at school and at work, everything is in Mandarin. When we were young, I remember our father speaking with us in Hakka. Why has that changed now that we have grown up?"

Fourth, in the context of talking about being Hakka, informants revealed that Hakka-language use is declining because intermarriage between Hakkas and other ethnics is becoming more common. When Hoklos and Hakkas intermarry, there is an increased likelihood that they and their children will not speak Hakka. #8 reported that it depends on which person is dominant. In her parent's case, her father, a Hakka, was more dominant than her mother, a Hoklo, so their family spoke Hakka. Most informants reported that when the husband and wife spoke different mother tongues and they could both speak Mandarin, they would use Mandarin to communicate. As a result, the children often followed the parents' habit and spoke Mandarin.

The final aspect of the symbol of the Hakka language that informants raised was how Hakkas feel about government programs which teach this language in elementary school. Those who are being Hakka have different perceptions about the need and the effectiveness of these efforts. Some of those who are being Hakka feel that, since use of the Hakka language was restricted for so many years in schools and other public settings, government programs cultivating the use of Hakka are justified to compensate for this past mistreatment. Most are happy that schools are helping to ensure that the younger generation has opportunities to learn Hakka. Some fear if something like this is not done soon, it will be even harder to rescue the Hakka language in the future. Others feel it is already too late. Still others wonder if it is really that important that Hakkas be able to speak Hakka. They argue that if proficiency in this language is advantageous at some point because of a change in residence or workplace, this language can be learned at that time. Most are of the opinion that these government efforts are motivated by a desire to gain the Hakka vote at the time of elections.

Some of those who are being Hakka see these efforts to teach Hakka in the schools as helpful, but others are more pessimistic. #10, an elementary school teacher, said that, while it is hard to teach effectively in just two hours a week, the fact that the schools are teaching Hakka makes parents pay more attention to speaking Hakka in the home. There are disadvantages though. #10 argued that the children are already overburdened. She also noted that since these Hakka classes are taught during the same years that students are learning Chinese characters, many students confuse Hakka with Mandarin. #5 said that children will not be interested in learning Hakka unless there is something to motivate them such as earning extra points on college entrance exams if they can demonstrate Hakka-language ability.

Traditions

As informants talked about being Hakka, they frequently raised the symbol of "traditions." While much of the discussion about being Hakka up to this point in this chapter and what follows has been and will also be about various Hakka traditions, the focus under this heading is on traditions in general. "Traditions" in this context are understood to be the "established habits" of those who venerate their ancestors together. Three aspects of these traditions will be discussed.

The first aspect of traditions that informants raised regularly as they talked about being Hakka is that traditions are perceived to be ways of doing things that have been passed down from generation to generation for as long as people can remember. Many Hakkas do not know the reasons behind these traditions. They value and follow these traditions primarily because they were passed on to them by their parents and grandparents. #16 said, "Because Hakkas are so conservative, they do not change things. They just do what their parents did before them, passed down from one generation to the next." #11 related that the reason he worships certain gods is not because he believes in these gods personally and feels that not worshiping them will result in something bad happening, but rather because these are the practices that were passed down from his ancestors. After listening to #4's description of how he worshiped two land gods, a comment was made that he was very sincere and faithful. His response was, "Tradition. My father worshiped them, and I am just following him."

The consensus among informants was that ancestor practices are passed on largely by the young family members repeatedly watching and participating in rituals with their older family members. #10 said her in-laws do not venerate their ancestors, so she, because she feels it is important for her children, takes them to attend her natal family's ancestor rituals so they can observe what is done there. She says the children learn by example when they see her relatives participating in these rituals. She has the expectation that her children will naturally venerate their own ancestors in the future. #1 described how he learned certain traditions through observation. As the oldest son, he has been involved in the ancestor rituals from the time he was little, so little he had to stand on a chair to put the incense into the burner. He continued, "Because early on in my life my grandfather required me to worship the gods and venerate the ancestors, these ways naturally have become very deeply rooted in me."

Many of those who are being Hakka also feel obligated to pass these traditions on to the next generation. For example, the wife of #9 said that if she did not pass on the traditions that she understood, she would feel unsettled. #14 told a story about how a senior member of the family, after overhearing two of his sister in laws speaking a kind of the Hakka language different from the kind traditionally used in their family, scolded them.

A second dimension of traditions that informants often surfaced is the way traditions are habitual. One of the traditional habits informants described in detail is the daily rituals performed in the place designated by the clan-grouping. For example, #4 described the tradition of worshiping the gods and ancestors that takes place in his home two times each day. First, he lights four sticks of incense. He then stands facing outside and, after bowing with the incense sticks in hand, pokes one of them in a small receptacle attached high on the wall of the balcony outside. This incense is for the heaven god. Next #4 takes the remaining sticks, turns, and moves to the front of the family altar bows before the images of the gods, Guanyin and Guangong, and pokes another incense stick in the sand in an urn on the altar in front of them. He does the same in front of the ancestor tablet sitting on the left side of the altar. Finally, he inserts the remaining stick of incense into the urn in front of the land god (*tudigong*) whose image is on the floor under the altar. #4 reported that this ritual has taken place in his home for as long as he can remember.

#19 explained that these kinds of traditions are passed on from generation to generation because, in the course of repeating certain behaviors over and over, they have become habit for each successive generation. People just follow certain habits without consciously thinking about what they are doing. For example, #19 described how the traditional way of relating to deceased relatives becomes habit: "People participate in ancestor veneration rituals at least twice each year, at the time of the Lunar New Year and at Tomb Sweeping. If someone dies, they participate again. They repeat these practices over and over, year after year. They start from the time they are small, and the practices naturally become habit. When they get to be about fifty and become the head of their family, what they have seen done for the last fifty years they continue doing and do not dare to stop." #8 told how even after people have not venerated their ancestors for a period of time, they, when faced with a problem, will automatically resort to their habit of reasoning that it is because they have neglected the ancestors that the problem has arisen. There may be many other possible explanations for this problem, but they will focus on this one out of habit. As a result, they will say, "My ancestors must not be protecting me. I must go and worship them."

A third aspect of traditions that informants raised regularly as they talked about being Hakka is that many of these traditions are changing. Informants pointed out that one of the reasons for these changes is that many traditions are not being passed down to the next generation. Some informants partly blamed themselves for not entirely understanding some of the more complex traditions, acknowledging that they would be unable to pass them on. Informants also blamed the younger generation, saying that youth do not always accept these traditions. For example, the wife of #9 reported that if her daughter likes the traditions, she follows them; if she does not like them, she does not use them. #8 also expressed pessimism about being able to pass on the traditions, saying that one can only do one's best. #5 said, "It is not like in the past when everyone lived together. Once children grow up, they move away. As a result, these Hakka habits will gradually get fewer and fewer."

Another of the reasons traditions are changing is that people are consciously adjusting some traditions. For example, her clan leaders have given #8 the role of planning important events in their clan-grouping, festive occasions such as engagement and wedding feasts, rituals, and birth celebrations, as well as mourning occasions like funerals. In this role, #8 sees herself as a person who takes what was passed on to her from the previous generation and adapts it to conform to today's situations. She said she omits parts that are too complicated or unnecessary. This changed tradition then becomes what is remembered and used by the next generation. For example, when planning for a recent wedding ceremony between one of their family members and a Hoklo, she created an event that included the most important elements of a Hakka wedding but also included things that Hoklos felt were important.

Informants reported that while change is happening, Hakkas expect change to happen slowly and in small increments. There is a perception that slow change will occur naturally if it is destined to be. #1 gave the example of how Hakkas have gradually changed their living arrangements over time. He explained that traditionally as many as five generations lived together in one house, but this tradition gradually changed to be four generations, and now it is not easy to find even three generations living together. #1 reported that this series of changes was the natural result of gradual changes in society.

Informants reported that when change is advocated too aggressively, people resist. For example, #11 said that he had recently had contact with a religion that taught that people should be vegetarians. He said he listened to their reasoning and felt their teachings made sense. The problem that caused him to discontinue attending their meetings was that they wanted him to change his habit of eating meat immediately. He said, "This is impossible! The only way to change is to do it slowly, one small step at a time." #3 reported that he is willing to accept change in ancestor practices since society is continuously changing, but he added, "I just do not want things to change too much, because the ancestors include those whom I have feelings of affection and devotion for, my grandfather and father."

Informants also gave several reasons that Hakkas use to justify change, explain change, or exhort older family members to change a particular tradition. These include saying that everyone is changing or that the traditions are too wasteful, complicated, inconvenient, unhealthy, harmful to the environment, and/or time consuming. When accused of making undesirable change, Hakkas often use the justification, "There is no other way." For example, #19 reported that when Hakkas in the city are scolded for not speaking Hakka well, they simply smile and reply, "There was no other way." #3 used this justification when discussing his inability, due to strong societal forces, to prevent his son from giving up many Hakka traditions. He said, "There was no other way" but to adjust his own thinking to fit with this reality.

Reciprocal Relationships

To those who are being Hakka, reciprocal relationships are important, with the family relationship at the core of social interaction.[17] One significant cultural value undergirding most of these reciprocal relationships is the expectation that one should repay the help and blessings others have provided. Consequently, informants said most Hakkas are very conscious

---

17. Lin, "Chinese Family Structure"; Chen, "Filial Piety"; Ching, *Chinese Religions*; Hwang, "Face and Favor."

of their indebtedness and pay close attention to repaying the debts they have incurred. An example that reveals the intensity of the pressure that comes as a result of this value is a custom Hakkas have of giving each other monetary gifts at occasions like engagements, weddings, and funerals to help with the expenses of these occasions. Usually relatives, neighbors, co-workers, friends, and others participate in this custom, and there is an understanding that accompanies each gift—that the recipient will give an equivalent gift back to the giver when the giver has a similar occasion. #28 described the social pressure that results: "I always have to be on alert, checking so that I know when the people in the neighborhood around my home have an occasion requiring a gift. . . . If I do not give a gift when I should, people will talk." #7 told how awkward this expectation is because he is often out of the country and so is not always aware of occasions that demand a gift. He reports that he would feel really ashamed if he missed giving a gift when he should have.

Some Hakkas, in order to avoid this feeling of indebtedness, are breaking with tradition and not accepting gifts at these occasions. For example, #28 had a big feast at his father's funeral but refused any monetary gifts. He said people reacted that he was "very strange," but, as a result, he does not have to worry so much about missing others' occasions. He said he continues to give money to others at similar occasions; he does not want to be indebted to others but does not mind if others are indebted to him.

The following symbols related to these reciprocal relationships regularly surfaced in discussions with informants about being Hakka: (1) "us," (2) ancestors, and (3) gods.

"Us"

As informants talked about those who are being Hakka, they pointed out that Hakkas have certain kinds of people who they treat as "us," or those persons who stand together with them on the same side of things as they face the challenges of life. One of the kinds of "us" that surfaced most often is that of the family or clan-grouping, often thought of as those who venerate the same ancestors. These "us" are those by whom Hakkas expect to be called on for help and those from whom Hakkas expect to receive help in times of need. These "us" sometimes act together to solve problems and seek the best interests of the group as a collectivity.

When within this family tie these "us" act according to expectations, the "us" bond is strengthened. Informants gave several examples of expectations in this area. For example, #13 stated, "If a male clan member dies an early death, other members are expected to join together to help support the family members who are left behind." Clan members are expected to help each other in their business dealings, providing startup loans and business. When one member has financial or other problems, these "us" are expected to help by providing money or other resources. When the ancestral hall or common mausoleum of the clan grouping needs repair or rebuilding, members are expected to donate money to help complete this project. When one person in the clan-grouping has a special occasion (e.g., a wedding or a funeral), other members are expected to attend and help or at least to send a monetary gift to help defray expenses. When the clan-grouping gathers to venerate the ancestors, every family is expected to have at least one representative participating.

In this area, informants reported a particular expectation that can be a significant force in strengthening the "us" tie; those who are helped by the clan-grouping often are expected to feel a sense of indebtedness to these "us." #13 gave an example of this expectation: "If a young person in the clan tests into college but does not have enough money to pay for tuition, clan members often join together and help this student to finish his education. Clan members provide the money needed with the hope that this young person, when older, will come back and help other clan members." The mutual aid that takes place between these "us" energizes and strengthens this relationship.

Informants reported another expectation that Hakkas have (as a part of this "us" thinking)—that the clan should take the lead in planning funerals. #35 described the way the clan takes over all of the funeral arrangements, "When my grandfather died, members of our clan took care of all of the arrangements. For example, they made decisions about where he would be buried, what procedures would be used, who needed to be contacted, and how to spend money. . . . They also decided who would carry the coffin, . . . who would cook meals for the funeral guests, and who would wear the mourning clothing." She continued, "Clan members expect to decide all of these minute details for you."

Informants reported that when a family member does not act according to expectations of the "us" relationship, this relationship is weakened. For example, #8 talked about what happens when a member of their clan-grouping ceases returning to participate in funerals, weddings, and ancestor rituals. She said, "If they come back, they are pulled into our group, and our relationships are deepened and thickened. . . . If they do not come back to participate in ancestor rituals, they have very little interaction with us." Consequently, when these clan members have needs, they do not really dare to ask for help. Instead of having the clan help with funerals and weddings, they must hire people to help them to make all the arrangements for funerals and celebrate their weddings in hotels.

Informants explained that when people seriously offend these "us," the consequence is often to be cut off to one extent or another from the resources and help that are usually procured through this relationship. #35 gave the example of one of her grandfather's friends who was the son of a wealthy family. Against his parents' will, this friend married a woman whom, due to her low social status, was considered to be an unsuitable daughter-in-law. As a result, this wealthy family disowned him, and his connection to the resources and help of those "us" was broken. He became a poor, common laborer.

ANCESTORS

As informants talked about being Hakka, they often mentioned reciprocal relationships between living Hakkas and their ancestors. There are two different aspects of these relationships with ancestors that will be mentioned here.

First, informants discussing being Hakka often talked about the way that living descendants maintain a reciprocal relationship with their ancestors. Informants reported that many of those who are being Hakka understand that their ancestors have needs that they can satisfy. For example, #24 said, "They believe that if no one worships them after death, they will become wandering and wild ghosts. . . . They believe that after death, people still need to eat, and that their descendants need to worship them so that they will not starve."

Desiring to be filial, these Hakkas do their best to meet the perceived expectations of their ancestors. For example, they provide food offerings for their ancestors at prescribed times. Some even go as far as to cater to the tastes of a certain ancestor (e.g., vegetarian) and to provide some variety in the offerings so that the ancestors will not tire of one kind of food. They also include the ancestors in the affairs of the family, telling them about the births of children and other significant events. They burn spirit money so that the ancestors will have money to spend in the spirit world. They express their gratefulness for the ancestors' blessing and protection by burning incense to them. They provide for the upkeep of the common mausoleum(s) where the urns of the ancestors' bones or ashes are kept. They often go to extraordinary lengths to ensure that the continuous line of venerating descendants will not be broken.

Informants reported that these Hakkas want to help meet these needs for two reasons. First, descendants want to be filial and repay the debt that they owe their ancestors. One saying that several informants used is, "When you drink water, think of its source" (*yinshuisiyuan*), meaning that one should not forget one's origins and should be grateful for favors received. #13 articulated the feeling of indebtedness that Hakkas can feel toward their ancestors: "I have a car to drive and a house to live in. If not for the hard work of my ancestors, would I have the opportunity to enjoy these things? Someone needed to sacrifice first so that today we can have a large tree that provides us with shade. If the ancestors had not planted that tree, how could the tree have grown to be so big?" #3 elaborated, "I exist today because of these ancestors. Any accomplishments I have achieved are the result of their blessing and protection." Sometimes, the fact that one's ancestors are Hakka brings out an ethnic dimension to this gratefulness. For example, #13 stated that the reason he is interested in preserving Hakka culture is because he feels responsible to repay the source of the blessings he has received. He said, "One should be grateful for all of one's blessings! This is the original spirit of Hakkas and is very important."

Second, some informants stated that, in return for caring for or fulfilling one's filial duty to one's ancestors, the ancestors will protect them and help them. For example, #4 said, "We Hakkas all have this thinking, 'If I worship you, you will bless and protect me.'" Ahern explained, "In the act of meeting [ancestor worship obligations], the living hope to inspire a further reciprocal response from the ancestors, to obtain through them the good life as they perceive it: wealth, rich harvests, and offspring who will ensure undying memory and sustenance in the afterlife."[18]

A second aspect of these relationships with the ancestors was expressed by informants talking about the belief among many Hakkas that ignoring obligations to ancestors results in bad consequences. #3 said that traditionally Hakkas believe that if you do not worship your ancestors, you will not receive their blessing and protection. So, when Hakkas encounter

18. Ahern, *Cult of Dead*, 91.

problems like car accidents, illnesses, financial struggles, hardships for their children, and deaths in the family, informants reported that many of them wonder if the ancestors are dissatisfied with them and, as a result, are not blessing and protecting them. When asked what traditions definitely should be passed down to the next generation, #8 stated, "If we do not worship our ancestors, the ancestors will not protect us, so we definitely need to pass down this practice." #7 told about a call-in television program that articulated this view as evidence that many people are making this connection between neglect of ancestors and illness. He explained that when people call in with health problems, the program host will counsel, "You have not worshiped your ancestors recently. They are up in the heavens crying. It is because of your neglect of your ancestors that you have contracted this illness."

#11 told the story of a relative who had a very difficult life that was attributed to her neglect of her ancestors. Her arranged marriage had fallen apart when her intended husband was not attracted to her. Later, she became crippled when she fell off of a train. #11 said that it was after this relative's illegitimate son died in a car accident that the gods she sought help from reminded her that she had never once worshiped her ancestors. This relative immediately made arrangements to set up a place in her home to worship her ancestors.

Some Hakkas believe that the connection between problems and neglect of ancestor worship is somewhat "superstitious." #15 pointed out that, while her family continues to venerate their ancestors, they are more educated and do not do so out of fear of reprisals if they stop. She elaborated, "Those who have had more education think about their ancestors differently; they have a different kind of a mindset when they venerate their ancestors."

Several informants said that the fear of losing the ancestors' blessing and protection is deep-rooted and not easily changed. Continuing to worship brings a certain psychological stability. For example, #8 related, "Sometimes, after seeing the practices of their family elders, young people decide that they are going to do things differently, that they are not going to worship their ancestors. Later, when things are not going smoothly for them, when they have health issues, they naturally question whether these problems are the result of not worshiping their ancestors. This deeply-rooted explanation will emerge, and they often return to worshiping their ancestors. Then their emotions are stabilized, and they feel like things go more smoothly."

Informants also pointed out that there are some bad consequences of neglecting one's ancestors that are not directly connected to the ancestors. For example, #34 reported that because veneration of ancestors is so important to them, many parents threaten their children who do not venerate with being disinherited when the family assets are divided among heirs. #34 said that, consequently, many people continue venerating their ancestors only to get an inheritance. #32 provided another reason some Hakkas do dare not give up venerating their ancestors. He reported that he lived in fear that if he did not venerate the ancestors and do other good things, he would be punished in hell. The pictures that he saw at funerals when he was a child of the kinds of punishment that a bad person could expect in hell were still vivid in his mind when he retired.

Gods

As informants talked about being Hakka, they often mentioned reciprocal relationships between many Hakkas and the gods, primarily talking about the *yiminye*, a *tudigong*, and Guanyin, Guangong, Tiangong, and Mazu. Four aspects of these relationships will be discussed.

First, informants reported that many of those who are being Hakka understand the gods to be able to protect and bless people. When life is going smoothly or when anything good happens, many Hakkas give the gods much of the credit. For example, #4 said, "Things like having twins, or making a lot of money . . . these things are the result of their protection." The gods that are typically given credit are those in the nearby temples and those that one's own ancestors worshiped.

Second, informants described the understanding these Hakkas had that those who experience the blessing and protection of the gods are expected to reciprocate and express their gratefulness through daily worship of the gods on the god shelf in one's home. Other ways to express gratitude to the gods include: giving money to maintain and/or build temples, donating to hire a drama group to perform in front of the temple on special days, chanting certain texts for the gods to hear, and going to the temple on specified worship days and offering food sacrifices, bowing with incense, and burning spirit money. #4 elaborated, "We Hakkas believe that if I worship a god, he will protect me, and . . . that the gods protect those who are good. Good people are those who worship the gods."

Informants reported that some Hakkas believe that when people do not express their gratefulness by worshiping the gods, the gods withdraw their protection and blessing. #5 said that they do not dare think that the gods will deliberately cause problems for them, but they fear that, without the benevolent care of the gods, bad things will happen to them.

Third, informants also described how many Hakkas also believe that the gods help those who come to them with specific problems. Typically, these Hakkas ask for guidance to make decisions or for help to solve a particular problem, to ensure the smooth completion of a certain endeavor (e.g., building a house), or to obtain something that they want (e.g., a grandson or success on the college entrance exam). For example, #8 told about when she was taking a test for an important promotion at work:

> I went to the temple and asked the gods to let me know if I had any hope of passing the test. [I decided that] if there was any hope that I could pass, I would study hard. If not, I would forget it and just go and take the test. I picked out one of the inscribed bamboo sticks (*qian*) and went and got the paper that corresponded with that stick. The answer was pretty good, so I went and studied hard and passed the test. At that time I remember feeling that, in my heart, I had someone to whom I could entrust myself.

At times, a particular god is invited to come to one's home to provide help temporarily. For example, #8 told how, when they built their house, the elder members of their family invited a particular god who was perceived to be especially powerful to come and oversee the process and ensure that things went smoothly. After a period of time, this god was taken back to the temple where he resided. #4 reported that because Hakkas have had things tougher than other ethnics in Taiwan, they like to worship the gods more than these others.

Sometimes, when Hakkas go to the temple, they also promise the gods that, if their wish is granted, they will do something special to repay this debt. The importance of making sure that all of these debts are paid is emphasized by the funeral ritual that ensures that even forgotten debts are repaid.

Fourth, informants also talked about the change in how those who are being Hakka relate to the gods. Some see this practice of seeking the help of the gods as superstitious. For example, #5 said that the reason people believed in the gods in the past was because medical science was not so developed. He said skeptically, "When a child got sick and was not getting better, parents would take the child to the temple. . . . If the child just happened to get better, the gods would get the credit."

Informants also talked about how the busyness of modern life is impacting the worship of the gods. #33 talked about how young people get tired at work and want to rest when they get home rather than get involved in worshiping the gods. #4 talked about how his grandmother used to chant some Buddhist scriptures for an hour, both morning and evening, and, when she was finished, she would kneel and worship before the god shelf. When asked if he continued his grandmother's practice he responded, "I do not have that much time. Just think what I can do with that hour of time. I do not have time."

Everyone

In this subsection, several symbols related to "everyone," the majority of people in any given setting, will be raised and discussed. As informants talked about those who are being Hakka, it was clear that what everyone thinks about things—how to live, how to handle certain situations, and so forth—is very important to Hakkas. The symbols that regularly surfaced in discussions with informants about being Hakka in this area include: "following everyone," "the favor of everyone," "the disfavor of everyone," "more independent from everyone," and "pockets where everyone is Hakka."

Following Everyone

The way Hakkas follow the social practices of those around them provides evidence that the opinions of everyone are important to them. Some informants connected this sensitivity to the opinions of everyone with the minority status of Hakkas, saying that they fear being bullied. The understanding is that those who stand out from the crowd often become the target of derision or prejudice. Consequently, many Hakkas look to what the majority of people around them are doing as a standard for what they should do.

This looking to others to set the standard was especially evident in the account #35 gave about her parents' particular sensitivity to the criticisms of neighbors. #35 said that when she was a child, if her parents or grandparents heard others in their neighborhood report that she or one of her siblings had misbehaved, they would not consider whether or not the accusations against their children were true or not. They would just punish them. "Since everyone said that you had done something wrong, there was no question that you were wrong." #35 gave another example of how her mother wanted her to give a monetary gift at a funeral for a distant family member solely because her cousin had done so. She said that her mother's starting point in making decisions like this is, "I do not want to be different from others. I am afraid that if I am different from others, people will talk." #35 continued, "Hakkas are all like this."

Hakkas also look to everyone to determine how to worship the gods and spirits. Informants explained that they or other Hakkas often do not understand much about certain religious practices they are involved in but participate in them because others around them are doing so. While many point to tradition to explain why they worship certain gods, Hakkas also talk about how widespread the worship of these gods is in their community.

To determine which god is the most powerful, many Hakkas also look to everyone for advice. A temple or a god which draws large numbers of people from many locations to worship and donate money is considered to be especially powerful, largely because everyone comes there to worship. #11 surmised that the hungry ghosts (*wanshanye*) must be powerful because everyone had given so much money to build a huge temple for them.

When everyone changed some aspect of a tradition, this development made Hakkas more willing to change this aspect as well. One example informants regularly raised is how everyone is simplifying the offerings they use in worship of the gods and in ancestors rituals. #16 told how his mother used to insist on offering three kinds of meat in sacrifices. When her daughter-in-law told her that people now are using fruit only, she gradually changed her perspective and now offers only fruit. The justification used is that everyone is so busy now and does not have time for all of the preparations. #9 used the argument of "everyone" to counter the suggestion that older people might criticize him if he did not offer certain kinds of offerings, saying, "Just look at what is happening with everyone in our society. You can worship however you want to worship. . . . I did not change anything. I am just making it not so complicated. Why do we have to have a duck? Who has time for all of this fuss?"

THE FAVOR OF EVERYONE

Another aspect providing evidence that the opinions of everyone are important to Hakkas which informants often mentioned is the strong value that is placed on being seen in a positive light by everyone. One symbol that often surfaced is that of "face." Hakkas want to be seen not only as having moral integrity and as living according to societal norms, but also as those who, having achieved socially desirable accomplishments, have prestige. Several informants indicated that while all Chinese value face, Hakkas value it even more than others.

The strong value of being seen in a positive light by everyone is also reflected in the way people respond when someone gives them face. Informants talked about how when a young person does something that gives face to the family elders, these elders are predisposed to treat them better than normal. For example, #35 said that when she was a child, her grandfather was very poor and treated as an inferior by wealthy Hoklos in his community. At that time, the education of girls was not typically viewed as important because they were needed at home and because they would leave the family when they got married. When she surprised everyone by secretly taking and passing the test to get into a good junior college (an achievement very few in their community could match), it gave her grandfather great face. As a result, her grandfather, against her mother's wishes and what was traditionally allowed for a girl like her, insisted that she be allowed to attend this school.

This desire to be seen positively by others is often connected to the ancestors since the face of ancestors is also considered to be important. #33 said, "We Hakkas place a stronger value [than others around us] on bringing honor to our ancestors." #11 talked about how his aunt was embarrassed when he prepared only one kind of meat in the ancestor ceremonies. She told him, "So many ancestors need to eat. If we want them all to have face, we need to prepare a lot of sacrifices for them." #19 reported that Hakkas are willing to adapt in areas that involve others (e.g., work, languages), but, when dealing with things that relate to ancestors, they are very stubborn; "They are afraid their family will be viewed as abnormal."

The desire to be seen positively often means hiding family problems from others. An example of this is a Hakka mother who labored to conceal the fact that her son was mentally ill. #36 told about this woman and said this mother, reflecting the values of Hakkas in general, feels mental illness is so shameful that she refused to let him go out in public. In an attempt to hide this situation from those around them, this family arranged for their son to live in an institution in another part of Taiwan.

Informants talked about how Hakkas feel when others discover their problems. #36 told about a family she knew who had an adult son with a drinking problem who was jobless and living with his parents. When another son who was quite successful visited his parents and went to buy some food from a vendor who parked everyday on a nearby street (and so was able to observe the happenings in this son's parents' home), the vendor said to him, "Your brother really has it nice. He does not have to work. Your mother must really love him." The visiting son was mortified at these comments because they revealed that this vendor had observed that his brother was not conforming to social norms of working regularly. He was furious with his brother for causing him and their family to lose face.

The desire to be seen positively means pushing oneself and one's children hard, seeking to acquire socially desirable achievements. #36 told about a situation where a Hakka family sought face through their daughter's academic achievements. This daughter was a good student and consistently got the best grades in her class in the first four years of elementary school. During the last two years, she never got below third place. Because of the girl's achievements, her mother, who worked at her school, received much face. When it came time for sixth grade graduation, the girl's mother and father expected she would be able to get the prize for having the best cumulative grade average for all of her elementary school years. On graduation day, not only did the daughter not receive first prize, she earned only sixth prize. Knowing how important it was to her parents for her to get the top prize, she began to cry. Her parents were mortified by their loss of face.

Informants also talked about the importance of receiving a positive evaluation of everyone at funerals. There is much at stake at the time of a funeral, especially one being held for a senior member of the family. Descendants are being evaluated by their community as to whether or not they are fulfilling their obligations to the deceased. In these settings, everyone includes the ancestors, clan members, neighbors, friends, and even those who make money on providing services at funerals. Informants pointed out that for Hakkas, clan members have an especially important voice at this time. Their opinions are very influential and their desires are hard to resist. Following traditional procedures which are widely accepted by everyone is one of the easiest ways to be evaluated positively.

Because so much is at stake in a funeral, Hakkas are very careful about making changes to past practices. #8 related how she and her husband had been chosen by her clan to be in charge of making the arrangements for weddings, engagements, and funerals of clan members. She said that she regularly makes changes to wedding and engagement arrangements but does not dare to do so with funeral arrangements. She said:

> These arrangements are the most important matters [in all of life].... I do not want to offend the deceased, the ancestors, and the senior members of my clan.... I am afraid they will not be satisfied. I have a huge responsibility.... If I am not sure about something, I ... ask my mother-in-law or one of the older generation. If they say something is okay, then there will be no problem. If they disagree with something, then I do not go against them because, when all is said and done, these arrangements are life's most important matters.

Everyone has clear ideas on what should happen at a funeral, and the pressure to conform to these standards is felt not only by those making the arrangements, but also by close family members of the deceased. For example, children of the deceased are supposed to demonstrate their filial piety in ways deemed appropriate according to the relationship they had with the deceased. For example, the oldest son is expected to carry the ancestor tablet of the deceased. Burning incense, offering sacrifices, and burning spirit money and other paraphernalia to provide for the welfare of the deceased are important parts of these rituals.

Ensuring the funeral is *renao* (bustling with noise and excitement) is one way to achieve a positive evaluation by everyone. #25 described this aspect of many Hakka funerals:

> [The family of the deceased] hire all kinds of groups of people. For example, they will have a parade [from the funeral venue to the burial location]. During this time, it is important to have a show of extravagance. The more *renao* things are, the more honor and glory the family of the deceased will feel. When there are a lot of people, this kind of an atmosphere is created. Knowing this, the family will hire all different kinds of instrumental groups. There will be a Western-style band playing and someone beating drums. Things will be *renao*. Sometimes people also hire a Chinese instrumental group. There will be two-string fiddles, flutes, and every kind of instrument. Anyway, they just want the funeral to be *renao*. The more people there are, the happier they are.... There are also people who hire a group of people just to weep to show their sadness. These people are just acting and do not know or have any

relationship with the deceased. They are given money, and then they weep. The louder they weep, the better.

The Disfavor of Everyone

Hakkas fear of the disfavor of others around them also provides evidence that the opinions of everyone are important to them. This disfavor or pressure comes in the form of being talked about, isolated, or blamed for misfortune.

Informants said that people want to be accepted by others, not to have them say bad things about them or reject them. Being talked about (in a bad way) is one way disfavor is expressed. #8 said, "[Hakkas] feel that as much as possible, they do not want to be different. [If you do things differently], people will talk badly about you, at least the traditional people, and especially the deeply entrenched older generation." When asked if he was afraid of people talking, #28 said, "Yes! Of course I am afraid!"

#35 said, "In Hakka communities, the societal pressure is very strong. If everyone does not accept some behavior of yours, there is no way you will be able to continue to do that. Everyone will talk." She also gave an example, "When I was a student . . . I studied in night school and worked during the day. Sometimes it was too late to catch the bus, so several of my male classmates would give me rides on their motorcycles. When my neighbors saw me doing this, they talked to some of my family members, especially to my grandparents. They said, 'Your granddaughter does not have any principles. She is always getting rides from boys, different boys every time.' Their meaning was that I was very wild. Because of this situation, my grandfather scolded me severely." In order to avoid being talked about in this way and the subsequent punishment from her grandfather, #35 changed her ways and no longer rode with her classmates but rather often walked home instead.

#35 gave another example of a time when she went against the wishes of her mother and others in the same community. Her mother had planned on her being home to help take care of the family and was against her going to school, so when #35 tested into a junior college, it created a crisis in their family. Her grandfather agreed she should go to study at this school, but everyone in her neighborhood sided with her mother and scolded #35 incessantly as a result. When neighbors met her on the bus coming home from school on the weekend, they would start scolding her and continue until they got off the bus and had walked to the point where their paths parted near their homes. They scolded her for wanting to go to school rather than fulfilling her duty to her family, that of taking care of her younger brothers and sisters. She said she was only able to withstand this pressure because of the importance she placed on attending this school and because she was only subjected to this pressure on weekends.

Informants noted that the words of some people in particular have more power and influence than others. #35 said:

> [A friend] told me that after you hear something over and over, you should just be able to get used to it. I told him that... when one of my own family is saying bad things about me, I cannot get used to it. When others say bad things about you, the first time you hear these things, you will probably get hurt. When they say them again, you think, "That is just the kind of a person they are." When they say bad things about you a third time, you acknowledge that their comments are just something to which you will have to get accustomed. But that is only the case with others. When your own mother and father incessantly berate you... it is impossible to become accustomed to it.

Informants talked about the isolation one feels when going against everyone. Because those who resist the group are viewed more as marginal members or those who are on the outside of the group, they find it harder to obtain the benefits of belonging to that group. The help of others is highly valued and needed, so when those who are considering resisting the group think of the possibility of not having anyone to help them when they grow old or have some other need, they often become anxious. #35 said, "When I become different, I may be attacked... be isolated... and not get any help in facing problems." #20 reported that if you go against the clan, you will have little position or influence in that group.

More Independent of Everyone

Informants also talked about how not all people are equally influenced by everyone. #33 reported that people who have prestige are more independent of everyone than the average grass-roots Hakka. Several informants said that people who have a higher level of education, have more abilities, or have been very successful in other areas are more confident and therefore do not need to worry as much about what others think as those who do not have these assets. #19 added that marginal people and those who are in an occupation where they do not need to depend on others for their livelihood are more likely to dare to be different. #6 added that those who live separated from their relatives and/or in urban areas where they are not so deeply involved in each other's lives are also less affected by the voices of everyone.

Pockets Where Everyone Is Hakka

One of the influences for fixity among those who are being Hakka is the presence of geographical pockets of Hakkas. Many areas of Taiwan that were originally populated primarily by Hakkas have had people of other ethnic groups migrate in on a large scale. But informants reported that some more rural areas are still largely Hakka. In these pockets, there is less influence from the outside, and people are embedded in long-term relationships with everyone around them.

The existence of these pockets is significant because traditional Hakka culture is more likely to be preserved in them. Being Hakka is the mainstream in these locations. Informants report that the pace of change in being Hakka is slower in these areas. Hakka is spoken by everyone, and so children have more opportunities to learn and speak Hakka. Conformity to certain norms is more enforceable. For example, #16 said if he had been living in the area of his family home at the time of his wedding, he would not have been able to marry a Hoklo as he did. The pressure would have been too great.

Some of the significant pressures to change existing practices (e.g., ancestor rituals) which exist in urban areas do not exist in these rural areas. For example, #19 pointed out that in urban areas, funerals are held in funeral parlors. The grieving family is given a certain time slot within which they can perform rituals. In rural areas, funerals are often held in a temporary structure built in the street outside one's house. Those planning the funeral rituals have few time constraints, and, as a result, funeral rituals are often spread out over several days. There is not as much pressure to simplify and shorten these ceremonies.

These pockets of Hakkas are often the places where the family home is located and where ancestor rituals take place. When those who have moved away to non-Hakka areas return to visit relatives or take part in ancestor rituals, they are reminded of their Hakka roots. #19 argued that this connection ensures that, even though being Hakka is not a primary identity for them in the place where they currently live, they do not totally forget their Hakka identity and what it means to be Hakka.

Christianity

In this subsection, two symbols related to Christianity will be raised and discussed. These symbols, "a foreign religion" and "one of many good religions," are categorizations of being Christian which are present in the cultural "stuff" of being Hakka. These Hakka categorizations of being Christian are not necessarily held by all those who are being Hakka, but they came to the minds of informants when they were asked about how Hakkas view being Christian. The data presented in this subsection comes from responses informants gave to interview questions emerging out of research question 2, "What tensions exist between being Hakka in northwestern Taiwan and being Christian?"

A Foreign Religion

One of the key parts of the cultural "stuff" of being Hakka is the categorization of being Christian as "foreign" (or "Western" or "barbarian"). There are two meanings associated with "foreign" that surfaced as informants talked about Christians and Christianity in the context of being Hakka.

First, when those who are being Hakka say Christianity is a foreign religion, they mean that the things they associate with this religion are different from what they are accustomed to and understand, different in a way that does not easily fit with being Hakka. Buddhism also came from outside traditional China, but this religion has been more widely accepted because, according to #16, "It is more in harmony with the Daoism and Confucianism of China and has a long history of integration with the culture of China." #34 described the perceptions that non-Christian Hakkas have of Christians: "They say, 'Those people who do not worship the gods and do not burn incense are those from another country, they are different from us. . . . They are not only just from another country, they are from another world.'"

Informants also described being Christian as confusing for many Hakkas, something with which they have had little substantial contact. Being Christian stands in stark contrast to their own practices which are familiar and routine. Those Hakkas who had previously attended a Christian church usually had done so as children and expressed that they often could not understand much of what was happening. Many Hakkas are also confused about what is considered to be "Christian" and what is not, often viewing any religion from the West (e.g., Christianity, Catholicism, Jehovah's Witnesses, and Mormonism) as "Christianity." For example, #8 said, "We think of anything that Americans believe as Christianity." Also revealing the shallow understanding that Hakkas have of Christianity is the frequency with which Hakkas ask Christians about the differences between Catholicism and Christianity.

The second meaning associated with "foreign" that surfaced as informants talked about Christianity is its connection to those who are not Hakka and not Chinese. This perception of a foreign connection has its roots in observable aspects of Christian churches. For example, one can often see Westerners in Christian churches and on Christian television programs. For many older Hakkas, the only exposure they have had to Christian churches was during World War II when they went to them to collect used clothing, flour, milk powder, and other relief items that were donated by Americans. Some if not many of the songs sung in churches in Taiwan are translated Western hymns or choruses.

A significant aspect related to this perception that Christianity is connected to what is not Hakka or Chinese is the view that Hakka or Chinese culture is superior. #19 explained that one term that Hakkas use for Christianity is "barbarian religion (*fanzijiao*)." He reported, "When they say 'barbarian religion,' they mean 'uneducated.' They feel Hakkas are superior and are more educated. [Outsiders] are barbaric and chaotic." Traditionally, the Chinese have seen themselves as the center of the world, not only in terms of geographical location (e.g., the name "China" literally means "Middle Kingdom") but also in the sense of moral superiority or being the most civilized of all peoples. Cranmer-Byng argues the traditional Chinese world order was based on the following assumptions, "Namely, that China possessed a universally valid system of beliefs which were ethically right and ought to be followed by all people; that China had a special role in the world as the guardian of these values, and that, although they could not be imposed on other peoples, China must herself live up to them and set an example by which others could learn how to follow the right path."[19]

#19 confirmed that this feeling of superiority is still affecting the way Hakkas view foreign things, arguing that the attitude of seeing oneself as better than others, this self-centeredness, is a part of human nature. He explained that as a result of this sense of superiority, "Hakkas see all things that come from the outside as not good. They have China's failures in the past one hundred years in mind and connect 'foreign' with

19. Cranmer-Byng, "Chinese View," 68.

the idiom 'blindly revering foreign things and pandering to foreign powers' (*chongyangmeiwai*). This is a really complicated situation. They send their children to the United States to study there and say American culture has some good things, so they want to learn from them. But . . . in their hearts, they are really not comfortable." #19 explained that when a Hakka becomes a Christian, there is a feeling they are not being loyal to their own—giving up what is Hakka and accepting what is foreign instead. This sense of disloyalty is felt more strongly by some Hakkas than by others.

One of Many Good Religions

Another important part of the cultural "stuff" of being Hakka is the judgment that all religions, including Christianity, are good and have the same goal, that of teaching people to be good. Each religion is seen as offering a different path to reach that goal. This judgment is widespread and surfaces often when non-Christians who are being Hakka encounter and think about Christianity.

A related aspect to the thinking of Hakkas that all religions being the same is the expectation that everyone should be tolerant of the religious beliefs of others. One comment that regularly surfaced as informants talked about the response of Hakkas to being Christian is, "Everyone should just follow their own religion." The wife of #9 expressed this thought this way, "Since all religions have the same goal, people will ask if I have a religion. If I say no, they will invite me to join them. If I say yes, they will not invite me to participate in their religion because religions are all the same. They will not reject or criticize me." Those who are being Hakka understand that people follow certain gods or religions either because these worship habits have been passed on to them by their ancestors or because they have what Hakkas call a predestined affinity with that god or religion.

Another meaning associated with this idea that "all religions have the same goal" is that religions are supposed to help people become better. Several informants talked about how family members, after discovering that they had become Christian, expected them to be good. For example, when #27 talked back to his parents, they scolded him, saying that, since he was going to church, he should not do that anymore. The mother of #35 also demanded a higher standard of behavior from her daughter after she identified herself as a Christian.

Boundaries of Being Hakka

In this second section, the focus is on the symbols that informants pointed to as the boundary markers of being Hakka. The data presented in this section comes primarily from responses informants gave to interview questions emerging out of research question 1, "What does it mean to be Hakka in northwestern Taiwan?" Scholars studying boundary markers among those who are culturally Chinese mention three criteria that have often been used to categorize people and structure interactions with them.[20] First, patrilineal links or genealogical connections are seen as vital. People are understood to inherit the social category of their father. In fact, patrilineal links have been considered to be so vital that at various points in history, non-Chinese who were judged to be sufficiently sinicized to become Chinese often sought and sometimes received constructed Chinese genealogical connections.[21] Second, provenance or one's ancestral home—"an identifiable village, township, county, or province in which a person's ancestors lived and were buried"—has been viewed as significant.[22] L. Ling-chi Wang argues that for a Chinese person, "The bond to one's roots is unique, sacred, and eternal."[23] Third, the use of a specific language or dialect has also been considered to be a distinguishing feature.

Other scholars studying Chinese argue that culture has also been an important boundary marker for being Chinese. For example, Melissa Brown argues that the cultural elements of "ancestor worship, ghost beliefs, mortuary practices, and property inheritance . . . [all deriving] from Confucian principles supporting strong parental authority" were the most important markers of the Han Chinese identity in Enshi prefecture of Hubei Province in China prior to 1949.[24] One dimension of this culture is the importance placed upon standardized rituals. Brown writes, "Han [Chinese] identity is most importantly based on culture—shared meaningful ideas, in this case Confucian moral principles."[25] Hence, "a person or group can be considered Han as a result of their cultural practices regardless of their ancestry."[26] Wang notes how the Han Chinese conceptualized their

---

20. Huang et al., "Chinese Context," 15; Blake, *Ethnic Groups*, 153.
21. Ebrey, "Surnames and Identity."
22. Huang et al., "Chinese Context," 15.
23. Wang, "Roots and Identity," 186.
24. Brown, *Is Taiwan Chinese?*, 192–95.
25. Ibid., 24.
26. Ibid.

world with themselves at the center and hierarchically divided and graded the barbarians (non-Han groups) they encountered according to their social behavior. He explains, "If the non-Hans showed a willingness to adopt the Han lifestyle, they were referred to by the Han Chinese as 'cooked' (*shou*), in contrast to the 'raw' (*sheng*) who resisted Han influence."[27] Li Yi-yuan points out that, while the Chinese did try to assimilate the "raw" barbarians, they were often "cautious and noncommittal" toward them.[28]

In 2004, the Council for Hakka Affairs of the Executive Yuan of the Republic of China commissioned a study of the Hakka population in Taiwan. One part of this survey dealt with what qualifies someone to be a Hakka. Researchers gave the informants eleven different options and broke them down into the following four categories of qualifications: (1) those involving self-identity, (2) those involving bloodline, (3) those involving an understanding of Hakka culture, and (4) those involving language.[29] Research results revealed that 41.8 percent of Hakka believed that the ability to speak and understand Hakka was something that qualified someone to be a Hakka. 38.9 percent thought bloodline was necessary, and only 14.6 percent believed that understanding Hakka culture was required. Self-identifying as Hakka was necessary for only 11.2 percent.

The symbols that regularly surfaced when informants talked about the boundaries of being Hakka primarily include "language" and "bloodline," with "ancestral home" also being mentioned. When these primary markers are not readily evident, when the Hakka-ness of someone's bloodline and ancestral home are ambiguous and they cannot speak the Hakka language, "customs" and "identity" also surfaced as boundary markers. The way informants talked about these different markers is closely tied to the contexts where they regularly encountered discussions about whether or not someone is Hakka.

In most cases, when those who are being Hakka talk about bloodline as a marker, they mean the bloodline of the father. In other words, the mother's bloodline does not influence the ethnicity of her children. But informants also mentioned some exceptions to this thinking. #15 stated that she felt the children of mixed marriages were "half-and-half." #6 told about a friend of his who has a Hakka mother and a Hoklo father. This friend feels he is both Hakka and Hoklo. #35 married a non-Hakka

27. Wang, "History, Space, Ethnicity," 286.
28. Li, "Ethnic Relations," 104.
29. Yang, "Preface," Section 1, 7.

and was troubled when she heard her children identify themselves according to the ethnicity of her husband. She taught her children that they were also Hakka.

When informants talked about those who are being Hakka who focus on language as an ethnic marker, some said there is a close connection between the language one speaks and one's ethnicity. They asserted that when one wants to determine the ethnicity of another person, language is a key distinguishing marker. Informants often spoke of how hard it is for Hakkas to hide their Hakka identity because they usually speak Hoklo or Mandarin with a unique accent which others can identify as a Hakka accent. #19 gave the example of a Mainlander family who lived close to them. Everyone knew they were not Hakka because they always spoke Mandarin. #1 told how his father had two wives, one Hoklo and one Hakka. #1 said he is Hakka because he was raised by the wife who was Hakka. She taught him to speak Hakka. If he had been raised by the Hoklo-speaking wife, he said he would probably have been Hoklo.

Ancestral home is another important marker that is used among those who are being Hakka to determine ethnic identity. In a situation where one wants to know the ethnicity of new acquaintances, informants pointed out that, outside of listening to them speak, one can just ask them where their ancestors lived in China before they came to Taiwan. There are some areas that are known to have been Hakka-speaking and others that are known to have been Hoklo-speaking.

One of the situations where informants and others who are being Hakka considered whether or not someone could be included in Hakka was when a person with a Hakka bloodline could no longer speak or understand Hakka. In this vein, informants raised the example of Hakkas whose ancestors moved into an area dominated by Hoklos and, over time, gradually assimilated with them. Consequently, the descendants of these people today cannot speak Hakka and often do not even know that they have Hakka roots. Informants also raised the case of the many Hakka young people who currently have little or no Hakka-language ability, a phenomenon which most anticipate will become more and more widespread in the future. In this kind of situation, some said non-speakers were still Hakka because of their Hakka bloodline; they were born as Hakkas. #28 said, "If one's roots are Hakka, then one is eternally Hakka." Others argued that when one cannot speak Hakka, one is no longer a Hakka. Language ability was the most important boundary marker for them.

Those informants who strongly value the Hakka language and want to stop its decline spoke harshly about those who call themselves Hakka yet cannot speak Hakka. They argued that these people should not bring shame upon themselves by calling themselves Hakka. Rather, they should voluntarily give up their Hakka identity. For example, #13 said:

> [In order to be considered a Hakka], you at least have to speak Hakka. If you are a Hakka but you cannot speak Hakka, then you should not call yourself a Hakka. Doing so would be humiliating. Presently there are a lot of people who have Hakka bones and Hoklo skin; they say their ancestors were Hakka in order to get some benefits. Really?! They cannot speak any Hakka. They are just like politicians; all they want is people to help them. In the past, one presidential candidate said his father and grandfather were Hakka and asked us to vote for him . . . but he could not speak Hakka. It was a scam.

Even those who made bloodline the primary marker were troubled by the absence of Hakka-language ability. For example, #14 said a Hakka who cannot speak Hakka is not a complete Hakka.

Another kind of situation that informants surfaced was how to classify a non-Hakka who has learned to speak Hakka. The most common examples raised include a non-Hakka wife who learns Hakka and embraces the traditions and practices of her husband's family and non-Hakkas who move into a Hakka area and learn to speak Hakka fluently. In these cases, some said since these non-Hakkas did not have Hakka bloodline, they could only be praised as those who have worked hard and have learned to live as Hakkas. Other Hakkas, however, included these kinds of people as Hakkas. For example, #29 reported that when non-Hakkas come to live in her small Hakka town and learn Hakka, people consider them to be Hakka.

Informants raised several examples of how people passed from one ethnic group to another, casting doubt on using bloodline as a primary boundary marker. #23 said using bloodline is unreliable because one does not know when one will discover that, in the past, one had Hoklo ancestors. He gave an example of someone who discovered later in life that his ancestors were Hakka rather than Hoklo. #36 gave the example of how her ancestors originally were Hakka, and then they became Hoklo and, later still, became Hakka again. She talked about how her father's ancestors came from an area in Fujian Province of China which is known to have been a Hakka-speaking area. When they moved to Taiwan, they lived in a Hoklo area in Taiwan and spoke Hoklo rather than Hakka. Later, her grandfather moved again to a Hakka area and, as a result, her father learned to speak Hakka and thought of himself as a Hakka even though he was the son of a Hoklo. All of #36's father's relatives still speak Hoklo. #21 is married to a Hoklo, but she reported that, originally, her relatives were Hoklo but moved into a Hakka area and became Hakka. Her husband's ancestors, on the other hand, were originally Hakka and became Hoklo after moving to a Hoklo area. #28 tells how in his past, several of his ancestors settled in different areas of Taiwan. The descendants of those who settled in Hoklo areas are Hoklo today, and the descendants of those who settled in Hakka areas are Hakka today. #18 tells of an "adopted" cousin of his who was originally a Hoklo but began presenting himself as a Hakka after he agreed to fill the role of a son for #18's childless uncle, ensuring this uncle had descendants and someone to venerate him after his death.

In some cases where the primary markers of bloodline, language, and ancestral home were not as evident, the markers of customs and identity were used. For example, #2 talked about a place where it has been reported that the residents were originally Hakka but have been largely assimilated with the Hoklos. No one speaks the Hakka language. She says, "It is only from looking at their customs that you can tell their ancestor veneration practices are Hakka practices." #18 described how at some point in the past, his Hakka ancestors moved into a Hoklo area and, in order to survive, began to speak Hoklo. He told how, even though no one in his family currently speaks Hakka, they still identify themselves as Hakka. He said, "We use the Hoklo language to explain to people that we are Hakka."

Relating to the Hakka Ethnic Identity

This third and final section recounts and discusses informants' perceptions of the way those who are being Hakka are relating to the Hakka ethnic identity. Informants talked about how Hakkas can: (1) have a sense of affection and devotion and of friendliness and familiarity when they encounter things or people connected to Hakka, (2) experience the Hakka ethnic identity as very thick, (3) actively work to distance themselves from Hakka, (4) experience the Hakka ethnic identity as thin, and (5) be triggered to suddenly thicken their Hakka ethnic identity. The data presented in this section comes primarily from responses informants gave to interview questions emerging out of research question 1, "What does it mean to be Hakka in northwestern Taiwan?"

First, those who are being Hakka often have a sense of affection and devotion and of friendliness and familiarity with things and people connected with Hakka. The sense of affection and devotion that informants spoke of was the result of commonalities and shared experiences between people—things like having a common language, common memories, common religious practices, belonging to the same group, and having a common residence. These are referred to in the literature as "ethnic attachments."

Informants spoke about the affection and devotion that those who are being Hakka have toward Hakka things in general. For example, #22 said when he is with older people who speak Hakka, he feels like he has returned to his own family. He elaborated:

> I can speak Hakka and feel I am a Hakka. Because of my parents, I have a certain kind of experience—Hakka experience. I guess my affection and devotion is connected to my whole clan—the love I have for my clan, and the love they have for me. I feel being able to belong to Hakka is like getting back to . . . a basic part of life. When I have the opportunity to visit those back home who still speak Hakka, I find I have a kind of feeling of affection and devotion for them. We Hakkas do not often feel such a sense of friendliness and familiarity. When I use Hakka to joke with them, I feel the words are so vivid. I can say things I would not be able to express in another language. All this is because being Hakka is something that is expressed in this language, in this affection and devotion, and in thinking. . . . As you and I are together here, the fact that we can speak like this [in Hakka about being Hakka], I feel almost like I have found a close and intimate friend or a shared connecting point.

#20, a teacher, gave another example of how Hakka things raise warm feelings for him. He said when he encounters a student in his classes who speaks Hakka, he feels a certain sense of friendliness and familiarity with him/her.

Informants talked about the importance of speaking the Hakka language for developing feelings of affection and devotion with those who are being Hakka. #8 said being able to speak Hakka is necessary for someone to be Hakka, because without this ability, there is a communication barrier. It is harder to feel affection and devotion for Hakkas who do not speak the language. #3 told about how his ability to speak Hakka helps him to gain a sense of mutual affection and devotion with Hakkas so that they are willing to trust him and to share more freely when he interviews them for television programs he is producing.

Nevertheless, it is important to note that those who are being Hakka in Taiwan can also feel a sense of affection and devotion for those who do not speak Hakka. To the extent to which Hakkas speak Mandarin or Hoklo, relationships filled with mutual affection and devotion with non-Hakka-speaking people can also develop using these languages as a communication medium. The most obvious example of this situation is the widespread intermarriage between Hakkas and non-Hakka speakers. It is not only young Hakkas who do not speak Hakka very well who are intermarrying with Hoklo speakers. Several older informants who spoke Hakka well also married Hoklos, speaking Mandarin with them. #2 provided another example. She told how a Catholic priest can live in a Hakka village in the mountains for a long time, and even though he cannot speak Hakka, he builds a certain sense of mutual affection and devotion with the people of that village.

Informants pointed out that when people have a sense of affection and devotion for each other, they do things to help each other. For example, there is a beef noodle shop close to where #26 works that is owned by a Hakka. He said he feels a sense of friendliness and familiarity with the owner because he is Hakka. #26 said he tries to go there often to give him business and also takes his friends and encourages them to eat there. #27 told about how his parents live in an apartment building in an urban area. There is a family living above them who is Hakka, and, because of this commonality, the two families help each other out. For example, when they have food they have made or grown themselves, they share it with each other.

Informants also pointed out that, among those who are being Hakka, those who are older often have more affection and devotion toward things that are Hakka than those who are younger. #3 reported that because his son grew up in a large city and has spent very little time at his family home several hours from the city, this son does not have the same feelings as he does toward his clan and the veneration of ancestors which brings the clan together. #3 acknowledged it will be hard for his son to have that same sense of affection and devotion for clan members since he sees those relatives only once a year and has not had the opportunity to develop a significant personal relationship with them. #22 also provided an example of the differences in feelings of affection and devotion between the young and older Hakkas: "The Hakkas I encounter [here in my urban community] are mostly in their forties and fifties. They identify with Hakka, and when we speak Hakka together, I feel friendly and familiar with them; I have a feeling we are Hakkas. The younger generation does not speak Hakka as well and identifies less with Hakka. I feel less friendly and familiar with them because I cannot speak Hakka with them.... Some of them say, 'My grandfather is a Hakka, my father is a Hakka'—what they mean is that they are not Hakka."

Second, informants also explained that the Hakka ethnic identity is quite thick and salient for some Hakkas. Being Hakka is one of the more important identities in their lives. Even though these Hakkas are culturally not very different from the others around them, they have a special interest in the areas where there are differences. For example, they may consciously think of handling certain situations in a Hakka way. They may give themselves to efforts that they think will help those who are being Hakka. They may work together with others to preserve the Hakka language and culture.

Several informants provided examples of those whose Hakka ethnic identity is thick. #6 spends vast amounts of time working with the Hakka language. He is especially interested in and proud of the dialect of Hakka that his family speaks. He has published many substantial resources for teaching this kind of Hakka on a deeper level. He offers two classes every year using his own material to teach adults. He also is a member of a group of like-minded people who are interested in promoting this kind of Hakka and who sponsor speech contests and other events to further this goal.

Hakka is also very important to #25, a professional musician and a professor of music. He explained that, from the time he was little, his father encouraged his siblings and him to value their Hakka identity. When he was a child, his father had a rule that, in their home, everyone spoke only Hakka. His father taught them that being Hakka was something of which to be proud. #25 said that, as a result, now when he introduces himself in groups, he naturally identifies himself first as a Hakka and then tells other things about himself. When he was a student over thirty years ago, #25 began to feel a burden and a responsibility to work with Chinese music, especially Hakka music. On school vacations, he often traveled to rural areas around Taiwan and recorded Hakka folk songs and other Hakka music. Returning home, he would listen to these recordings, record the songs on paper, and then study and work with these songs. Later, he used what he had learned to compose and perform his own Hakka music. #25 currently participates in a music group that performs only Hakka music.

The Hakka identity is also thicker for #31 than for many other Hakkas. The salience of his Hakka identity is evident as he insists on speaking Hakka even when other Hakkas do not. Most Hakkas in his workplace usually speak Mandarin and Hoklo with each other and others. #31 encourages them to speak Hakka because he wants people to know he is Hakka and that Hakka is not something shameful. He is particularly troubled by people who downplay the fact that they are Hakka and try to ingratiate themselves with other ethnics by speaking their languages while neglecting their own.

Third, informants also reported that many Hakkas distance themselves from the Hakka ethnic identity. This phenomenon was especially evident in the past, but even today, many Hakkas reject or hide their connection with Hakka for fear they will be looked down upon or have fewer opportunities to advance in school or in their work. #18 explained that Hakkas who distance themselves from the Hakka ethnic identity feel they have no other choice if they are going to survive and thrive in a competitive environment where being Hakka is not a social advantage. For example, #19 said, "[Many Hakkas in Taipei] deliberately do not identify themselves as Hakka.... If others find out they are Hakka, they will have difficulty advancing to higher levels. So, when Mainlanders are in the majority, these Hakkas identify with Mainlanders and the people around them do not know they are Hakka.... As a result, these Hakkas get opportunities based on their abilities. They can climb as high as their abilities warrant." #25 told about a Hoklo he knew many years ago who owned a large factory. If he found out a job applicant was a Hakka, he would not hire them.

#35 also provided an example of this distancing. She said that after she had worked together with one of her colleagues for a long time and was well-acquainted with him, she asked him about his roots. This colleague said he was a Hoklo. When she asked him where his Hoklo ancestors came from, he said he did not know. She was puzzled that he did not know and kept asking questions. He finally admitted his father and mother were both Hakkas. #35 challenged him saying, "If your father and mother are both Hakka, how can you not be a Hakka?" He defensively replied, "If I say I am not a Hakka, then I am not!" #35 said she has two or three colleagues like this. Her evaluation was, "Maybe they feel if they admit they are Hakka, they will be weaker and there will be people who will look down on them."

Several informants also argued that distancing oneself from Hakka is more common in the lower classes of Hakkas. #20 said Hakkas who understand their own history and have a higher education level and higher status in society are less likely to hide the fact that they are Hakka.

Fourth, informants also explained that the Hakka ethnic identity is thin for many Hakkas. These Hakkas are not so culturally different from other ethnics around them, and, where they are different, they do not emphasize these differences. When they are asked directly if they are Hakka, they will not hide their Hakka identity, but this identity is not very important to them. Using Patterson's distinction between a cultural and an ethnic group, the way these Hakkas relate to being Hakka suggests they are more of a cultural group than an ethnic group.[30] Since one of the more observable differences in ethnicity is the Hakka language, when these Hakkas lose their ability to speak Hakka, their identity becomes what Gans calls "symbolic ethnicity."[31] These Hakkas have other identities (e.g., social status, education level, or occupation) which are more relevant and important to them.

Hakka young people, in general, are another example informants raised as those whose Hakka identity is thin. For example, #16 postulated that all young people in Taiwan are very similar culturally and do not distinguish between Hakka, Hoklo, and Mainlander. #22 pointed to a trend in Taiwan where young people primarily speak Mandarin, and their ethnic identity is weak. #27, a college student, confirmed this situation in his experience, saying that even though he can discern a classmate's ethnicity by listening to them speak Mandarin, ethnic distinctions are not very important for him and other classmates.

#23 raised another reason for Hakkas having a thin ethnic identity. He said that many middle-aged people (like himself) are experiencing an identity crisis because of the political situation in Taiwan. He said:

> Am I a person connected to the Republic of China [the official name of the government currently ruling Taiwan, one that claims not only to rule Taiwan but also all of mainland China] or to

---

30. Patterson, "Context and Choice," 309.
31. Gans, "Symbolic Ethnicity," 9.

Taiwan? Do I belong to the country of Taiwan or the country of China? I do not know who I am. From the time I was little until I became an adult, as I was growing up, this crisis flavored things for me. I do not have much of a sense that I am a Hakka. The whole environment around me has been emphasizing that I should speak Mandarin; that I should identify with Mainlanders. That is the environment I grew up in. Because of this, from the time I was little, I have not especially identified myself with Hakkas or myself as a Hakka. . . . I do not know what kind of a person I am.

Fifth, informants also reported how a thin Hakka ethnic identity can thicken when those who are being Hakka encounter certain triggering situations. Three triggers were mentioned most often: (1) situations that made them aware that Hakka may become extinct, (2) situations where they perceived that Hoklos were seeing themselves as superior to Hakkas, and (3) situations where a close connection to Hakka brought benefits. It is important to note that an increase of saliency in the Hakka identity after a triggering situation is not necessarily permanent and often thins out again as other priorities vie for their attention.

One kind of situation informants often raised as triggering an increased salience in the Hakka identity is one that raised the awareness that Hakka is threatened. #15's experience is one example. When she was young, she said she downplayed and was a bit embarrassed about her Hakka identity. She remembers thinking that Hakkas looked like country hicks. She married a man from another ethnic group and moved to a Hoklo area. Later, when circumstances led her family to move back to a Hakka area, she began to feel differently about Hakka. She noticed that even in that Hakka area, very few people were speaking Hakka, and she began to worry that if she and other Hakkas did not do something, Hakka would become extinct. She described her feeling as a sense of crisis. At the same time, she started really appreciating other Hakkas. She began to be drawn to things Hakka. She started deliberately seeking opportunities to speak Hakka and to teach her children the Hakka language.

Another kind of situation that triggered increased salience in the Hakkas that informants talked about is when something happened to give these Hakkas a sense that the Hoklos around them thought they were superior. #33 talked about this kind of a situation, "When Hoklos have a sense of superiority, when they stand on my head, I have a consciousness that emerges which says, 'I am a Hakka,' and I am unwilling to yield to them. This is really the only time where I have a consciousness that I am a Hakka. Normally, when everything is harmonious, I do not have this awareness." He explained further that the trend in Taiwan has been to use Mandarin as the national language which all ethnic groups can speak. Recently, some Hoklos, who are the majority ethnic group in Taiwan, have been campaigning for Hoklo to become the national language. #33 continued, "When they talk like this, I get a little uncomfortable." #2 had a similar feeling when she attended a seminar where the speaker expected everyone to be able to understand Hoklo. Hearing people around her call the Hoklo language "Taiwanese" (as if Hakka and other languages used in Taiwan were somehow not Taiwanese) triggered a desire in her to stand up for Hakka.

Still another kind of situation that informants often raised as triggering an increased salience in the Hakka identity in Hakkas is when benefits could be gained by having a connection to Hakka. Informants talked about several politicians who previously had not identified with Hakka and did not speak the Hakka language, but began to report that they had Hakka ancestors in the context of campaigning for election in order to court votes from Hakkas.

Concluding Remarks

This chapter focused on the ways Hakkas in northwestern Taiwan construct being Hakka in the areas that relate to the perceptions Hakkas have of being Christian. In the first section, the words of informants regarding some shared symbols of being Hakka were presented and arranged according to five themes. "Hakka history" was the first theme, and in this area informants talked about the symbols of "good roots, "disadvantaged guests," and "shaped by history." Under the symbol of "disadvantaged guests," informants described how Hakkas, due to their unique history, encountered great hardship and were often bullied and scorned by others around them. When informants talked about the symbol of "shaped by history," they reported that the historical experiences of the Hakkas have shaped them to have a stiff-necked Hakka spirit, to be hardworking, frugal, and conservative, to sing mountain songs, to have solidarity and adaptability, and to be people with ability.

The second theme that emerged as informants discussed the meaning of being Hakka was that of "family," and four symbols regularly surfaced as informants conversed in this area. The symbols of "respect," "incense fires," "ancestors' language," and "traditions" were raised and their meanings spelled out by informants. One particular phenomenon that was observed in this area is that, while many Hakkas highly value and feel responsible to pass on the Hakka language to the next generation, most are unsuccessful at ensuring that their children and grandchildren are able to speak Hakka. As informants talked about the reasons for a decline in the use of the Hakka language, one can note that tremendous energy is required and high costs are involved in order to resist this decline in Hakka-language ability in one's own family.

"Reciprocal relationships" was the third theme that came into view as informants talked about being Hakka, especially in relation to Hakka perceptions of being Christian. The three symbols informants raised and filled with meaning under this theme were "us," "ancestors," and "gods." Those who are being Hakka were shown to feel relationship obligations in each of these areas.

The fourth theme used in this chapter to organize symbols informants raised was "everyone." Informants regularly talked about the symbols of "following everyone," "the favor of everyone," "the disfavor of everyone," "more independent than everyone," and "pockets where everyone is Hakka." "Everyone" was shown to have a significant influence on the thinking of those who are being Hakka.

"Christianity" was the final theme used to group the two symbols informants discussed at length, those of "a foreign religion" and "one of many good religions." Christianity was shown to be foreign in the sense that it is not well understood, but also in the sense that it has connections with the West. The idea captured in the symbol of being "one of many good religions" was that tolerance between religions is expected and that all religions have the same goal, namely that of teaching people to be good.

The second section of this chapter related the insights of informants regarding the boundaries of being Hakka. The boundary markers used most often were shown to be the presence of a Hakka "bloodline," "language ability," and "ancestral home," but when these markers were not evident, Hakka "customs" or "self-identity" were also used to determine who qualified to be Hakka. Informants varied greatly on the fixity and fluidity they attributed to these boundaries. For example, some argued that a Hakka is a Hakka even when they are unaware of it. Many others argued that the boundaries are porous and that Hakkas can cross over the boundaries and assume a different ethnicity. The fluidity that can be present in these boundaries is important to note and contrast with the perspectives of many that reify and essentialize ethnic boundaries.

The final section of this chapter recounted the comments of informants as they talked about the way Hakkas relate to the Hakka ethnic identity. While these Hakkas were shown to have a sense of affection and devotion and of friendliness and familiarity when they encounter things or people connected to Hakka, these feelings were not limited to Hakka connections alone. Hakkas were shown to vary in the salience with which they experienced Hakka in their lives, some experiencing Hakka as very salient and "thick," others experiencing this identity as "thin," and still others even actively working to distance themselves from this identity. Informants also related how certain triggering events can make this identity suddenly thicken and become very salient for Hakkas. The fluidity or variety in the way Hakkas relate to the Hakka ethnic identity is important to note and contrast with the perceptions of some scholars (e.g., McGavran) that ethnic groups are homogeneous units.

Christians who want to engage Hakkas in northwestern Taiwan more effectively and intentionally should note the fixity and fluidity in being Hakka in northwestern Taiwan. First, there is fixity to being Hakka, and this fixity makes certain habits, traditions, practices, and ways of thinking feel commonsensical and necessary to Hakkas and makes change difficult. This cultural "stuff" has not only shaped these Hakkas but also serves as a reservoir of symbols and habits on which they draw as they construct their identity in encounters with Christians and Christianity. Second, it is also important to note that there is fluidity in being Hakka in northwestern Taiwan. In every area of the cultural "stuff" of being Hakka, change is taking place, and Hakkas vary in the way they are shaped by and locate themselves in regard to this change.

5

Non-Christian Hakkas in Northwestern Taiwan and Being Christian

THE SECOND STEP IN exploring tensions between being Hakka in northwestern Taiwan and being Christian is to look closely at the way Hakka non-Christians negatively categorize being Christian. These categorizations are expressions of these tensions and emerge as Hakkas encounter differences between their cultural "stuff" and the things they associate with being Christian and choose to make these differences significant. These Hakkas access the symbols and other resources contained in their cultural "stuff" and construct being Christian as something that does not fit with being Hakka. This chapter explores these negative categorizations and then reflects on the fixity and fluidity evidenced in these categorizations.

Non-Christian Hakka Categorizations of Being Christian

The focus in this section is on the categorizations that non-Christian Hakkas make of being Christian. The data presented in this section comes from responses informants gave to interview questions emerging out of research question 2, "What tensions exist between being Hakka in northwestern Taiwan and being Christian?" Some of these responses are the personal constructions of non-Christian informants as they talked about their perceptions of being Christian. Other responses are those that informants have encountered, either as a reaction to their own practices as a Christian or as they have listened to non-Christians talk about being Christian. These categorizations, spoken in a context where Hakka was the focal point, are one aspect of the interactive process of ethnic identification. In this case, the only ethnic "other" present was this researcher. Non-Christian informants often tried to solicit this researcher's response to their statements (e.g., "Am I right about Christians?"). In order to avoid influencing informants, this researcher attempted to limit (or avoid entirely) a response to these kind of inquiries (both verbally and nonverbally) and tried not to address or challenge any of the categorizations of the informants.

The comments of informants in this area are arranged and discussed according to the same themes as in the previous chapter: (1) Christianity, (2) Hakka history, (3) family, (4) reciprocal relationships, and (5) everyone.

Christianity

Some of the categorizations that Hakka non-Christians make of being Christian access themes and symbols contained in their cultural "stuff" directly related to the theme of Christianity. As informants talked in this area, two symbols stood out: (1) a foreign religion, and (2) one of many good religions.

A Foreign Religion

Informants reported that non-Christian Hakkas often categorize being Christian as "foreign" in one way or another. For some, this categorization is simply an easily accessible label (from their cultural "stuff") to use when a well-meaning Christian friend or relative seeks to proselytize them. For others, this foreign nature has deeper roots.

Some non-Christian Hakkas, when constructing being Christian as difficult for Hakkas to accept, often make significant the way the things they associate with being Christian are largely unfamiliar and not well-understood. Consequently, these Hakkas categorize being Christian as "foreign to Hakkas." #1 provided an example of the unfamiliar nature of the things they associate with being Christian as he talked about his feelings when attending a Christian memorial service for a relative in his neighbor's home. #1 was uncomfortable because he "did not know what to expect next." When he arrived and was handed a songbook, he was nervous because he was not familiar with any of the songs. In fact, he lamented that everything the Christians were doing was foreign to him. He reported that he regretted attending and argued that many Hakkas would anticipate having the same feeling and simply decide not to attend this kind of gathering. #27 provided another example of this unfamiliar nature, telling about the response of his parents to his baptism, "When I was a senior in high school, I told my parents I was attending church, . . . but they did not really understand Christianity. Then one day I brought home my baptism certificate and told them I had been baptized. Because they did not know much about this religion, they were shocked and very afraid. They looked at my certificate and said, 'What is this? What are all of these signatures?' They felt this situation was very serious." When #19 heard about the conversion of a woman who lived with her non-Christian mother-in-law, he expressed concern that if this mother-in-law was not exposed to more Christians, she would naturally see her daughter-in-law's conversion as a bad thing. He pointed out that the lack of understanding and exposure can influence even the most open-minded people to be troubled when a family member joins this foreign group. #19 anticipated that unless something was done, this older Hakka would begin to see her daughter-in-law as belonging to "another country."

The unfamiliarity of the things Hakkas associate with being Christian is often contrasted with the familiarity of Hakka things. For example, when he talked about how ancestor practices are a focal point that links his family together, #3 said, "The idea of having Christian beliefs bring our family together feels so distant. Having our ancestral line as the focal point is much more natural. When my father and my grandfather passed away, their names were added to the ancestor tablet. In the future, my name will also be added."

Also with the different-ness of being Christian in mind, some non-Christian Hakkas categorize Christianity as "a good religion for Westerners but not for Hakkas." These Hakkas say they have their practices and Westerners have Christianity. For example, #1 said, "It is like the difference between a . . . cow and a water buffalo. Christianity is Western and is just different from Hakka." #2 also recounted how her mother thought Christianity was good but just not something for Hakkas.

Another of the differences many non-Christian Hakkas make significant as they construct being Christian as hard for Hakkas to accept is Christianity's foreign connections. Informants reported that some Hakkas access the idea in their cultural "stuff" that Hakka and Chinese are superior and categorize being Christian as "inferior and barbarian." For example, #28 related how his parents talked about him, saying, "When I went to church, my parents opposed me. They went to my relatives and said, 'This son is worthless. Every day he goes over there to *Jesus*,'" strongly emphasizing the first syllable of the word "Jesus" and explaining, "In the Hakka language, [this first syllable] sounds like [*wild* as in] wild person." #28's parents said these kinds of things in many different settings.

Other Hakkas access the idea in their cultural "stuff" that giving up what is Hakka and accepting what is foreign is being disloyal, and they categorize belief in Christianity as "being disloyal to one's own." For example, #19 said, "When we preach the gospel to Hakkas, they all really do not want to listen. When they hear us talk about Jesus, they cover their ears. They feel Christianity is a Western religion and therefore [those who convert are] disloyal; they are not being loyal to their own but rather are enamored with the West." #25 said, "Non-Christians think Christianity is Western, not Chinese, so they are not interested. . . . They say, 'This is not ours. This history is not our history. We Chinese people have Chinese religions; Chinese people have Chinese gods. Why should we go and follow foreign gods?'"

Part of the desire to be loyal to one's own has its roots in the historical relationship between China and the West. #20 articulated this connection, "[Before I became a Christian], because I had been taught in school that, especially in the eighteenth and nineteenth centuries, China had been mistreated by Western powers, I connected Western missionaries with this mistreatment and rejected them to some extent." #19 provided an example of the desire of Hakkas to be loyal to their own, telling the story of how a Christian Hakka taught English classes at her church because she wanted to use her English abilities to build relationships with non-Christian children and their parents. #19 reported that several parents rejected her and her class because they felt she was following a Western religion and, in doing so, was admiring foreign things and pandering to foreign powers. #35 also gave an example, telling about the feeling of her family when she became a Christian: "[My non-Christian family members] said that [Christianity] is not something Chinese and that, when you become a Christian, you show that you do not want your ancestors, that you do not want this clan."

One of Many Good Religions

Christianity's exclusivity is another aspect many of those who are being Hakka notice as different and make significant as they construct being Christian as something hard for Hakkas to accept. These Hakkas access the idea from their cultural "stuff" that all religions are good and categorize Christianity's exclusive message as "offensive."

Informants reported that Hakkas encounter this exclusiveness most often in the active evangelism efforts of Christians. Rather than just practicing their religion and only proselytizing those who seek them out and express interest in exploring Christian teachings, Christians often aggressively try to convert non-believers. Shaped to see all religions as equally good and to be tolerant of other religions, many Hakkas view any Christian evangelism efforts that go beyond a more passive witness as offensive and something that does not fit with the ways of those who are being Hakka. #19 told about a common response of Hakkas when Christians seek to evangelize them. He related how others often say something like, "All religions are good, so you do not need to teach me. I follow Buddhism. I already have a religion. I already know how to do good, so you do not have to teach me."

#8 told about a junior high school teacher who had originally been "quite stable." After this teacher became a Christian, #8 said she started to deviate from what was normal. Before and after class, she began calling students to come over and sit with her on the edge of a flowerbed outside her classroom and talking to them about becoming a Christian. The students were all afraid of her. #8 said this teacher really "went bad" when she became a believer, "The students are in school to study. It is okay if you talk about your religious beliefs once in a while, if you gradually influence students one small step at a time. If your students have a predestined affinity with Christianity, they will naturally believe. But when you aggressively try to pull them in . . . you are going too far."

#1 provided another example. He talked about how troubled he was when his aunt was baptized as a Christian on her deathbed. She had become seriously ill and had died quickly, but before his aunt passed away, a cousin (her son) who had been witnessing to her for many years had arranged to have her baptized as a Christian. #1 was furious. Part of his anger came from the fact that this cousin had been so aggressive—taking advantage of a situation in the hospital where there was much fear and no one was thinking clearly. #1 felt his uncle's willingness to let his wife be baptized in the hospital was a desperate last-minute attempt to grasp at anything that might possibly help her, not a true change of beliefs. His aunt's baptism seemed completely contrary to all of her former behavior and beliefs. #1 said, "She worshiped the gods on the first and fifteenth of every month. She *never* forgot. . . . How is it possible that my aunt could suddenly become a Christian overnight? I cannot accept that. . . . If my cousin wanted her to become a Christian so badly, he should have found a way to convince her to be baptized when things were not so crazy. . . . Religions are supposed to respect each other."

#15 gave another example of the offensive behavior of Christians. She said Christians in Taiwan are very egocentric. She elaborated, "They all feel they are right and everyone else is wrong." She continued, saying these Christians feel their God is the highest, that He is the only God. When asked how she and her friends feel about this, she said, "We all say, 'Nonsense!'" She asked incredulously, "Is it really only the Christian god who is a god, and all the other gods are not gods?" She felt it would be obvious to anyone that Christians were unreasonable, that they did not respect the religious beliefs of others. For her, the fact that there were so many Christian denominations, suggesting Christians could not even agree among themselves, was also evidence of this strong egocentric consciousness among Christians. She offered another example of when a group of Christians came to her home to study the Bible, saying, "Every one of them had a different way of explaining the scripture passage they studied together."

#18 told about a Christian relative's actions which communicated a flagrant lack of respect. At Chinese New Year, this new Christian, in order to prevent his relatives from worshiping the gods and ancestors, cut off the heads of the ducks and chickens that had been prepared as offerings, thus rendering them unfit for an offering. #18 reported that this act was extremely offensive to those in his clan-grouping, and, as a result, this new Christian's relationship with these relatives was severely strained for many years. In contrast, #18 reported that many Christians applauded this new Christian's act as outstanding and encouraged him to give testimonies about his actions.

#36 provided another example of the offensive behavior of Christians. She reported that years ago a Christian, in an attempt to proselytize her father, told him the temple gods were made out of wood just as urinals (used before the advent of indoor plumbing) were made out of wood. #36's father was extremely offended that this person had put the gods on the same level as urinals.

As Hakkas put Christianity in the category of "religion" and access the idea from their cultural "stuff" that all religions are the same, they make the differences between being Hakka and practices associated with being Christian significant and construct conversion to Christianity as something "unnecessary" for Hakkas. For example, #27 reported:

> Hakkas do not reject Christianity but just feel they do not need to change their beliefs. They feel Christianity is a religion which is good but comes from the outside. For example, if a missionary comes to a Hakka area to spread the gospel, [Hakkas] will not get angry or reject you saying you are a foreigner and are not welcome here. They will receive you but [say], "You have your beliefs, and I have my religion. I want to worship the gods I feel are good. Of course, your religion is good too, but everyone should just follow the beliefs they believe to be true." They will feel believing in the Lord is unnecessary.

Another aspect of being Christian that many of those who are being Hakka notice as different and make significant is the way Christians do not appear to be living exemplary lives. Shaped to see all religions as having the same goal of helping people become good, many Hakkas are troubled when they see Christians doing things that are, in the eyes of these Hakkas, less than "good," and, consequently, they categorize Christians as "substandard" or "hypocritical." In the eyes of these Hakkas, identifying oneself as a believer in a religion raises expectations of a higher level of behavior.

#15 provided several examples of Christians doing bad things to the point that she said she did not want her Christian husband to go to church anymore because she was afraid he would learn to be like them. She said the Christians around her are always saying "Praise the Lord" but not doing what the Bible says. She also gave the example of a Christian government official who had been in the news the day before. This official had aided a politician in illegal ways and originally denied his involvement when these acts were discovered. #15 reported that this official had just held a news conference where he confessed that he had actually acted illegally. In his confession this official said that a fellow Christian had exhorted him saying Christians should not cover up their wrongs but should confess them. #15 was indignant saying, "What happened to his beliefs when he committed the crime in the first place?" #15's Christian husband, sitting in on the interview, offered, "Everyone has times of weakness." #15 retorted to her husband, "I really dislike it when you say stuff like that . . . finding excuses for people, saying that everyone makes mistakes, that God says all people make mistakes, that they should be forgiven. . . . If that is the case, then everyone can do a lot of bad things." #15 also told about how a Christian had tricked her out of a job. As she told this story, she kept repeating that this woman was the wife of a pastor. The assumption she had was that if anyone should be expected to be better than others, it should be the leaders of the church.

#13 provided an example of the substandard behavior of the Christian pastors he knows:

> My impression is that [a large percentage of] pastors in Taiwan see their work as just a way to make a living.... When I was overseas maybe I just had good luck, but, outside of church services and when they had time, pastors would go and care for the handicapped or the poor. Even though they did not make a lot of money, they were still willing to deny themselves and spend time with you, putting their whole heart into communicating with you.... But pastors in Taiwan come to evangelize only because they have a goal to get more believers. Normally, they are not interested in visiting those older people who cannot give them any benefit. What kind of evangelism is this?

#13 articulated the level of expectations many non-Christian Hakkas have of Christians and related the behavior of Christians to their success or lack of it in gaining converts, opining, "If you want people to believe in Christ, the behavior of Christians must be exemplary so that people are moved to ask, 'Why are you always so joyful and happy? Why are you so successful at whatever you do? Why do your children do so well in school?' Then you can answer, 'It is because I believe in Christ; my family is blessed, everything is going well; I am making a lot of money because I have this source of light. You should come and join me in becoming a Christian.'"

Hakka History

Some of the categorizations Hakka non-Christians make of being Christian access themes and symbols contained in their cultural "stuff" relating to Hakka history. As informants talked in this area, two themes stood out: (1) disadvantaged guests; and (2) shaped by history.

Disadvantaged Guests

As informants talked about the categorizations non-Christian Hakkas make of being Christian, they related their responses to their history of being disadvantaged guests who, because they arrived in Taiwan later than the Hoklos, often struggled to make a living.

One of the differences informants made significant as they constructed being Christian as something that does not easily fit with being Hakka is the dearth of opportunities Hakkas have had to be influenced by Christians. These Hakkas accessed the symbol of "hard life" from their cultural "stuff" and categorized being Christian as something that, because they struggled to make a living and have not had time or opportunities to encounter and explore it, is "unrelated to me." For example, when asked about what his parents said about Christianity when he was young, #7 said his parents knew very little about this religion. He explained, "In the past, thirty or forty years ago, when missionaries first came, when Christianity and Catholicism arrived on the scene, the living standard in Taiwan was very low; everyone was struggling to make a living. It was not like now where, after they eat, people have free time where they can inquire about the church and analyze these teachings. No. Everyone was trying to get enough to eat. They just did their job and did not think about much else."

#5 gave another example, saying that, in the past, the schools that Christians established were for the upper class. He reported that the reason there are fewer Hakkas who are Christians now is because, early on, most Hakkas were poor and very few had opportunities to be exposed to foreign teachings in these schools.

Shaped by History

As informants talked about the negative categorizations of being Christian of some Hakkas, they also connected these responses with the way Hakka history has shaped them.

Stiff-necked Hakka Spirit

Informants constructed conversion to Christianity as difficult for Hakkas to embrace because doing so means changing. Informants accessed the "stiff-necked Hakka spirit" symbol in their cultural "stuff" and said Hakkas categorize conversion to Christianity as a "change to stubbornly resist." For example, #10 said:

> Hakkas are more stubborn than others. . . . When they decide things should be done in a particular way, they are hard to change because they feel this is the way things are. . . . Western religions conflict with Hakkas in the area of ancestor rituals. You Christians

believe venerating ancestors and worshiping other gods is bad and we should not do these things. But Hakkas feel we have all been doing this kind of veneration and worship from the past all the way up until today. It will not be easy to break this firmly established tradition. They will rebel against Christian teaching. Additionally, the more they insist on their own viewpoint and do not try to understand Christianity, the more possibilities for misunderstandings there will be. Not only will they not understand, they will also have significant misunderstandings.

Hardworking

Some of those who are being Hakka categorize being Christian as "something that does not fit with my busy lifestyle." Shaped by history to value working hard, these Hakkas are very busy and do not feel they have the time or energy to go to church. The idea of being required to attend church every Sunday is very unattractive to them. For example, #4 said:

> If someone asked us to go to church, to come and listen and pray, we do not have that much time to let you control and restrict. [Christianity] is hard for Hakkas to accept because you constantly have to go and pray, have meetings, and so forth. The gods we worship . . . it is like we have more freedom. I can burn incense whenever I want. In the morning, I can get up early or later and burn the incense. . . . In the evening, I can burn incense at six, seven, or eight o'clock, it does not matter. . . . Look at those Christians, they are very devout. On Sunday they go to church to pray and stuff. We Hakkas do not have that kind of time because . . . we want to work more. . . . We Hakkas are people who work hard so we do not have that much time.

Shaped by their cultural "stuff" to work hard for the good of their family, some Hakkas make the many activities of the church significant as they construct being Christian as something that does not fit with being Hakka. These Hakkas categorize being Christian as "something that keeps people from working as hard as they should." They view church activities as hindering family members from working hard for the family's benefit, and this neglect makes being Christian unattractive to non-Christian family members. For example, #13 expressed frustration that his Christian wife sometimes does not cook for him and take care of other family matters because she is at church. He said, "I blame the pastor for not teaching my wife properly. This is not okay. Christianity should not be the first priority. She should be taught to take care of her family responsibilities first and then go to church."

The Hakka value of working hard has as its goal gaining wealth for oneself and one's family. Many Hakkas have been shaped to be careful with their money and therefore find the common Christian practice of giving 10 percent of one's income to the church very unattractive. These Hakkas categorize Christianity as "wanting my money." For example, #34 said, "Christians have a practice of giving a tithe, and Hakkas have a big problem with this practice. In an agricultural society, one only bought as much as one had money for. Now [in our more urban society], you can buy a car on credit, you can take out a loan to buy a house, you can buy a lot of things on credit. Often, the money you make is not enough to pay these loans, but if you are a Christian, you still have to give a tenth of your salary to the church."

Adapting

Informants also reported that being Christian is difficult for Hakkas to embrace because they make Christianity's unwillingness to adapt itself to Hakka culture and religions significant. In the context of a world where adapting is very important, Hakkas categorize being Christian as "confining." Rather than adapting to the thinking of Hakkas like other religions do, #2 said that Christianity insists on maintaining differences. She told how her friend asked her why she would want to believe in Christianity when it is so restrictive at certain times (e.g., not allowing the burning of incense in ancestor rituals). This friend felt Christian restrictions did not allow the flexibility necessary for her to respond to different situations. She also thought it strange that one would deliberately insist on being different rather than trying to adapt to those around them.

Family

Because of the high value Hakkas place on filial piety and their ancestors, any differences between practices associated with being Christian and traditional practices often result in becoming a Christian being categorized as "unfilial" and as "turning your back on the ancestors." Each of the four subsections under this theme of family details an aspect of being "unfilial" and "turning your back on your ancestors."

Lack of Respect

Informants reported that many Hakkas make Christians' lack of deference to their parents or the senior members of their clan-grouping significant as they construct being Christian as something that does not fit with being Hakka. Raised in an environment where this kind of deference is assumed or at least considered to be important, those who are being Hakka are often troubled by the actions of younger family members who converted to Christianity or act in Christian ways against the wishes of their parents. Hence, these Hakkas categorize Christians as "disrespectful to elders."

Especially in more traditional families, this habit of seeing things hierarchically often creates conflicts when a young family member converts to Christianity. #17 gave an example of such a conflict that took place in a church where he served. A young man had become a Christian when he was away in college, and after graduation, he moved back home. He secretly attended #17's church for many years, knowing his father would become angry if he found out he had become a Christian. Eventually, this young man decided to get baptized. While preparing for his baptism, he decided he should discuss his plans with his father. Upon hearing about his son's desire to be baptized, his father forbade him from doing so. When his son insisted, the father became furious and threatened that if he took another step towards Christianity, their father-son relationship would be broken. The level of the threat was elevated even further when the father shouted that if his son went through with baptism, he would come to the church during the ceremony and attack his son with a knife. Assuming the hierarchical nature of relationships, this father's expectation was that his son should obey him unquestioningly.

Even those Hakkas who are less traditional in their understanding of hierarchy in family relationships say Christians who ask their parents to change their religious beliefs are being disrespectful to them. #1 made this point when discussing the way his Christian cousin had pressured his parents, #1's aunt and uncle. Believing a junior family member should defer to his parents and allow them to function in their usual manner, #1 was troubled when this cousin put pressure on his parents to convert to Christianity shortly before the death of the mother. #1's thinking his uncle should not have been expected to change his beliefs when in his eighties was confirmed when, after the Christian funeral, this uncle expressed fear that his wife was starving in the afterlife. #1 and other relatives were very angry that his uncle had been put into this situation.

Informants reported that many Hakkas also make the way Christians handle ancestor tablets significant as they construct being Christian as something that does not fit with being Hakka. In the past, when a person converted to Christianity, the ancestor tablet was often taken outside the house and burned in front of all of the neighbors. #17 said that early in his ministry he handled ancestor tablets in this way. The neighbors would say things like, "They are turning their back on their ancestors and their religion. Look, they are destroying and burning their ancestor tablet. That is inconceivable!" Regarding their ancestor tablet as something precious, requiring special care and respect, many of those who are being Hakka are troubled by these kind of Christian practices, leading many Hakkas to categorize Christians as "disrespectful to their ancestors."

#35 told the story of how her grandfather, at a time when they were quite poor, had agreed not to venerate his ancestors as a condition for receiving relief from the Catholic church near his home. One day, the Catholic priest came over and found the ancestor tablet still present. He took the tablet and threw it into a manure pit. #35 reported, "As a result of this experience, my grandparents decided that these foreign religions teach people to disrespect their ancestors. This feeling was deeply ingrained in their hearts, and so that is the reason that, when I wanted to become a Christian, I had so much difficulty. [My grandparents and the rest of my family] were fiercely opposed to me going to church. The actions of the priest came to the forefront of their thinking, and they angrily said that Christians disrespect their ancestors."

#13 also told of a situation where a Christian pastor demanded that the ancestor tablet in a new convert's home be destroyed. He elaborated on the awkward situation that resulted, pointing out that the convert would not be the only one influenced by such an action: "There were other people in his family—brothers, uncles. Those who had not become Christians were in the majority. What were they supposed to do?"

Breaking the Continuity of Incense Fires

Informants also constructed being Christian as something hard for those who are being Hakka to embrace based on the way Hakkas make the refusal of many Christians to use incense significant. Shaped to see continuity with the past through the veneration of ancestors as extremely important and as "the way things are," those who are being Hakka find hard to accept the Christian practice of not using incense. Many Hakkas use the symbol of "incense fires" from their cultural "stuff" and categorize practices associated with being Christian as "breaking the incense fires." #3 reflected the viewpoint of many Hakkas which informants talked about when he succinctly said, "The problem with Christianity is that you are not allowed to use incense."

One of the implications that comes to the minds of these Hakkas when they think about "breaking the incense fires" is that the continuous linkage of their family all the way back to their first ancestors will be broken because of their actions. #7, talking about how he would feel if his son converted to Christianity, said:

> This is the way Hakkas think. . . . I still venerate my ancestors, burning incense daily. If my son converted and did not offer incense anymore . . . well, I just have one son, so of course I cannot accept that. Our ancestor practices have been passed on from one generation to the next. If this tradition stops with my son, of course it would be hard for me to accept. . . . If the continuous ancestral incense fires are broken, if there is no one to continue them, if no one venerates my ancestors, if these fires stop with me, if my grandfather, father, and I have no one to venerate us, if no one venerates at the common mausoleum at Tomb Sweeping when the other relatives are venerating, if my family did not have anyone to take over these veneration practices, this would be a very big and serious problem. . . . I would feel *extremely* ashamed.

Other Hakkas also expressed fear that the ancestors would not protect their family any more if the incense fires were discontinued.

Another implication of "breaking the incense fires" that informants talked about is the perception that doing so will break important family relationships. The perception that these Hakkas have of Christians is that they often do not return when the family gathers for ancestor rituals. This perception is not unfounded. Many Christians do not believe Christians should be present at clan-grouping gatherings where ancestor rituals take place. Christian informants explained that the reason some Christians avoid these gatherings is that their churches encourage them not to attend. Others do not attend because they fear their relatives will pressure them to venerate ancestors in ways that contradict Christian teachings. Still others do not attend because they, wanting to distance themselves from ancestor worship practices, have often not buried their dead in the common mausoleum of their clan-grouping. The absence of Christians at these times is very distasteful to many non-Christian Hakkas. #3 expressed this sentiment, "My generation has no problem accepting [that a Christian does not burn incense]. What I cannot accept is that you do not come back and participate. If you have time, but you do not return for ancestor rituals just because you have become a Christian [that is not acceptable]. . . . [You do not need to burn incense]; bowing is sufficient. I can accept that you do not worship the other gods because you have a different god that you worship. But you cannot change your ancestors; there is no substitute for your ancestors."

When Christians do attend ancestor rituals, the atmosphere is often awkward and sometimes antagonistic when they insist on doing things differently. For those non-Christian Hakkas who look forward to and cherish the sense of belonging and the opportunity to gather with family which these gatherings provide, the prospect of not attending or of attending and having to do things differently because of a belief in Christianity is very unattractive. They do not want to lose touch with or strain relationships with relatives whom they see only at these times.

Not Using the Language of My Ancestors

Some informants made the way many Christian churches do not regularly use the Hakka language significant in constructing being Christian as something which does not fit with being Hakka. Shaped to habitually use Hakka or to view speaking Hakka as very important, informants reported that some Hakkas categorize being Christian as "cold" and "disrespectful to Hakkas."

Informants reported that for those Hakkas who habitually speak Hakka and have limited abilities in other languages, Christians' use of the Mandarin or Hoklo language in their ministries can not only complicate the communication process but also creates a very "cold" feeling. #24 raised as an example the non-Christian parents of Hakka Christians in his church. He said, "When these parents want to convert or we want to reach out to them, they are not comfortable using the Mandarin language. . . . When Hakka is used, it brings a sense of friendliness and familiarity."

#26 gave two other examples of this feeling of "coldness." He told of a group of older Hakkas who did not believe him when he told them their neighbor of many years had become a Christian on his death bed. He said it was only when he used the Hakka language at the funeral that they began to trust him and accept his words. A second example #26 raised is of a funeral that was held in a Hakka area. The pastor of the deceased could not speak Hakka very well, so he used Mandarin in a pre-funeral memorial service for close family members. In doing so, this pastor discovered that all of these relatives were accustomed to speaking Hakka, and that, because of his use of Mandarin, he felt a great distance between himself and the family as he tried to minister to them in their grief. He called #26 to help him so that he could have a Hakka-speaking person lead the funeral service in order to help alleviate this problem.

Informants also talked about how those Hakkas who highly value the Hakka identity relate to the language customs of churches and those representing them. These Hakkas feel Christians should use the Hakka language when the church is in a Hakka area. Some feel not doing so is disrespectful. For example, #13, a non-Christian who has had some contact with the church, said he would welcome Christians (as well as a representative of any religion) to visit him as long as they did not try to speak to him in anything but Hakka. He surmised that anyone would expect the same. Speaking about the language used in church services, #13 said, "If you are a Hakka, and you come to a Hakka area, get up on the church platform, and preach in Mandarin, then you might as well give up right then and there because no one will listen to you. I am certainly not going to listen to you."

#15 talked about how she, after moving back from Taipei to her former hometown in a Hakka area, started to value her Hakka identity more. At the same time, she heard about a church in her area that used the Hakka language. Even though she dislikes most Christians and often tries to stop her non-Hakka Christian husband from attending church, she reported that she had less problems with him attending a Hakka-speaking church. "At least he can hear some Hakka there," she said.

Different from Traditions

Informants said many Hakkas highlight the differences between practices associated with being Christian and the traditions of their families as they construct being Christian as something those who are being Hakka cannot accept. Shaped to habitually do things in certain ways and to see these traditions as "the way we have always done things," Hakkas have a variety of responses as they contemplate change in these ways. Some Hakkas categorize practices associated with being Christian as "impossible." #9 provided an example as he described his interaction with his sister when she refused to burn incense at his mother's funeral, "When you go to church, you do not burn incense, but . . . [with your] mother . . . that is different. It is not the same situation. You can burn incense . . . because she is your own close relative. . . . Do not keep saying the rules say you cannot! Did God really say you absolutely cannot burn incense? That is impossible!" To him, it just did not make sense that the Christian God would not allow a daughter to burn incense at her mother's funeral. He continued to explain, "Now she burns incense. Mother died; . . . my sister is her daughter. Being filial means burning incense." #4 provided another example, "When someone dies, we Hakkas all weep when we are mourning. But the Christians sing. How is it possible that I could sing at a time like this? . . . I cannot accept this. I could not sing, even if I wanted to do so." #7 articulated the position of many Hakkas when they encounter what they perceive as the Christian rejection of the veneration of ancestors: "These are rules of propriety from ancient times. We are required to do these things. One cannot throw them out."

Some Hakkas categorize the variance from traditions which being Christian would require as "unsettling," "strange," or "awkward." Accustomed to habitually performing certain ritual tasks at specific times, these Hakkas anticipate a large upheaval in their routine if changes are made. For example, in the context of talking about Christians not venerating ancestors, #7 said, "These traditions have come down to me [from my ancestors], and every day I burn incense, worship the gods, and venerate the ancestors; at Lunar New Year and on festival days I also do this. If all of a sudden I decided not to continue these practices, I would feel unsettled . . . like there was something I had forgotten, like there was something I have to do that I had not finished yet." #4 described the feelings of Hakkas regarding Christian funerals, saying, "When Hakkas do not burn incense during death rites, they feel very strange . . . this is not their habit." #27, the only son in his family, provided another example. He described his parents' response and the discomfort he felt after telling them he could not burn incense at a Lunar New Year ancestor ritual: "They were not adamant [against me], . . . but they felt awkward . . . when I did this. Of course, I also felt very awkward. They felt it was strange not to burn incense."

When Hakkas encounter the call of Christians to change their traditions and follow Christian ways, some of them draw on the idea in their cultural "stuff" that things should be allowed to evolve slowly and categorize being Christian as "wanting to change too much too fast." #1's reaction after he attended a Christian funeral is an example. As he discussed the funeral service that took place in a church, he repeatedly stated that the Christians tried to change too much in their funeral rituals. For him, the absence of incense was the deciding factor which made the change too great. He declared, "[Burning incense] is something all Chinese do. We automatically burn incense [at a funeral]." For many Hakkas, the step of forsaking the burning of incense and ancestor veneration is too huge for them to make. #10 articulated her feelings on this prospect, "I am more than fifty-years-old. I have venerated my ancestors for a long time. If you want me to come and listen to your teaching and are willing to let me continue this ancestor veneration, I might become a Christian. If you want me to get baptized and I have to cut myself off from my past practices, I will probably not be willing to become a Christian."

Reciprocal Relationships

Many of the categorizations Hakka non-Christians make of being Christian relate to the value reflected in their cultural "stuff" on reciprocity in their relationships with: (1) people who are thought of as "us," (2) the ancestors, and (3) the gods.

Related to "Us"

Many Hakkas construct being Christian as hard for Hakkas to accept as they focus on the way Christians do not fulfill their roles appropriately in their relationships with others who are included in "us." These Hakkas categorize Christians as "not acting like 'us.'" When Christians do not follow the normal practices of "us," they do not fulfill the expectations that come with being in relationship with others, thus weakening or even jeopardizing these relationships.

Informants said a death in the family is one significant occasion where differences between Christians and the expectations of these "us" who are being Hakka are often encountered. When the deceased is a Christian, rather than following the practice of allowing the clan to make all the funeral arrangements, Christian family members expect there should be a Christian funeral and turn to the pastor of their church for leadership. Informants reported that even under normal circumstances, this expectation is difficult, but when the deceased family member converted to Christianity shortly before their death, this expectation is especially hard for non-Christian members of "us" to accept. In addition, the practice that some Christians have of burying Christian family members separate from the mausoleum of their clan-grouping is significantly different from the Hakka way where the bones or ashes of family members are buried together. Many non-Christians also perceive that Christian funerals are contrary to the common interests of "us" because they lack the significant money-making opportunities that non-Christian funerals provide for members of the clan who are involved in related businesses (e.g., providing food, musicians, tents, and other commonly used things).

When the deceased is a non-Christian, Christian family members often do not cooperate fully, if at all, in the rituals and other activities that the family leaders plan. For example, Christians do not act like "us" when they refuse to use incense in funeral rituals or to contribute money to hire a Daoist priest to perform certain rituals. They do not act like "us" when, for various reasons, they do not attend clan-grouping gatherings for ancestor rituals. #22, a Christian, reported the response of non-Christian clan members to the absence of Christians at important clan events, "If you do not attend [the ancestor rituals at Tomb Sweeping and Lunar New Year], your relatives will say you now belong to a different family." #19 pointed out another difference, saying that non-Christian Hakkas often are troubled when their Christian relatives are not as interested as they are in spending money on maintaining or remodeling the mausoleum of their clan-grouping or other ancestor-related things.

Informants also pointed out that some Hakkas view Christians as not acting like "us" when they give money and energy to the church rather than to "us." #13 offered the following example:

> When a person in his sixties or seventies from a family with five or six brothers hears several of his good friends say to him, "Believing in Christ is good," he may listen to them [and consider the possibility of becoming a Christian]. But then one day, when his clan decides to build an ancestral hall, he will be stimulated to think, "Oh my! If I become a Christian and invest all of my energy and donations in Christianity rather than investing with my ancestors, my Daoism, and my many brothers, . . . [as I get older, they will say], 'Those of you who are Christians [and did not give toward building the ancestral hall], do not plan on being placed in the common mausoleum.'" As a result, this man will be afraid of converting.

#13 told of several Hakkas who previously were Christians or were interested in Christianity but have returned to their old ways, being unwilling to jeopardize this "us" relationship with their clan-grouping.

Related to Ancestors

Some Hakkas notice differences between the way Christians relate to their ancestors and their own ways of interacting with ancestors and make these differences significant as they construct being Christian as something difficult for Hakkas to embrace. Informants pointed out that some Hakkas view the relationship between themselves and the ancestors as a reciprocal relationship and categorize what they perceive as the refusal of Christians to venerate their ancestors to be "neglect" and therefore "unfilial" and "turning your back on your ancestors."

Informants reported that many Hakkas feel if they follow the ways of Christians and do not worship their ancestors, the needs of their ancestors will go unmet. #1 provided the example of an older relative who, because the Christian funeral of his wife did not include food offerings, was very troubled because she might possibly be starving. #4 described Hakka feelings regarding Christian funerals: "If Hakkas do not burn spirit money for the deceased or provide some meat for them to eat, they will feel very apologetic . . . they will feel that the deceased will be deprived." The wife of #23 told of a relative who converted to Christianity, but, while she herself did not burn incense and make offerings for her deceased husband, she still prepared everything and made sure someone worshiped him at the proper times. This relative did not want her deceased husband to be neglected.

Some Hakkas fear they themselves will starve after they die if no one worships them, and this fear motivates them to find means of ensuring that the next generation will adequately care for them. Hence, it is disturbing when a son, especially an only son, becomes a Christian and does not want to participate in ancestor rituals.

Informants related that many Hakkas feel the Christian refusal to meet the needs of the ancestors ignores or forgets the debt they owe to their ancestors. In this vein, some Hakkas accused Christians of "turning your back on your ancestors" or of "being unfilial." For example, #19 said, "[When the ancestor rituals take place], people will say to [Christians], 'Everyone else is venerating the ancestors. Why are you not venerating?' They will say things like, 'You are so unfilial. In the past, your father loved you so much. Will it kill you to venerate him a little bit now? . . . Your father paid for you to go to college. Are you really unwilling to venerate him a bit now?'"

Informants reported that many Hakkas also feel if they follow the ways of the Christians, they will forfeit the blessing and protection of the ancestors and/or misfortune may fall upon them. For example, when #9 saw that his Christian sister was unwilling to perform certain ritual acts at her mother's funeral, one of his concerns was that relatives would blame her when they encountered misfortune in their lives. These relatives worried that the mother would punish them all for her daughter's unfilial behavior at her funeral.

Related to Gods

Some of those who are being Hakka make significant the differences between their ways of relating with the gods and the Christian perspective on these gods. These Hakkas categorized Christians as "those who do not worship the gods." For example, #3 reported that when his family went to worship the gods at the temple (a practice which he emphasized he had been involved in since he was very young), his Christian relatives did not go in and worship. He said, "It was as if they were not willing to recognize these gods as gods."

Informants revealed that there are several implications of this categorization. When Hakkas notice that Christians do not worship the gods, they naturally view these Christians as "others" rather than "us." #34 stated, "Hakkas say the Christians, those who do not worship the gods, those who do not use incense, are people from a different country. They are different from us. . . . When they say 'a different country,' they do not mean a different nation. Rather they mean persons from a different world."

Another implication of the categorization that Christians do not worship the gods is that these Hakkas do not dare to convert to Christianity because they fear doing so might cause them to lose the blessing and protection of the gods. For example, #36 talked about an older woman who was afraid of going to church because doing so would offend the god her family worshiped on a daily basis. Because she had been experiencing some health problems and was unable to burn the daily incense to this god, she feared she had already offended this god. To attend a church would be an even worse affront. #20 says, "[A potential convert] will wonder if the gods that they served before will do something to them. . . . They fear if they leave their original gods, something [bad] will happen to them."

Everyone

As informants discussed the reasons Hakkas construct being Christian as something hard for those who are being Hakka to accept, the cultural value placed on "everyone" often surfaced. Informants' words in this topic area will be grouped into the following themes: (1) following what everyone does, (2) acting to gain the favor of everyone, and (3) working to avoid the disfavor of everyone.

Following Everyone

Informants reported that many of those who are being Hakka categorize being Christian as "something everyone does not embrace." Many informants also stated that there are very few Christians in their communities and clan as well as among those who are being Hakka in general. For those who are in the habit of looking to everyone around them to determine how they should live, the fact that being Christian is accepted by just a small minority of people is a huge obstacle. To follow a small minority belief, especially when it is so different from and conflicts with what everyone is doing, is contrary to the deeply felt desire to conform to the practices and expectations of everyone. #19 explained that even when people are attracted to your descriptions of Christianity, when they see everyone around them worshiping the gods or venerating ancestors, it is difficult for them not to participate with them. Even if they wonder if these rituals are really necessary or meaningful, they still prepare the offerings and participate because everyone is doing so. One of the feelings common among everyone in the circles of most Hakkas is that, in the words of #3, "Not being able to venerate your ancestors is unacceptable." #3 reported, "In my experience, the reason Christianity has not grown fast, especially in the past when it first entered Hakka areas, is because of this prohibition."

Because many of those who are being Hakka are in the habit of listening to everyone, when misinformation about Christianity spreads, many people believe it. For example, several informants raised the perception many Hakkas have that Christians do strange things to the corpse (e.g., twist the head around so that it is facing backwards) during their funeral ceremonies. #13 reported, "Christianity is like a branch, being pulled this way and that.... The things everyone is saying create fear; some people are naive, some are stupid; when they suddenly hear these things, they believe them and do not dare to convert."

The Favor of Everyone

Many of those who are being Hakka categorize belief in Christianity as "something that creates challenges in the area of gaining the favor of everyone." The more being Christian is viewed negatively by everyone, the greater these challenges. For those who habitually emphasize bringing face and honor to ancestors in the eyes of everyone, who push their children to achievements that will bring them face in the eyes of everyone, and who work hard to hide things that will cause them to lose face in the eyes of everyone, identifying themselves with something (e.g., being Christian) that may jeopardize their face is ludicrous. For example, Christians are often accused of being unfilial, something #19 reported as causing a major loss of face, because they do not venerate their ancestors. #35 told about the reaction of her mother when #35 married a Christian. #35 and her fiancée planned a simple ritual for their wedding day. They wanted to kneel and show respect to #35's ancestors and use this means to express their thanks to her family for raising her. This kind of ceremony is common among Hakkas. Usually, incense is burned during this ritual, something #35 had told her mother in advance that they would not do. When they arrived in front of the ancestor tablet on their wedding day, they discovered her mother had covered the ancestor tablet with a big cloth. #35 said, "She did not want my ancestors to see . . . something that would cause them to lose so much face."

One of the venues those who are being Hakka typically use to display their filial piety to everyone is the funeral of their parents. In this venue, practices associated with being Christian are often quite different from the practices of everyone. Traditional Christian funerals are known to be solemn occasions, often very similar to a normal church service, rather than being bustling with noise and excitement, the funeral environment typically valued by everyone. For example, #17 remarked that Christians do not hire mourners to wail loudly at key points in the funeral. This diversion from customary practices not only makes it hard to gain the favor of everyone, but can also lead to criticism like, "Christians do not even cry when their parents pass away." #19 reported that many non-Christians do not understand Christian funerals. This lack of understanding is especially troubling for non-Christians when they feel everyone is watching at the time of a funeral.

#19 also pointed out that, rather than gaining face at funerals, Christians often lose face. This venue can become a public opportunity for the community to express their opposition to being Christian. As an example, he told about Christian funerals he has attended where there were non-Christian Hakkas who sat in the back of the funeral parlor and conversed loudly with each other in order to disrupt the service.

Garnering the Disfavor of Everyone

Informants also frequently talked about how those who are being Hakka categorize being Christian as "something that brings the disfavor of everyone." For example, #21 said, "Would anyone dare to not venerate the ancestors? The older generation would be very unhappy, so they would talk." Disfavor is often expressed by everyone "talking," a force that is extremely hard to resist among those who are being Hakka. This "talking" includes gossiping about the subject, or scolding, berating, or shaming the subject directly. Consequently, the fear that change will result in everyone talking is a strong force for fixity in the way Hakkas relate to being Christian.

#35 provided many examples of the power inherent in everyone talking. For example, as she talked about her own conversion to Christianity and her desire to have a Christian funeral for her grandfather, a death-bed convert, she said, "The power of the clan suppressed me." When asked to expand on this power, she said:

> What I mean is the power of public opinion.... Everyone will talk about you, saying that you are unfilial, that you are breaking faith and neglecting your ancestors, and that you have forgotten who your ancestors really are. They will ... attack you. One minute, one uncle will talk about you, the next moment another uncle will talk about you, and another moment, someone else from your clan will talk about you. Could you bear this? People keep talking about you, and every time they berate you, you get so many hurts that, in the end, you give in and cannot continue to insist on your way.... You think, "Why do I want to have so many people talking about me? ... Do I want to keep persisting?" Everyone will have an unrelenting stream of representatives coming to see you.

In this vein, #28 argued, "People do not necessarily always follow their parents' desire just because they want to be filial. They do so because they do not want to listen to their constant scolding all day long."

#19 gave another example of the power of everyone talking, expressing their disfavor, which Christians often face: "When you do not go with everyone to participate in the ancestor rituals [e.g., at Chinese New Year], the pressure is huge. The older family members will scold and berate you, many other relatives will talk about you behind your back, and your parents will say that you, this unfilial child, are not willing to go and participate. You end up with a huge problem and complications not only in your relationship with your parents but also with those in your clan."

#35 gave another example of the power of everyone talking when she described part of the pressure she received from her siblings when she became a Christian, "My brothers and sisters cried and said, 'Why do you insist on wanting something that is so bad? . . . Sister, they are tricking you; do you not see what is happening?' My older sister cried and said, 'How can you do this? Christianity is not something that is our kind of thing; why do you insist on wanting it?' My heart is not made of stone. When they cried like this, I really had no way out."

Another way the disfavor of everyone is expressed is in blaming. Informants reported that whenever misfortune strikes someone in the clan, a convert to Christianity may be blamed as the cause of this misfortune. #21 gave an example of this when talking about one of her relatives who became a Christian. This relative began to use flowers rather than the normal sacrifices used in ancestor rituals, and as a result of this change, whenever misfortune struck, people would blame her and her practice of using flowers for bringing misfortune on them. The pressure became so great that she finally gave up using flowers and started preparing sacrifices again. #35 told about her friend whose Hakka boss worshiped the hungry ghosts on the fifteenth day of ghost month: "He prepared everything, and then each of the employees came out to participate, all except for my friend. The boss came in looking for her and asked her, 'Why are you not coming out to worship?' She told him she did not believe in that kind of thing. Her boss replied, 'What happens if by some slim chance our company has a problem? What will you do then?'" #35 said the boss's meaning was that if something bad happened, her friend could be blamed because she did not cooperate and join in the worship of the hungry ghosts. #35 said no one would dare not go and worship when he put things that way.

Reflecting on Fixity and Fluidity in the Categorizations of Non-Christian Hakkas

This section explores the fixity and fluidity of ethnic identification present in non-Christian Hakka categorizations of being Christian. Reflecting on this fixity and fluidity can provide insights into tensions between being Hakka and being Christian.

Fixity

Several dimensions of the fixity of ethnic identification described in the literature on ethnic identification can be seen in the categorizations constructed by Hakka non-Christians.

The Way Things Are

One of the most common sources of fixity in the categorizations Hakkas make of being Christian is the assumed nature of the way they see themselves and the world around them. The categorizations of being Christian raised by informants surface in encounters with Christians and Christianity because they are perceived to advocate something that, in the minds of Hakkas, does not fit well with "the way things are." For example, the assumption that all religions are good and have the same goal of helping people to be good is the foundation that led #15 to categorize the exclusive Christian message as "offensive" and Christians who did bad things as "substandard" or "hypocritical." The assumption that certain traditions are "the way things are done" led #9 to categorize the Christian idea that his sister could not burn incense at the funeral of her mother as "impossible." The given nature of the understanding among Hakkas that the favor of everyone is important led the colleague of #2 to categorize being Christian as "confining" and to puzzle why #2 would even consider conversion to Christianity. The way the reciprocal nature of relationships is embedded in the thinking of Hakkas led the Hakkas #19 talked about to categorize the unwillingness of their Christian relatives to participate in ancestor rituals as "unfilial" and to berate them for not being willing to repay their debt to their deceased parents.

Deep Human Needs

Another source of fixity underlying Hakka categorizations of being Christian is the way current practices, the ones that those who are being Christian seek to abolish or change, meet deep needs—needs such as wanting to be connected to others in deep and lasting ways, such as desiring to have stability in a changing world, such as hungering for familiarity rather than uncertainty, and such as being perceived positively by others. For example, many Hakkas categorized practices associated with being Christian as "breaking the incense fires." There is much about the incense fires of ancestor veneration that meets deep needs for Hakkas. Seeing oneself as a part of a continuing line of ancestors that can be documented in the ancestor record and on the ancestor tablet, relishing the shared memories and relationships that have been built with others through the veneration of the same ancestors, enjoying the fellowship each time relatives gather to burn incense in ancestor rituals, valuing the help that those whose relationships revolve around venerating the same ancestors give to each other, and appreciating the help in making important transitions that ancestor rituals and clan cooperation at the time of the death of a family member provide, one naturally resists anything that might introduce a "break" in these practices. When Hakkas categorize being Christian as "wanting to change too much too fast," they do so because change introduces uncertainty and removes them from the practices that are familiar to them. When those who are being Hakka categorize being Christian as "foreign to Hakkas," one of the dimensions of this foreignness is that it is unfamiliar and not understood. When Hakkas categorize being Christian negatively because of the potential that doing so will make it hard to gain the favor of or will garner the disfavor of everyone, they reveal that they value being perceived positively by everyone.

Reifying Christianity

Another dimension of fixity evident in these negative categorizations is the way Christianity is reified based on limited experience with and understanding of Christians. For example, Hakkas who categorized being Christian as "offensive" often based their perspective on the actions of the Christians they had encountered and assumed were representative of all of Christianity. When Hakkas categorized practices associated with being Christian as "breaking the incense fires," they often assumed that, based on what they had heard from others or on personal encounters, no converts to Christianity would attend when the relatives gather for ancestor rituals. Those Hakkas who categorized being Christian as "something everyone does not embrace" often did so because they misunderstood or had an incomplete understanding of what Christians do at the time of a death. For example, some believed that Christians do strange things to the corpse or that all Christian funerals are identical. Those who are being Hakka were often unaware of the diversity of practices associated with being Christian, and, consequently, they related to this religion as a homogeneous whole that was hard to accept.

Accessible Ethnic Label

Another form of fixity evident in these categorizations is the way that, when many of these Hakkas encounter cultural differences in certain areas and see the connections between Christianity and Westerners, they often construct being Christian as "other" because the "not Hakka" label is so easily accessible. Rather than engaging and exploring the differences, they focus on the foreign origin, connections, and the unfamiliar nature of practices associated with being Christian, categorize Christianity as "foreign to Hakkas" and as "good for foreigners but not for Hakkas," and do not seek to add to their limited understanding of this religion. Other less accessible categorizations are not used. For example, Christianity could be categorized as "one of the many religions that Hakkas follow," a categorization that would make it more likely that Hakkas would engage and explore this religion more deeply at some point.

Fluidity

The dimensions of the fluidity of ethnic identification described in the literature are also present in the categorizations constructed by Hakka non-Christians. As informants talked about Hakka non-Christian categorizations of being Christian, they also discussed and/or provided examples of fluidity in these categorizations. They pointed out that not every Hakka categorizes being Christian in the same way. The following examples are those that surfaced most often as informants talked about these categorizations.

Fluidity as Individual Hakkas Change Their Categorizations

Fluidity stemming from the active nature of the ethnic actor in ethnic identification can be seen in the non-Christian Hakka categorizations of being Christian. Informants and the Hakkas they discussed provided examples of non-Christians changing their categorizations as they sought to present themselves in ways that bring them the best results. For example, #28 told how his father was originally *very* opposed to him going to church but changed his mind when #28's daughter, a Christian, tested into one of the top girl's high schools in Taiwan. As a result, all of the neighbors and relatives praised #28's father and often gushed to him, "Your granddaughter is *really* great!" He gained much face in the eyes of everyone and credited his granddaughter's success to the fact that she was a Christian and that she had spent a lot of time with the pastor's family next door. Consequently, rather than seeing being Christian as something unacceptable, #28's father began to see being Christian as a source of blessing for him and his family. #28 reported that his father started to come to church quite frequently after this development and often said to others, "Being a Christian is not a bad thing." #28's father eventually became a Christian.

Fluidity as Hakkas Respond Differently to Being Christian

Fluidity which arises as different ethnic actors respond differently in the process of ethnic identification is also evident in the non-Christian Hakka categorizations of being Christian. One example of this kind of fluidity is the variety of responses that non-Christian Hakkas have when Christian family members are unwilling to use incense in ancestor rituals. By refusing to use incense, these Christians are, either implicitly or explicitly, categorizing this practice as "unacceptable." While some, primarily older, Hakkas respond by categorizing these Christians' unwillingness to burn incense as "breaking the incense fires" and therefore unfilial and unacceptable, others are willing to accept those who do not use incense. For example, informants reported that some Hakkas are troubled if someone in their family or clan-grouping does not use incense in ancestor rituals, and so they use the power available to them to pressure this person into using incense. Other non-Christian Hakkas in the same situation have a different strategy. They are willing to consider the possibility of not needing to use incense in ancestor rituals and do not necessarily categorize Christians who do not burn incense as "breaking the incense fires." For example, while many middle-aged and young Hakkas still burn incense when they attend ancestor rituals, they are willing to accept when other family members attend but do not burn incense. These Hakkas often say, "One's heart is most important."

Informants provided several other examples of differing categorizations. #2's colleagues categorized being Christian as "confining," while #2 was open to exploring this religion. #35 was willing to embrace Christianity even though she knew this choice was "different from everyone" and consequently, would result in the disfavor of everyone. This attitude contrasts with Hakkas whom other informants talked about who dared not convert because they were unwilling to take that risk. Many

Hakkas categorize being Christian as foreign because practices associated with being Christian go against Hakka traditions. But when #9 was asked if he categorized Christianity as a Western religion, he said, "We do not feel that way . . . the people we know. The way I look at things is that this is a different time. You can believe what you want to believe; everyone chooses for oneself."

As informants discussed differences in the way Hakkas view being Christian, they provided many examples of how different factors affect things. For example, when #15 was told about a Hakka who categorized being Christian as "foreign to Hakkas" and the refusal of Christians to provide sacrifices and burn incense for a newly deceased family member as "neglect" and "being unfilial," she responded by asking many questions about this Hakka—questions about this person's age, gender, occupation, education level, and whether or not this person had grown up in a rural area—to confirm the relationship in her mind between this categorization and the factors that were influencing this person. To her, the fact that this Hakka was an older businessman who was not highly educated and had received his primary socialization in a rural area was consistent with his appraisal of being Christian.

The fluidity in categorizations that results from differences in age was the most common of informants' comments in this area. For example, older Hakkas were often presented as being resistant to change in traditional practices. Middle-aged Hakkas were characterized as being more open to change but also as continuing many of the traditional practices out of respect for the older generation. Younger Hakkas were presented to be the least involved in these traditional practices, and informants often suggested that it is possible that in the future, younger generations of Hakkas will embrace being Christian.

Another source of fluidity in non-Christian Hakka categorizations of being Christian that informants raised is differences in places of residence. #17 said, "Most Hakkas who become Christians do so when they leave their homes for business purposes, for school, and for work." For those who live in rural areas, the pressure to continue traditional practices is greater than for those in urban areas. #25 explained:

> In the country, everyone knows you, and if you become a Christian, your neighbors will push you aside, thinking you have betrayed their traditional beliefs. . . . People living in Taiwan's cities do not have this problem because they do not live in a small community.

No one knows their neighbors on either side of them, so they do not have this kind of pressure. If they go overseas, this pressure is less evident. If they want to become a Christian, the elders in their family will not be at their side obstructing them; their relatives and friends will not be opposing their actions. Consequently, it is a bit easier.

#34 provided an example of this pressure in a rural area as she talked about the reason why her younger brother does not dare to become a Christian. She said, "If you could see the place where he lives, you would know the reason. His neighbors are all his aunts, uncles, and cousins. . . . Even though he is bored with the veneration, he still forces himself to participate. He goes out and buys offerings that have been prepared by others. He feels he would lose face if he did not participate in these ceremonies with the rest of the extended family." #23's description of the difficulties of starting a church in a rural Hakka town also revealed why rural Hakkas are more likely than urbanites to categorize being Christian as "something that will bring the disfavor of everyone" and hence, as something they dare not pursue,

> It is very hard to plant a church in [that town]. Why is it so hard? Because people are afraid they will not be able to satisfactorily explain themselves to those in their clan-grouping. There have probably been close to twenty people [since the beginning of ministry in that town] who have wanted to become Christians, but when they thought of the pressure to burn incense to their ancestors that they would receive from their relatives and others, they dared not convert. [In this environment], it takes the faith of a martyr to become a Christian.

Several informants also pointed out that it was much easier for someone to become a Christian if they went to live in another country. There they are more likely to be outside the influence and scrutiny of everyone at home and have more opportunities to come into contact with Christians.

An additional factor influencing those living in rural areas is that there are often fewer opportunities to have contact with Christianity and Christians. Regarding this factor, #16 said, "In Hakka areas, everyone follows everyone else and does not want to change. They do not try to understand Christianity and have little contact with Christians. If they had more contact, they would probably gradually be more willing to convert." Often, those churches that do exist are not very visible, and church members are not active participants in the life of their communities. For example, #13 reported that the Christian church that his wife attends in their small rural town is very disconnected from the rest of the community. He related how Christians there hire only Christian workers (e.g., building contractors) even if they are not as skilled as non-Christian workers in the same field and how his wife's church never sets up a booth at community events to provide people with an opportunity to have more contact with Christianity and Christians.

Another factor that contributes fluidity to the non-Christian categorizations of being Christian is the influence of differences in level of education. Those who as children received little formal education have also had less exposure to outside influences and, as a result, are more traditional in their thinking. For example, in the context of explaining her mother's strong opposition to her conversion to Christianity, #35 said, "My mother never went to school, so she was very traditional in her thinking. The things her parents and her mother-in-law taught her she insisted on continuing. She feels she has to hold on to these things and cannot change." Through education, some of the traditional practices of Hakkas that differ from practices associated with being Christian are challenged. For example, #8 reported,

> As a result of the influence of educators, my generation feels . . . when you burn a huge stack of spirit money, it creates a lot of pollution. We think this way, but the older generation does not. They feel one must definitely burn spirit money. . . . Actually, burning spirit money is not necessary. My opinion is that burning is only efficacious for someone because they believe in it sincerely. The feeling of my generation is that when you worship, if your heart is there and is communicating with the spirits of the ancestors, that is enough.

A final factor that contributes to differences in the categorizations that non-Christian Hakkas have of being Christian is differences in the status someone has in society. Those who are more independent because of their status are less likely to make cultural differences between being Hakka and being Christian significant and construct being Christian as something not for Hakkas. #23 gave the example of a retired politician who became a Christian. This person's status in society allowed her more freedom to choose to convert to Christianity than other women her age who were deeply dependent on their clan-grouping.

Fluidity in the Meaning of Symbols

Another kind of fluidity in ethnic identification that can be seen in non-Christian Hakka categorizations of being Christian is the way the symbols used have different meanings. The symbol of burning incense is an example. Two groups of non-Christians may both burn incense in ancestor rituals but attach slightly different meanings to this practice. For the first group of Hakkas, burning incense is seen as an indispensable part of expressing one's filial piety to one's ancestors. For example, #9 said, "Being filial means burning incense." For #1, the failure to burn incense at a Christian funeral was "changing [the culture] too much." For the second group of Hakkas, burning incense is viewed rather as one possible way among many to express one's filial piety to one's ancestors. For these Hakkas, gathering for ancestor rituals remains important, but those who use other methods to express their filial piety are also accepted. For example, when #4 was asked about whether people would feel a family member who did not burn incense was unacceptable, he said, "Not anymore. Things are much more open in this day and age." #14 reported that to him, the Christian practice of bowing while holding flowers and bowing with a stick of burning incense were equally acceptable.

Concluding Remarks

This chapter focused on the negative categorizations non-Christian Hakkas in northwestern Taiwan use to construct "Christianity" as something not easy for Hakkas to embrace. These categorizations were detailed in the first section of this chapter, organized around the five themes used to discuss the shared symbols of being Hakka in chapter 4. In the second section of this chapter, the fixity and fluidity present in these categorizations was raised and discussed.

Under the first theme of "Christianity," the categorizations of "foreign to Hakkas" and "a good religion for Westerners but not for Hakkas" were shown to emerge out of a lack of exposure to things "Christian." Christianity's foreign connections were shown to be made significant as being Christian is categorized as "inferior and barbarian" and as "being disloyal to one's own." The categorizations that Christians are "offensive" and that being Christian is "unnecessary" were shown to be rooted in the assumption found in the cultural "stuff" of being Hakka that all religions are good. The Hakka non-Christian categorizations of Christians as "substandard" and "hypocritical" were also raised, and the connection between them and the Hakka cultural stuff's assumption that all religions teach one to be good was pointed out.

"Hakka history" was the second theme used to group the negative categorizations of non-Christian Hakkas in this section. Shaped by and accessing symbols from their cultural "stuff" like "hard life," "stiff-necked Hakka spirit," "hardworking," and "adapting," Hakkas were shown to categorize being Christian as "unrelated to me," "wanting my money," "confining," "something that does not fit with my busy lifestyle," as well as "something that keeps people from working as hard as they should," and conversion to Christianity as "change to stubbornly resist."

Under the third theme of "family," the ways Hakka non-Christians negatively categorize being Christian as "unfilial" and as "turning your back on your ancestors" were raised and discussed. In this vein, informants raised the categorizations that Christians are "disrespectful to their elders" and "disrespectful to their ancestors" and that following practices associated with being Christian means "breaking the incense fires." Some Hakka non-Christians were also shown to categorize practices associated with being Christian as "cold" and "disrespectful of Hakkas" when the Hakka language is not used and to view Christian demands that taken-for-granted practices should be changed as "impossible," "unsettling," "strange," "awkward," and as "wanting to change too much too fast."

The categorizations placed under "reciprocal relationships," the fourth theme raised in this section, were revealed to emerge out of obligations that many non-Christian Hakkas feel towards "us," their ancestors, and the gods. Hakka non-Christians were seen to categorize Christians as "not acting like 'us'" and "those who do not worship the gods" and the refusal of Christians to venerate and care for their ancestors in the socially accepted way as "neglect" and therefore "unfilial" and "turning your back on your ancestors."

Under the fifth theme of "everyone," the negative categorizations that reflect the high value many Hakka non-Christians place on the habits and opinions of the majority of people who surround them were brought into focus. Being Christian was shown to be categorized in this area as "something that everyone does not embrace," "something that creates challenges in the area of gaining the favor of everyone," and "something that will bring the disfavor of everyone."

In the second section of this chapter, the fixity and fluidity that can be found in the negative categorizations constructed by Hakka non-Christians was highlighted and discussed. Fixity in being Hakka as it relates to being Christian was traced to the way Hakkas are shaped by their cultural "stuff" to see certain habits, traditions, practices, and ways of thinking as commonsensical and necessary and to notice differences between being Hakka and being Christian that they make significant as they categorize being Christian as something hard for Hakkas to embrace. Fixity in being Hakka was also found to have roots in the way the current habits of Hakkas meet deep needs. The way Hakka non-Christians reified Christians and viewed being Christian as a homogeneous whole was also revealed as a dimension of the fixity found in being Hakka. In addition, fixity in being Hakka was shown to be tied to the accessibility of the ethnic label of "not Hakka."

Fluidity in being Hakka as it relates to being Christian was highlighted in the way individual Hakkas can change their categorizations over time and in the way Hakkas respond with diversity to the same cultural differences they encounter in the things they associate with being Christian because of the different factors influencing them. The variety of meanings that can be associated with the same symbol was also shown to be a kind of fluidity present in being Hakka.

6

Christian Hakkas in Northwestern Taiwan in the Context of Negative Categorizations of Being Christian

THE THIRD STEP IN exploring tensions between being Hakka in northwestern Taiwan and being Christian is to look closely at the way Hakka Christians respond in the context of the negative categorizations that non-Christian Hakkas have of being Christian. The data presented in this section comes from responses informants gave to questions related to research question 3, "How are Hakka Christians in northwestern Taiwan responding in the context of tensions between being Hakka and being Christian?" The attitudes and actions of Christian Hakkas that surfaced in the comments of informants are arranged in separate sections according to the following three themes: (1) the variety in the importance placed on Hakka in ministries, (2) challenging non-Christian categorizations of Christianity, and (3) constructing Hakka in order to justify prioritizing ministry to Hakkas. At the end of this chapter, the lens of the literature on ethnic identification is used to highlight the way the actions of Hakka Christians discussed in the previous three sections can be seen as a part of the process of ethnic identification.

Variety in the Importance Placed on Hakka in Ministries

Informants revealed that Hakka Christian leaders vary in the importance they place on Hakka in their ministries. Some make the Hakka aspect of their ministry primary and significant, while for others, the Hakka dimension of their ministries is balanced with other ministry priorities or completely set aside as they pursue other burdens or interests.

Focusing on Hakka

Informants reported that, in the context of negative categorizations of being Christian, some Hakka Christian leaders sometimes choose to make an ethnic distinction, namely Hakka, significant in their ministries—making evangelizing Hakkas rather than one of the other ethnic groups in the context around them the focal point of their ministries. Other possible non-ethnic foci (e.g., denomination, geographical location, class, age group) are seen as secondary. For example, rather than saying that their desire is to reach young families, intellectuals, the working class, a certain community, or to have an "X" denomination church in a particular city or town, these leaders articulate something like, "Our goal is to evangelize Hakkas," or "This church/group/institution/ministry is for Hakkas."

The actions of many informants or other Hakka Christian leaders they discussed reflect the importance some of these leaders place on distinguishing Hakkas from other ethnic groups and focusing on them as opposed to something else. These leaders who make this ethnic distinction significant are primarily those who are heavily promoting, supporting, and/or involved in the Hakka Mission Seminary and efforts coordinated by the Christian Hakka Evangelical Association (CHEA). Some examples of these efforts include the translation of the Hakka Bible, the compilation of Hakka hymnbooks, the composition of new Hakka songs and other worship resources, the preparation and sales of Hakka music recordings, the organization of a Hakka choir, and the planning of seminars and other events and programs where Hakka is the emphasis. These Hakka Christian leaders often seek to use the Hakka language in sermons and Bible studies, providing a translation into Mandarin for those who do not speak Hakka. They are often involved in the development, use, and/or promotion of contextualized ancestor rituals. They usually desire to read and use the portions of the Hakka Bible which have already been translated and distribute them to others. They often challenge other Hakka Christians to become involved in ministering to Hakkas and encourage those Christian Hakkas who do not speak Hakka to learn so that they can become more effective in evangelizing Hakkas.

Balancing Hakka with Other Pressing Priorities

As informants talked about the ways these Hakka Christian leaders relate to Hakka in their ministries, they revealed that there are many of these leaders who view ministry to Hakkas as only one of many priorities. The fluidity of ethnic identification is evident as these leaders balance their Hakka identity with other things they value. Much of the pressure that informants talked about related to the maintenance and expansion of churches in light of the fact that emphasizing Hakka was often perceived to make it hard for a church to grow and effectively reach out. A phrase that often surfaced was "the market for Hakka is very small." For example, #22 reported about the situation where his church is located, saying, "In [the area where my church is located], only 20 percent of the residents are Hakka. They are a minority. If we focus on Hakka, we will be really lonely. . . . I feel that, living in a city, the people we touch each day and who are interested in our community outreach efforts are so varied. If we focus on Hakka, we will chase some of these people away." When asked about whether or not he thought he would participate in planning a large-scale joint contextualized memorial service (described in greater detail below), #22, a strong advocate of this kind of event, said he was in "a bit of a quandary." He told how people are very busy and noted that his church is not made up entirely of Hakkas, saying, "Sometimes, even the Hakkas in our own churches are not that supportive. . . . The older Hakka Christians in my church have 'cooled off' and do not set a good model for others. . . . When I am focusing on Hakka in these outreaches and the Hakkas in my church are not supportive (the non-Hakkas are more supportive), I feel a little embarrassed." #22 continued, discussing how even when Hakka is emphasized and some Hakkas are attracted and attend, that does not mean Hakka is the primary factor that continues to attract or keep them attending:

> They will look at how this church fits with their system of relationships; they will look at the facilities; they will look at the worship style; they will consider many different things. Maybe they think Hakka is important, but they are conservative. When they see that your church is one where people jump and dance [during worship times], they will not feel at home and may leave. Maybe they have a very strong Hakka identity, but they feel your church is not very supportive of [one political party or another], and so they will stop coming. Or they do not like the pastor or someone else in the church, and they will leave because of that.

#25 agreed with this assessment, reporting that just because someone is Hakka does not mean he/she will be strongly attracted to Hakka things. Discussing ministry using Hakka music, he reported, "Those who do not value Hakka culture, those who are Hakka but do not like Hakka, will probably not be moved by this Hakka music."

As informants talked in this area, one skill that emerged as important is the skill of knowing when it is appropriate and when it is not appropriate to emphasize Hakka, both in ministry to individuals and in the formal ministries of the church. Informants reported that Hakka Christian leaders varied the extent of their Hakka focus depending on the context in which they found themselves. For example, in ministry to older Hakkas, #19 uses strictly Hakka. In his own church that is composed primarily of grass-roots Hakkas, he preaches in Hakka with a simultaneous Mandarin translation. In the context of a seminar focused on Hakka ministry and attended primarily by Hakka speakers but also by a few people who could not understand Hakka, he used Mandarin in order to communicate effectively with everyone.

Other Burdens or Interests

Informants also reported that some Hakka Christian leaders have other burdens and interests and are not involved in Hakka-focused ministry. Several examples surfaced as informants discussed this phenomenon. #23 talked about a Hakka pastor he knows who is concerned instead with working to correct some of the heretical teachings he sees present in the Christian church in Taiwan. Several informants mentioned the way some Hakka pastors serve in Hoklo-speaking churches. #23 explained, "Most Hakka churches are in the country and are not very large or the work is very difficult. . . . If a pastor is very talented, preaches well, and is filled with love, maybe city churches will call him to come [and serve there]. To a Hakka pastor, this is a good opportunity. His children will be able to get a good education and things will be more convenient."

Challenging Hakka Non-Christian Categorizations of Being Christian

Christian informants told how, in the context of the negative categorizations by non-Christian Hakkas of being Christian, many Christian Hakkas work to undermine and otherwise challenge these categorizations, seeking to remove as many of the reasons that Hakkas use to construct being Christian as something that does not fit with being Hakka as possible. The goal of these Christians is to find ways to help non-Christian Hakkas understand and be able to accept and enjoy God's love for them (for some other examples of Hakka Christians who are contesting the categorizations of non-Christian Hakkas around them, see Nicole Constable's research on Shung Him Tong in Hong Kong).[1]

It is important to note that not all Hakka Christians seek to challenge some or all of these categorizations, and the way they approach these categorizations can change over time. Some Christian Hakkas have had a time in their lives when they were more active in challenging these categorizations. For example, at the time of her conversion, #35 put much effort into challenging the categorizations of her non-Christian family members. Recently, she expressed, "After I have tried to help them once, twice, three times . . . continually being disappointed, when I think about trying again, I am without hope that it will help."

It is also important to note that the challenges to the categorizations of non-Christians mentioned in this section are far from exhaustive. Those included below are those that informants raised as they talked about the way Christian Hakkas respond to the actions of non-Christian Hakkas. Some of them are direct responses to certain categorizations while others are more general responses (some Christian informants discussed what Hakka Christians do to help non-Christian Hakkas become Christians without focusing their comments on any particular categorization). The more general responses are included under the categorizations where they relate.

As informants talked about the responses of Hakka Christians to categorizations of being Christian, there were also several categorizations which informants or the Hakka Christians they discussed did not address. For example, the categorizations that being Christian is "something that does not fit with my busy lifestyle" or is "wanting money" were not discussed. There are many possible explanations for these gaps. For example, informants could have forgotten to mention them or did not think responses in these areas were significant enough to mention. Another possibility is that these gaps reveal that there are categorizations which Hakka Christians are less actively challenging.

1. Constable, "Christianity and Hakka Identity"; Constable, *Christian Souls*; Constable, "Poverty, Piety, and Past."

The responses to non-Christian categorizations detailed in this section were spoken in a context where Hakka was the focal point and are one aspect of the interactive process of ethnic identification. The fluidity of ethnic identification can readily be seen in these efforts. Some of the symbols (e.g., filial piety, ancestor rituals) remain the same, but Christians are seeking to change the meanings associated with these symbols. The comments of informants in this section will be arranged and discussed according to the following themes and topics: (1) family, (2) reciprocal relationships, (3) everyone, and (4) not as foreign as you think, and (5) all religions are not the same.

Family

Many of the differences between Hakka and practices associated with being Christian that have led many non-Christian Hakkas to categorize Christians as "unfilial" and as "turning one's back on one's ancestors" have their roots in the obedience of Hakka Christians to the biblical prohibition of worship of anyone or anything except God (see Exod 20:3–4 or Deut 5:7–8). Hakka Christians perceive non-Christian Hakkas to be worshiping their ancestors—serving them and looking to them for help—in traditional ancestor rituals, and so, many have refused to attend these rituals or to participate if they do attend. The words of informants as they talked about the ways Hakka Christians contest the categorizations in this area of family will be organized around the following themes: (1) contextualized ancestor practices, (2) showing respect to elders and ancestors, (3) filial piety without burning incense, (4) challenging the grip of traditions, and (5) using the Hakka language.

Contextualized Ancestor Practices

In an effort to undercut or directly challenge the categorizations of non-Christians that have resulted from the unwillingness of many Christians to participate in ancestor rituals, several Hakka Christian leaders have developed various contextualized practices which they believe will enable Hakka Christians to express their filial piety and commemorate their ancestors in concrete ways without worshiping them or being perceived as worshiping them. The desire of these leaders has been to create contextualized practices that are similar enough to non-Christian practices to be acceptable to Hakka non-Christians but different enough to ensure that these non-Christians understand that Christians are not worshiping their ancestors and rather only commemorating them. They anticipate that while Hakka non-Christians will not be completely satisfied with these practices, many will be willing to accept them as a better alternative than totally abstaining from attending or participating. #24 pointed out that when Christians lack concrete means (e.g., rituals) they can use to express their filial piety, the natural response of many non-Christian Hakkas is to postulate that these Christians do not care about their ancestors. Many Hakka Christian leaders advocate that Christians should use these practices at the same time and place as when non-Christian ancestor rituals are taking place, while others recommend using them in totally separate settings.

One example of these contextualized practices that Christian informants often mentioned is a ritual called the Three-Memorials Ceremony (*Zhuisisanli*), designed to replace the Three-Offerings Ceremony (*Sanxianli*), an important ritual in non-Christian Hakka funerals. In the non-Christian Three-Offerings Ceremony, three offerings (e.g., wine, flowers, and fruit) are ritually presented to the deceased. The contextualized Christian Three-Memorials Ceremony, on the other hand, is understood to be a part of a service of worship to God (see appendix 2 for a translation of the Three-Memorials Ceremony). The three ritual acts (pouring water, offering flowers, and lighting candles) that make up this ceremony are performed by persons specifically chosen beforehand (e.g., family members, community or church leaders, and associates of the deceased). While some Christian leaders regularly use this and other contextualized rituals in funerals, others choose not to because of various concerns. One concern often raised is that non-Christians family members are often asked to perform these ritual acts. Some Christian leaders feel the involvement of non-Christians in such important roles in a Christian service is not appropriate and are concerned that these non-Christian participants will view their involvement as ancestor worship. #24 countered these concerns by pointing out that these non-Christians are only performing an act that is set in a context where the meaning of what is happening is being clearly defined by the words used in the ritual. He believes these participants clearly sense they are doing something different. For more information about some of the concerns raised about this contextualized ancestor ritual and one response to them see Wen.[2]

The Three-Memorials Ceremony consists of certain ritual acts and some prayers and responsive readings (usually printed out for those in

---

2. Wen, *Transforming Chinese Ancestor Worship*.

attendance to read) which seek to present the Christian perspective on the ceremony's meaning. For example, as water is being poured into flower vases, the prayers and responsive readings focus on declaring that God is the source of all life. As the flowers are raised and then placed in the vases, the focus is on asking God to help those present to follow the good example of the deceased. As candles are being lit, the prayers and responsive readings express a desire that God would help those present to live a life that glorifies God, benefits man, and honors one's clan and ancestors. Some Hakka Christians also use this Three-Memorials Ceremony at Tomb Sweeping and other times when non-Christians gather to perform ancestor rituals.

Another example of a contextualized practice that informants frequently mentioned is the use of flowers to replace incense and sacrifices in ancestor rituals. For example, instead of bowing with incense at funerals, some Christian Hakkas bow with a flower or bow and then place a flower in a basket in front of the picture of the deceased. Also, instead of offering a sacrifice of meat or fruit during the family ancestor rituals at Tomb Sweeping, some Christian Hakkas prepare flowering plants and place them in front of the common mausoleum. This ritual is being used by some Christian leaders in Taiwan, but others have voiced concerns. One concern that some Hakka Christians have with this practice is the possibility that, when performed in the context of others who are venerating their ancestors, these plants, just like the food offered by non-Christians, will be seen as sacrifices to the ancestors who will come to enjoy them. #4 provided an example of this kind of misunderstanding, commenting about the flowers his Christian relative brings when he attends family ancestor rituals, "Adding beautiful flowers for the ancestors to come and enjoy is a good thing." Discussing this problem, #18 emphasized the importance of clearly explaining one's different perspective to non-Christian relatives or, preferably, commemorating one's ancestors at a separate time.

These contextualized practices provide Hakka Christians with concrete examples to point to when they seek to challenge the categorization that Christians are unfilial and that they turn their backs on their ancestors. When they encounter these categorizations, many Hakka Christians explain that, while they are not willing to worship their ancestors, Christians do have a way of expressing their filial piety and honoring their ancestors. In this attempt to change what it means for those who are being Hakka to express their filial piety and to honor their ancestors, the fluidity of ethnic identification is readily evident.

Some informants also described the way that they or other Hakka Christian leaders are actively working to encourage the more widespread use in Christian circles of these contextualized rituals. For example, #26 talked about efforts to include the Three-Memorials Ceremony in the ritual book of the Presbyterian Church in Taiwan (PCT). Hakka Christian leaders participate in seminars to demonstrate this ritual for other pastors and Christian leaders, engaging them in discussions about the benefits of using this ritual and seeking to address any of their concerns or questions.

Showing Respect to Elders and Ancestors

Informants also reported that Christian Hakkas challenge the categorization that practices associated with being Christian are "disrespectful to elders" and "disrespectful of ancestors," and therefore "unfilial," by consciously seeking to be very respectful of their family members and ancestors. One expression of this respect that informants raised is the way some Hakka Christian leaders encourage new converts to delay baptism for a short period of time in order to give other family members a chance to understand Christianity better before the baptism takes place. For example, when asked about a situation where a middle-aged woman converted to Christianity and was concerned that her actions would cause serious problems with her mother-in-law, #19 affirmed her decision to delay baptism for a few months. He recommended that the new convert and her Christian friends invite other Christians who were about the same age as the mother-in-law to visit her and make friends with her so that she would have a chance to know that believing in Jesus is not something scary or bad and to help her understand what the Bible says about ancestors and family relationships.

Another expression of this respect that surfaced several times is the way some Hakka Christians delayed their baptism (sometimes many, many years) until after their parents died so that they could perform their visible role in the ancestor rituals that take place at their funerals. While most Hakka Christian leaders do not condone this practice, several informants gave examples of Christian Hakkas who delayed baptism in this way. #22 gave the example of his mother:

> My mother went to church for many years [and accepted the gospel] but was not baptized until much later because her mother and

father were still living. She wanted to be able to venerate and serve them at the time of their death. She waited until both her parents and her husband had passed away before she was baptized. She believed in the Lord; . . . maybe she felt the pressure was too great or her responsibilities or obligations to the clan had not been satisfied, and so once they were satisfied, she did not hesitate to follow through and be baptized.

Yet another expression of efforts to be respectful in the context of the categorization that Christians are disrespectful is the way Hakka Christians are encouraged to take advantage of opportunities to express their filial piety to living relatives. Informants offered examples in this area of many Hakka Christians greatly sacrificing themselves to be filial, talking about caring for ailing parents and grandparents and contributing resources to help solve problems encountered by the family. #19 elaborated:

> We Christians know being filial to one's parents does not mean burning incense in veneration of them once in a while; rather, being truly filial is a heart attitude that is expressed daily. . . . Parents, if they are alive, know who treats them better, although it sometimes takes a long time. [After someone converts to Christianity], he/she needs to fight a long war of resistance, put up with surface conflicts, and work hard to maintain a normal relationship. Maybe it will take ten or twenty years of living out one's faith before things will get better. . . . One's family watches you to see if you will become a bad person. In the beginning, they feel like you are not a part of their family anymore, but later, they begin to see that you have not given up your family. They originally thought you would be unfilial but gradually discover that you are not unfilial. Instead, you are polite to your father and mother, and you love and care for them. In the end, one's family will come to the conclusion, "Believing in Jesus is not a bad thing," and they may gradually change. Typically, this takes a long time because this is a huge problem, and it is hard for change to happen quickly. Originally, one's parents might be very angry with their child, but as they watch him or her over the years, they come to the conclusion that Christianity is not a bad thing.

The desire to be more respectful can also be seen in the way some Hakka Christian leaders are changing the way they dispose of the ancestor tablet of a new convert. #17 explained, "The old way of burning the ancestor tablet and gods in front of the neighbors is very disrespectful.

Instead, I just wrap things up, carry them away, and dispose of them later." When #29 became a Christian, Hakka church leaders encouraged her not to destroy the tablet (which other relatives were still using) but rather to contact her relatives, asking them to come and take the ancestor tablet to another place.

Filial Piety Without Burning Incense

In response to the categorization that Christians "break the incense fires," informants reported that some Christian Hakkas challenge the belief that burning incense is necessary to express filial piety to one's ancestors. They intentionally act in ways aimed at clearly expressing their filial piety to the ancestors without burning incense. They seek to help non-Christian Hakkas understand the Christian perspective on expressing filial piety to the ancestors. #19 emphasized that these efforts are not just to satisfy the expectations of non-Christian relatives but are efforts to express one's heart attitude of filial piety in ways these relatives can understand.

One common strategy that informants reported that many Hakka Christian leaders have in this area is to encourage Christians to attend when relatives gather for ancestor rituals and to use these opportunities to show Christian ways of expressing filial piety to their ancestors and commemorating them. Hakka Christians who attend clan-grouping gatherings where ancestor rituals take place often commemorate their ancestors by standing before the common mausoleum, praying a prayer of thanksgiving to God for their ancestors, and bowing to show one's respect. They also prepare flowers and place them in front of the common mausoleum. #22 explained the importance of attending,

> [Attending and using a Christian way to participate] will let the whole clan-grouping know there is no conflict between believing in the Lord and [being filial to] ancestors. There is only a conflict between God and other gods. By attending, we show that we still commemorate our ancestors, we just do not make them into gods and worship them. We commemorate our ancestors and honor them; we do not throw out our ethical and filial obligations [when we become Christians].

When accused of being unfilial because they do not use incense, these Hakka Christians often contest the meaning of "unfilial." For example, #32 said, "What does it mean to be unfilial? Not attending the ancestor rituals is unfilial, but I attend and have done so every year since I was baptized. . . . [My relatives] do not dare to criticize me because I am sincere and do not renege on my obligation as a descendent. I am more sincere and diligent [than they are] in commemorating our ancestors." By redefining "unfilial" as "not attending ancestor rituals" rather than "not burning incense in ancestor rituals" and by being more intentional and sincere in his commemoration of his ancestors during the time of ancestor rituals, #32 expressed hope that his non-Christian relatives would not be justified in categorizing Christians as "unfilial" and as "breaking the incense fires."

#22 provided another example of intentional efforts to express filial piety to ancestors in Christian ways. He reported how he had traveled to China and labored to locate the grave of his ancestors pre-dating the family's immigration to Taiwan. He photographed this ancestral grave and some distant relatives he met there. After returning to Taiwan, he wrote an account of his efforts ("My Journey to Find My Roots") and the simple Christian method he had used at the ancestral grave to express his honor for his ancestors. He printed this account and pictures, as well as a narrative detailing the names of his ancestors and tracing his ancestral line back to the first man God created, and gave a copy to each of his relatives when they gathered to venerate their ancestors at Tomb Sweeping. His efforts to make connections with his ancestral past and to express his filial piety to those ancestors went beyond what most if not all the others in his clan-grouping had done, and he anticipated his diligence would communicate to all of his relatives gathered there that Christians, rather than turning their backs on the ancestors and neglecting the continuity of the family line, consider the ancestors to be *very* important. His version of his clan-grouping's ancestral record that started with "the man God created" sought to redefine the origin of this continuous line and to locate their first ancestor in the creative act of the Christian God.

Challenging the Grip of Traditions

Informants reported that Christian Hakkas challenge the categorizations of practices associated with being Christian as "impossible" and "wanting to change too much too fast" by highlighting how traditions and traditional ways are changing and by challenging non-Christian Hakkas to evaluate traditional ways and explore Christian ways to determine if there are better ways of doing things. For example, #19 described how he handled things in this area, saying:

> I do not quarrel with [Hakka non-Christians who are habitually following traditions] but rather try to joke with them as I talk. First, I say, "In the past, our ancestors all used kerosene lamps. The light was very small, about as bright as a small candle. Why did we replace these lamps with electric lights? Using electric lights is not our traditional way. We replaced them because electric lights are better." Second, I point out, "Traditions are slowly changing. In the past the bride wore red clothing at weddings. Now everyone wants to wear a white wedding dress [Red is often associated with blessing and good fortune whereas white is a color often associated with death]. How do we know what is the right way to do things?" I do not argue with them but try to find other ways to help them see that traditions are not necessarily right; that we should keep the good traditions and, if there are bad ones, we should replace them with other ways. We have to challenge them a little bit in order to help them develop a new way of thinking about these things.

The main point many Hakka Christians make is that since traditions can change and better options for handling certain things are often available, non-Christians should explore Christianity to determine whether or not this religion is better than traditional ways.

#19 also pointed out that, in order to combat the forces of tradition, Christians need to work together to encourage change in what is acceptable to Hakka non-Christians in the area of ancestor practices. He elaborated, "This kind of change happens gradually and slowly, so the church needs to be persistent and move slowly. If we are not committed to seeking change, we will lack power. Maybe it will take five years or ten years to make a few small changes. . . . There needs to be a group of people who are working hard in this area." #19 emphasized that challenges to some of the traditional ways of venerating ancestors will be more effective if Christians are more uniform in the way they handle ancestor practices. He explained:

> We cannot have each church handling things differently. . . . If we do that, we will not be able to change people. The church is already only 2 or 3 percent of the population; the Hakka percentage is even lower. . . . [Only if we have more uniformity in our ancestor practices] will people know the church also has a good method. . . . If things are done differently each time, people will not be able to keep track of what we are doing and will not be able to understand our ways. If someone has seen Christians using one method in one place and then goes to a different town and another method is being used there and to another location where

still another method is being used, if every place is different, they will feel churches are all just carelessly doing whatever they please.

In challenging the grip of traditions, some Hakka Christians access themes being used by others in society. For example, #22 told how he presents Christian rituals as being more environmentally friendly, accessing the teaching that many younger non-Christian Hakkas have had in school that burning spirit money in the worship of the gods and in ancestor rituals is pollution.

Informants also reported that some Christian Hakkas challenge categorizations of practices associated with being Christian as "awkward," "strange," or "unsettling" by developing and encouraging widespread use of contextualized ancestor practices (described above) that are similar enough to Hakka ways to evoke a feeling of familiarity among Hakka non-Christians but different enough in significant and noticeable ways to alert them to the fact that Christians are not worshiping their ancestors. For example, several informants reported that at the end of funeral services led by many Hakka pastors, attendees follow a traditional, non-Christian funeral practice of queuing to pay their respects in front of a picture of the deceased (placed in the front of the funeral parlor). Rather than bowing while holding sticks of burning incense or bowing and then adding incense powder to an urn filled with burning incense as they would do in a traditional, non-Christian funeral, attendees at these Christian funerals bow in front of the picture of the deceased, place a flower provided for them into a basket in front of the picture, and then turn and bow to the immediate family of the deceased who are standing to one side. There are several variations of this practice that are currently being used in Hakka Christian circles. For example, sometimes a Styrofoam cross is placed in front of the picture of the deceased, and attendees are instructed to poke the stem of a provided flower someplace on that cross. In this way, Christians provide an opportunity for non-Christians to pay their respects to their deceased friend or loved one and to the family of the deceased in a way that has a familiar feel to it but is significantly different because of the absence of incense.

Encouraging Hakka Christians to be present at the ancestor rituals of their clan-grouping and to use methods to commemorate their ancestors that are compatible with Christian teachings is another example of efforts that Hakka Christians are using to help expose non-Christians to Christian teachings and practices. For example, when Hakka Christians attend family gatherings where ancestor rituals take place, informants reported that these Christians are better able to maintain and develop their relationships with non-Christian members of their clan-grouping; through these relationships and time spent together, non-Christian relatives have opportunities to observe Christians and better understand Christian teachings, and Christians have more natural opportunities to interact with their relatives about practices associated with being Christian and to challenge their categorizations of being Christian.

Informants also reported that, in the context of the non-Christian categorization of being Christian as "wanting to change too much too fast," some Christian Hakkas are trying to be cautious about not pressuring people to change too quickly. An example of this is the way some advocate being flexible about the rate at which new converts, especially those who are older, are expected to change their practices, giving them time to work out the implications of their conversion to Christianity. For example, #26 said, "When we lead someone to believe in Jesus, especially an older person, we need to be flexible in the way we make arrangements for their ancestor tablet; we need to move slowly." He pointed out that many Hakkas worship their ancestors because they fear they will be punished if they discontinue this practice. He explained, "I inform them that we will not remove the ancestor tablet immediately, but instead, set it aside for a while and focus on worshiping Jesus. . . . After one month of not worshiping the ancestors, they can see if their life is less peaceful. They will find their life is more peaceful. They pray to God, and He gives them more strength. They will still have problems, but after they pray and read the Bible, they will be changed by God."

Several Christian informants expressed a need for caution in this area, pointing out the danger that sometimes people never give up their old ways. For example, #23 told about an older Hakka convert who, while she did not perform the ancestor rituals herself, made sure someone in her immediate family did so at the required times, even after she had been a Christian for many years.

Using the Hakka Language

Informants also reported that many Christian Hakkas challenged the categorization of being Christian as "cold" and "disrespectful to Hakkas" by intentionally using the Hakka language in evangelistic encounters with those who are limited to using or prefer speaking Hakka. These

Christians expected the use of Hakka rather than Mandarin or Hoklo would not only facilitate better communication but would also add a measure of friendliness and familiarity to their words and provide better ministry opportunities.

Informants reported that one visible expression of this strategy is the intentional and significant use of the Hakka language in some churches, small groups within churches, and special evangelistic meetings. #20 reported that one important role these ministries play is that of helping Christians who do not speak Hakka very well to reach out to their non-Christian friends and relatives who are limited to or prefer speaking Hakka. He continued by saying that, in addition to facilitating better communication and creating a warm, inviting environment through the use of the Hakka language in conversation, scripture readings, prayer, music, preaching, and teaching, these ministries often have leaders who better understand the obstacles to conversion that Hakkas often face and, consequently, can better help non-Christian Hakkas overcome these obstacles. Another role these ministries play is helping Hakka Christians who are younger and have only a basic level of Hakka-speaking ability to learn, through attending, the vocabulary necessary to talk about Christianity with their older relatives and friends who are limited to or prefer using the Hakka language. #26 argued, "If you say that, since most Hakkas do not speak Hakka, we do not need to use Hakka in evangelism, you are wrong. If you turn that thinking around and work hard to train people in the church to use Hakka, then the church can become a leader in Hakka culture. We can do things so that people will think, 'If I want to learn the Hakka language, the best place to come is to the church.'"

Several Christian informants reported the difficulties they had encountered and the tremendous commitment it had taken for them to learn to talk about the Bible on a deeper level using Hakka. These informants felt their efforts were worth it so that more Hakka non-Christians would have better opportunities to hear about Christian teachings in Hakka.

Informants also talked about how many Hakka Christians reported that using the Hakka language with non-Christian Hakkas had helped facilitate ministry with them. For example, in response to the question, "Is using the Hakka language important in sharing the gospel with Hakkas?" #19 recounted some stories from his own experience of evangelism working with Hakka-speaking missionaries:

> I went to visit a Hakka acquaintance with [a Hakka-speaking missionary]. The grandmother who came to the door asked us what we wanted and, seeing a foreigner standing there, nervously said, "We are Buddhists." She continued to stand in the doorway, clearly communicating to us that she did not want us to come in.... Then I told her, "This foreigner can speak Hakka." "Really?" she said. Then [the missionary] spoke perfect Hakka with her. She started to smile and said, "Wow! This is great! Please come in and sit down." When I told her [the missionary] could also sing Hakka songs, she was moved further and immediately went in and began to prepare some tea for us. She went from a person who wanted to chase us away to someone who, just because we spoke Hakka, invited us in, and just because we could sing Hakka songs, made some tea for us.

He continued, "Does that answer your question?" and then added:

> One time I went out with a foreign missionary to do some evangelism.... We decided to get a bite to eat.... As we sat in this small restaurant, the missionary spoke loudly in Hakka.... Soon the owner came over and said to him, "You can speak Hakka?" We talked to him for a bit. When it came time for us to pay the bill, the owner refused to take any money from us. We had very quickly become friends with him. Normally, people think of Christianity as a foreign religion, a disloyal and unfilial religion, but when you missionaries can speak Hakka, you can really quickly move to a deeper level and discuss spiritual things.

#26 provided another example of the power of using the Hakka language in ministry, telling a story of an old non-Christian Hakka man who was very sick and his middle-aged Christian daughter who could not speak Hakka. He recounted how the daughter brought some Hakka-speaking pastors to visit her father in the hospital and how they read from the Hakka Bible, sang Hakka songs, and shared and prayed using the Hakka language. The daughter related that as her father listened to these Hakka speakers, his face "began to shine." #26 reported, "In this way, her father became a Christian before he passed away." He said as a result of the role the Hakka language played in her father's conversion and believing in the power of using this language in ministry to non-Christian Hakkas, this Christian woman began to diligently study Hakka and gathered together as many of the Hakkas as she could find in the large city church she attended, and together they started a separate Hakka service.

#29 provided another example of the benefits of using the Hakka language in ministry to those who prefer to speak Hakka. As this woman, whose Mandarin abilities were very weak, talked about a Mandarin-speaking church that she attended with her grandson before she became a Christian, she said, "I did not fit there. It was all young people, and there was no one like me. . . . There were a couple of old people and some Hoklos. I can understand some Hoklo, but I cannot speak it. I wondered what I was going to do because I did not know how to find other churches." Eventually, a friend of her grandson connected her with a Christian woman who, in the words of her grandson, "just happened to be able to speak Hakka and so was really able to connect with Grandma." After #29 became a Christian and began attending a Hakka church, she told another person about this church: "There are Hakkas there, so you do not need to worry. The pastors are all very good, and [even though they are foreigners] they can all speak Hakka," a reflection of the importance she placed on the Hakka dimension of this church.

Reciprocal Relationships

The comments of informants as they discussed the ways Hakka Christians contest the categorizations that non-Christians have of being Christian related to reciprocal relationships will be organized around the following three themes: (1) acting like "us," (2) redefining relationships with ancestors, and (3) worship of the highest god.

Acting Like "Us"

Informants reported that many Hakka Christians challenge the non-Christian categorization that Christians are "not acting like 'us'" by seeking to act as much like "us" as possible. Obviously, there are times when Christians cannot act like "us" in the way their non-Christian relatives desire. For example, informants reported that most Christian Hakkas do not allow the clan to take over the planning for the funerals of Christian family members. However, they seek to act like "us" by still hiring clan members to provide certain services in connection with the funeral (e.g., mortuary arrangements, catering the meals, printing bulletins and funeral announcements, providing small gifts for funeral attendees who give money, providing and setting up the temporary structures often used for funeral activities, etc.). Many Hakka Christian leaders also invite non-Christian clan leaders to participate in contextualized rituals during funerals. #24 reported that, as a result, "These leaders feel we are really valuing them," rather than ignoring them and/or forbidding them to be involved.

Informants provided other examples of the way Hakka Christians tried to act as much like "us" as possible. #33 talked about how each Lunar New Year his relatives on his mother's side of the family expect him to pay a visit on the second day of the holiday. Usually he is able to meet their expectations, but one year when he was not going to be able to go on that particular day, he made a special effort to go a few days early. He feared family members would say that after he became a Christian, he did not do any "us" things anymore. #33 elaborated:

> Now that we are Christians, we need to be especially careful about things. What I mean is, in the area of interacting with our relatives, we want to make sure we understand their needs and reach out to them. This is really important. If we do not do this, they will not have a good impression of Christians.... [When my cousin was in intensive care at the hospital], of all of my relatives, I was the one who went to visit him the most. I did so because I am a Christian. I know Christians need to do this.

#18 told how his mother needed someone to care for her for a period of time before she died. There was no one available in his family to do this, so he quit his job to care for her. In doing so, he acted like "us," and, as a result, he reported that his relationship with his family (which had been strained since his conversion) became much better.

Informants also reported that many Hakka Christians acted like "us" as much as possible by continuing to bury their dead in the common mausoleum, by being present when the members of "us" gather for ancestor rituals, and by contributing toward the construction and maintenance of the common mausoleum or ancestral halls because they want to fulfill their responsibilities to "us" and maintain relationships with other members of "us."

#35 provided another example of deliberately acting like "us." When she became a Christian, her mother became so angry with her for not acting like "us" and making what Christians say more important than the traditions and directives of her clan that her mother treated her like she was no longer a part of the family. #35 described what she hoped her attitude and actions would say to her mother at that time: "I will do absolutely everything you ask me to do [e.g., household tasks of caring for children, cooking, and cleaning]. Through my sacrificial labors for this household,

I intend to say that, even though I am a Christian, I am still a member of this family. You cannot drive me away just because I have become a Christian, because if you do, there will be no one to do all of these things for you."

Redefining Relationships with Ancestors

Informants reported that many Hakka Christians counter the non-Christian categorization that Christians are "neglecting their ancestors" by challenging the idea that the ancestors need things their descendants can supply for them. One example that surfaced often as Christian informants talked in this area is the way Hakka Christians disputed the idea that the ancestors are present and partake in the sacrificial offerings provided for them as a part of ancestor rituals. #19 said when he asked non-Christians if the ancestors really come and eat the sacrifices, "It is very troublesome for them. They do not know how to answer." #28 called the beliefs of the non-Christian Hakkas contradictory, saying, "They envision more than ten generations of people coming to eat. If they really eat and you only feed them five or six times a year, they will have already starved to death.... If there are several hundred or more than a thousand people coming and you only prepare a few chickens, how are they going to eat?" #19 detailed some of the things he says to non-Christian Hakkas in this area:

> "If the ancestors eat the sacrifices, do you give them something to eat every day?" No. "If not, will they not get really hungry?" [When I challenge them in this way, many non-Christian Hakkas] respond that the sacrifices are just an expression, a commemoration. "Since these sacrifices are just an expression and a commemoration, the church also has an excellent way of commemorating the ancestors, right? We present flowers, pour water, and light candles. We pray and sing songs to commemorate our ancestors, to tell about the good things our ancestors have done." [In saying these kinds of things] we slowly change their thinking. Originally they think their way is the only way that is right. When we use a soft approach to challenge this thinking, it helps them to come to the conclusion that their thinking is not necessarily right.

When this subject comes up at the death of a Christian, #19 described what he often says: "[The deceased] does not need to eat food we prepare for him or her. Jesus would not let them come unless he had completed all of the preparations for them. The preparations Jesus makes are definitely better than anything we could do."

Many Hakka Christians, thinking about the debt they owe to their parents and ancestors, challenge the categorization that Christians neglect their ancestors by arguing that there are other appropriate ways to respond in light of this debt. Informants reported that many Hakka Christians tell their non-Christian relatives that, while they do not worship their ancestors, that does not mean they neglect to do anything in this area. These Hakka Christians point out that, rather than worshiping their ancestors, they honor and commemorate them and give thanks to God for the ancestors' influence on their lives. For example, when his mother stated that, because he had become a Christian, he would probably not venerate his father and her after their deaths, #27 responded, "It is not that I will not venerate you; it is just that the meaning of what I will be doing will be different."

Regarding the implications of "neglecting the ancestors" that many non-Christian Hakkas accept—that those who do not worship the ancestors will not be protected and might even be punished by them—some Christian Hakkas challenge the accuracy of this understanding. For example, #19 argued that most parents want the best for their children, so it does not make sense that, after their deaths, they would come back and deliberately hurt their children. Several Christian informants also challenged this understanding by emphasizing how, rather than living in fear of punishment from the ancestors and gods after their conversion, they felt great peace. For example, #32 testified, "I kept thinking [about my worship of the gods and ancestors], 'I worship you, but I am still afraid. It is only because of fear that I worship you.' After I trusted in the Lord and read 1 John 4:18 which says, 'There is no fear in love . . . ' (NIV), I was greatly comforted. Because I trusted, all of my previous fears disappeared."

Worship of the Highest God

In response to the non-Christian Hakka categorization that Christians "do not worship the gods," informants reported that some Hakka Christians are looking for ways to contextualize Christian worship to address this categorization. #19 gave an example:

> Once we planned a service where we burned incense. The pastor who officiated went to the Chinese medicine pharmacy of [one of his relatives] and used the frankincense, myrrh, and so forth talked

> about in the Bible to make a kind of incense that would only be used in worship of God. [At the experimental service], we beat drums outside the church . . . and Christians lined up, and when they entered . . . the incense had been placed on the communion table. [The worship leader] picked up the burning incense and declared, "This incense represents our prayers that are given to the triune and true God. He set the incense back down, and letting it burn, he knelt down in front of the table and prayed. . . . All of the Christians prayed quietly.

These attempts often receive mixed reactions and are discarded. For example, the use of incense in Christian worship services has not gained a following in Taiwan. #19 reported that about half of those who were involved in the ensuing discussions (after this experimental service took place) about the possibility of regularly using incense in Christian churches responded positively, saying, "This is truly indigenous worship." The other half said, "This is heresy."

Other informants talked about Hakka Christians who respond to the issues behind the categorization that Christians "do not worship the gods" by emphasizing that the Christian God has the highest authority and power. This emphasis on the God above all gods counters the fear many non-Christians have that if they stop worshiping the gods they and their ancestors have worshiped for so many years, the gods will no longer protect and bless them. For example, #20 described one of the ways he helped his mother overcome her fear in this area:

> There was a spirit medium who operated close to the home of one of my brothers. . . . Once, when my mother was staying with my brother, . . . I walked past the medium, and she told me that at the first hour of the day, she was going to start [being possessed by the spirit]. . . . [At the appointed time,] I told my mother, "That is nothing to be amazed about. If I pray, the medium will not be able to become possessed and speak for the spirit." My mother replied, "You are just talking big. Look the spirit is coming." Then I prayed out loud so that my mother could hear, and I asked God to bind this evil spirit in the name of Jesus so that the medium would not be able to become possessed. . . . The medium worked for more than thirty minutes and could not become possessed. . . . I was not there every day, so on the days when I was not present, the medium became possessed, but whenever I went and prayed in the name of Jesus, the spirit would not possess the medium. After this happened several times, my mother told the people she met

> that Jesus has the highest authority and power. As a result, she did not fear me leaving my original beliefs and trusting in Jesus. . . . We definitely have to help Hakka non-Christians understand that when they seek Jesus, He has the highest authority and power and can protect them from other [gods and spirits]. They need this kind of assurance before they will be willing to, without fear, leave the false gods they serve.

Other informants reported that some Christian Hakkas respond to the categorization that Christians "do not worship the gods" by talking about the power of the Christian God. They emphasize the ability of God and his church to meet the needs of Hakka families and individuals. Their testimonies are similar to testimonies of non-Christian Hakkas who often will tell about a particular god in a specific temple that is especially able to meet certain needs. #29, a convert for less than a year, provides an example of such a Christian testimony: "Everyone says when people become Christians, their families are happy and harmonious and safe and sound, and so everyone wants to become Christians. Take me for example—in the past I had a lot of troubles, but since the time I connected with the church, my family has been trouble-free, life has been good, and things have been comfortable." #21 also told about a testimony that was instrumental in drawing her into the church and in her eventual conversion to Christianity. She described how a Christian teacher in the community outreach classes of a church shared her experience of the power of God to meet needs:

> She told us how her child had worked hard and, without attending a cram school, had tested into college. She asked us if we wanted our children to be that obedient and well-behaved. "Take them to Sunday School," she said. At that time, I thought of my only son, and my immediate response was, "Of course I want my child to be like that!" It was too good to be true—[my son] testing into [a top university in Taiwan] without the help of a cram school and being so obedient and well-behaved. I began to look for a Sunday School for my son.

Everyone

The observations informants made as they related the ways Hakka Christians contest the categorizations that non-Christians have of being Christian related to "everyone" will be divided into the following three themes: (1) blindly following everyone, (2) gaining the favor of everyone, and (3) fighting the disfavor of everyone.

BLINDLY FOLLOWING EVERYONE

Informants reported that many Hakka Christians counter the non-Christian categorization that being Christian is "something everyone does not embrace" by highlighting the meaninglessness of doing something you do not understand just because others are doing it. For example, #28 said, "Most people [in my hometown] go to worship [the gods], but they have no idea what they are doing. They worship at the temples and just do what everyone else is doing there. In the end, they are unclear about the meaning of what they are doing; they only observe how others are worshiping and imitate them." #28 continued, telling how on worship days, many of these people "eat, and after they have drunk some alcohol, they stagger around, and foul words spew from their mouths." He emphasized the fact that there appeared to be nothing more to their worship than just imitating the actions of others.

#35 provided an example of how some Christian Hakkas work to undercut the idea that one should follow everyone, telling about her interaction with a sister who wanted her to do something just because a cousin had done it. A distant relative had died, and this cousin had given a monetary gift, visiting and burning incense at the place where the body of the deceased was kept. #35 reminded her sister that they hardly knew this relative, and challenged her saying, "Think about it for a second. If we have to go just because one of our cousins went, then logically, all of our cousins should also go, [which is unreasonable]." #35 reported that, after her sister thought about what she had said and evaluated things from a different mindset, she decided that they did not need to go. #35 said she used this opportunity to challenge her sister (and her mother who had initiated the idea) to counter the thinking that you should blindly follow what everyone does and, at all costs, avoid being different.

GAINING THE FAVOR OF EVERYONE

Informants also reported that, in the context of the non-Christian categorization that being Christian is "something that creates challenges in the area of gaining favor with everyone," many Hakka Christian leaders seek to plan funerals (a very visible venue where the evaluations of everyone are particularly important) that can be evaluated positively by non-Christian

Hakkas. Rather than planning funerals where there are very few differences from a Sunday worship service in church, these Hakka Christians work to make the funerals they plan as similar as possible to those of non-Christians without compromising Christian teachings. The most important aspect of these funerals is the use of contextualized ancestor rituals, but they can also include things such as the decoration of the funeral parlor or church and the music and musicians that are used. For more information about the practices that are used by these Hakka Christian leaders see "The Christian Funeral and Ancestor Memorial Handbook."[3]

Several informants reported that non-Christian Hakkas had very positive impressions of these contextualized Christian funerals. For example, #31 told of the response of his non-Christian friends to his father's funeral: "All I heard was praise, saying that the way we did things was *very good*. There were even some people who asked, 'Can I have a funeral like this, even though I am not a Christian?'" #24 described the funeral of a church member that left a deep impression on him:

> This was the first time I had seen the [non-Christian family members of the deceased] sitting, diligently and intently engaged in a Christian funeral, from the beginning to the end, including the sermon time. I felt we Christians were really honoring and respecting them. Originally, the family had vocalized that they were not happy with Christianity and with God. But when we told them we were going to use the Three-Memorials Ceremony and include some of them as ritual participants, their attitude changed, and they agreed to attend. When they came, those who represented the family as ritual participants sat up front. Quite a few of the other family members sat in the audience, unlike at other Christian funerals where the non-Christians often do not come inside or they stand in the door and talk loudly.

Fighting the Disfavor of Everyone

Informants also described some of the ways Hakka Christians challenged the categorization that being Christian is "something that brings disfavor with everyone." One of the most common ways that surfaced was the desire to have Christians engage with Hakka non-Christians to serve as "witnesses" who could help them get to know Christian beliefs and practices better and correct some misunderstandings they have. For example, #19

---

3. Jidujiao Kejia Fuyin Xiehui Bianji Xiaozu, *Ancestor Memorial Handbook*.

argued that the reason being Christian is viewed so negatively is that very few Christians spend time with non-Christians "cultivating the ground" and "preparing it for harvest." #22 argued that his presence and use of contextualized ancestor practices when his relatives gather for ancestor rituals "paved the way" for other relatives to convert since they knew Christians could express their filial piety at these times in ways the other relatives could accept.

#19 articulated another method Hakka Christians are using to fight the disfavor of everyone, that of focusing evangelism on families rather than on individuals. He gave the example of a situation where twenty-six relatives were baptized together and said, "I feel the concept of whole families converting to Christianity together is needed among Hakkas." He elaborated:

> When a whole family trusts in the Lord, it is easier to develop family devotional practices and to remain strong in the faith. There will not be so much turmoil—there are so many Christians [in predominantly non-Christian Hakka families] who have so much turmoil in their homes, so much tension with their clan, problems in their marriages, problems with family worship and veneration practices . . . they really have an inexhaustible amount of problems on every level. Hakkas do so many things together with their clan . . . so it is really hard for individuals who convert alone. Consequently, a lot of people are afraid to trust in Jesus.

#19 described one related strategy he uses when he visits non-Christian Hakkas: "It is best if three generations go visiting together so we can have a Christian who is the same age as each person in the home we are visiting. We can eat and chat with them and give them gifts. The older Christians can make friends with the older family members, the middle-aged with the middle-aged, and the young with the young. This is the best strategy. Take a group of people so you can gain a group of people, a family, a clan."

#20 described another method his urban church is using to evangelize in the context of the disfavor of everyone. He talked about the difficulty of ministering in Hakka areas where the power of everyone is very strong, "If you want to get . . . dozens of clans of people to change quickly, it will not be easy." He highlighted the way many Hakkas have moved to the larger cities where the influence of everyone in their clan is not so strong. With this in mind, #20's church targets city-dwelling non-Christian Hakkas and plans seasonal special evangelistic events which Christians can invite their city-dwelling non-Christian Hakka friends and relatives to attend.

Not as Foreign as You Think

As informants talked about the attitudes and efforts of Christian Hakkas, it was readily evident that the non-Christian Hakka categorization of Christianity as a foreign religion was one they felt was important to challenge. These Christians sought to emphasize Hakka in their ministries, to redefine "foreign," and to provide opportunities for Hakkas to better understand Christian beliefs and practices.

Emphasizing Hakka

One of Hakka Christians' strongest responses to the categorization that being Christian is "foreign" is the way some intentionally emphasize Hakka in their ministries. This is done in an attempt to show that the Christian God is the God of Hakkas, that Christianity is not only not foreign, but it is something that is Hakka. For example, #19 said he wants to have a Hakka emphasis in his church "to communicate that the Christian God does not belong to foreigners but belongs to Hakkas—He is the God of Hakkas. I want this concept to be very clear. . . . If there are foreigners present, they also love Hakkas and speak Hakka." In placing a strong emphasis on Hakka, Hakka Christians also become more appealing to those who have good feelings toward Hakka and those Hakkas who are concerned about the decline of the Hakka language and Hakka culture.

Several Christian informants pointed out the positive effects of emphasizing a particular language and other aspects of a particular culture. #26 referred to the incident in Acts 2 where the Holy Spirit descended upon those present so that they were able to speak in other languages and foreigners heard these people talking about the wonders of God in their native languages. #26 explained that, as a result of this situation, these foreigners understood that the Gospel belonged not only to the Greeks; it also belonged to them. Hakka Christians use this account to point out that the use of the Hakka language in Christian ministries helps remove the perception that being Christian is foreign and belongs to others. #19 added, "If a church in a Hakka area uses Hakka, this practice communicates that we are the same as those who live there." He continued, talking about a Christian senior citizens' meeting where Hakka is used, saying, "Those meetings are not that special. We just sing Hakka songs and speak

Hakka, but those seniors really like to come. They feel a sense of belonging [in this Hakka environment]."

Other informants described how many Christian Hakkas believe the use of Hakka music rather than Western music in churches helps take away the foreignness of being Christian for Hakkas. #25 discussed how the use of music that is Hakka feels different than the use of Western music:

> When non-Christian Hakkas first come to church and the songs are all Western, of course they will feel the God we are worshiping is a Western God. They do not feel this God is also the God of the Chinese. . . . "Christian" becomes equated with "Western." . . . But if in the church you preach in Hakka, and the music is Hakka, Hakkas will feel everything is very familiar. They will be drawn closer to God and will feel this God is the God of the Hakkas. . . . This is the kind of task that music and language can easily accomplish. The language of song can bring things to a different level, to a heightened state, to a place where it can be more easily experienced. Preaching in Hakka already takes away the distance, and then when you start to sing, immediately it is easier for people to be moved, . . . church has a different feel to it. . . . That does not mean they need to know every melody. Music is something very abstract. There are traditional melodies, but there are also newly created ones that people do not know. . . . These new melodies can have a Hakka flavor to them. Even though Hakkas do not know them and need to learn them, these melodies sound very familiar to them.

Some Hakka Christians seek to challenge the foreign flavor of being Christian in the minds of their non-Christian fellow ethnics by relating being Christian with Hakka ways. For example, #19 told how he explains to non-Christians that the Christian God is the god many Hakkas refer to as the Heaven God. #18 told about how he uses stories from Hakka history in evangelism. For example, he tells a story about how, during an encounter with the leader of the Huang Chao Rebellion in the late Tang Dynasty, a Hakka woman displayed such exemplary filial piety that the leader was deeply moved. When he told her to go home and attach a certain kind of grass to the doorposts of her house so that his troops would know not to harm her family, this woman went home and instructed everyone she knew to do the same, and, in doing so, saved her whole village from being destroyed by rebel troops. #18 highlighted the similarity between this story and the biblical story where the Israelites were protected from death by putting the blood of a lamb on their doorposts (see Exod 12:1–13). He continued, "From here we can talk about the story of salvation provided by the Lord Jesus Christ." He elaborated on the benefits of using stories from Hakka history: "When you start [your evangelistic presentation with a story from Hakka history], a Hakka will feel affirmed since you are talking about their things and not about the things of others.... When I want to share the gospel with you, I need to look at things from your perspective and relate my words to your historical and cultural background."

Other efforts to emphasize Hakka that informants raised include doing things as closely to Hakka ways as possible without compromising Christian teachings. For example, Christian Hakka leaders have developed contextualized rituals like the Three-Memorials Ceremony (discussed in greater detail above) that provide a method for Hakka Christians to express filial piety to ancestors at funerals and at the time of Tomb Sweeping. Another example is the development and use by Hakka Christians of ancestor-memorial plaques which are a visible reminder for non-Christian Hakkas that Christians still value and respect their ancestors and their ancestral roots.

In order to have this Hakka emphasis, several tools are necessary. Informants reported that some Christian Hakkas were working to translate the entire Bible into the Hakka language. The "Today's Taiwan Hakka Version" of the Hakka New Testament and Psalms as well as Proverbs were already available at the time the interviews for this study took place, and the remaining books of the Old Testament were in their final stages of translation (the Hakka Bible has since been published).[4] They also talked about Hakka hymnbooks, Bible studies using the Hakka Bible, and books and pamphlets written as tools for Hakka evangelism that have been published. In addition, informants reported that others have composed Hakka music which can be used in Hakka churches and performed by Hakka choirs.

REDEFINING "FOREIGN"

Informants also reported that Christian Hakkas challenge the negative categorization of being Christian as "foreign" by seeking to change the meanings associated with this symbol in the thinking of Hakkas in at least

---

4. Zhonghuaminguo Shengjing Gonghui, *New Testament and Psalms*; Zhonghuaminguo Shengjing Gonghui, *Proverbs*; Taiwan Shengjing Gonghui, *Hakka Bible*.

three ways. First, Christian Hakkas often point out that foreign things are not necessarily unsuitable for Hakkas. #20 told how, in the past when his mother and other relatives rejected being Christian because it is "foreign" or "Western," he would talk to them about all of the other things that they use that are "Western." He related his words to them:

> How about if we light an oil lamp, the kerosene lamps that we used to use? Or . . . you say you want to wear Western-style clothing, you want to live in a foreign-style house, not one made out of brick from olden times; cement is also called "Western powder." Did we use it in olden times? No. How about televisions and refrigerators? No. Of all of the things we use daily, which of them is not foreign? Do you still want to write with a brush? No. Of course you want to write with a pen or pencil. Did our ancestor invent the pen or pencil? No. Why did you scold me for not being diligent when I did not do well in English class, and now you say believing in Jesus is a "Western religion"? Why do you have a different standard? . . . If you believe "Western" is bad, then you should give everything up. If these things are good, you want to use them. Is not a pen better than a brush? Are electric lights not better than your oil lamps? You want to use things that are good, right?

Second, Christian Hakkas also seek to help Hakka non-Christians understand that just because Christianity was brought to China and Taiwan by Westerners, this does not necessarily mean it is "Western." #20 provided the following example of what he often says to Hakka non-Christians:

> Why is Christianity called a "Western religion"? When the game of Go (*weiqi*), invented by Chinese, is taken to Japan and becomes popular there, does it become Japanese? Of course not! Whether we are talking about Europeans or Americans, they only received the Lord's blessings after they believed in Jesus. Originally, they did not believe, and before they believed, they were not blessed, right? . . . So, Christianity is not a Western religion; it is for the whole world. God wants to give it to us; He wants to share it with everyone so that everyone can have it. Westerners accepted it earlier, so they have also been blessed earlier.

Third, informants reported that Hakka Christians have also sought to change the meaning of "foreign religion" or "Western religion" from "inferior" to "a blessing Hakkas have missed." #20 provided an example of the way Christians seek to make this change. He said he often talks to non-Christian Hakkas about how China was so strong during the Tang, Song, and Ming Dynasties and then poses the question, "Why did Westerners suddenly become stronger in the last few hundred years?" He responds, "It is because they believed in Jesus. . . . Countries that believe in Jesus are more scientific and democratic."

Providing Opportunities to Get to Know Christianity

Informants also reported that in the context of the categorization of being Christian as "foreign," Christian Hakkas seek to provide opportunities for Hakkas to get to know Christianity better. These efforts are motivated by the perception that a large part of the foreign flavor of being Christian has its roots in the fact that many Hakkas have had little or no contact with Christianity and just oppose this religion because they do not understand it. #19 elaborated, "There are lots of misunderstandings, but many people do not see them as misunderstandings—[they see them] as the way things really are."

In this area, informants told stories of how they themselves or other people who had originally been opposed to Christianity had changed their opinion after an encounter with Christians or after they had attended a Christian service in some setting (e.g., at a funeral or wedding). As Christian informants talked about their own ministries or those of their churches, it was readily evident that many of them and other Christian Hakkas were actively and creatively working in a variety of ways to give non-Christians opportunities to encounter Christianity in deeper ways.

One example of this desire to actively engage non-Christians is how several Christian informants talked about the need to build relationships that facilitate interactions with non-Christians where practices associated with being Christian and perspectives can be explained. #19 pointed out that without personal contact with Christians, non-Christian Hakkas naturally continue to believe the categorizations that have been passed on to them. He said, "If a person is going to trust in Jesus, we need to make friends with them. If we do not, it is really hard to take the next step." Several informants lamented the fact that many Christians often do not have much interaction with non-Christian relatives. #21 said, "[The reason many Hakkas have a problem with their Christian relatives using practices associated with being Christian] is that Christians have not built relationships with them. If there is a relationship, differences in practices are not so important." She continued, telling about her own situation as a new Christian, "I have not explained to my relatives that I now believe in Jesus as well as the reason why I do not worship or prepare sacrifices anymore, why I use flowers . . . commemorating our ancestors [rather than worshiping them]. If I were to go and explain things to them, they would not have a problem with these things. Those people do not know the good things Christians enjoy; they just know [their traditions]." She told of her intention to go and visit her older relatives and seek appropriate, non-confrontational opportunities to explain and share with them.

Another example of this intentional engagement is how Hakka Christians hold events that will help non-Christian Hakkas better understand practices associated with being Christian. For example, #22 told about the large-scale ancestor-memorial services which Christian churches sponsor together each year around the time that many Hakkas are returning to their ancestral homes for Tomb Sweeping. During these services, contextualized rituals are used to commemorate ancestors. #22 told how, in Taipei, Christians invite many non-Christian Hakka leaders, politicians, and other non-Christians to attend and participate. He said:

> This is a way of helping these non-Christians [better understand Christianity]. It is good for them to see the church sponsor this type of event and paves the road for more to happen in the future. After attending, they will say, "Being a Christian is also very good, because Christian churches do not reject ancestors [like I thought]." . . . Since we have paved the road in this way, in the future when they have an opportunity to come in contact with Christianity again [and desire to know more], we can continue to reach out to them. . . . We use this ancestor-memorial service as a starting point for evangelism. These non-Christians would never come to church or attend an evangelistic meeting, but when we invite them to come and bow [as a part of the Christian ritual] and commemorate the ancestors together, they are interested. As a result, they have an opportunity to see how Christian Hakkas [commemorate their ancestors].

An additional example of this desire to help Hakka non-Christians get to know Christianity better is the way Hakka Christians seek to involve non-Christians in funerals. #19 talked about how, in contextualized rituals, the involvement of respected clan members in the rituals means they and those who respect them are engaged and Christian funerals are not seen as just something for Christians. #24 elaborated, "[Hakka non-Christians who are involved in the Three-Memorials Ceremony in this way] feel we really value them. They have a chance to see how Christians commemorate their ancestors and value their ancestors. They can only hear our sermons, the songs we sing, and worship God together with us if they are present. This is a good opportunity."

All Religions Are Not the Same

As informants talked about the attitudes and efforts of Hakka Christians in the face of the non-Christian Hakka categorizations of being Christian as "unnecessary," "disrespectful," "offensive," "substandard," or "hypocritical," they revealed that sometimes Hakka Christians challenge these categorizations and the assumptions undergirding them, and other times they seek to adjust their actions in ways that will undercut these categorizations. The following themes were evident in the observations informants had made of Hakka Christians in this area: (1) clearly different, (2) offense is sometimes necessary, (3) trying to be less offensive, and (4) doing good works.

CLEARLY DIFFERENT

Informants reported that many Hakka Christians make efforts to challenge the assumption of non-Christian Hakkas that all religions are the same and have the same goal, that of teaching people to be good, undergirding the negative categorizations discussed in this area. One common assertion that Christian informants made in this vein is how some Hakka Christians believe it is important to be able to clearly explain to non-Christians how Christianity is different from other religions. For example, as he talked about his sacrificial care for his mother, #18 said, "I feel it is not enough to just model Christian beliefs. . . . Being able to explain things is very important." #19 also provided some examples:

> They do not understand when we say God's grace and love are free. They feel going to church every week is a bother. There are a lot of things like this that they do not understand. When they hear Christians say Jesus died on the cross for us, they think He is so pitiable, and they do not understand. Because they do not understand, when we talk about God, they see our God as one to be added to all of the gods they serve. We always talk about sin, right? Because they are not clear about what we mean by sin, they have a hard time accepting that they are sinners and rather insist that they are good. When they do not understand these

important points, it is hard for them to believe. We really need to have a good explanation.

One issue that surfaced often, revealing the importance some Hakka Christians place on challenging the assumption that all religions are the same and have the same goal, is their concern for how non-Christians perceive their actions. It was readily evident that these Hakka Christians want the message their actions are meant to communicate to be very clear—that all religions are not the same and that any beliefs or practices incompatible with the Bible are wrong. For example, #18 pointed out:

> [Christians] should not only consider what they themselves are thinking [as they consider how to be involved in ancestor rituals]. They should also think about the interpretation that others have of their actions. Some people feel there is no problem when the Catholics burn incense because, in doing so, the Catholics are not thinking of the ancestors as gods. The problem with using incense in these settings is that we do not know what others are thinking and cannot determine the meaning that our actions are communicating to them. I feel it is best for Christians to have their own ways and use a set of methods for commemorating ancestors that is as distinctive as possible while still exuding filial piety.

Offense Is Sometimes Necessary

Some Hakka Christians respond to the categorization of non-Christians that conversion to Christianity is "unnecessary" by arguing that sometimes being offensive is unavoidable. For example, responding to the non-Christian categorization of conversion to Christianity as "unnecessary," #27 said, "Since non-Christian Hakkas feel that foreign and local religions are all equally good, they do not think much about conversion to Christianity, or feel attacked by the presence of Christians. I feel . . . Christians need to create an attack or express opposition to these non-Christian Hakkas to prompt them to really think about some of these things."

Other Hakka Christians challenge the categorization that the aggressive and persistent witness of Christians is "offensive," arguing that, while there are some non-Christian Hakkas who are offended, there is also a positive dimension to this kind of witness. #35 explained, "There are people who become Christians as a result of an aggressive witness. The Holy Spirit moves them, and they understand what is being said. . . . But there is also another group that this approach misses. They are filled with antipathy and want nothing to do with Christianity. They end up not even being willing to listen to anyone talk about Christianity."

Trying to Be Less Offensive

Some Hakka Christians responded to the categorization that being Christian is "offensive" by seeking to interact with non-Christians in ways that would create fewer conflicts when possible. Many of the responses of Hakka Christians to any of these categorizations of non-Christian Hakkas are examples of this desire to act in ways that respect Hakka ways without compromising Christian truths. For example, talking about how Hakka Christians challenge the categorizations that Christians are "unfilial" and that they "turn their backs on their ancestors," #19 mentioned doing things in the area of ancestor rituals that, while they might not totally satisfy non-Christian Hakkas, might be seen as valid substitutes which are better than doing nothing (for the ancestors). Some informants talked about the need to be less confrontational in interactions with non-Christian relatives. For example, #18 told about a Hakka Christian who strongly regretted being so strident with his non-Christian relatives after his conversion because they shut him out of further interactions with them and he lost opportunities to share the gospel with them. He told how this Christian was now using less offensive ways to rebuild broken relationships. #18 added that Christians need to be more "skillful" in their interactions with non-Christian Hakkas, finding positive aspects of what they do to affirm. For example, he said even though we cannot affirm any actions that elevate ancestors to the level of gods and worship them, we can still praise a non-Christian who is especially diligent in ancestor veneration for his or her desire to be filial. #21 talked about non-confrontational opportunities to explain practices associated with being Christian to the senior members of her Hakka family. She said, "You should not say, 'When you venerate in this way, you are wrong.' They will immediately ask you to leave. You need to go and gradually build relationships with them."

Christian informants also talked about the need for Hakka Christians to be less offensive in their evangelistic efforts. One principle that came up regularly in this area was the need to move slowly and to be sensitive to the feelings and needs of Hakka non-Christians. For example, #34 said, "If you want them to come and listen to a sermon, no one will come. We need to chat with them, starting with more superficial topics and connect with them. Only if we are slow and deliberate will we be able to do anything. If you start by talking about Christianity and call the pastor to come and give a sermon, I guarantee you that no one will be interested." #21 elaborated further:

> It is important to make friends with them and not to push them to immediately become Christians. When as friends we ask them to come and listen, they will be willing to come. They are willing to be friends, and to eat, chat, and sing together with us. Sometimes we can talk about some of the things God has done for us but not say anything more. If we say too much, they will be scared off and leave, and we will not have another opportunity to share with them.... Our focus should not be on what we want to give to them but on their felt needs and relating the gospel to those needs.

#19 added that Christians need to look for "points of intersection" between Christian teachings and the desires of non-Christian Hakkas—relating the Christian gospel to their desires and needs.

Informants reported that, in the context of the categorizations that Christians are "substandard" and "hypocritical," many Hakka Christians are more attentive to their behavior in areas where Christians have been criticized and choose instead to focus on the way conversion to Christianity has changed them. For example, #19 talked about honoring one's father and mother, one area where Christians are often criticized: "Since [non-Christian Hakkas] place so much emphasis on this area, we need to be very diligent and work hard to express our filial piety. We want to truly be filial though, not just doing these things because they are watching us." #20 elaborated and gave an example from his own life,

> We need to take the love of Christ and live it out ... to show a life of love to Hakka people so that they will really feel our love. For example, when I was sharing the gospel with my mother, I told her how the God of Heaven sent his only Son, Jesus. When I talked to her about these kinds of things, she was not willing to believe. So I asked her if I had become more filial to her after becoming a Christian. At that time, one of my brothers was always smoking, drinking, and gambling. My mom said, "Yes." I had really changed, and she had observed and felt a difference in me.

Another method of seeking to be less offensive is being proactive in potential areas of conflict. One area that surfaced several times in informants' comments is ensuring that the children and other relatives of older people who convert and are baptized shortly before their deaths understand what has happened. #19 reported that he tries to be very careful to take pictures or video recordings of baptisms so that, when it comes to planning funerals for the deceased, there is no dispute as to whether or not they were Christians.

Some of these Hakka Christians seek to hide their Christian identity for fear of providing evidence to non-Christians that Christians are "substandard" and "hypocritical." For example, #31 explained that he is sometimes afraid to tell people he is a Christian, ". . . because I am not such a good person, and everyone knows it. . . . I feel I need to change in a lot of areas, but I feel doing so is impossible. How can a person who struggles [like I do] be a Christian? I feel very embarrassed."

Doing Good Works

In the context of Hakka non-Christians who assume that the role of all religions is to teach people to do good and who categorize Christian behavior in this area as "substandard" and "hypocritical," some Hakka Christians encourage the church to be more involved in ministries of compassion. For example, #18 pointed out that in the past, Christians were more involved in these kinds of ministries—establishing hospitals and institutions that help those with special needs (e.g., the blind). He suggested that the church should provide non-Christian Hakkas who want to do good deeds with opportunities to do so in Christian settings rather than only in those organized by other religious groups. This kind of involvement would have a two-fold benefit; these volunteers would have a better chance to be exposed to the tenets of Christianity, and non-Christians would see Christian organizations as more involved in ministry to the disadvantaged.

Constructing Hakka in Order to Justify Prioritizing Ministry to Hakkas

As informants talked about the ways Christian Hakkas relate to Hakka in their ministries, they revealed that many of them are constructing Hakka in ways that justify prioritizing ministry to non-Christian Hakkas—highlighting the reasons they believe they and other Christians who desire to share the gospel with non-Christians should see evangelism of Hakkas as a high priority. Like all self-identification in the ethnic-identification process, these Hakkas construct Hakka in a way that will help them achieve their goals. Several different themes emerged as informants discussed and gave examples of the attitudes and actions of Christian Hakkas as they related to other Christians: (1) a difficult situation, (2) not hard ground, (3) neglected, (4) needing our sacrifice, and (5) needing immediate attention.

A Difficult Situation

As informants talked about the situation Christian Hakkas face as they encounter non-Christian Hakka categorizations of being Christian and the implications of these categorizations, they reported that many articulate that the growth of Christian church among Hakkas faces significant challenges. Informants often used words like "complicated," "not easy," and "hard" as they talked about the situation that Christian Hakkas and those ministering to Hakkas face. While discussing these difficulties, #19, a pastor who has been involved in ministry to Hakkas for most of his life, used a recently deceased older Hakka woman as an example:

> She lived as a Christian in a Hakka area for forty years and was only able to lead two or three people to believe in Jesus. It was very hard for her. Her son [a Hakka pastor] was one of the only fruits of her efforts. It was very hard for her to live as a Christian. Hakkas have so many misunderstandings [about Christianity]. . . . If you want to reach out to Hakkas you have to spend a lot of time. . . . Leading people to Christ in a Hakka area is *very* difficult. . . . In the past, there were many Christians, including Hakkas, who worked [in Hakka areas] for five to ten years and then felt they had done enough. . . . They felt they had done their best and could do no more.

#20 compared the challenges of ministering to Hakkas with the challenges that the Israelites faced in biblical times of taking the land of Canaan that God had promised to them (see Numbers 13). He told how ten of the twelve men sent to spy out the land felt the people who lived in the land of Canaan were too strong and would be too hard to defeat. He compared these ten fearful spies with missionaries and others who dare not join in ministries to Hakkas. The two brave and faith-filled spies were compared with those who dare to take on the task of ministering among the Hakkas. Presenting ministry to Hakkas as *very* challenging can justify prioritizing this ministry and lead to a respect for those who dare to join in ministry among Hakkas and a desire to support and maybe even sacrifice oneself to join in these ministries.

When Christian informants discussed the challenges Christian Hakkas face, they often cited the statistic that only three out of every one thousand Hakkas are Christian as evidence of these challenges. For example, as #32 talked about his desire to learn how to evangelize better, he said, "Why is it that we have been evangelizing [Hakkas] for so long and only have 0.3 percent of Hakkas [who are Christians]?" Some informants referred to this statistic using the number "997" to talk about the nine hundred and ninety-seven non-Christians out of every one thousand Hakkas. Informants never raised the figures of Swanson or Xia, and all but one had not been exposed to the TSCS data. Interviews took place before the CHEA and the HMS began reporting that the 0.3 percent figure had improved to 0.4 percent.

For some Hakka Christians, the stark need evidenced by this 0.3 percent statistic motivated them to want to become more involved in ministry to Hakkas. For example, when asked to talk about his strong desire to invest his life so that Hakkas could have better opportunities to hear the gospel, #18 explained about the different ethnic groups in Taiwan and then told how the percentage of Christians among Hakkas was much lower than in other groups. He then cited the 0.3 percent statistic and compared it with a 2.6-3.0 percent statistic of Christians among all residents of Taiwan.

Some Hakka Christians use this 0.3 percent statistic in settings where they want to convince others of the need to get involved in Hakka ministry. For example, in a setting where he spoke to a group of people regarding the need to prioritize ministry to Hakkas, #24 told the following story about an expatriate missionary: "I have heard . . . that in his car, the number '997' was written on his steering wheel. Why? Because in every one thousand Hakkas, there are 997 who are lost. So . . . every time he drove his car, he reminded himself . . . of the 997 who do not know Jesus, who are still unsaved. Hearing this really moved me." With the important nature of this need voiced by a non-Hakka in this way, #24 moved on to encourage listeners to join in meeting the need and enumerated specific ways they could be involved.

One place where this statistic is currently being used in a foundational role is in the "Double the Hakka Church in Ten Years Movement" organized by the Christian Hakka Evangelical Association (CHEA). Some Hakka Christians are appealing to other Christians to join this movement and help address the stark need reflected in the 0.3 percent statistic. #19 reported, "We have found that when we appeal like this, more and more [people come to help].... It is really amazing. People find things they can do and work diligently to see if it will help. They are moved to help in this area where Hakkas are weak. [For example, they say,] 'My church can do a little; we can send a team, or we can give money.'" He gave the example of a famous non-Hakka pastor of an urban church who, in response to the need reflected in this statistic, was willing to make time in his busy schedule to travel to Hakka areas and lend his talents to Hakka ministry. For example, #19 reported that this gifted pastor had recently led a large funeral service for a Hakka Christian and had been particularly effective in connecting with many of the non-Christian Hakkas in attendance. #19 also told about how, as a part of the "Double the Hakka Church in Ten Years Movement," new churches have been intentionally planted in Hakka areas, Hakka-language services and small groups have been started in existing churches, and many Christians have joined together to pray for Hakka ministry. #19 added, "When everyone works together, there is strength."

Informants and the Hakka Christians they described accept the 0.3 percent statistic as being reflective of the current spiritual need among Hakkas. For example, #19 explained why this statistic made sense to him, calculating the percentage of Hakka Christians in two locations in the Hakka area where he lives by dividing the average attendance at all churches in those locations by the total population in those same locations, "In [City A] there are [W number of] churches which, if we err on the high side, have roughly fifty people each. That calculates to be 0.6 percent. [City A] has more churches than most areas; there are some places with only one or two churches.... [City A] has [X number of] people.... [Town B] has a population of [Z] and only [Y number of] people attending church.... So, the percentage there is only 0.15 percent." For him, averaging his figures of 0.6 percent and 0.15 percent in these locations supports the 0.3 percent figure.

Not Hard Ground

As informants talked about the small size of the Hakka Christian community in the context of Hakka non-Christian categorizations of being Christian, a categorization or ascription of Hakkas as "hard ground" often surfaced, one that is closely connected to the ascription of Hakkas as having a "stiff-necked Hakka spirit." Christian informants constructed Hakka in the context of this categorization in ways that reveal their desire to present Hakka in ways that make the evangelism of Hakkas achievable and worthwhile. For example, some informants acknowledged the connection between the stiff-necked Hakkas and the small size of the Hakka Christian community. Using the metaphor of farming, they talked about the Hakkas as "hard ground" that has not been properly prepared for "planting." In doing so, they blamed the "farmer" rather than the "soil" for the lack of a bountiful "harvest." For example, #19 argued, "Hakka areas are like hard ground that has not been plowed. When everyone casts the seed on the ground, they find out that the ground is hard, and so they decide to wait until the ground is looser before they go and spread more seed. The problem is [not that it is hard, but one must ask], 'Who is going to do the plowing and loosening?'"

Other Christian informants rejected this categorization that Hakkas are "hard ground" or that, when given the same opportunities as other ethnics, Hakkas are resistant or less responsive to Christian evangelistic efforts. #25 articulated this perspective, "When comparing Hakkas to Hoklos, many [Christians] mistakenly think Hakkas are hard-hearted. Actually, this is not true; it is a misunderstanding. Hakkas are not hard-hearted. Do they really reject things that come from the outside? I do not think so." Wen Yongsheng, president of the Hakka Mission Seminary, explained, "When people say, 'Hakkas are "hard ground,"' the underlying meaning is . . . that Hakkas are hard-hearted and find it very hard to believe in the Lord; [in other words], no matter how we evangelize, it is of no use. Those who say these words push the blame [for the small size of the Hakka church] off on Hakkas."[5] Wen countered, "Hakkas are not 'hard ground'; all we need to do is plow the ground, and then there will be a great harvest."[6]

A positive dimension of the stiff-necked Hakka spirit surfaced often as Christian informants discussed Christian attitudes and actions in the context of the categorizations of being Christian they face. Several informants reported that once a Hakka becomes a Christian, they are "good Christians." For example, #29 said, "The nature of Hakkas is that when we truly believe in Jesus, we will persist in our beliefs until the end; we are more loyal." #26 said, "When Hakkas become Christians, they are stiff-necked to the point that they will still believe even if they are beheaded for

5. Wen, "Double in Ten," 161.
6. Ibid.

doing so." #20 added, "Once Hakkas believe in Jesus, they are much more diligent about their beliefs and do more work for their Lord."

Neglected

Many Christian informants argued that the reason for the low percentage of Christian Hakkas is that Hakkas have been neglected by the Christian church. Informants described neglect as not working to prepare the "soil" of Hakka hearts by doing ministry in ways that take into consideration the special characteristics of Hakkas. In doing so, informants suggest a reason more workers should get involved in Hakka ministry. For example, #26 said, "Hakkas have the reputation of being stiff-necked, but they are this way because we have not tried to understand why they are stiff-necked. They are stiff-necked when they are not acknowledged [as different], so of course their neck will become harder and harder."

One of the aspects of this neglect that surfaced often is that of not using the Hakka language to minister to Hakkas. Most churches, even those churches which are in Hakka areas, use either Hoklo or Mandarin in their services. #19 commented: "[There have been] 140 years of mission work done in Hakka areas, and there is still no complete Hakka Bible and not enough Hakka hymnbooks and songs. This is *very* strange." #26 told about the strange situation that often results because Christians are used to "being Christian" in another language. He said:

> You come to share the gospel with me [when I am sick] and use Hakka to say, "How are you today? I understand you are not feeling well. Would you mind if I prayed for you?" Then suddenly in your prayer you switch to speaking Hoklo. Do you not feel this is strange? When you talk with me, you use Hakka, but when you pray, you use Hoklo. It feels like the gospel does not belong to Hakkas but belongs to Hoklos. [When this situation happened to me several years ago], I had no other way to handle things, because at that time I could only pray in Hoklo, I could not pray in Hakka.

Prominent in informants' comments about this aspect of neglect are the words and actions of early missionaries, especially those of George Mackay. Several informants pointed out the strong influence that early missionary George Mackay is perceived to have had in this area. For example, #17 said:

> The main reason [for the low percentage of Hakka Christians] is that Christians have not been diligent and focused in their Hakka work. [Early on,] missionaries influenced things in this way. They felt that since, when Hakkas come to the cities to do business they learn Hoklo, [it was not necessary to use the Hakka language in ministry]. Mackay wrote in his journal that in one hundred years the Hakka language would disappear. This had a profound impact. After this, in the outreach ministries of the Presbyterian Church in Taiwan to Hakkas, Hoklo was the language that was always used. [PCT missionaries and national pastors] did not realize that to Hakkas, the language of their ancestors is extremely important . . . The average missionary [and national pastor] did not understand this part.

#19 added, "Because of Mackay's decision, the Hakka church in Taiwan has not had a period of time when it could grow well."

Informants also told stories of local Christians who had acknowledged their neglect of ministry to Hakkas. For example, in 2003, when Christians participating in the *Taiwan xunhui daogao yundong* (Touring Taiwan prayer movement) came to Hakka areas, #24 reported, "They prayed and said that, in the past, evangelism to the Hakkas had been neglected, and they admitted that this neglect was sin."

Another aspect of this neglect that informants raised is the lack, until 1999, of a Hakka seminary. To many informants, if one wants to evangelize Hakkas and strengthen the Hakka church, a Hakka seminary is an obvious necessity. Without this kind of institution, informants reported that Hakka seminary students not only do not have as many opportunities to learn about the unique needs of Hakkas and how to use the Hakka language in ministry, but they often get channeled into non-Hakka ministries. #22 elaborated, "When Hakka students go to a seminary that does not emphasize Hakka, after three or four years, they no longer have a burden for Hakka ministry. Other churches probably have a stronger attraction [to them]." #24 talked about how having a Hakka seminary helps:

> Those in the Hakka Mission Seminary [HMS] are always discussing a vision for Hakkas or outreach to Hakkas. When students are [in this environment] for one year, two years, or three years, when they are constantly hearing about Hakkas and praying for Hakka churches, pastors, and ministries, . . . when they often hear about the needs of Hakkas, it is easier for this vision for Hakkas to be in their hearts. . . . Also, [HMS] assigns students to do their

practicum in Hakka churches or churches that have a burden for Hakka ministries. . . . As a result, these students have many more opportunities to become acquainted with Hakka churches. . . . After they graduate, these students [are more likely] to stay and serve in Hakka areas.

Informants also pointed out that a Hakka seminary can also serve as a place where pastors and scholars discuss and research the unique challenges in Hakka ministries.

Also, in the area of seminary training, one of the common examples Christian informants raised of the neglect of Hakkas was the way many prospective leaders in the Presbyterian Church in Taiwan (PCT) were required to use the Hoklo language in seminary. #26 told about his own experience:

> The PCT seminary made Hoklo their "national" language, and no Mandarin was spoken there. This focus on Hoklo was really hard, because even though I had learned some simple Hoklo when I did my military service . . . the Hoklo used in seminary was not the same. From the Lord's Prayer, to the creeds, to the Apostles' Creed, to praying, to preaching, to reading the Bible, all of these things were done in Hoklo. When I first started, it was *very* difficult, and I wanted to give up. I asked myself, "Why do I need to speak Hoklo when I study in seminary?" The teachers all taught in Hoklo.

An additional aspect of this neglect that often surfaced in the comments of informants is the way Hakkas have been neglected in the organizational structure of the PCT. The events that finally led to the establishment of a Hakka presbytery (*Kejia xuanjiao zhonghui*) in 2007 were fresh in the minds of several informants. For example, #17 told about how, in the late 1960s, he had called for the establishment of a Hakka presbytery. He said, "At that time I argued that Hakka churches needed to step out and work to establish a Hakka presbytery. In the Presbyterian church . . . a presbytery is a basic unit; whether administration, church planting, or finances, everything happens in the presbytery. If you do not have a presbytery, you cannot do anything. . . . Everyone laughed and said this would be impossible." Several informants and the Hakka Christians they talked about actively supported efforts to prioritize Hakka ministry in the PCT organizational structure.

Needing Our Sacrifice

Informants also talked about how Christian Hakkas presented Hakka as needing our sacrifice, again in order to motivate more people to join in ministry to Hakkas. For example, speaking to other Hakkas and evoking the loyalty to "us" present in the Hakka cultural "stuff," #25 said, "For the sake of our own Hakka people, we also need to make some sacrifices. If we cannot speak Hakka, we should go and learn it. Foreign missionaries are willing to come to Hakka areas and learn Hakka in order to evangelize. We are locals, and this is our language. If we cannot speak Hakka, there is no excuse. We should go and learn it. We should restore our own culture."

Speaking to all potential workers, Wen argued, "Hakkas can change; we just need to be willing to pay a price, and then Hakkas will probably believe in the Lord."[7] #19 argued that this price was paid in other areas of ministry in Taiwan but not in Hakka areas. He stated, "When missionary George Mackay went to Hoklo areas [in the late 1800s], he learned their language, preached, started a seminary, pulled teeth, started other schools . . . he did not just preach and, if his listeners rejected his words, move on to other areas. No. Those who come to Hakka areas need to do the same."

Another sacrifice that informants reported that some Hakka Christians are asking other Christians to make is being willing to give up some of their habits or church traditions. #19 reported:

> Change is hard for the church. . . . Every church has traditions. After they do something five times it becomes a tradition . . . It is really hard to change the traditions of the church. Together, pastors and seminaries especially need to research, discuss, and think, evaluating [Christian] practices in the light of the culture of the grass-roots people around us and looking for connecting points and practices that are more acceptable to them. We really need to think about these things. There are some who never think about things outside the walls of the church. Because it is easier for them, after they do something for five years, they do not want to change.

#25 talked about the way many Christians oppose using Hakka music in the church: "They are not used to this kind of music, so they oppose using it in the church. . . . They do not think about the fact that if we added Chinese songs, gaining converts will be easier and faster. . . . They are selfish and only think of their own preferences. . . . They have never been

---

7. Ibid.

exposed to good Chinese music, so they feel Chinese music is backward and not good, that only Western music is good music."

Needing Immediate Attention

As informants related how Hakka Christians talked about the need to prioritize ministries to Hakka, the importance of the present moment often surfaced. Two perspectives were evident. There are those who believe Hakkas in Taiwan are standing on the threshold of a renewed interest in things Hakka by those who are being Hakka. The motivation to begin prioritizing Hakkas in ministry immediately is that timely action will allow the church to take advantage of this trend. For example, #24 described the recent efforts of the Taiwan government to value Hakkas and said:

> Hakka mission in Taiwan is facing a crucial time. Of course, everyone in society sees our government beginning to value Hakkas—establishing the Council for Hakka Affairs of the Executive Yuan—everyone sees there is a new hope for Hakka ministries. Even though we see things that make us worry (including the way Hakka youth, in the current environment in Taiwan, are less and less interested in the Hakka language and only a few are able to speak this language), through the government programs to encourage the use of mother tongues, the next generation has the opportunity to learn their mother tongue. So, we feel this coming period of time is key for Hakka mission. If we do not take advantage of this period of time, maybe in ten years, outreach to Hakkas will be even more difficult.

Other Hakka Christians have a more pessimistic view, believing that the interest that those who are being Hakka in Taiwan have towards Hakka things will continue to diminish. They suggest that if Christians do not quickly take advantage of those who currently express interest in using the Hakka language and focusing on their Hakka identity, this opportunity to use Hakka to connect with people will be wasted. For example, #22 argued that the time to use Hakka in ministry is now, saying, "My feeling is that, in Taiwan, it is possible that there is only one more period of time left when we can use the Hakka language in evangelism. We want to take advantage of this time to give the gospel to Hakkas because there is still this Hakka identity. Thirty years from now, those who can speak Hakka, those who identify themselves as Hakka, those old-fashioned Hakkas, will all have died. Consequently, these things will naturally drop off and disappear."

Reflecting on the Responses of Christian Hakkas Through the Lens of Ethnic Identification

The focus of this section is on using the lens of ethnic identification to look briefly at the responses of Hakka Christians discussed in the previous three sections of this chapter. Looking at these responses through the lens of ethnic identification can provide greater depth to an understanding of these responses.

The way Hakka Christian leaders vary in the importance they place on Hakka in their ministries reveals the fluidity of ethnic identification. This diversity in focus on Hakka in ministries can be seen to reflect the variety of ways that those who are being Hakka relate to Hakka. For example, it is probable that those leaders who are heavily emphasizing Hakka in their ministries are expressing the strong salience they feel for Hakka. In the same way, it is probable that the thinness of Hakka identity or the desire to downplay or even reject their Hakka identity is reflected in the actions of those leaders who balance their ministries with other priorities or who have other burdens and interests that they are pursuing in their ministries.

The fact that there are those Hakka Christian leaders who look at the non-Christians around them and choose to focus their ministries on Hakka rather than on other ways of differentiating people (e.g., geographical area, age, job, education level) could be the result of the fact that ethnic categories are easy, very accessible, and plausible ways of grouping people, something that contributes to fixity in ethnic distinctions.[8] When some Hakka Christian leaders are reported by informants to be balancing an emphasis on Hakka with other ministry foci, they reveal the fluidity present in the ethnic distinction. Rather than insisting on making Hakka primary in their ministries at all costs, they construct Hakka in such a way that this identity and their Hakka connection can be balanced with other ministry priorities in order to achieve the results that are the most beneficial to them.

The way Hakka Christians actively contest the categorizations of non-Christian Hakkas also reveals the process of ethnic identification. Whether conscious or not, these efforts to challenge these categorizations reveal that the meaning of being Hakka, especially as it relates to being Christian, is being negotiated through these interactions. As informants

---

8. Brubaker, *Ethnicity without Groups*; Hale, "Explaining Ethnicity."

talked about the endeavors of Hakka Christians, it was evident that these Hakka Christians are seeking to define Hakka in a way that will produce the positive results they are seeking—in this case, that of tensions between being Hakka and being Christian being diminished or removed so that more Hakkas will see being Christian as something they can and want to embrace.

The way some Hakka Christians construct Hakka as "a difficult situation," "not hard ground," "neglected," "needing our sacrifice," and "needing immediate attention" can be seen as one act in the drama of ethnic identification. These Christians can be seen as constructing Hakka in ways that will help them achieve the positive results they desire—in this case, having other Christians join them in prioritizing ministry to Hakkas and, ultimately, more Hakkas becoming Christians. Other Christians who hear these constructions actively make choices about how to respond to them: with acceptance, with rejection, or in another way. Some may accept them and join in prioritizing ministry to Hakkas. Others may reject this construction and argue that Hakkas, rather than being "neglected," are "hard ground." Still others may respond that the prioritizing of Hakka is good for others but not for themselves.

The origins and continued justification of the use of the 0.3 percent statistic to talk about the spiritual needs among the Hakkas can also be shown to have ethnic dimensions. When Liao and other Hakka Christians calculate the percentage of Hakka Christians in predominantly Hakka areas and then extrapolate that figure to represent the situation among all Hakkas in Taiwan, they reveal the reification and dual accentuation that scholars argue accompanies the use of ethnic categories. Individuals ascribed to belong to a certain category (in this case Hakka) are viewed and attributed characteristics based on certain exemplars of that group. In other words, the implicit assumption is that Hakkas are a homogeneous whole; the spiritual condition of the many Hakkas living outside Hakka areas is consciously or unconsciously assumed to be the same as that of those living in Hakka areas.

The way the words of Mackay, "the younger generation learn the Hoklo dialect, and in time, the Hakkas may become extinct,"[9] are handled by Hakka Christians who want others to join them in prioritizing ministry to Hakkas can also be shown to have ethnic dimensions. An important part of constructing Hakka as "neglected" is to be able to affix blame on

---

9. Mackay, *From Far Formosa*, 1896 #1925

someone. The way blame is placed on Mackay, when a case can be made that his words were only part of an off-hand observation in a certain context and were not intended to articulate his views on and strategy for ministry to Hakkas, can be understood to be part of a construction of Hakka that will bring the best possible results. Placing a significant amount of blame on Mackay's words and the influence of these words as the underlying reason for the neglect of Hakka among PCT churches in Taiwan can be seen as an ingenious way for these Hakka Christians to avoid offending some of those whom they are seeking to recruit to join in prioritizing Hakka ministry. If, for example, rather than blaming Mackay, the blame for the neglect of Hakkas was placed on Mainlander or Hoklo Christians and these Christians were accused of ethnic discrimination or domination, the construction of Hakka as "neglected" could evoke entirely different emotions. Perhaps placing blame on these groups of Christians might elicit a defensive or an otherwise unfavorable response rather than a sympathetic one.

Concluding Remarks

This chapter explored the actions of Hakka Christians in the context of the negative categorizations that Hakka non-Christians articulated regarding Christians and Christianity. In the first section, the focus was on the way Hakka Christians vary in the extent to which they make Hakka important in their ministries. Some Hakka Christians were shown to make Hakka the strong focal point of their ministry efforts. Others were presented as valuing their Hakka roots and articulating an understanding of the spiritual needs of the Hakkas but being forced by their context to balance Hakka with other ministry priorities. Still other Hakka Christians were pointed out to have ministry burdens or interests in other areas.

The second section highlighted the different efforts Christian Hakkas have made to challenge the categorizations of non-Christian Hakkas. These challenges were organized under five themes. Under the first theme of "family," the efforts of Christian Hakkas were divided under the subthemes of "contextualized ancestor practices," "showing respect to elders and ancestors," "filial piety without burning incense," "challenging the grip of traditions," and "using the Hakka language." One effort of Hakka Christians that surfaced several times under this theme and others and which is important to note is the development and strategic use of contextualized ancestor practices.

"Reciprocal relationships" was the second theme used in this section to discuss the responses of Christian Hakkas to some categorizations of being Christian in this topic area. Christians were seen to be consciously seeking opportunities to do and say things that would convey that they were "acting like 'us,'" that would "redefine relationships with ancestors," and that would help Hakka non-Christians understand "worship of the highest God."

Under the third theme of "everyone," challenges to the Hakka non-Christian categorizations of being Christian in this topic area were raised and discussed. Hakka Christians were shown to be doing and saying things that would undercut the practice of "blindly following everyone" and that would be effective in "gaining the favor of everyone" and "fighting the disfavor of everyone." #19's words emphasizing the need to have more Christians engaged with and spending time with non-Christians "cultivating the ground" and "preparing the harvest" are important to note.

The fourth theme, "not as foreign as you think," was divided into three subsections detailing the endeavors of Hakka Christians in the context of categorizations of being Christian as "foreign." The ways these Christians did and said things that "emphasized Hakka," that "redefined 'foreign,'" and that "provided opportunities to get to know Christianity" were highlighted and explained.

Under the final theme of "all religions are not the same," the actions and words of Hakka Christians in the face of the assumption found in the cultural "stuff" of being Hakka that all religions are good and have the same goal and the categorizations of Hakka non-Christians that are built on this assumption were raised and discussed. Hakka Christians were shown to be arguing that being Christian is "clearly different" and that "offense is sometimes necessary." The ways these Christians made conscious efforts to "try to be less offensive" and to "do good works" were also noted. Considering the extent to which the assumption that "all religions are the same and have the same goal" significantly undergirds many categorizations of non-Christian Hakkas, the limited efforts to challenge this assumption are important to note.

The third section of this chapter related how many Christian Hakkas construct Hakka in order to justify prioritizing ministries to Hakkas and was arranged around four themes. Under the first theme of "a difficult situation," Hakka Christians were shown to be constructing the spiritual need among the Hakkas as a significant challenge, both in the difficulty of the job and the quantity of the work needing to be done. Significant in this topic area is the emphasis placed on the 0.3 percent statistic.

Discussions under the second theme of "not hard ground" captured the efforts of many Hakka Christians to contest a categorization that many Christians have of Hakkas—that they are a spiritual "hard ground." The way this categorization was problematized by shifting the blame from the "ground" to the "farmer" and the "farmer's" lack of cultivation of the "soil" was detailed.

Under the third theme used in this section, the endeavors of many Hakka Christians to construct Hakka as "neglected" were raised and discussed. These Christians were shown to be highlighting and puzzling over the small number of Hakka-focused efforts, resources, and organizations in existence as well as some mistakes made by early missionaries to Taiwan.

In a discussion focused on the fourth theme used in this section, that of "needing our sacrifice," the way some Hakka Christians called for other Hakka Christians to be loyal to their own and for other Christians to sacrifice for Hakkas in ways that have been characteristic of the Christian missionary efforts among other ethnic groups in Taiwan was detailed. The perception that there is a need to sacrifice for Hakkas is significant because it suggests that there is a substantial cost involved in having a Hakka ministry focus. The inclusion of, as a dimension of this sacrifice, the need for pastors, seminaries, and churches to think "outside the walls of the church" and to be willing to change church traditions so that Hakka non-Christians can be more effectively evangelized is also important to note.

Under the final theme in this section entitled "needing immediate attention," the effort of some Hakka Christians to encourage others to focus on Hakka in their ministry efforts was reported. Motivations were revealed to be rooted in both optimistic and pessimistic outlooks on the future of Hakka in Taiwan. These differences in outlook are also worth noting.

In the fourth section of this chapter, some of the ethnic dimensions of the efforts of Christian Hakkas were briefly discussed. Both the fixity and fluidity of ethnic identification were shown to be evident in these efforts.

7

Summary, Implications, and Recommendations

THIS CHAPTER SUMMARIZES THE findings of this exploratory study of tensions between being Hakka in northwestern Taiwan and being Christian. Implications of these findings and some recommendations based on these findings for ministry to the Hakkas of northwestern Taiwan as well as for mission outreach throughout the world are also detailed. This chapter also includes some recommendations for further research on this topic.

Summary of Findings

This research reveals that tensions between being Hakka in northwestern Taiwan and being Christian are rooted in the cultural "stuff" of being Hakka, "stuff" which shapes the perceptions and actions of Hakkas. As informants constructed Hakka for this researcher in the context of thinking about the way Hakkas relate to being Christian, five areas of "stuff" surfaced: Hakka history, family, reciprocal relationships, everyone, and Christianity. The symbols informants raised in each of these areas evidence both fixity—that they are resistant to change—and fluidity—that they are changing. The boundaries of being Hakka were found to vary and be porous for some. The way Hakkas relate to being Hakka was also found to vary between the extremes of those who make the Hakka identity primary and salient and those who distance themselves from or reject this identity.

This study also reveals that tensions between being Hakka in northwestern Taiwan and being Christian surface and are expressed in the negative categorizations that many non-Christian Hakkas have of being

Christian when they notice and make significant cultural differences between being Hakka and being Christian. These categorizations relate to topics of Hakka history, family, reciprocal relationships, everyone, and Christianity and are constructed using the raw materials of their cultural "stuff." Both fixity and fluidity were observed in these constructions. Fixity resulted from the way Hakka practices are perceived to be "the way things should be done," the way these practices meet deep needs, the way being Christian is reified, and the accessibility of the "not-Hakka" category. Fluidity was seen in the way that these categorizations change over time, vary between different persons in the same situation, and vary depending on age, education, and location. Fluidity was also seen in the way that the meanings of symbols used in these categorizations are often unstable.

This research further reveals that Christian Hakkas respond, in the context of the categorizations of Hakka non-Christians, in ways they hope will bring positive results. The responses of Hakka Christians vary in the emphasis Christian Hakka leaders place on Hakka in their ministries, with some choosing a primary focus in this area rather than other possible foci and other Hakka Christian leaders balancing this priority with other pressing priorities. Other responses include Christian Hakkas using their words and actions to challenge the categorizations of non-Christian Hakkas and to construct Hakka in ways that justify prioritizing ministry to Hakkas.

Implications and Recommendations for Mission

While this research does not reveal easy answers that will rapidly increase the size of the Hakka church in Taiwan, highlighting the dimensions of this situation is expected to help both expatriate missionaries and local Christians and their leaders working in Taiwan to be more intentional and strategic in their outreach efforts. LeCompte and Schensul assert the value of this highlighting: "In many ways, the job of the ethnographer is, in fact, to attribute meanings and importance to patterns and regularities that people otherwise take for granted in everyday life—until a researcher points them out, highlights them, and gives them broader significance by associating them with other experiences, situations, and literature."[1] This discussion will first focus on some general implications and recommendations for Christian workers in various contexts and then on those related to the perspective of people groups. The focus will then move to implications

---

1. LeCompte and Schensul, *Analyzing and Interpreting Data*, 214.

and recommendations that relate specifically to ministry among Hakkas in northwestern Taiwan.

Some General Thoughts for Christian Workers in Various Contexts

There are several general implications of this research project for Christian workers ministering in various contexts throughout the world. One important implication of looking at any mission context through the social constructionist lens on ethnicity and ethnic groups is the need to be cautious about the way the term "ethnic group" is understood and used. Missiologists and ministry practitioners need to be careful not to think of these "groups" as static, homogeneous, and clearly bounded or as something people possess (such as a nose on their face). Rather, these "groups" should be thought of as something people do together (as in a game they are playing), something perceived to be "fixed" and yet that is "fluid" or changing. Only when "ethnic groups" are viewed in this way will the insights that can be gained from this theoretical lens be readily evident.

It is also important for those who are crossing cultures and ethnic boundaries in order to present the gospel to others to understand that, in their ministry contexts, there are often conversations taking place about being Christian that have ethnic dimensions. The importance of working to understand the various elements of these conversations—(1) the cultural "stuff" that shapes people and makes some differences between habitual practices and practices associated with being Christian seem significant enough that they reject being Christian as something not for "us," (2) the negative categorizations of being Christian that are voiced, and (3) the way local Christians and others are contesting these categorizations—is evident. The development of the skills necessary to appropriately, effectively, and intentionally recognize, understand, challenge, and interact with non-Christians about their negative categorizations and the presuppositions upon which they are built promises to be strategically helpful. Christians can join the conversations, not by simply relying on rational arguments that articulate a Christian perspective on something, but by raising questions that stimulate their conversation partners to think more about beliefs that they have unquestioningly accepted as fact. Rather than simply pointing out the unbiblical nature of the practices of non-Christians, Christians can work to develop new practices that can effectively replace these non-Christian ones and talk about these new alternatives as counters to the negative categorizations that often surface when Christians do not participate in unbiblical practices. In addition, an awareness that aspects of the cultural "stuff" may be changing due to challenges from within the ethnic boundaries (e.g., the practice of burning spirit money in ancestor practices is being challenged as "bad" because it creates pollution) also highlights the importance of looking for and understanding this kind of change and, when appropriate, of incorporating these voices into interactions with non-Christians about being Christian.

The importance of Christian workers laboring to understand the ways and the extent to which the non-Christians they are attempting to evangelize are relating to their ethnic identity and working to develop understandings and skills that enable them to relate appropriately and strategically as they interact with people who are located differently in this process is also evident. For example, workers can ask questions like, "When do you speak and not speak [the ethnic language of interest]?" or "When do you feel the most and least [the ethnic label of interest]?" This strategic sensitivity may mean doing things in a way that affirms how each individual or group in each context is relating to their ethnic identity—so for Hakkas, having ministries only be as Hakka as or Hakka in the way of the Hakka individual or group with whom one is currently interacting. For example, in the area of the language used to communicate, the Christian worker would ideally follow the language habits of each person with whom they are interacting. Practically, in contexts where more than one language is commonly used, this means developing the language skills to be able to build relationships and interact about being Christian in the one or many languages that the individuals and groups one is seeking to evangelize are in the habit of using. This sensitivity may also mean sometimes, for strategic reasons, deliberately positioning oneself in ways that fit with only one way of relating to ethnic identity. For example, some Christian workers can choose to physically locate themselves among those in a particular area whose ethnic identity is consistently very salient and to reflect that salience in their ministry by using language or cultural "stuff" in ways that would be appropriate in this setting but not in other settings where that identity is less salient.

A related implication of this research is the importance of the Christian worker understanding that there is variety in the way local Christians are relating to a particular ethnic identity. For some, a particular identity will be primary and salient. For others, this identity may be salient only in certain situations. For still others, they may be actively distancing themselves from that identity. An awareness of this variety will help Christian workers to understand how and why these Christians are handling this ethnic identity in different ways. The different perspectives Christians articulate about this ethnic ministry can be understood in the context of their location within the conversation about the importance of that ethnic identity.

Another important implication of this research relates to the way meanings are socially constructed and the way the meanings ascribed by the powerful are often the meanings which are most widely accepted. Christian workers, understanding the dynamics of the way meanings are arrived at in relationships between people with differing degrees of power, can more appropriately and effectively engage people who are located at different places in this power structure. For example, Christian workers can work to identify non-Christians who have some power in determining meanings in any particular setting and seek to contest meanings with them in appropriate ways, working out the implications of any change. In the same way, as Christian workers share the gospel with those who are not in positions of power, it is essential to understand the implications that the change they are advocating may have on these people and to help work out ways to avoid unnecessarily challenging or threatening those in positions of power.

Understanding the variety of ways that non-Christians perceive and respond to being Christian raises the importance of not assuming that the same strategy and/or tool(s) can be used "as is" with each non-Christian whom Christians engage in their evangelistic efforts. Once a Christian has learned a particular way of presenting the gospel, it is often tempting for him/her to assume that using this gospel presentation will enable each and every person being evangelized to understand and respond to the gospel, regardless of who they are. It is also very tempting for some Christians to think back to their own conversion experience, remember the things that were said or done that significantly helped them to respond positively to the gospel, and seek to duplicate these words and actions with those they are seeking to evangelize. While some non-Christians may respond to these approaches and/or tools, others will not and may even be alienated in the process. In evangelistic encounters, the importance of seeking to first understand the way non-Christians perceive and respond to being Christian is clear. A deeper understanding will greatly facilitate efforts to develop effective strategies and/or tools (or to incorporate existing ones) that will enable Christians to graciously interact with each non-Christian in such a way that, as much as possible, their negative categorizations of being Christian will gradually lose their intensity and the voice of the Word of God will become clearer, helping these non-Christians to be able to see themselves as God does.

One potential danger is that, as Christians see the vital nature of surfacing, understanding, and dealing with the negative categorizations that non-Christians have of being Christian, they can easily be led to view themselves more highly than they ought—to overemphasize the importance of the role they play in evangelism. Ultimately, God is the one who does everything necessary to make it possible for people to come to faith in Him. He created each person with a heart which cannot totally be satisfied with anything unless it has Him. He enables each individual to see their sin and turn to Him. He prepared a way through the death of His Son, Jesus, so that all who are outside of His will can be forgiven and restored to Himself. He raises up and empowers people to bring His Word to the ends of the earth and, in doing so, actively pursues each non-Christian rather than passively waiting for them to seek Him out. He also empowers Christians to live in obedience to Him in a world that is evil and uses them as lights which can help non-Christians around them to see the blessings that can come from a right relationship with God. Christians who are seeking to surface, understand, and respond to negative categorizations are doing so because God is at work in them, giving them the power and wisdom to use the analytical and creative gifts He has given them for His glory.

Some Thoughts Related to the People Group Perspective for Christian Workers in Various Contexts

This research implies that the way people are interacting about Christianity in many ministry contexts is much more complex than the people group lens can adequately explain. This subsection will discuss the use of the people group perspective and some of the weaknesses of this perspective. An alternative lens—that of negotiating identity—will be described and the usefulness of this lens will be described.

Using the People Group Perspective

Many Christian workers are accustomed to using the lens of people groups to view existing and potential ministry settings. In *Operation World*, an influential resource that many Christians use to help them understand

and pray for the nations and different people groups in the world, Jason Mandryk offers the following definition of a "people group": "A significantly large sociological grouping of individuals who perceive themselves to have a common affinity. From the viewpoint of evangelization, this is the largest possible group within which the gospel can be spread without encountering barriers of understanding or acceptance."[2] Mandryk suggests three types of people groups—the ethnolinguistic, the sociological, and the incidental people groups. His first category, the "ethnolinguistic people group," "defines a person's identity and primary loyalty according to language and/or ethnicity."[3] The Hakka Chinese ethnic group fits into this category. Mandryk's "sociological people group" is "a grouping defined by its long-term relation to the rest of society, such as by migration or traditional occupation or class, but not having a self-contained culture or identity as an ethnic group."[4] The working class in Taiwan is an example of this category. Mandryk's final category, the "incidental people group," is understood to be "causal associations of individuals that may be temporary and are usually the result of circumstances rather than personal choice."[5] The examples he provides for this category include drug addicts and commuters.[6]

The primary attraction of the people group perspective is the way it allows Christian workers to divide the world's population into "easy to think" categories of people (which often are already being used by others) which feel much more manageable than the whole to talk about, to seek to understand, and to engage in ministry. When an individual is perceived to belong to a particular people group, it easily follows for many that this individual's thinking and actions, to a significant extent, are predictable, and, as a result, evangelism and church-planting strategies that uniquely fit this individual and other people in this group can be developed. Also, Christian workers can compare the spiritual needs and the responses to Christianity of different people groups and prioritize ministry among groups according to their perceived responsiveness to the gospel.

---

2 Mandryk, *Operation World*, 961.
3 Ibid.
4 Ibid.
5 Ibid.
6 Ibid.

Some Weaknesses of the People Group Lens

While the people group lens has been very attractive for Christian workers in different social and/or geographical locations around the world, this perspective is not without significant weaknesses. Christian workers looking at ministry settings through this perspective can and often do fall into the temptation of viewing people in static HUP ways, expecting individuals to be grouped together with others in groups that are internally homogeneous, well-bounded, and clearly distinct from other "groups." They often assume that insiders in these groups have a common affinity that is salient in every situation and that, in the case of ethnolinguistic people groups, members have a primary loyalty to the group. Furthermore, once the gospel is understood to have penetrated group boundaries (e.g., a person understood to be in a people group becomes a Christian), many of these Christian workers expect this good news to spread more naturally throughout the group as insiders (rather than outsiders) share with other insiders.

The problem, as this study has shown in the case of the Hakka ethnic group, is that these expectations often do not correspond with the complex realities found in ministry settings. Christian workers often encounter a great deal of variety in the thinking and actions of individuals identified or categorized as belonging to a particular people group. The people group identity of individuals they encounter in ministry is not always the most salient identity these individuals possess, and these individuals often trust and feel more affinity with and are more loyal to those who are not considered to be group insiders. Group boundaries are often fuzzy and even porous. Consequently, predicting how someone identified or categorized to be in a particular people group will think or act is often difficult, and expecting the individuals perceived to be in this group to trust and feel affinity with and loyalty to other people group insiders in a way that will significantly facilitate the spread of the gospel among these insiders is often unrealistic.

The influence of these problematic expectations is great. Often, large amounts of energy and resources are invested in seeking to understand the kind of person envisioned to be in a particular people group and to develop strategies and tools that will enable Christian workers to evangelize and plant churches in ways that fit with this kind of person and those like him/her (other members of this same people group). When these strategies and tools are used in actual ministry settings—settings where there is

Summary, Implications, and Recommendations 273

great variety in the way people are thinking and acting—they are limited in their effectiveness, and the well-intentioned and sacrificial investments made do not facilitate the spread of the gospel in the way that is expected. For example, if Christian workers in Taiwan envision individuals they encounter in ministry settings to be in the Hakka people group and come to believe that individuals in this group highly value the Hakka language (to the extent that, as long as one is a Hakka speaker, differences in social class, political persuasion, age, personality, geographical location, etc. that normally separate people are considered significantly less important), these Christian workers will likely follow a strategy of learning the Hakka language, developing Hakka language resources, and insisting on using this language in ministry settings. This strategy, based on an inadequate understanding of the variety of ways that Taiwan Hakkas relate to their language, while helpful for those Hakkas for whom the Hakka language is a high priority, will not be as effective with the many Hakkas who value their language to a certain extent but do not prioritize it to the point where this language becomes a primary symbol around which they gather with others or even something that leads them to really hear God's Word. A further influence of these problematic expectations is that Christian workers often become frustrated and disillusioned when those understood to be group insiders do not respond to the ministries and tools designed to fit insiders and when the gospel does not spread as naturally as expected among these insiders.

The weaknesses of the people group lens raise the question of whether or not there are more helpful and accurate ways to think about, to develop understandings of, and to engage people in ministry settings around the world. In the discussion below, an alternative lens will be proposed, not as a mature and "easy to think" alternative to a focus on people groups, but rather as a preliminary idea that is hoped will stimulate Christian workers to search for better ways to think about and engage the complexities they encounter in ministry settings around the world.

The Alternative Lens of Negotiating Identity

The lens of negotiating identity offers the promise of being an alternative to that of people group. Looking thought this lense highlights the way individuals whom Christian workers encounter in ministry contexts are actors who, while their identity has been and continues to be shaped by their world and their place in it, play an active role in determining their identity in general and, more specifically, in regards to "being Christian." These individuals are actively pursuing an identity which they perceive will bring well-being (as they understand it) using the resources available to them to construct and reconstruct identifications of themselves and categorizations of others in the context of being influenced by the self-identifications of others and the categorizations that others have of them.

The Helpfulness of the Lens of Negotiating Identity

Highlighting the way people are negotiating their identities as Christian workers interact with them about being Christian helps Christian workers choose ministry locations, mobilize Christians for missions, incorporate new believers into the church, refocus existing ministries, and engage strategically in interaction with those they encounter in ministry.

Choosing a Ministry Location

Instead of choosing to minister to a people group, Christian workers can use the lens of negotiating identity as they search for a geographical and/or social location in which to minister. Christian workers can choose to enter those locations where there are few or no Christians available to respond to the identifications and categorizations that relate to being Christian. They can also choose locations where the Christian response to one or more key negative categorizations is weak or ineffective. They can choose to focus on a location where there is a lack of understanding and necessary tools (e.g., narratives, illustrations, strategies, contextualized options to existing practices, arguments, literature, training, biblical exegesis, etc.) to effectively contest and problematize these categorizations and the presuppositions upon which they are built.

Mobilize Christians for Mission

As Christian workers seek to increase awareness among other Christians about the spiritual needs of others in the world and to be used by God to call and send gifted Christians to serve as cross-cultural Christian workers, they often use statistics depicting the low percentage of Christians in a particular people group. While these kinds of statistics are "easy to think," they are often hard to gather and can promote a static way of viewing "groups" of people. Looking through the lens of negotiating identity, comparisons of and explanations about the spiritual needs of the world can be focused on negative categorizations that are being articulated in different locations as individuals and groups negotiate their identities. Sending Christian workers to develop effective responses to particular negative categorizations of being Christian that are persistently strong and widely used by non-Christians in a particular geographical or social location could be shown to be a ministry priority. Sending Christian workers to live and work in geographical and social locations where the loving influence of Christians and the voices of Christians responding to the negative categorizations that non-Christians construct are non-existent, weak, or ineffective could also be articulated as a concrete and compelling ministry need.

Incorporating New Believers into the Church

As the aspects of each non-Christian's identity that keep them from becoming a Christian are gradually dealt with and they come to faith, the importance of working to understand the way they are negotiating their identity continues. New Christians need help finding a place in the body of Christ where they and the primary aspects of their identities fit together with others in the body well enough so that they can draw close and have these aspects shaped by encounters with the Word and fellowship with other Christians. Perhaps one of the reasons that many new Christians leave the church is that the church they initially enter is not compatible with some primary aspects of their identity. For example, a sixty-five-year-old new Christian for whom the identity of "not old" was important stated that she did not want to attend a particular church that had been recommended to her because, "They are all old people there."

Refocusing Existing Ministries

Those Christian workers who are already located in a particular ministry setting and who have already invested much time, effort, and money in developing the understandings, skills, and tools needed to minister to a particular people group can refocus their ministries using the lens of negotiating identity while continuing to be good stewards of these investments. Christian workers seeking to reach these people groups can hold their existing understandings of the ways people are relating to each other loosely and explore the complexities involved. They can view those around them as those who are negotiating their identities and more deeply explore these identities (e.g., the symbols being used, the meanings being associated with these symbols, the way individuals are locating themselves with respect to these symbols, and the way these identities relate to the pursuit of well-being). As Christian workers discover geographic and/or social locations around them where the skills and understandings they have developed can help them to cultivate trust and to interact about being Christian in concrete and strategic ways, they can refocus their efforts on these locations.

Existing people-group-focused ministries (e.g., CHEA, HMS) that have been established to train Christian workers for and/or to facilitate ministry to a particular people group (and would lose their reason to exist if this emphasis was abandoned) can work to better understand and help their constituencies to better understand the complexity of meanings encountered among those who have identified themselves or been categorized with this people group label, especially those meanings related to "being Christian." If there is a language associated with this label, these organizations can train people to use this language and develop useful tools in this language that can be used to contest negative categorizations of being Christian and to teach new Christians how to live and grow as Christians. If there is a significant number of individuals for whom this particular people-group identity is salient, these ministries can also focus their efforts on training workers for and facilitating ministry that targets these individuals.

Engaging Strategically with Individuals

Looking at ministry settings through the lens of negotiating identity can help Christian workers to engage strategically in interaction with the individuals they encounter in these settings. First, the lens of negotiating identity can provide Christian workers with a framework in which to work that helps them better understand the individuals with whom they are interacting so that they can build trust and avoid words or actions that unnecessarily create distance. Pursuing this end, Christian workers can work to understand the symbols these individuals are using to identify themselves and categorize others. They can also explore the complex meanings associated with these symbols and where these individuals are located in regard to these symbols. As Christian workers grow in their understanding of the way these individuals are identifying themselves, they can defer to or value these identities and strategically locate themselves in ways that will open up deeper relationships. For example, if they discover individuals who have a thick ethnic identity, they can intentionally value and respect that identity and do things that support it as much as possible (e.g., learning and using ethnic language and music in ministry settings). On the other hand, when Christian workers encounter individuals who have a thin ethnic identity and for whom another identity is primary, they can work to do and say things that match the thinness of their ethnic identity while deferring to or valuing the primary identity.

Second, the lens of negotiating identity can help Christian workers engage strategically in interaction with individuals in the geographical and/or social locations of those around them by highlighting the importance of surfacing and understanding the negative categorizations of being Christian prevalent in those locations. Pursuing this end, Christian workers can seek to explore the way the individuals in these locations are identifying themselves and categorizing others in regards to "being Christian" and the meanings they are attaching to this phenomenon. Christian workers can also explore the cultural "stuff" out of which negative categorizations are being constructed and how this "stuff" is being used in a variety and complexity of ways by the individuals who are embedded in these locations as they seek to identify themselves in ways they perceive will bring them well-being. Christian workers can also seek to understand how these individuals define well-being and the complexity of ways they use in responding to challenges to and opportunities for well-being in their contexts. Christian workers can carry out their explorations informally in the context of interactions with these individuals and in more formal ways, conducting and sharing the results of ethnographic research which explores these issues at a deeper level and reveals more of the complexities surrounding the way individuals in this geographical and/or social location are constructing their identity as it relates to "being Christian."

Third, the lens of negotiating identity can help Christian workers engage strategically in interactions with non-Christians in various locations by surfacing the need to develop tools and strategies that will enable them to effectively respond to the prevalent negative categorizations of "being Christian" and to problematize the taken-for-granted nature of the presuppositions underlying these categorizations. Tools that can be developed include things like stories, literature, illustrations, ways of handling certain problems, music, contextualized rituals, paintings, Bible studies, language abilities, relationships, diagrams, gospel presentations, and the like. "Strategies" in this context are plans of how to graciously interact with the non-Christians who articulate negative categorizations of "being Christian" in such a way that these categorizations, as much as possible, gradually lose their intensity and eventually are deemed unimportant or unsatisfying (unnecessary to raise any more) and that these non-Christians are able to see themselves as God sees them and to have credible opportunities to thoughtfully respond to the good news of the gospel.

Fourth, understanding the way non-Christians in their ministry settings are negotiating their identities, Christian workers can seek opportunities to engage these non-Christians and respond to their negative categorizations in both the personal and public arenas of life. In the personal arena, Christian workers can engage in face-to-face discussions with the non-Christians they encounter, seeking to give voice to the Christian perspective on issues that arise. These workers can also intentionally act in ways that will be a "voice" in the interaction with non-Christians about being Christian in a particular geographical and/or social location. For example, in order to contest the negative categorization by Hakka non-Christians that Christians are unfilial, a Hakka Christian can deliberately seek to be sacrificially filial, taking on the role of primary caregiver to his/her elderly and ailing parents.

In the public arena, Christian workers can work to cultivate a public voice that effectively responds to the identifications and categorizations non-Christians have that relate to being Christian in a particular location. For example, presentations in the media and literature and well-organized activities that use creative and well-tested ways of responding to the negative categorizations of being Christian can effectively shape the understandings of non-Christians and become useful tools that Christians can access in their personal interactions with the non-Christians around them.

Some Thoughts for Those Working among the Hakkas of Northwestern Taiwan

The implications of this research for those who are ministering among the Hakka in Taiwan are also many. The thoughts raised here are divided into (1) those related to the cultural "stuff" of being Hakka, (2) those related to the categorizations of non-Christian Hakkas, and (3) those related to the actions of Hakka Christians.

Related to the Cultural "Stuff" of Being Hakka

Knowing the crucial role that the cultural "stuff" of being Hakka has in shaping and serving as a reservoir of symbols used by Hakka non-Christians to construct their identity as it relates to being Christian reveals the need for Christians who want to evangelize Hakkas to work to deeply understand this "stuff." Deeply understanding and feeling what it means to be Hakka in any particular context will not only enable these Christians to better understand the reasons Hakka non-Christians say and do what they do but will also enable them to use this cultural "stuff" strategically in their ministries to these non-Christians—to craft well-thought-out presentations of the gospel in each setting that are easily understandable and not unnecessarily threatening and that answer the questions and contest the categorizations that are often thought but not expressed.

An awareness that the cultural "stuff" of being Hakka is changing highlights the value of Christians understanding that change so that they can relate appropriately to Hakkas who are located differently in respect to this change and harness this change when appropriate. For example, knowing the way the meaning of "being filial" is changing enables Christians who are sharing the gospel in a certain context to look for clues as to how an individual or a group of Hakkas feel about that change and to adapt their presentation of the gospel accordingly.

Alerted to fluidity or variety in the way Hakkas relate to being Hakka and speaking Hakka, Christians can be sensitive to differences in these areas as they determine how much of a Hakka emphasis and the Hakka language to include in their ministry to individuals or groups in any given setting. For example, the use of the Hakka language and a ministry emphasis on Hakka will most likely be more effective with Hakkas for whom a Hakka identity is primary than it would for one whose Hakka ethnic identity is very secondary, only salient in certain situations, or something being downplayed or rejected because of the perceived high cost of asserting this identity.

Understanding that to some extent or another, most Hakkas feel a sense of friendliness and familiarity when they hear the Hakka language or encounter Hakka things in some settings, Christians can develop skills at knowing when, how, and to what extent to relate to being Hakka in a way that will appropriately resonate with and feel friendly and familiar for Hakkas. For example, a Hakka word or saying can occasionally be added to sermons preached in Mandarin. Also knowing that the presence of this friendly and familiar feeling does not necessarily reflect a desire to have Hakka be salient in their lives at all times or even at any time reveals that, while Christians can take advantage of the connections that speaking

Hakka with Hakkas can create, they should not expect that these connections will necessarily continue and overshadow other differences.

Being conscious of the way many Hakkas value Hakka to a certain extent but do not treasure this aspect of their identity enough to sacrifice to continually make it primary at the exclusion of other priorities (e.g., because they want to fit in with and/or respect those around them) in all or even some contexts in their lives, Christians can realize that the assertion of Liao that Hakkas respond better to a "separate approach"—one where Hakka is made salient, without regard to the context, in every aspect of ministry—is not as unequivocal as Liao envisioned it to be. Christian ministries that forefront Hakka to a greater extent than those they are trying to evangelize, rather than attracting Hakkas, risk being perceived as (1) irrelevant or uninteresting by those Hakkas who are actively and aggressively pursuing other priorities; (2) constricting to Hakkas who feel unable to fully understand or freely express their ideas in the Hakka language; (3) embarrassing to those Hakkas who are weak in their Hakka-speaking, -listening, or -reading abilities; and/or (4) awkward when ethnic differences are emphasized in a society where many Hakkas and other ethnics are downplaying these differences for the sake of ethnic unity. Christian ministries that desire to pursue a "separate approach" in spite of the context will also require a great deal of effort to maintain this emphasis when the habits of Hakkas in many contexts run counter to this emphasis.

Knowing that there are Hakkas for whom a strong Hakka emphasis is desirable or for whom using the Hakka language is preferred, Christians and Christian churches can search for and learn to use Hakka-language resources to facilitate ministry to these people and plan and invite these Hakkas to attend Hakka-language evangelistic events, small groups, and/or church services. The value of having specialists or resource people—those who really understand and have the gifts necessary and who have learned skills to help certain segments of the Hakka population overcome the challenges they face as they consider conversion to Christianity and as they live as Christians—is also evident. Specialists can also include those who speak Hakka well, those who sing, play, and can lead others to sing Hakka music, those who can translate materials into Hakka, those who can teach others to speak Hakka and to understand the Hakka cultural "stuff," those who can effectively lead contextualized rituals in a public setting, those who can create Hakka resources that can be used in the evangelism of Hakkas, and those who work to better understand the categorizations that Hakka non-Christians have of being Christian and to develop more effective ways to undercut or challenge these categorizations.

Related to Contesting the Categorizations of Hakka Non-Christians

As understanding of the interactive nature of the way the meaning of Hakka in relation to being Christian is determined increases, the importance of listening to the categorizations of non-Christian Hakkas, not as an articulation of something "fixed," but rather as a construction that makes the most sense for these Hakkas in a particular context and of looking for appropriate ways and times to contest these categorizations becomes evident. The need for Christians working among Hakkas to strive to identify and understand these categorizations—their roots in the cultural "stuff" and the contexts where they do and do not surface—and to develop and improve responses that can be used and taught to others is also readily apparent. Hakka Christians can be proactive and intentional in doing and saying things that appropriately and strategically contest these categorizations.

The benefits of not only challenging categorizations at a surface level but also strategically challenging the fundamental assumptions upon which they are built is also clear. For example, in the same spirit that Hakka Christians are working hard to challenge the categorization that Christians are "unfilial" by doing things like developing contextualized rituals (e.g., the Three-Memorials Ceremony), the fundamental assumption that "all religions are the same and have the same goal" underlying many of the categorizations of non-Christian Hakkas can be singled out and efforts made to more effectively challenge it.

The strategic value of being more visible and public in the way these categorizations are challenged is also evident. For example, a large-scale Christian ancestor-memorial service that Hakka non-Christians are familiar with because television stations reported about it can be used by Hakka Christians to construct being Christian as very filial and respectful of ancestors. Christian Hakkas can raise the profile of Christians in appropriate ways at community events (e.g., set up a booth), seeking effective ways to publicly problematize the categorizations of Hakka non-Christians and the assumptions underlying them. For example, they can play a video taken at a large-scale Christian ancestor-memorial service to raise an awareness of what Christians are doing in this area and to stimulate conversations about different ways to be filial.

Understanding the interactive nature of the way the meaning of Hakka in relation to being Christian is determined, Christians will see value in locating with and engaging with non-Christian Hakkas in as many contexts and using as many different communication avenues as possible. Meaningful encounters with Christians provide significant opportunities for the categorizations of non-Christian Hakkas to be challenged. Being deeply involved in relationships with Christians enables non-Christians to have more opportunities to hear and discuss their categorizations of being Christian and to observe the lifestyle of Christians. Without close contact, conversations about being Christian between Christians and non-Christians will more likely be forced and harder to relate to the specifics of a particular context. When they are not being appropriately challenged, many non-Christian Hakkas will continue experiencing these categorizations as "the way things are" and will not have good opportunities to really understand and digest Christian truth. With the goal of being well-placed witnesses, Christians can take advantage of appropriate training to learn how to be more effective in their encounters with non-Christians. They can seek ways to aptly engage non-Christian neighbors, colleagues, classmates, relatives, and friends, and for some, even relocate to contexts where there is a need for a stronger Christian voice. They can fight the tendency to seek out those who share their beliefs and values and rather sacrifice so that non-Christian Hakkas will have the chance to hear the good news. They can work to become more visible as Christians in their communities in strategic and appropriate ways.

As Christians recognize that habit and emotional attachments contribute to fixity in being Hakka, the value of developing alternative ways of handling things that can effectively replace the Hakka non-Christian practices that are incompatible with the Bible without changing them more than is necessary is apparent. The experience gained while developing contextualized ancestor rituals can be used to develop alternatives in other areas. An awareness that fixity in being Hakka stems in part from emotional needs being met by non-Christian practices also highlights the need for Christians to find other ways to meet deep needs for continuity, stability, and belonging in this rapidly changing world. For example, a strong emphasis on the continuity of the ancestral line that began with

Adam as well as the way the Christian community can provide a sense of belonging could be helpful.

Related to the Actions of Hakka Christians

Understanding the variety of ways Hakkas relate to being Hakka, those Hakka Christians who attempt to involve other Hakka Christians in prioritizing Hakka ministry will not be surprised when many of these other Christians are not as responsive to their appeals as they would like. This lack of interest in Hakka ministry may reflect the low level of salience that being Hakka has for these Christians. In addition, a Hakka Christian who feels gifted and led by God to be involved in non-Hakka-focused ministries may also view Hakka in a more secondary way. The answers to questions like, "Should Hakka Christians focus their ministries on Hakkas?" and "Are Hakkas who do not choose a Hakka ministry focus being disloyal?" are not clear-cut, and the different answers to these kinds of questions may be seen simply as the diverse voices in a conversation about what it means to be a Hakka in this context.

Recognizing that there is a high cost (besides those issues that have led people to categorize Hakkas as "hard ground") of maintaining a primary ministry focus on Hakka (e.g., the energy and resolve required for a group of people to continue to use the Hakka language together when doing so is inconvenient), many Hakka Christians will not consider it unusual when Hakka Christian leaders find it difficult to justify this kind of focus when other less difficult ministry foci are readily available (e.g., a geographical area, an age group, a certain kind of occupation, an educational level, or a particular need). Even in non-Hakka-focused ministry settings, Hakka Christians, alerted to the value of their Hakka connection, their understanding of the Hakka cultural "stuff," and their Hakka-language ability, can choose to use these God-given gifts as ministry tools that can be used to minister to those Hakkas they encounter.

Knowing that the idea that ethnic identities are constructed rather than "fixed" is often threatening to people, Hakka Christians can identify and understand any reluctance in their own thinking about embracing the assertion that Hakka is constructed. Alerted to this constructed nature, these Christians can also better determine their own location in the conversation about the meaning of Hakka and how this location affects their perspective on the necessity of ministry focused on Hakkas.

Recommendations for Further Research

The Bible identifies mankind as being created in the image of God and, after the fall in the Garden of Eden, as having a sinful nature. This study did not directly explore the way these dimensions of being human influence how individuals interact with others regarding identity. Further exploration in this area promises to be very fruitful for Christian workers who are seeking to understand and more effectively respond to the negative categorizations of being Christian expressed by the non-Christians around them. For example, Christian workers could explore questions like: "How is the fact that the non-Christians around me are created in the image of God affecting their responses to being Christian and providing 'stuff' which can be used to construct effective responses to their negative categorizations?" and "How is the old nature affecting the identifications and categorizations that the non-Christians around me voice in regards to being Christian?"

As people grow in their understanding of the importance of effectively contesting the categorizations that non-Christian Hakkas have of being Christian, the value of doing more research in this area becomes evident. Each categorization being used needs to be isolated and better understood and a variety of responses to these categorizations needs to be developed, tested, and taught to other Christians. Hakka Christians who have strong social skills and those who have had success in this area could be included in this process.

Alerted to the widespread use of the statistic that only 0.3 percent (or 0.4 percent) of Hakkas are Christian and to the limitations of the research upon which this statistic is based, those interested in evangelizing Hakkas in Taiwan should consider whether or not more information in this area would be helpful. In addition to the possibility of developing new original research, the results of academic research being done by other scholars could be sought out and analyzed (e.g., existing and future data from the Taiwan Social Change Survey). Additional resources could prove useful to triangulate with existing statistics in order to provide a fuller picture of the spiritual need among the Hakkas of Taiwan.

For those interested in evangelizing Hakkas in Taiwan, the question of whether or not an ethnic ministry focus is the best way to reach many non-Christian Hakkas with the gospel is worth exploring. In other words, would other primary ministry foci (e.g., a focus on a certain community or a kind of community, an age group, a class of people, or those who are articulating a particular negative categorization) bring Christians closer to certain kinds of Hakka non-Christians, giving these Hakkas opportunities that they would not otherwise have to hear and respond to the gospel? For example, since many unreached Hakkas live in rural areas, further research could explore the challenges, opportunities, and needed skills and understandings related to a rural ministry focus in Taiwan and evaluate the kinds of situations where this kind of a primary focus would be more beneficial than a sole ministry emphasis on Hakka.

More broadly, Christian workers and missiologists are encouraged to use the social constructionist lens on ethnicity and ethnic groups in order to better understand the thinking and ways of people in different mission contexts throughout the world. In doing so, they can move beyond Homogeneous Unit Principle thinking without ignoring the ethnic dimensions of those contexts.

Closing Comments

This study has been motivated by a desire to bring glory to God by helping Christians better understand the way those who are being Hakka in northwestern Taiwan are interacting about being Christian so that Christians can more effectively and intentionally engage these Hakkas. Christians involve themselves in evangelistic ministries among those who are not yet Christians, not because they want to force their ideas on them, but because they want to be used by God to challenge the misunderstandings and misconceptions that non-Christians have of Him so that these non-Christians can know and experience God's love for them. While much of what we take for granted around us is socially constructed, there is ultimate Truth, God's way, which is crucial for each person to understand. This researcher is grateful to be one who is being used by God to share this Truth among those who are being Hakka in Taiwan.

Appendix 1

Interview Questions

RQ1. WHAT DOES IT mean to be Hakka in northwestern Taiwan?

A. How are Hakkas different from other Han Chinese in Taiwan? (*Kejiaren gen Taiwan qita de hanren you zenyang butong?*)

   1. What characteristics do Hakkas have? How are Hakkas different from other Han Chinese in Taiwan in these areas? Please provide some examples. (*Kejiaren you shenme tezhi? Zai zhexie tezhi zhong kejiaren gen Taiwan qita de hanren you zenyang butong? Qing tichu yixie lizi.*)

   2. What are some of the more important Hakka traditions and habits? How are these different from those of other Han Chinese in Taiwan? (*Kejiaren you na yixie bijiao zhongyao de chuantong yu xiguan? Gen Taiwan qita de hanren de chuantong yu xiguan you zenyang butong?*)

   3. How does a child learn to be Hakka? (*Kejia xiaohai ruhe xuexi chengwei yi ge kejiaren?*)

   4. When did you first become aware that you were Hakka? (*Qingwen ni diyici juecha dao ziji shi kejiaren shi shenme shihou?*)

   5. What are some things Hakkas fear? (*You naxie shiqing shi kejiaren suo jihui de?*)

   6. Where do Hakkas turn for help in time of need? (*Dang kejiaren yudao wenti shi hui xiangyao cong nali dedao jishi de bangzhu?*)

B. What are the boundary markers of the Hakka ethnic identity? (*Kejiaren yong naxie wenhua tezhi zuowei zuqun bianjie biaoji?*)

1. What qualifies someone to be called a Hakka? *(Yao jubei shenme yang de tiaojian caineng suan kejiaren?)*

2. Do you know or have you heard of people who were once Hakkas but no longer consider themselves or are no longer considered by others to be Hakka (or those who were not Hakka but became Hakka)? Would you please tell me more about these people and their situations? *(Ni shifou renshi huoshi tingshuoguo youren cengjing shi kejiaren danshi houlai buzai chengren ziji shi kejiaren huoshi buzai bei bieren renwei shi kejiaren [huoshi yuanlai bushi kejiaren dan houlai you chengwei kejiaren]? Guanyu zhexie ren he tamen de qingxing qing duo jia shuoming.)*

C. What factors are contributing to the maintenance and persistence of being Hakka? *(Na yixie yinsu hui yingxiang kejiaren jixu jianchi zuo kejiaren?)*

1. Some say Hakkas are conservative and are slow to change. Would you please tell me more about this and provide some examples? *(Youren shuo kejiaren henbaoshou erqie bijiao bu gan huo bu yuanyi gaibian. Qing duo tan zhe fangmian de xianxiang bing tichu yixie lizi.)*

2. What are some Hakka traditions that have changed a lot in your lifetime? Some that have changed only a little bit? Some that have not changed at all? *(Zai ni yisheng dangzhong you naxie kejia de chuantong gaibian le xuduo, you naxie you shaowei de gaibian, naxie ze shi yidian dou buceng gaibian guo?)*

3. Some people say the Hakka ethnic identity will gradually fade away. What are your thoughts in this area? *(Youren renwei kejia zuqun de rentonggan hui suizhe shijian jianjian de xiaoshi. Ni juede ne?)*

4. Some people talk about the importance of maintaining the Hakka identity, culture, and language. Would you please give some examples of what they are saying and doing? *(Youren renwei weihu kejia zuqun rentong, wenhua, yu yuyan shi yi jian zhongyao de shi. Qing duo tan zhe fangmian de xiangfa yiji ren, weile wehu zhexi, suo zuo de shiqing.)*

5. Has there been a time or times in your life when your Hakka identity has become more important to you? Have you seen this

phenomenon in others? (*Ni shibushi zai shenghuoshang yudao yixie qingkuang shi ni ganjuedao kejia zuqun shenfen shi feichang de zhongyao huoshi cengjing cong qita de kejiaren shenshang ganshou dao?*)

D. How are Hakkas relating to the Hakka ethnic identity? (*Kejiren dui ziji de kejia zuqun shenfen ganjue ruhe?*)

1. What are some situations where it is beneficial for Hakkas to identify themselves as Hakka? (*Zai zenmeyang de qingxing zhixia rang bieren zhidao ziji shi kejiaren shi youli de?*)
2. What are some situations where it is inconvenient for Hakkas to identify themselves as Hakka? (*Zai zenmeyang de qingxing zhixia bufangbian rang bieren zhidao ziji shi kejiaren?*)
3. When do Hakkas use the Hakka language? (*Kejiaren zai shenme qingkuangxia hui shiyong kejiahua?*)
4. Some people say that speaking or hearing the Hakka language has a friendly feel to it. Would you please talk more about this phenomenon and provide some examples? (*Youren shuo, shuo kejiahua yu ting kejiahua hui dai lai qingqiegan. Qing duo tan zhe fangmian de xianxiang bing tichu yixie lizi.*)

RQ2. What tensions exist between being Hakka in northwestern Taiwan and being Christian?

1. When you have heard your family or other Hakkas talking about Christians, what are some of the things they said? (*Ni jiaren huoshi ni zhouwei de kejiaren tidao jidujiao shi, tamen hui zenme shuo?*)
2. When was the first time you heard about Christianity? What was the situation? (*Ni diyici tingdao jidujiao shi shenme shihou? Dangshi qingxing ruhe?*)
3. Have you or other Hakkas you know ever felt Christians were acting rather strangely or offensively? (*Ni ziji huo ni renshi de kejiaren zhong, you meiyou ganjuedao youdeshihou jidujiao de xingwei yu qitaren bu tai yiyang huoshi hui maofan ren?*)
4. Some people say it is hard for a Hakka to become a Christian. Would you talk more about this difficulty and provide some examples?

(*Youren shuo, kejiaren hen burongyi chengwei jidutu. Qing duo tan zhe fangmian de nanchu bing tichu yixie lizi.*)

RQ3. How are Hakka Christians in northwestern Taiwan responding in the context of tensions between being Hakka and being Christian?

1. How do Hakka Christians respond when relatives and friends give them pressure about their Christian beliefs? (*Kejia jidutu ruhe miandui laizi qinyou fandui jidujiao xinyang suo shijia de yali?*)

2. What are some things Hakka Christians do to make it easier for non-Christian Hakkas to become Christians? (*Weile rang kejia feijidutu bijiao rongyi xin jidujiao, kejia jidutu zuo shenme?*)

3. Some people say the church in Taiwan is not taking the spiritual needs of the Hakkas seriously. Would you please talk about this situation and give some examples? (*Youren shuo Taiwan de jiaohui meiyou kanzhong kejiaren de shuling xuyao. Qing duo tan zhe fangmian de shiqing bing tichu yixie lizi.*)

Appendix 2

Three-Memorials Ceremony (*Zhuisisanli*)[1]

1. Water-Pouring Ritual—Contemplating Our Roots

    Heavenly Father God, everything is from You and belongs to You. Our ancestors were created by You, and all the good we have is given by You. May You receive the glory until eternity.

    Leader: God, today we respectfully stand in your presence and remember our beloved _____.

    Congregation: All rivers have their source; all blood relationships have been passed down to us from others.

    Leader: Therefore, as we think with gratitude about the source of our blessings,

    Congregation: Teach us not to forget that only You are the source of life.

    Together: Yes, Holy Trinity and True God, You are the source of all life. We are willing to return to You and submit to You and drink from the spring of salvation. Amen.

2. Flower-Placing Ritual—Extolling the Virtues of Those Who Have Preceded Us

    Thank You, Jesus, for dying on the cross for the people of the world, for taking away our sins and those of our ancestors and rising from

---

[1] This text is a translation (by this author) of a version of the Three-Memorials Ceremony found in Jidujiao Kejia Fuyin Xiehui Bianji Xiaozu, *Ancestor Memorial Handbook*, 56–60.

the dead. In the wisdom and strength You gave them, our ancestors and loved ones have left beautiful footprints. May their virtues be like the fragrance of flowers and last forever. Amen.

Leader: God, today we reverently stand before You,

Congregation: Bringing a little bit of fragrance in our hands.

Leader: As this bouquet of flowers emits a fragrant smell, our beloved _____ left behind a good example.

Congregation: We ask You now to help us give off the fragrance of life, in order that our virtues might exert an edifying influence on our descendants.

Together: Yes, Holy Trinity and True God, we are willing to accept and pass on the teachings of those who have gone before us and persist in doing good deeds. Amen.

3. Candle-Lighting Ritual—Glorifying God and Serving Others

May the Holy Spirit fill us, enlighten us, lead us, and, as we live in this world, enable us to shine like lights, glorifying God, serving others by good deeds and virtuous acts, and bringing honor to our ancestors. Amen.

Leader: God, we respectfully come before You,

Congregation: Lifting up the small light in our hands.

Leader: All fires have been ignited,

Congregation: Just as all big trees grow from a seed.

Leader: Today we come and remember our beloved_____, how he/she burned himself/herself for his/her clan and for society.

Congregation: Today, we ask You to help us to emit light and heat for our age.

Together: Yes, Holy Trinity and True God, we want to honor our ancestors, to bring glory to God, and to serve others. Amen.

Bibliography

Ahern, Emily. *The Cult of the Dead in a Chinese Village*. Stanford, CA: Stanford University Press, 1973.
Babbie, Earl R. *The Practice of Social Research*. 10th ed. Belmont, CA: Thomson/Wadsworth, 2004.
Band, Edward. *Barclay of Formosa*. Tokyo: Christian Literature Society, 1936.
Bandura, Albert. *Social Foundations of Thought and Action: A Social Cognitive Theory*. Englewood Cliffs, NJ: Prentice-Hall, 1986.
Barth, Fredrik. "Introduction." In *Ethnic Groups and Boundaries: The Social Organization of Culture Difference*, edited by Fredrik Barth, 9–38. Boston: Little, Brown, and Company, 1969.
Bentley, G. Carter. "Ethnicity and Practice." *Comparative Studies in Society and History* 29 (1987) 24–55.
Berger, Peter, and Hansfried Kellner. "Marriage and the Construction of Reality." *Diogenes* 46 (1964) 1–24.
Berger, Peter L. *The Sacred Canopy: Elements of a Sociological Theory of Religion*. Garden City, NY: Doubleday, 1967.
Berger, Peter L., and Thomas Luckmann. *The Social Construction of Reality: A Treatise in the Sociology of Knowledge*. London: Penguin, 1966.
Bernard, H. Russell. *Research Methods in Anthropology: Qualitative and Quantitative Approaches*. 4th ed. Lanham, MD: AltaMira, 2006.
Blake, C. Fred. *Ethnic Groups and Social Change in a Chinese Market Town*. Honolulu: University Press of Hawaii, 1981.
Bolton, Robert J. *Treasure Island: Church Growth among Taiwan's Urban Minnan Chinese*. South Pasadena, CA: William Carey Library, 1976.
Bourdieu, Pierre. *Distinction: A Social Critique of the Judgment of Taste*. Cambridge: Harvard University Press, 1984.
———. *In Other Words: Essays Towards a Reflexive Sociology*. Cambridge: Polity, 1990.
———. *The Logic of Practice*. Stanford: Stanford University Press, 1990.
———. *Outline of a Theory of Practice*. Cambridge: Cambridge University Press, 1977.
Brown, Melissa J. *Is Taiwan Chinese? The Impact of Culture, Power, and Migration on Changing Identities*. Berkeley: University of California Press, 2004.
Brubaker, Rogers. *Ethnicity without Groups*. Cambridge: Harvard University Press, 2004.
———. "Ethnicity without Groups." *European Journal of Sociology* 43 (2002) 163–89.
Butler, Judith. *Undoing Gender*. New York: Routledge, 2004.
Carpenter, Mary Yeo. "Familism and Ancestor Veneration: A Look at Chinese Funeral Rites." *Missiology* 24 (1996) 503–17.

Char, Andrew. "Social Origins of Ethnicity: The Hakka in Central Kwangtung." *Stone Lion Review* 9 (1982) 53–78.

Chen, Carolyn. "From Filial Piety to Religious Piety: Evangelical Christianity Reconstructing Taiwanese Immigrant Families in the United States." *International Migration Review* 40 (2006) 573–602.

Chen Yundong. "Yuan liu pian" [Origins]. In *Taiwan kejia yanjiu gailun* [The introduction of Taiwanese Hakka studies], edited by Cheng-kuang Hsu, 19–41. Taipei: Xingzhengyuan Kejia Weiyuanhui, Taiwan Kejia Yanjiu Xuehui, 2007.

Chen Zhiping. *Kejia yuanliu xinlun* [New perspectives on Hakka origins]. Nanning: Guangxi Jiaoyu Chubanshe, 1997.

Ching, Julia. *Chinese Religions*. Maryknoll, NY: Orbis, 1993.

Chiu, Hei-yuan. "Education and Social Change in Taiwan." In *Taiwan: A Newly Industrialized State*, edited by Hsin-Huang Michael Hsiao, Wei-yuan Cheng, and Hou-sheng Chan, 187–205. Taipei: National Taiwan University, Department of Sociology, 1989.

Chu, John S. T. "2009 nian Taiwan Jidu jiaohui jiaoshi baogao" [2009 Report on the trends in Taiwan Christian churches]. Jidujiao Ziliao Zhongxin, No pages. Online: http://www.ccea.org.tw/church/adlink/statics/one.htm.

Chuang, Ying-chang. "A Comparison of Hokkien and Hakka Ancestor Worship." *Bulletin of the Institute of Ethnology, Academia Sinica* 69 (1990) 133–60.

———. "Settlement Patterns of the Hakka Migration to Taiwan: The Case of the T'ou-Fen Ch'en Family." *Bulletin of the Institute of Ethnology, Academia Sinica* 66 (1988) 169–93.

Cohen, Myron L. "The Hakka or 'Guest People': Dialect as a Sociocultural Variable in Southeast China." In *Guest People: Hakka Identity in China and Abroad*, edited by Nicole Constable, 36–79. Seattle: University of Washington Press, 1996.

Cohen, Shaye J. D. *The Beginnings of Jewishness: Boundaries, Varieties, Uncertainties*. Berkeley: University of California Press, 1999.

Constable, Nicole. *Christian Souls and Chinese Spirits: A Hakka Community in Hong Kong*. Berkeley: University of California Press, 1994.

———. "Christianity and Hakka Identity." In *Christianity in China: From the Eighteenth Century to the Present*, edited by Daniel H. Bays, 158–73. Stanford: Stanford University Press, 1996.

———. "History and the Construction of Hakka Identity." In *Ethnicity in Taiwan: Social, Historical, and Cultural Perspectives*, edited by Chen Chung-min, Chuang Ying-chang, and Huang Shu-min, 75–89. Taipei: Institute of Ethnology, Academia Sinica, 1994.

———. "Introduction: What Does It Mean to Be Hakka?" In *Guest People: Hakka Identity in China and Abroad*, edited by Nicole Constable, 3–35. Seattle: University of Washington Press, 1996.

———. "Poverty, Piety, and the Past: Hakka Christian Expressions of Hakka Identity." In *Guest People: Hakka Identity in China and Abroad*, edited by Nicole Constable, 98–123. Seattle: University of Washington Press, 1996.

Cornell, Stephen E. "The Variable Ties That Bind: Content and Circumstances in Ethnic Processes." *Ethnic and Racial Studies* 19 (1996) 265–89.

Cornell, Stephen E., and Douglas Hartmann. *Ethnicity and Race: Making Identities in a Changing World*. 2nd ed. Thousand Oaks, CA: Pine Forge, 2007.

Cranmer-Byng, John. "The Chinese View of Their Place in the World: An Historical Perspective." *The China Quarterly* 53 (1973) 67–79.

Creswell, John W. *Research Design: Qualitative, Quantitative, and Mixed Method Approaches.* 2nd ed. Thousand Oaks, CA: Sage, 2003.
Crotty, Michael. *The Foundations of Social Research: Meaning and Perspective in the Research Process.* Thousand Oaks, CA: Sage, 1998.
Cushman, Philip. *Constructing the Self, Constructing America: A Cultural History of Psychotherapy.* Reading, MA: Addison-Wesley, 1995.
De Vos, George A. "Introduction: Ethnic Pluralism; Conflict and Accommodation." In *Ethnic Identity: Problems and Prospects for the Twenty-First Century*, edited by Lola Romanucci-Ross, George A. De Vos, and Takeyuki Tsuda, 1–36. Lanham, MD: AltaMira, 2006.
De Vos, George A., and Lola Romanucci-Ross. "Conclusion: Ethnic Identity; A Psychocultural Perspective." In *Ethnic Identity: Problems and Prospects for the Twenty-First Century*, edited by Lola Romanucci-Ross, George A. De Vos, and Takeyuki Tsuda, 375–400. Lanham, MD: AltaMira, 2006.
Durkheim, Émile. *The Division of Labor in Society.* New York: Macmillan, 1933.
Ebrey, Patricia Buckley. "Surnames and Han Chinese Identity." In *Negotiating Ethnicities in China and Taiwan*, edited by Melissa J. Brown, 19–36. Berkeley: Institute of East Asian Studies, University of California, 1996.
Eller, Jack D., and Reed M. Coughlan. "The Poverty of Primordialism: The Demystification of Ethnic Attachments." *Ethnic and Racial Studies* 16 (1993) 185–202.
Fan Zhengan. "Wenhua shehui yundong pian" [Cultural and social movements]. In *Taiwan kejia yanjiu gailun* [The introduction of Taiwanese Hakka studies], edited by Cheng-kuang Hsu, 417–47. Taipei: Xingzhengyuan Kejia Weiyuanhui, Taiwan Kejia Yanjiu Xuehui, 2007.
Fenton, Steve. *Ethnicity.* Malden, MA: Oxford, 2003.
Gans, Herbert J. "Symbolic Ethnicity: The Future of Ethnic Groups and Culture in America." *Ethnic and Racial Studies* 2 (1979) 1–20.
Gao, Ge, Stella Ting-Toomey, and William B. Gudykunst. "Chinese Communication Processes." In *The Handbook of Chinese Psychology*, edited by Michael Harris Bond, 280–93. Oxford: Oxford University Press, 1996.
Gates, Hill. "Ethnicity and Social Class." In *The Anthropology of Taiwanese Society*, edited by Emily Martin Ahern and Hill Gates, 241–81. Stanford: Stanford University Press, 1981.
Geertz, Clifford. *The Interpretation of Cultures: Selected Essays.* New York: Basic Books, 1973.
Giddens, Anthony. *The Consequences of Modernity.* Stanford: Stanford University Press, 1990.
———. *Modernity and Self-Identity: Self and Society in the Late Modern Age.* Stanford: Stanford University Press, 1991.
Gil-White, Francisco J. "Are Ethnic Groups Biological 'Species' To the Human Brain?" *Current Anthropology* 42 (2001) 515–54.
———. "How Thick Is Blood? The Plot Thickens . . . : If Ethnic Actors Are Primordialists, What Remains of the Circumstantialist/Primordialist Controversy?" *Ethnic and Racial Studies* 22 (1999) 789–821.
Goffman, Erving. *The Presentation of Self in Everyday Life.* Garden City, NY: Doubleday, 1959.
———. *Strategic Interaction.* Philadelphia, PA: University of Pennsylvania Press, 1969.
Government Information Office. *The Republic of China Yearbook.* Taipei: Government Information Office, Republic of China, 2010.

Hale, Henry E. "Explaining Ethnicity." *Comparative Political Studies* 37 (2004) 458–85.
Handelman, Don. "The Organization of Ethnicity." *Ethnic Groups* 1 (1977) 187–200.
Ho, David Y. F. "Filial Piety and Its Psychological Consequences." In *The Handbook of Chinese Psychology*, edited by Michael Harris Bond, 155–65. Oxford: Oxford University Press, 1996.
Hogg, Michael A., and Dominic Abrams. *Social Identifications: A Social Psychology of Intergroup Relations and Group Processes*. New York: Routledge, 1988.
Hsiau, A-chin. *Contemporary Taiwanese Cultural Nationalism*. New York: Routledge, 2000.
Hsu, Francis L. K. *Under the Ancestors' Shadow: Kinship, Personality, and Social Mobility in China*. Stanford: Stanford University Press, 1967.
Huang, Shu-min, Chen Chung-min, and Chuang Ying-chang. "Introduction: Problems of Ethnicity in the Chinese Cultural Context." In *Ethnicity in Taiwan: Social, Historical, and Cultural Perspectives*, edited by Chen Chung-min, Chuang Ying-chang, and Huang Shu-min, 3–22. Taipei: Institute of Ethnology, Academia Sinica, 1994.
Huang Shuanfan. "Language, Identity and Conflict: A Taiwanese Study." *International Journal of the Sociology of Language* 143 (2000) 139–49.
Hutchinson, John, and Anthony D. Smith, eds. *Ethnicity*. New York: Oxford University Press, 1996.
Hwang, Kwang-kuo. "Face and Favor: The Chinese Power Game." *American Journal of Sociology* 92 (1987) 944–74.
Isaacs, Harold R. "Basic Group Identity." In *Ethnicity: Theory and Experience*, edited by Nathan Glazer and Daniel P. Moynihan, 29–52. Cambridge, MA: Harvard University Press, 1975.
———. *Idols of the Tribe: Group Identity and Political Change*. New York: Harper and Row, 1975.
Jenkins, Richard. *Pierre Bourdieu*. London: Routledge, 2002.
———. *Rethinking Ethnicity*. 2nd ed. Thousand Oaks, CA: Sage, 2008.
———. "Rethinking Ethnicity: Identity, Categorization, and Power." *Ethnic and Racial Studies* 17 (1994) 197–223.
———. *Social Identity*. 2nd ed. New York: Routledge, 2004.
———. *Social Identity*. 3rd ed. New York: Routledge, 2008.
Jidujiao Kejia Fuyin Xiehui Bianji Xiaozu [Christian Hakka Evangelical Association Editorial Committee]. *Jidutu sangli yu jingzu shouce* [Christian funeral and ancestor memorial handbook]. Taipei: Tianen Chubanshe, 2010.
Johnstone, Patrick, and Jason Mandryk. *Operation World*. 21st Century updated and revised ed. Carlisle, Cumbria, UK: Authentic Lifestyle, 2001.
Kefu jianxun [Christian Hakka Evangelical Association newsletter]. 246 (2010).
Keshen jianxun [Hakka Mission Seminary newsletter]. "Zui weida de jihui" [The greatest opportunity]. 107 (2010) 2.
Knapp, Ronald G. "The Shaping of Taiwan's Landscapes." In *Taiwan: A New History*, edited by Murray A. Rubinstein, 3–26. Armonk, NY: M. E. Sharpe, 2007.
Lakoff, George. *Women, Fire, and Dangerous Things: What Categories Reveal About the Mind*. Chicago: University of Chicago Press, 1987.
Lamley, Harry J. "Subethnic Rivalry in the Ch'ing Period." In *The Anthropology of Taiwanese Society*, edited by Emily Martin Ahern and Hill Gates, 282–318. Stanford: Stanford University Press, 1981.

LeCompte, Margaret D., and Jean J. Schensul. *Analyzing and Interpreting Ethnographic Data*. Edited by Jean J. Schensul and Margaret D. LeCompte. Vol. 5, *The Ethnographer's Toolkit*. Walnut Creek, CA: AltaMira, 1999.

Lee Fong-mao. "The Daoist Priesthood and Secular Society: Two Aspects of Postwar Taiwanese Daoism." In *Religion in Modern Taiwan: Tradition and Innovation in a Changing Society*, edited by Philip Clart and Charles Brewer Jones, 125–57. Honolulu: University of Hawai'i Press, 2003.

Leong, Sow-theng. "The Formation of the Hakka Ethos in the Nineteenth Century." In *Migration and Ethnicity in Chinese History: Hakkas, Pengmin, and Their Neighbors*, edited by Tim Wright, 69–81. Stanford: Stanford University Press, 1997.

———. "Hakka Migrations in Lingnan and Southeast Coast." In *Migration and Ethnicity in Chinese History: Hakkas, Pengmin, and Their Neighbors*, edited by Tim Wright, 39–68. Stanford: Stanford University Press, 1997.

———. "The Origins and Historiography of the Hakkas." In *Migration and Ethnicity in Chinese History: Hakkas, Pengmin, and Their Neighbors*, edited by Tim Wright, 19–36. Stanford: Stanford University Press, 1997.

Levine, Hal B. "Reconstructing Ethnicity." *Journal of the Royal Anthropological Institute* 5 (1999) 165–80.

Li, Yih-yuan. "Four Hundred Years of Ethnic Relations in Taiwan." *New Asia Academic Bulletin* 8 (1989) 103–15.

Li Zhenglong. *Taiwan jidujiao lishi* [Christian history in Taiwan]. Taipei: Tianen Chubanshe, 2001.

Liao, Chao-chih. "Changing Dominant Language Use and Ethnic Equality in Taiwan since 1987." *International Journal of the Sociology of Language* 143 (2000) 165–82.

Liao, David C. E. *The Unresponsive: Resistant or Neglected?* Chicago: Moody Press, 1972.

———. *The Unresponsive: Resistant or Neglected? The Homogeneous Unit Principle Illustrated by the Hakka Chinese in Taiwan*. Pasadena, CA: William Carey Library, 1979. First published 1972 by Moody Press.

Lin, Nan. "Chinese Family Structure and Chinese Society." *Bulletin of the Institute of Ethnology, Academia Sinica* 65 (1988) 59–129.

Liu, Li. "Yang and Yin in Communication: Towards a Typology and Logic of Persuasion in China." *Diogenes* 55 (2008) 120–32.

Lofland, John, and Lyn H. Lofland. *Analyzing Social Settings: A Guide to Qualitative Observation and Analysis*. 3rd ed. Belmont, CA: Wadsworth, 1995.

Luo Xianglin. *Kejia yanjiu daolun* [An introduction to the study of the Hakkas, in its ethnic, historical and cultural aspects]. Taipei: Nantian Shuju, 1992. First published 1933 by Xishan Shucang.

Mackay, George L. *From Far Formosa. The Island, Its People, and Missions*. Edited by J. A. MacDonald. Taipei: SMC Publishing Inc., 2002. First published 1896 by Oliphant Anderson and Ferrier.

Mandryk, Jason. *Operation World*. 7th ed. Colorado Springs, CO: Biblica Publishing, 2010.

Martin, Howard J. "The Hakka Ethnic Movement in Taiwan, 1986-1991." In *Guest People: Hakka Identity in China and Abroad*, edited by Nicole Constable, 176–95. Seattle: University of Washington Press, 1996.

———. "Hakka Mausoleums in North Taiwan." *Ethnology* 30 (1991) 85–100.

May, Stephen. *Language and Minority Rights: Ethnicity, Nationalism and the Politics of Language*. New York: Routledge, 2008.

McClintock, Wayne. "Sociological Critique of the Homogeneous Unit Principle." *International Review of Mission* 77 (1988) 107–16.

McGavran, Donald A. *The Bridges of God: A Study in the Strategy of Missions*. London: World Dominion, 1955.

———. *The Clash between Christianity and Cultures*. Washington: Canon, 1974.

———. "Homogeneous Populations and Church Growth." In *Church Growth and Christian Mission*, edited by Donald A. McGavran, Robert G. Guy, Melvin L. Hodges, and Eugene A. Nida, 69–86. New York: Harper & Row, 1965.

———. "The Priority of Ethnicity." *Evangelical Missions Quarterly* 19 (1983) 14–23.

———. *Understanding Church Growth*. rev. ed. Revised and edited by C. Peter Wagner. Grand Rapids, MI: Eerdmans, 1990.

McKay, James. "An Exploratory Synthesis of Primordial and Mobilisationist Approaches to Ethnic Phenomena." *Ethnic and Racial Studies* 5 (1982) 394–420.

Merriam, Sharan B. "Evaluating Qualitative Research." In *Qualitative Research in Practice: Examples for Discussion and Analysis*, edited by Sharan B. Merriam, 18–33. San Francisco: Jossey-Bass, 2002.

———. "Introduction to Qualitative Research." In *Qualitative Research in Practice: Examples for Discussion and Analysis*, edited by Sharan B. Merriam, 3–17. San Francisco: Jossey-Bass, 2002.

Michael, Franz H. *The Taiping Rebellion: History and Documents*. Seattle: University of Washington Press, 1966.

Nagata, Judith. "In Defense of Ethnic Boundaries: The Changing Myths and Charters of Malay Identity." In *Ethnic Change*, edited by Charles F. Keyes, 88–116. Seattle: University of Washington Press, 1981.

Nagel, Joane. *American Indian Ethnic Renewal: Red Power and the Resurgence of Identity and Culture*. New York: Oxford University Press, 1996.

———. "Constructing Ethnicity: Creating and Recreating Ethnic Identity and Culture." *Social Problems* 41 (1994) 152–76.

Padilla, C. René. "The Unity of the Church and the Homogeneous Unit Principle." *International Bulletin of Missionary Research* 6 (1982) 23–30.

Pang, Keng-fong. "Being Hui, Huan-Nang, and Utsat Simultaneously: Contextualizing History and Identities of the Austronesian-Speaking Hainan Muslims." In *Negotiating Ethnicities in China and Taiwan*, edited by Melissa J. Brown, 183–207. Berkeley: Institute of East Asian Studies, University of California, 1996.

Park, Robert Ezra, and Ernest Watson Burgess. *Introduction to the Science of Sociology*. Chicago: University of Chicago Press, 1924.

Patterson, Orlando. "Context and Choice in Ethnic Allegiance: A Theoretical Framework and Caribbean Case Study." In *Ethnicity: Theory and Experience*, edited by Nathan Glazer and Daniel P. Moynihan, 305–49. Cambridge, MA: Harvard University Press, 1975.

Phinney, Jean S. "Ethnic Identity in Late Modern Times: A Response to Rattansi and Phoenix." *Identity* 5 (2005) 187–94.

Priest, Robert J. "Afterword: Concluding Missiological Reflection." In *Power and Identity in the Global Church: Six Contemporary Cases*, edited by Brian M. Howell and Edwin Zehner, 185–91. Pasadena, CA: William Carey Library, 2009.

Qiu Changtai. "Zhengce" [Policy]. In *Taiwan kejia yanjiu gailun* [The introduction of Taiwanese Hakka studies], edited by Cheng-kuang Hsu, 534–62. Taipei: Xingzhengyuan Kejia Weiyuanhui, Taiwan Kejia Yanjiu Xuehui, 2007.

Raber, Dorothy A. *Protestantism in Changing Taiwan: A Call to Creative Response.* South Pasadena, CA: William Carey Library, 1978.
Rin, Hsien. "The Synthesizing Mind in Chinese Ethno-Cultural Adjustment." In *Ethnic Identity: Cultural Continuities and Change*, edited by George A. De Vos and Lola Romanucci-Ross, 137–55. Chicago: University of Chicago Press, 1982.
Roosens, Eugeen. *Creating Ethnicity: The Process of Ethnogenesis.* Newbury Park, CA: Sage, 1989.
———. "The Primordial Nature of Origins in Migrant Ethnicity." In *The Anthropology of Ethnicity: Beyond 'Ethnic Groups and Boundaries,'* edited by Hans Vermeulen and Cora Govers, 81–103. Amsterdam: Spinhuis, 1994.
Rosch, Eleanor. "Principles of Categorization." In *Cognition and Categorization*, edited by Eleanor Rosch and Barbara B. Lloyd, 27–48. Hillsdale, NJ: Lawrence Erlbaum Associates, 1978.
Rubinstein, Murray A. "Taiwanese Protestantism in Time and Space, 1865–1988." In *Taiwan: Economy, Society, and History*, edited by E. K. Y. Chen, Jack F. Williams, and Joseph Wong, 251–82. Hong Kong: University of Hong Kong, Centre of Asian Studies, 1991.
Schensul, Stephen L., Jean J. Schensul, and Margaret Diane LeCompte. *Essential Ethnographic Methods.* Edited by Jean J. Schensul and Margaret Diane LeCompte. Vol. 2, *Ethnographer's Toolkit*. Walnut Creek, CA: AltaMira, 1999.
Schermerhorn, R. A. *Comparative Ethnic Relations: A Framework for Theory and Research.* Chicago: University of Chicago Press, 1978.
Seidman, Irving. *Interviewing as Qualitative Research: A Guide for Researchers in Education and the Social Sciences.* 3rd ed. New York: Teachers College Press, 2006.
Shepherd, John R. "The Island Frontier of the Ch'ing, 1684–1780." In *Taiwan: A New History*, edited by Murray A. Rubinstein, 107–32. Armonk, NY: M. E. Sharpe, 2007.
Shils, Edward. "Primordial, Personal, Sacred and Civil Ties: Some Particular Observations on the Relationships of Sociological Research and Theory." *British Journal of Sociology* 8 (1957) 130–45.
Simpson, Andrew. "Taiwan." In *Language and National Identity in Asia*, edited by Andrew Simpson, 235–59. New York: Oxford University Press, 2007.
Smith, Anthony D. *The Ethnic Origins of Nations.* Oxford: Basil Blackwell, 1988.
Smith, David. "The Church Growth Principles of Donald McGavran." *Transformation* 2 (1985) 25–30.
Spradley, James P. *The Ethnographic Interview.* New York: Holt, Rinehart and Winston, 1979.
Swanson, Allen J. *The Church in Taiwan: Profile 1980; A Review of the Past, a Projection for the Future.* Pasadena, CA: William Carey Library, 1981.
Tajfel, Henri, and John Turner. *An Integrative Theory of Intergroup Conflict.* Edited by Mary Jo Hatch and Majken Schultz. New York: Oxford University Press, 2004.
Taiwan Shengjing Gonghui [Bibe Society in Taiwan]. *Keyu shengjing: Xiandai Taiwan keyu yiben [The Hakka Bible: Today's Taiwan Hakka Version].* Taipei: Taiwan Shengjing Gonghui, 2012.
Thompson, Laurence G. *Chinese Religion: An Introduction.* 5th ed. Belmont, CA: Wadsworth, 1996.
Thornton, A., T. Fricke, L. S. Yang, and J. S. Chang. "Theoretical Mechanisms of Family Change." In *Social Change and the Family in Taiwan*, edited by Arland Thornton and Hui-sheng Lin, 88–115. Chicago: University of Chicago Press, 1994.

Thornton, Arland, and Hui-sheng Lin. "Continuity and Change." In *Social Change and the Family in Taiwan*, edited by Arland Thornton and Hui-sheng Lin, 396–411. Chicago: University of Chicago Press, 1994.

Ting-Toomey, Stella. "Identity Negotiation Theory: Crossing Cultural Boundaries." In *Theorizing About Intercultural Communication*, edited by William B. Gudykunst, 211–33. Thousand Oaks, CA: Sage, 2005.

Tong, Hollington Kong. *Christianity in Taiwan: A History*. Taipei: China Post, 1961.

Tönnies, Ferdinand. *Community and Society*. New York: Harper and Row, 1963.

Tsao, Feng-fu. "The Language Planning Situation In Taiwan." *Journal of Multilingual and Multicultural Development* 20 (1999) 328–75.

Tse, John Kwock-ping. "Language and a Rising New Identity in Taiwan." *International Journal of the Sociology of Language* 143 (2000) 151–64.

van den Berghe, Pierre L. *The Ethnic Phenomenon*. New York: Elsevier, 1981.

———. "Ethnic Pluralism in Industrial Societies: A Special Case?" *Ethnicity* 3 (1976) 242–55.

Vermeer, Edward B. "Up the Mountains and out to the Sea: The Expansion of the Fukienese in the Late Ming Period." In *Taiwan: A New History*, edited by Murray A. Rubinstein, 45–83. Armonk, NY: M. E. Sharpe, 2007.

Wagner, C. Peter. "Homogeneous Unit Principle." In *Evangelical Dictionary of World Missions*, edited by A. Scott Moreau, 455. Grand Rapids, MI: Baker, 2000.

Wang, Cecil Kwei-heng. "Ancestor Veneration Practices and Christian Conversion in Taiwan: A Study of Perceptions of Chinese College Students in Urban Taiwan." PhD diss., Trinity International University, 2001.

Wang Dong. *Kejiaxue daolun* [An introduction to Hakkaology]. Taipei: Nantian Chubanshe, 1998.

Wang Fuchang. *Dangdai Taiwan shehui de zuqun xiangxiang* [Ethnic imagination in contemporary Taiwan]. Taipei: Qunxue Chuban Youxian Gongsi, 2003.

Wang, L. Ling-chi. "Roots and Changing Identity." In *The Living Tree: The Changing Meaning of Being Chinese Today*, edited by Tu Wei-ming, 185–212. Stanford: Stanford University Press, 1994.

Wang, Li-jung. "Diaspora, Identity and Cultural Citizenship: The Hakkas in 'Multicultural Taiwan.'" *Ethnic and Racial Studies* 30 (2007) 875–95.

———. "Multiculturalism in Taiwan." *International Journal of Cultural Policy* 10 (2004) 301–18.

Wang, Q. Edward. "History, Space, and Ethnicity: The Chinese Worldview." *Journal of World History* 10 (1999) 285–305.

Wang, Sping, Jan Kok, and Ying-chang Chuang. "Who Married How? Modeling Marital Decisions in Early-Twentieth Century Taiwan." *Journal of Family History* 33 (2008) 430–51.

Weber, Max. *Economy and Society: An Outline of Interpretive Sociology*. New York: Bedminster, 1968.

Wen Yongsheng. "Cong xuanjiaoshi kan Shinian Beijia Yundong" [Looking at the Double in Ten Years Movement from the perspective of mission history]. In *Kejia xuanjiao xin langchao: Zai suo ding de rizi, da dao beijia* [The new wave of Hakka missions: The day for doubling has come], edited by Zeng Zhengzhong, Qiu Shanxiung, Wen Yongsheng, and Wu Ruicheng, 161–70. Taipei: Huashen Chubanshe, 2008.

———. "Shang tonghua xiang '997' Kejia xuanjiao" [Enjoying tong blossoms and thinking about the "997" Hakka mission]. *Jidujiao luntan bao* [*Christian Tribune*], May 17, 2008.

———. *Shenzhongzhuiyuan ying fuxing zhuanhua huaren jizu wenhua* [Paying careful attention to one's parent's funerary rites invites revival: Transforming the culture of Chinese ancestor worship]. Taipei: Tianen Chubanshe, 2010.

Wilson, Robert Scott. "The Invisible Ones: The Politics of Culture Work among Taipei's Hakka." PhD diss., Stanford University, 2005.

Wu Xueming. "Yiken kaifa pian" [Settling and developing]. In *Taiwan kejia yanjiu gailun* [The introduction of Taiwanese Hakka studies], edited by Cheng-kuang Hsu, 42–61. Taipei: Xingzhengyuan Kejia Weiyuanhui, Taiwan Kejia Yanjiu Xuehui, 2007.

Xia Zhongjian. *Yincang de yi qun: Taiwan ke zhuang he ke zhuang jiaohui* [The hidden group: Taiwan Hakka community and Hakka churches]. Taipei: Jiaohui Gengxin Yanjiu Fazhan Zhongxin, Kejia Xuanjiao Xiehui, 1983.

Xu Wenxiong. "Shibaji shijiuji Taiwan Fulao Kejia xiedou" [Violent conflict between Hoklo and Hakka in Taiwan in the eighteenth and nineteenth centuries]. In *Guojia, shichang yu mailuohua de zuqun* [State, market, and ethnic groups contextualized], edited by Jiang Bin and He Cuiping, 151–204. Taipei: Zhongyang Yanjiuyuan Lishi Yuyan Yanjiusuo, 2003.

Yang Changzhen. "Zuqun guanxi pian" [Ethnic relationships]. In *Taiwan kejia yanjiu gailun* [The introduction of Taiwanese Hakka studies], edited by Cheng-kuang Hsu, 389–416. Taipei: Xingzhengyuan Kejia Weiyuanhui, Taiwan Kejia Yanjiu Xuehui, 2007.

Yang, Kuo-shu. "Chinese Responses to Modernization: A Psychological Analysis." *Asian Journal of Social Psychology* 1 (1998) 75–97.

———. "Chinese Social Orientation: An Integrative Analysis." In *Chinese Societies and Mental Health*, edited by Tsung-Yi Lin, Wen-Shing Tseng, and YingKun Ye, 19–39. Hong Kong: Oxford University Press, 1995.

Yang, Li-shou, Arland Thornton, and Thomas Fricke. "Religion and Family Formation in Taiwan: The Decline of Ancestral Authority." In *Family, Religion, and Social Change in Diverse Societies*, edited by Sharon K. Houseknecht and Jerry G. Pankhurst, 121–46. New York: Oxford University Press, 2000.

Yang, Philip Q. *Ethnic Studies: Issues and Approaches*. Albany: State University of New York Press, 2000.

Yang Wenshan. "Jihua zhuchiren xu" [Research leader's preface]. In *Quanguo kejia renkou jichu ziliao diaocha yanjiu baogao* [Report on the National Hakka Population Basic Data Survey], edited by Yang Wenshan. Taipei: Xingzhengyuan Kejia Weiyuanhui, 2004.

———, ed. *Quanguo kejia renkou jichu ziliao diaocha yanjiu baogao* [Report on the National Hakka Population Basic Data Survey]. Taipei: Xingzhengyuan Kejia Weiyuanhui, 2004.

Zelinsky, Wilbur. *The Enigma of Ethnicity: Another American Dilemma*. Iowa City, IA: University of Iowa City Press, 2001.

Zeng Zhengzhong, ed. *Jidujiao kejia fuyin xiehui sanshi jounian jinian tekan* [Christian Hakka Evangelical Association thirty-year anniversary commemorative publication]. Zhudong, Hsinchu Xian, Taiwan: Jidujiao Kejia Fuyin Xiehui, 2009.

Zeng Zhengzhong, Qiu Shanxiung, Wen Yongsheng, and Wu Ruicheng. *Kejia xuanjiao xin langchao: Zai suo ding de rizi, da dao beijia* [The new wave of Hakka missions: The day for doubling has come]. Taipei: Huashen Chubanshe, 2008.

Zheng Lianming, ed. *Taiwan jidu zhanglao jiaohui bainianshi* [A centennial history of the Presbyterian Church of Formosa]. Tainan, Taiwan: Jidujiao Zai Tai Xuanjiao Baizhounian Jinian Congshu Weiyuanhui, 1965.

――― . "Zi jiaoshihui chengli zhi Wu Weilian Mushi shishi" [From self-governance until the death of Pastor William Gauld]. In *Taiwan jidu zhanglao jiaohui bainianshi* [A centennial history of the Presbyterian Church of Formosa], edited by Zheng Lianming, 144–67. Tainan, Taiwan: Jidujiao Zai Tai Xuanjiao Baizhounian Jinian Congshu Weiyuanhui, 1965.

Zhonghuaminguo Shengjing Gonghui [Bible Society in the ROC]. *Keyu Shengjing: Xiandai Taiwan keyu yiben: Xinyue shipian [The Hakka Bible: Today's Taiwan Hakka Version: New Testament and Psalms]*. Taipei: Zhonghuaminguo Shengjing Gonghui, 1993.

Zhonghuaminguo Shengjing Gonghui [Bible Society in the ROC]. *Keyu zhenyan: Qiannian zhihui shu [Hakka Proverbs: Wisdom of the Ages]*. Taipei: Zhonghuaminguo Shengjing Gonghui, 1995.

Index

aboriginal languages. *See under* language
Aborigine, 9–10, 72, 75–78, 81–84
Abrams, Dominic, 51
age
 as a factor affecting attitudes, 121, 124, 130–31, 151, 171–72, 208, 210
 of informants, 100–101
agriculture, 57–58, 66, 113
Ahern, Emily, 150
ancestor practices (including ancestor rituals, ancestor veneration, ancestor worship)
 baptism and, 222–23
 change in attitudes toward, 55, 146, 161, 171, 207, 211: heart attitude in, 129–31, 223; necessity of practices, 200, 233; some beliefs considered superstitious, 151; waning interest in practices, 68, 151–52, 209
 change in and respect for senior family members, 121–22
 children and, 143–44
 Christians' responses to: concern Hakkas, 187, 189, 192–93, 196–97, 202, 205; reject traditional practices, 188, 191, 195–98, 200, 203–5, 207, 219, 224–25, 233–34; seek to address concerns of non-Christians, 215, 219–28, 232–34, 238–39
 contextualized, Christian: ancestor-memorial services, 95, 245; designed to challenge negative categorizations, 221; development of, 215, 219, 227, 242, 277; failure to use, 91, 216; positive reception

ancestor practices *(continued)*
 by non-Christians, 238–39, 245–46; promotion of, 215, 222, 227, 280; use of, 95, 216, 220–21, 231, 238, 245, 280–82. *See also* Three-Memorials Ceremony
 definitions of, 7–8
 feelings of non-Christians associated with non-Christian: affection and devotion, 121, 126–28, 146; belonging, 127, 193; conflicted, 130–31; continuity, 121; fear, 151–52, 190, 192, 198, 202, 228, 232, 234; indebtedness, 147, 150; respect, 120–22, 125–26, 201, 227
 functions of: bring protection/blessing/help of ancestors, 145, 150–52, 199, 234; connect clan members, 126–28, 131, 147–49, 161, 171, 192–93, 196–97, 205, 211, 227–28, 232; express filial piety, 122, 132, 149–50; give face to ancestors, 156; make transitions, 128–29, 205; provide continuity with the past, 129, 150, 191–92, 205; provide for the needs of ancestors, 158, 198; repay debts to ancestors, 150, 204, 234
 habit and, 144
 Hakka distinctives in, 89, 126, 128, 169
 inclusion of one's first Taiwan ancestor in, 128
 influences affecting use and views concerning: age, 121, 123–24, 126, 130–31, 208; education, 151, 208, 210; habitualization,

303

304　*Index*

ancestor practices *(continued)*
　　143–45; occupation, 160–61, 208; residence, 129–30, 209–10; societal change, 131; status in society, 160–61, 210; time pressures, 130, 155, 161, 187, 193; urban versus rural settings of practices, 161, 208–10; wealth, 130, 191
　necessity of, absolute, 120, 122, 195
　negative effects of non-participation: blamed for misfortune, 203; loss of protection/blessing/help of ancestors, 145, 150–52; seen as being unacceptable, 122, 187–88, 192, 196, 200, 202; seen as neglecting ancestors, 149–51, 198, 202, 208, 212, 254; seen as unfilial, 198, 202, 204, 208, 212; worry that deceased loved ones are not being cared for, 149, 190, 198; punishment, 152, 228
　non-traditional, 129–32, 210–11
　obligations of descendants in: ensure continuity of family line, 120, 169; follow and pass on family traditions, 143–44, 192; perform ceremonial duties, 120, 124, 150, 152; repay the ancestors, 150; provide for welfare of ancestors, 198
　pollution and, 130, 210
　practice of: clan-grouping leaders' involvement in, 196–97; daily nature of, 123, 125, 144, 192, 195; at funerals, 128, 205; on important holidays and festival days, 122, 126, 128, 144, 184, 195, 197, 202, 225, 245; sacrifices in, 121, 130–31, 149, 155, 198, 221, 233; use of incense in, 121–29, 131, 143–44, 150, 158, 192, 195, 197–98, 205, 207, 211, 223; use of spirit money in, 121, 131, 158, 198, 227
　pressure to participate in, 158, 202–3, 207
　reciprocal nature of, 149–52
　related to ethnic identity: being Chinese, 165; being Hakka, 161
　something everyone does, 200
　standardized, 165
　tradition and, 143–45

ancestor practices *(continued)*
　traditional thinking in this area seen as the way things are, 124, 191
　translation issues regarding related English and Chinese words, 7–8
ancestor record, 125, 205
ancestor tablet, 123, 125, 127–29, 144, 158, 181, 191, 201, 205, 223–24, 228
ancestors
　Christians' disrespect of, 183–84, 190–91, 201–4, 223–24
　communicating with, 8, 125, 129–32, 149
　language of. *See* language: of the ancestors
　worship of. *See* ancestor practices
ascription, 20, 26, 28, 46, 80, 253
assertion, 29
assignment, 30
assimilation
　of ethnic groups not God's plan, 90
　of Hakkas. *See under* Hakkas
attachments
　ethnic, 22, 24, 53, 170
　primordial, 20–22, 43

Babbie, Earl R., 105, 107
Band, Edward, 42, 77–78, 158
Bandura, Albert, 39
Barclay, Thomas, 75, 77–78, 91
Barth, Fredrik, 23, 25–28, 46, 52
basic interpretive qualitative research, xiv, 96–97
basic social constructionist anthropological model of ethnicity, 28–29
being Christian
　definition of, 7
　negative categorizations by non-Christian Hakkas in northwestern Taiwan of, 179–203
being Hakka in northwestern Taiwan
　boundary markers of, 165–69
　definition of Hakka, 7, 70–71, 73, 85
　important shared symbols of, 111–64
　negative categorizations asserted about Christianity in, 179–203
　relating to the Hakka ethnic identity and, 169–76
being Hakka in Taiwan
　fixity and fluidity in, 94
　historical development of, 54–65
　modernization and, 65–68

being Hakka in Taiwan *(continued)*
  recent developments in, 68–75
  Christian ministry and, 75–95
Bentley, G. Carter, 45
Berger, Peter L., 11, 44
Bernard, H. Russell, 104–5
Blake, C. Fred, 165
blaming
  for misfortune, 159, 199, 203
  for the small size Hakka church, 79, 87, 254, 261–62, 264
Bolton, Robert J., 81
boundaries, ethnic
  actions involving: generating, 26; maintaining, 26
  characteristics of: constructed in the context of interaction with others, 30; crossable, 17, 124–25, 168; differences made significant, 25; fuzzy, 272; impermeable, 19; porous, 265, 272
  cultural "stuff" and, 26–27, 47
  Homogeneous Unit Principle and, 2, 17, 88, 272
  made by a group, 27
  relationships across, 17, 25, 35
  salience of varies, 47
  See also boundary markers
boundary markers
  of being Hakka in northwestern Taiwan, 165–69
  different meanings attached to, 42
  of Hakka used in the Taiwan Social Change Survey, 85
  some symbols more accessible and plausible as, 52
  See also boundaries, ethnic
Bourdieu, Pierre, 44–45
Brown, Melissa J., 165
Brubaker, Rogers, 6, 26, 33, 50–52, 260
burden for Hakka ministry, 3, 172, 215, 217, 256–57, 260, 262
Burgess, Ernest Watson, 19
Butler, Judith, 50

Carpenter, Mary Yeo, 120
categorizations
  that Christians have of Hakkas, 77–79, 87–93, 250–59
  that Hakkas in northwestern Taiwan have of being Christian, 179–203: fixity in, 204–6; fluidity in, 206–11

categorizations, cognitive
  accessible, plausible, and easy-to-think nature of, 51–52
  benefits of, 50–51
  reifying nature of, 51
categorizations, one part of the process of identification, 27–32, 36–41, 46–48
Catholics, 83, 86, 162–63, 171, 187, 191, 247
Chang, J. S., 61, 128
Char, Andrew, 56–57
CHEA. *See* Christian Hakka Evangelical Association
Chen Yundong, 55
Chen Zhiping, 55–56
Chen, Carolyn, 146
Chen, Chung-min, 165
China, central plain of, 54–56, 58, 112–13
Ching, Julia, 68, 146
Chiu, Hei-yuan, 66
Christian ancestor practices. *See* ancestor practices: Christians' responses to; ancestor practices: contextualized, Christian
Christian ancestor rituals. *See* ancestor practices: Christians' responses to; ancestor practices: contextualized, Christian
Christian Hakka Evangelical Association, 80–81, 83, 95, 215, 252, 276
Christian Resource Center, 86
Christian worship
  use of Hakka language and music in, 229–31, 241
  of the highest god, 235
  use of incense in, 234–35
  plurality of languages in, 92
Christianity, as categorized by Hakkas in northwestern Taiwan, 179–203
Christians, as categorized by Hakkas in northwestern Taiwan, 179–203
Christians, categorizations of Hakkas by, 77–79, 87–93, 250–59
Christians, challenges to Hakka non-Christian categorizations in northwestern Taiwan of, 217–50

Christians, response in the context of the negative categorizations that Hakka non-Christians in northwestern Taiwan assert about being Christian by, 214–64
Chu, John S. T., 86
Chuang, Ying-chang, 7, 61, 128
church planting, 1–2, 4, 14–17, 79–80, 257, 271
circumstantialism, 23–25
Cohen, Myron L., 56–57
Cohen, Shaye J. D., 27
Constable, Nicole, 11, 54, 218
constructionists, social, 28, 30, 32, 36, 42–44, 48–50, 52. *See also* lens: social constructionist; ethnic identification: constructionism and
contextualized ancestor practices. *See* ancestor practices: contextualized, Christian
contextualized ancestor rituals. *See* ancestor practices: contextualized, Christian
Cornell, Stephen E., 19, 21, 23–24, 29–36, 38, 43–44, 47, 49
Coughlan, Reed M., 22
Council for Hakka Affairs of the Executive Yuan, 72, 85, 118, 166, 259
Cranmer-byng, John, 163
Creswell, John, 97, 99, 105–9
Crotty, Michael, 96
cultural "stuff"
  accessed by Christian Hakkas to construct their response to categorizations, 214–59
  accessed by non-Christian Hakkas to construct categorizations of Christianity, 179–203
  Barth and, 25–27, 46
  of being Hakka in northwestern Taiwan, 110–78
  of being Hakka in Taiwan, 53–75
  categorizations and, xv, 162, 281
  current changing nature of, 178, 268, 279
  difference and, 46, 179, 267
  Jenkins and, 46–47
  Liao and, 93
  researcher's understanding of Hakka, 108

cultural "stuff" *(continued)*
  as a reservoir of symbols and habits, xiv, 13, 53, 75, 110, 178–79, 265, 278
  shaping effect of, xiv, 13, 53, 75, 110, 178, 213, 265, 267, 278
  used in a variety and complexity of ways to construct identity, 94, 277
culture, definition of, 6–7
Cushman, Philip, 49–50

De Vos, George A., 32, 48
Double the Hakka Church in Ten Years Movement, 80–81, 83, 95, 252–53
Durkheim, Emile, 20

easy-to-think nature, 52–53, 260, 271, 273–74
education
  diligence and, 114, 156
  emphasis on, 58, 64, 157, 217
  of girls not as important, 114, 156, 158–59
  influence on attitudes, 65–66, 123, 133, 151, 208, 210
  level of informants, 100–101
Eller, Jack D., 22
English language. *See under* language
essential nature of groups, 43, 51, 93, 178
essentialism, 19
  David C. E. Liao and, 93
ethnic boundaries. *See* boundaries, ethnic; boundary markers
ethnic groups
  Barth's perspective on, 25–26: critique of, 26–28
  definition of, 6–7
  detailed, 25–26
  playing the same game and, 25, 93, 267
  plurality of, 92
  in Taiwan, 9–10
ethnic identification
  Barth and, 25–28
  circumstantialism and, 23–25
  cognitive dimensions of, 50–52
  constructionism and, 28–52
  definition of, 6–7
  fixity and fluidity, double-sided discourse of in, 28–53

ethnic identification *(continued)*
  fixity in, 6, 19–22, 43–52
  fluidity in, 6, 23–43
  influences affecting: active strategizing role of individual or group, 29–32; cognitive dimensions, 50–52; contexts, 36–41; group assets and characteristics, 33–36; the nature of symbols, 42–43; needs, 32, 47–50; primary socialization and habit, 37, 43–47
  primordialism and, 19–23
  saliency in: active strategizing role of individual or group, 29–32; cognitive dimensions of, 50–52; contexts affecting, 36–41; group assets and characteristics affecting, 33–36; nature of symbols affecting, 42–43; other social identities and, 32–33; symbolic ethnicity and, 32; thick/thin distinction, 32; triggers of, 33, 169, 175–76, 178
  something people do, not something people possess, 6–7, 267
ethnic identity. *See* ethnic identification
ethnicity. *See* ethnic identification
ethnography. *See* research project underlying this book
everyone, the phenomenon of
  areas where everyone is Hakka, 161
  disfavor of everyone, 159–60, 202–3, 238–40
  favor of everyone, 155–59, 201–2, 237–38
  following everyone, 154–55, 200–202, 237
  more independent of, 160–61
external definition, 11, 28–30, 37–38, 43
evangelism
  efforts engaging Hakkas should be prioritized, 250, 256
  efforts of George Mackay, 78, 90
  of families, 239
  as God's work, 270
  methods that offend non-Christians, 183, 186
  people groups and, 14–15, 272
  strategy of Apostle Paul in, 92
  tools for use in, 243, 280–81
  understanding of non-Christians important in, 5, 267–70, 276–83

evangelism *(continued)*
  use of Christian ancestor-memorial services, 245
  use of Hakka language in, 229–30, 259
  use of stories from Hakka history in, 92–93, 241–2
  See also Hakkas: Christian ministry to, strategies for; implications of this research project

family
  ancestors and. *See* ancestor practices; filial piety
  as one kind of "us," 147–49
  changes in related to: hierarchy of relationships, 123; secularization, 68; traditions, 145; westernization, 68
  conversion of a whole, 239
  funeral practices and. *See* funerals: family involvement in
  hierarchical nature of, 104, 120–23, 190: changes in, 65–68, 123
  home of the: ancestral home, 64, 82, 165–67, 169, 177, 245; family home, 127, 161; original home, 126
  incense fires and the, 123–32: breaking of the, 191–93
  influences on, 65–68, 123
  male heir, importance of, 124–25
  power of, 202
  respect in, 120–23, 157–58: Christians' lack of, 184, 190–91; Christians showing, 222–25, 249
  responsibilities in: of children to parents, 120; Christians fulfilling, 132, 278; Christians not fulfilling, 196–98; related to funerals, 148, 158; related to giving face, 156–57, 159–60; related to money, 66, 123, 146–47; related to the needs of other members of, 148, 232; to marry appropriate spouse, 137, 149, 161; to pass on traditions, 144–45; to teach Hakka language to children, 137–38; to the deceased, 120, 122, 144, 194–95, 198, 222–23
  roles of women in: daughter, 114, 156, 159–60; wife, 114, 188–89

family *(continued)*
  socialization of children in, 37, 39, 65–66, 143–45, 170, 172, 210
  traditions in the, 143, 146: differences with Christian practices, 194–96
  See also filial piety
Fan Zhengan, 63, 70–71
Fenton, Steve, 20, 32
festivals, 36, 72, 89, 117, 130
filial piety
  ancestors and. *See* ancestor practices
  burning incense and, 132, 195, 224–25
  contesting the traditional meaning of, 224–25
  defined, 120
  expressed in: Christian ways, 223–25, 239, 242, 247, 249; non-traditional ways, 132, 211, 219, 221, 224–25, 239, 242; traditional ways, 126, 158, 201, 211, 241
  funeral as venue for displaying, 158, 201, 242
foreign religion, 162–64, 180–82
  redefining foreign, 240–46
Fricke, Thomas, 65–66, 68
funerals
  practice of: giving monetary gifts at, 147–48, 155; languages used at, 193–94; mourners at, 201; use of incense in, 130, 158, 195–97, 204, 211; use of spirit money at, 158
  baptism and, 222–23
  change and, 145, 157–58, 211
  Christian, 190, 211, 245, 253: of new converts, 250; perceptions of non-Christians regarding, 195–97, 199–202, 204–5, 237–38, 244; use of contextualized rituals in, 220–21, 227, 238; use of the Three-Memorials Ceremony in, 220
  family involvement in: clan-grouping leads in planning, 148; clan members have significant money-making opportunities at, 157, 197, 231; and those who have distanced themselves from "us," 149
  fear of deviance from norms inculcated at, 152

funerals *(continued)*
  function of: caring for deceased through, 198; draw clan-grouping members together, 149; draw participants back to their roots, 161; venue for displaying filial piety, 158, 201, 242
  misfortune and, 199
  positive evaluation of others is sought, 157–59, 238
  renao atmosphere (bustling with noise and excitement) valued at, 158, 201
  urban versus rural settings and, 161
  See also ancestor practices: practice of

Gans, Herbert J., 32, 174
Gao, Ge, 120
Gates, Hill, 62–65
Geertz, Clifford, 21–22
gender
  as a factor affecting attitudes, 97, 123–24, 208
  of informants, 100–101
  female. *See* education: of girls not as important; family: roles of women in; Hakka women; women
  male. *See* family: male heir, importance of
ghost month, 203
Giddens, Anthony, 44, 48
Gil-White, Francisco J., 19–20
gods
  finding powerful, 153, 155, 235–36
  given credit when good things happen, 152
  reciprocal relationship with, 152
  worship of, 60, 144: change in general attitudes toward, 68, 153–55; and children, 144; and Christianity, 234–36, 246; deeply rooted, 144; on festival days, 195; on first and fifteenth of every month, 183–84; at Lunar New Year, 195; sacrifices used in, 131, 155; daily nature of, 123, 144; use of incense in, 144
  worshiped: Guangong, 144, 152; Guanyin, 144, 152; heaven god (Tiangong), 144, 152, 241, 249; land god (*tudigong*), 131, 143–44, 152; Mazu, 152; those of the ancestors, 143;
  See also idols

Goffman, Erving, 30
graves. *See* mausoleums, common
groups, evangelism of, 89
Gudykunst, William B., 120

habits, 43–47
  characteristics of: change slowly, 146; not taught, 124, 144; passed down from generation to generation, 164; repetition creates, 144
  cultural "stuff" and, 110, 178
  provide sense of constancy and predictability, 48–49
habitus, 44–46
Hakka Bible, 3, 95, 215, 242
Hakka choir, 95, 215
Hakka Christian leaders in Taiwan
  opinions of in Liao's survey, 78–79
Hakka Christians in northwestern Taiwan
  challenges to the negative categorizations of non-Christians of, 219–50, 260–61
  construct Hakka in order to justify prioritizing ministry to Hakkas, 250–59, 261–62
  implications of the research project underlying this book for, 266–83
  importance of Hakka in ministries varies, 214–17, 260
Hakka Christians in Taiwan
  challenged to pray for ministries to Hakkas 93
  indifferent toward evangelizing Hakkas, 91–92
  migrating out of Hakka areas, 91
  number of, 81–87
  use of Hoklo Bibles and hymnbooks, 88
Hakka churches in Taiwan
  financial weakness of, 91
  manpower shortages of, 79, 87
  methods used to count, 80–81, 85
  number of, 79–80
  planted by the PCT. *See* Presbyterian Church in Taiwan: Hakkas and the
  rural location of, 217
  use of the Hoklo language in, 88, 255
Hakka ethnic identity in Taiwan
  being Hakka in northwestern Taiwan and, 169–76
  desire to preserve, 87, 89, 175

Hakka ethnic identity in Taiwan *(continued)*
  the Hakka ethnic movement and, 69–72
  multiculturalism and, 72–75
Hakka history. *See* history related to Hakkas
Hakka language. *See under* language
Hakka Mission School, 95. *See also* Hakka Mission Seminary
Hakka Mission Seminary, 81, 83, 95, 215, 252, 254, 256–57, 276
Hakka mountain songs. *See under* music
Hakka music. *See under* music
Hakka non-Christians' in northwestern Taiwan
  negative categorizations of being Christian, 179–203
  negative categorizations of being Christian, challenged by Christians, 217–50
  negative categorizations of being Christian, fixity and fluidity in, 203–11
Hakka women, 57–58, 241. *See also* education: of girls not as important; family: roles of women in; gender
Hakkas
  assimilation of, 63, 69, 90, 167, 169
  burial practices of, 128
  categorizations others have of, 58, 77–79, 87–89, 114–15
  change and, 93, 145–46, 195, 205, 210, 212, 225, 228
  Christian ministry to, implications of this research project on. *See* implications of this research project
  Christian ministry to, strategies for: articulated by Christian Hakkas in northwestern Taiwan, 214–64; and the Homogeneous Unit Principle, 14–17; and the lens of negotiating identity, 273–78; evidenced in the author's use of the lens of people groups in Taiwan, 1–5; seen in past ministry to Hakkas in Taiwan, 75–79, 94–95; suggested by David C. E. Liao, 87–89; suggested by Zeng, Qiu, Wen, and Wu, 90–93
  difficulty of Christian ministry to, 78–79. *See also* hard ground

310 Index

Hakkas *(continued)*
  good feelings for things Hakka and, 171–72, 178
  as Han Chinese, 9–11, 54–59, 91, 112–13
  handling problems and: become more diligent in relationships with gods and ancestors, 150–51, 153; hide them, 156–57; turn to "us" for help, 147–48, 160, 223
  have highest percentage of Han Chinese Christians, 91
  hiding their Hakka identity, 4, 69, 167, 173–74
  history of. *See* history related to Hakkas
  marriage of non-Hakkas and, 142, 171
  neglect of, 87–94
  passing to another ethnic group, 168–69, 173–74
  prejudice against, 57–58, 60–61, 114–16, 118, 140, 173: lower social class than Mainlanders, 64
  solidarity of, 58–59, 61, 89, 115, 118–19, 128, 176
  superiority and, 58, 119, 163, 175
  Taiwan government policies regarding, 62–63, 72–73, 118, 136–37, 140, 142, 259. *See also* Council for Hakka Affairs of the Executive Yuan
  Taiwan politics and, 70–75, 142, 168
  Taiwan residents with ancestral home in Guangdong Province, 10, 60, 82
  yiminye worship and, 71
  See also being Hakka in northwestern Taiwan; being Hakka in Taiwan; stiff-necked Hakka spirit
Hale, Henry E., 48, 51–52, 260
Handelman, Don, 26
hard ground, 78, 90–91, 251, 253–54, 261, 264, 283
Hartmann, Douglas, 19, 21, 23–24, 29–36, 38, 43–44, 47, 49
heart
  attitude of is most important, 129, 131–32, 164, 186, 207, 210
  for Hakka ministry. *See* burden for Hakka ministry
  hard, 254
heart language, 3–4

heaven god (Tiangong). *See* gods: worshiped
hell, 152
hidden peoples, 15
history related to Hakkas
  conflicts between Hakkas and: Hoklos, 60–61, 90; Puntis, 57–59, 113
  Hakka heartland, 55–56
  historical development of being Hakka for Hakkas in Taiwan, 54–65
  an important symbol in the Hakka ethnic movement, 71
  key to the Hakka identity, 54
  migration of Hakkas from rural to urban areas in Taiwan, 66–67
  migration of Hakkas to Taiwan, 59–60, 71, 113
  migrations of Hakkas in mainland China, 54–55, 113, 119
  self-identifications of Hakkas in, 58–59
  stories from used in evangelism, 92–93, 241–42
HMS. *See* Hakka Mission Seminary
Ho, David Y. F., 120
Hogg, Michael A., 51
Hoklo language. *See under* languages
Hoklos
  conflicts with Hakkas and, 60–61, 90
  perceived as a lower social class than Mainlanders, 64
  Taiwan residents with an ancestral home in Fujian Province, 9, 59, 82
Homogeneous Unit Principle
  critiques of, 15–17
  David C. E. Liao and, 93
  described, 14–15
  examples of use of, 1–5, 93–94
  influence on missiology, 15
  people group lens and. *See* lens: of people group
  response of missiologists to, 18
Hsiau, A-chin, 70, 76
Hsu, Francis L. K., 120
Huang Shuanfan, 63, 74
Huang, Shu-min, 165
hungry ghosts, 149, 155, 203
Hutchinson, John, 26
Hwang, Kwang-kuo, 108, 111, 146

identification, 38
identity
  characteristics of: constructed actively, 29–32; fixity in, 43–52; fluidity in, 29–4; thick-thin, 32–36
  confusion about, 174–75
  definition of, 6
  pre-existing, 33
  seeking a positive, 30–31
  social types of: future-oriented, 32; past-oriented, 32; present-oriented, 32
idols, 79. *See also* gods
implications of this research project
  for Christian workers in various contexts, 267–78: related to use of the people group perspective, 270–78
  for those working among the Hakkas of northwestern Taiwan: related to the actions of Hakka Christians, 283; related to contesting the categorizations of Hakka non-Christians, 281–83; related to the cultural "stuff" of being Hakka, 278–81
incarnation, principle of, 90
incense fires, 123–32
  breaking of, 191–93
  See also ancestor practices; incense, use of
incense, use of
  Catholics and, 247
  change in attitudes toward, 193, 207–11: refusal is acceptable, 207–8
  Christian alternatives to, 211, 221, 223–25, 227
  Christians reject, 189, 192–93, 195, 197, 205
  convenient, 188
  deep needs and, 205
  functions of: carry prayers to gods and ancestors, 125–26; connect one with others in one's clan, 127; enable appropriate engagement of gods and ancestors, 126; express filial piety, 132, 195, 224–25; express gratefulness to ancestors, 150; express gratefulness to gods, 152, 199; provide for the welfare of ancestors, 158
  habit and, 195
  hard to give up, 196, 198, 211
  in marriage ceremony, 201

incense, use of *(continued)*
  meanings attached to vary, 211
  pollution and, 130
  something all Chinese do, 196
  those who do not embrace: are not "us," 162, 197, 199; reject their ancestors, 132, 207
  See also ancestor practices: practice of; funerals: practice of
internal definition, 27, 29–30, 37–38, 43
interview
  questions, 104–5, 287–90
  sample, 99–104
Isaacs, Harold R., 21

Japanese, 121, 243
  language. *See under* language
  music. *See under* music
  rule of Taiwan, 54, 62, 64, 75–76, 117
  treatment of Christians, 75–76
Jenkins, Richard, 6, 24, 26–32, 37–39, 42–48, 50
Johnstone, Patrick, 81

Kellner, Hansfried, 11
KMT, 62, 64, 68–69, 72. *See also* Nationalists, Chinese
Knapp, Ronald G., 60
Kok, Jan, 124

Lakoff, George, 50
Lamley, Harry J., 60–61
language
  aboriginal, 62, 68, 76
  of the ancestors, 132–43
  as a boundary marker, 166–69
  English and other international languages: pressure to learn to speak, 63, 139
  ethnicity in Taiwan and, 71, 167–68
  geographical areas of Taiwan and, 167–69
  habits and change, 141–42
  Hakka: age and, 132, 136, 141–42; benefits of decrease in use of, 138–39; children and, 63, 139–43, 161, 175, 177; Christians' use of, 76–77, 92, 228–31; churches' use of, 76–77; concerns regarding, 69, 136–39, 142; decline in use of, reasons behind, 139–42;

language *(continued)*
  demands related to, 69–70, 135–38; discrimination and, 139–40; education and, 132–33, 140–43; good feelings and, 2, 134–35, 138–39, 170–72, 193, 229, 279; Hakka culture and, 138–39; Hakka ethnic movement and, 70–72; higher levels of competence in, 133, 136, 141; identity and, 133; incompetence of many Hakkas in, 135–36, 168, 173; limitations of, 135, 138, 141, 170; Mandarin and, 139; marriage and, 139, 142; missionaries and, 76–77, 87, 229–30; mother-tongue classes and, 72, 140, 142–43; preservation of, 69–72, 133, 135–36, 140–43; private use of, 133, 136, 138, 142; restrictions and, 62, 68; stigma and, 62
  Hoklo: churches and, 75–77, 257; Hakka accent in speaking, 167; mother-tongue classes and, 140; Mainlanders and, 69, 76–77; as the national language in Taiwan, 69, 176, 257; non-speakers and, 176; restrictions and, 62, 68, 76; stigma and, 62; as Taiwanese, 176
  Japanese, 62, 76, 135–36
  Mandarin: churches and, 75–77; as a common language, 74, 139, 142; considered high class, 133; education and, 74, 140; Hakkas' habit of speaking, 137, 141–42, 217; as the national language in Taiwan, 2, 62, 74, 176; as a neutral language, 74; Hakka accent in speaking, 167, 174; use of Chinese characters habitually connected with, 106
  mother tongues, 21, 72, 139–40, 142, 259
  use of language that brings most benefit in a particular context, 69, 133, 142, 259
Lecompte, Margaret D., 106–7, 266
Lee, Fong-mao, 68
lens
  of negotiating identity, 273–78: helpfulness for Christian workers, 274–78

lens *(continued)*
  of people group, xiii, xiv–xv, 266, 270–73: attractiveness of use in ministry, 271; author's use of in a missionary ministry in Taiwan, 1–5; rooted in homogeneous unit principle, 13, 15; weakness of use in ministry, 272–73
  social constructionist, xiii–xiv, 5, 93, 109, 267, 285
Leong, Sow-theng, 10, 54–60
Levine, Hal B., 51
Li Zhenglong, 81
Li, Yih-yuan, 60, 166
Liao, Chao-chih, 69, 72
Liao, David C. E., 2, 57, 77–85, 87–89, 93–94, 261, 280
Lin, Hui-sheng, 65, 67
Lin, Nan, 146
Liu, Li, 36
Lofland, John, 107
Lofland, Lyn H., 107
Luckmann, Thomas, 44
Luo Xianglin, 54–56, 59

MacKay, George, 78–79, 90, 108, 255–56, 258, 261–62
Mainlanders, 10
  effect of intermarriage with other ethnics in Taiwan, 74
  Hakkas presenting themselves as, 63–64, 173, 175
  perceived to be foreign, 64–65
  perceived to be of a higher social class, 64
  Taiwanese/Mainlander distinction and the Hoklo/Hakka distinction, 64–65
Mandarin. *See under* language
Mandryk, Jason, 1, 5, 81, 271
marriage, 37
  choice of spouse limited to a Hakka, 137–38, 161
  marital status of informants, 100–101
martial law, 68
Martin, Howard J., 64–65, 69–71, 122, 128
mausoleums, common, 122, 126, 128, 148, 150, 192
  Christians and, 192, 197, 221, 224, 232
May, Stephen, 45
Mazu. *See under* gods

McClintock, Wayne, 16–17
McGavran, Donald A., 14–18, 88, 178
McKay, James, 22
Merriam, Sharan B., 96–97, 99–100
Michael, Franz H., 75
migration of Hakkas. *See* history related to Hakkas
ministry strategies. *See* Hakkas: Christian ministry to, strategies for; implications of this research project
missionaries
  Hakka-speaking, 76–77, 87, 229–30
  neglect of Hakkas and, 77, 87
  number working with: Aborigines, 77; Hoklos, 75–77; Mainlanders, 76–77; Hakkas, 77
modernization, 65–68
music
  aboriginal, 117
  good feelings for certain kinds of, 117, 135
  Hakka, 3, 172–73, 215, 217, 241–42, 258, 280
  Hakka Christians, of: hymns, 215; new songs, 241
  Hakka mountain songs, 115–18, 176: strong feelings for, 117; connected with low-class things, 118
  Hakka music used to make Christianity feel less foreign, 241
  Hakkas also enjoy non-Hakka kinds of, 117
  Hoklo music, 75, 88, 135
  Japanese music, 117, 135
  Western, 163

Nagata, Judith, 42
Nagel, Joane, 26–28
National Hakka Population Basic Data Survey, 10, 82, 100, 166
national language. *See under* language: Hoklo; language: Mandarin
Nationalists, Chinese, 54, 62–64, 76 . *See also* KMT
needs, deep human, 47–50
negotiating identity
  definition of, 6
  lens of. *See under* lens
  See also ethnic identification

Padilla, C. Rene, 16

Pang, Keng-fong, 11, 111
Park, Robert Ezra, 19
Patterson, Orlando, 23–24, 56, 174
PCT. *See* Presbyterian Church in Taiwan
people group
  definition of, 271
  lens/perspective of. *See under* lens
Perspectives on the World Christian Movement course, 1
Phinney, Jean S., 48
power, social
  Christian ministry and, 269
  desire to limit, 57
  Mainlanders have disproportionate amount of, 10
  of person categorizing related to strength of their categorizations, 28, 31, 38, 40–41, 160, 202–3, 239
practices, ancestor. *See* ancestor practices
predestined affinity, 164, 183
Presbyterian Church in Taiwan
  churches in the, 79–80
  Hakkas and the: church-planting efforts among Hakkas, 79–80; Hakka presbytery, 90–91, 95, 257; lack of coordinated outreach among Hakkas, 87, 92; neglect of Hakkas, 88, 262; survey regarding ministry to Hakkas, responses of pastors, 78–79
  Hoklo language, use of in the, 75–76, 256–57
  influence of George MacKay on the, 78, 90, 256, 262
  integration policy of the, 88
  one-language policy of the, 88
  Three-Memorials Ceremony and the, 222
presentation
  of the gospel, 14, 242, 269, 277–79
  of self, 30, 99, 112
Priest, Robert J., 18, 33, 171, 191, 197
primordialism, 19–23
Punti (*bendiren*)
  relationship with Hakkas, 57–59

Qiu Changtai, 72–73
Qiu Shanxiung, 78, 80–81, 87, 89–91, 93–95

Raber, Dorothy A., 81

research project underlying this book
  assumptions of, 11
  concern of, 5
  context surrounding, 9–11
  data analysis process used in, 105–9
  definitions used in, 6–7
  delimitations of, 12
  findings of, 265–66
  implications of. *See* implications of this research project
  interview questions used, 104–5, 287–90
  interview sample of, 99–104
  limitations of, 99
  problem statement of, 11
  procedures used, 85–87, 99–109
  questions addressed, 4, 12
  recommendations for further research of, 284–85
  significance of, 5
  translation issues affecting important words in, 7–8
researcher
  impact on research study of, 97–99, 111–12, 179–80
  personal experience using people group lens of, 1–5
  presentation of self and, 104
residence
  as a factor affecting attitudes, 161, 169, 175, 193–94, 208–10, 239
  of informants, 100–101
rituals, ancestor. *See* ancestor practices
Rin, Hsien, 42–43
Romanucci-Ross, Lola, 48
Roosens, Eugeen, 24–25, 27, 47–48
Rosch, Eleanor, 51
Rubinstein, Murray A., 76

sacrifices
  used in ancestor practices. *See* ancestor practices: practice of
  used in worship of the gods. *See under* gods: worship of
saliency in ethnic identity. *See under* ethnic identification: saliency in
Schensul, Jean J., 100, 106–7, 266
Schensul, Stephen L., 100
Schermerhorn, R. A., 6
secularization, 68
Seidman, Irving, 106
self-ascription, 46
self-identification, 29, 31, 39, 41

separate approach, 93
She people/group, 56–57
Shepherd, John R., 9, 60–61
Simpson, Andrew, 62, 64, 69, 72, 74
Smith, Anthony D., 26–27
Smith, David, 15–16
social constructionist lens. *See under* lens
social science, xiii–xiv, 5, 13, 16
socialization
  primary, 6, 31, 37, 43–45, 208
  secondary, 39
solidarity
  during the Qing Dynasty, 61
  facilitated by the joint burial practices of Hakkas, 128
spirit money, use of
  in ancestor practices. *See* ancestor practices: practice of
  changes in attitudes toward, 121, 131–32
  at funerals, 158
  pollution and, 130, 210, 227, 268
  providing for the needs of the deceased and, 158, 198
  reciprocal nature of, 152
  unthinking nature of, 132
Spradley, James P., 104–7
statistics related to Christianity
  Allen J. Swanson, 83–84
  Christian Resource Center, 86
  David C. E. Liao, 81–83
  difficulty in obtaining accurate figures, 82–83, 87
  Han Chinese Christians, highest percentage are Hakka, 91
  Sabah, number of Hakka Christians in, 91
  Taiwan: number of Hakka Christians in, 81–87; number of Hakka churches in, 79–80
  Taiwan Social Change Survey, 85–87
  Xia Zhongjian, 85
  0.3% of Hakkas in Taiwan are Christian, 81–83
  0.4% of Hakkas in Taiwan are Christian, 83
stiff-necked Hakka spirit, 91, 115, 187–88, 253–55
Swanson, Allen J., 76–78, 81, 83–85, 252
symbols
  accessed by Hakkas in northwestern Taiwan: related to Christianity,

symbols *(continued)*
  162–64; related to everyone, 154–61; related to family, 120–46; related to Hakka history, 112–20; related to reciprocal relationships, 146–54
  accessed by non-Christian Hakkas in northwestern Taiwan to categorize being Christian: related to Christianity, 180–86; related to everyone, 199–203; related to family, 189–96; related to Hakka history, 186–89; related to reciprocal relationships, 196–99
  accessed by Hakka Christians as they respond in the context of the negative categorizations that non-Christian Hakkas in northwestern Taiwan assert about being Christian: related to Christianity, 240–50; related to everyone, 236–40; related to family, 219–31; related to prioritizing ministry to Hakkas, 250–59; related to reciprocal relationships, 231–36
  fixity of often imagined, 42–43
  nature of, 42–43
  nominal-virtual distinction of, 42
  fluidity of meanings of, 42

Taiwan
  economic change in, 67
  education in, 65–66
  Japanese rule of, 62, 64, 75–76
  KMT rule of, 62–64, 76
  language use in, 68–69
  modernization and, 65–68
  multiculturalism and, 72–75
  present situation of, 9
  secularization and, 68
  transitions and, 38
Taiwan Social Change Survey, 85–87, 108, 252, 284
Tajfel, Henri, 51
talking, as a means of showing disfavor, 38, 155, 159–60, 202–3
tensions
  between being Hakka and being Christian: described, 265–66; three steps used to explore, 110, 179, 214
  definition of, 7
Thomas Barclay, 77, 91

Thompson, Laurence G., 7, 120, 124, 129
Thornton, Arland, 65–68
Three-Memorials Ceremony, 220–22, 242, 281, 291–92
  concerns of some Christians with, 220
  involving non-Christians in, 238, 245–46
  promoting the use of, 222
  use in funerals, 220
  use in Tomb Sweeping, 221
Ting-Toomey, Stella, 30, 49
tithing, 189
Tong, Hollington Kong, 75, 77, 218
Tönnies, Ferdinand, 20
traditions
  changes in, 145–46
  habitual nature of, 144–45
  as institutionalized habit, 44
  passed down from generation to generation, 143–44
Tsao, Feng-fu, 63
TSCS. *See* Taiwan Social Change Survey
Tse, John Kwock-ping, 69, 72, 74
Turner, John, 51

unfilial, being
  brings the disfavor of everyone, 201–3
  challenging accusations of, 221–25, 230, 248, 278
  fluidity regarding the definition of unfilial, 207–8
  in treatment of ancestors, 198–99
unity without ethnic distinctions, 88
unreached people group
  definition of, 1
  rooted in the homogeneous unit principle, 15
us, 147–49, 177, 196–99, 212, 231–32, 258, 267

van den Berghe, Pierre L., 20, 22
veneration of ancestors. *See* ancestor practices
Vermeer, Edward B., 9

Wagner, C. Peter, 15
waishengren, 10, 65. *See also* Mainlander
Wang Dong, 55
Wang Fuchang, 65
Wang, Cecil Kwei-heng, 8
Wang, L. Ling-chi, 165

Wang, Li-jung, 72–75
Wang, Q. Edward, 165–66
Wang, Sping, 124
Weber, Max, 23
weddings
　ancestors and, 201, 226
　ceremonies, change in, 121–22, 145, 220
　Christian, 201, 244
　clan leaders' role in planning, 145, 158
　gift giving at, 147
　participation of relatives in, 148–49
Wen Yongsheng, 77–78, 80–81, 87, 89–91, 93–95, 220, 254, 258
West, the, 162, 177, 182
　influence of, 67–68
　people enamored with, 182
　See also Western; Westerners
Western
　God, 241
　missionaries, 182
　music, 241, 259
　products widely used in Taiwan, 243
　redefining this word, 243
　religion, 181–82, 187, 208, 243. *See also* foreign religion
　worldview, 99
　See also West, the; Westerners
Westerners
　Chinese, mistreatment of by, 182
　Christianity is connected with, 206, 211, 243. *See also* foreign religion
　Hakka language use and, 3, 98
　See also West, the; Western; Westerners
Wilson, Robert Scott, 73
women
　achieving higher social status brings more independence, 210
　Hakka. *See* Hakka women
　education of, 156, 210
　expected to learn the language of their husbands, 133, 136, 168
　See also education: of girls not as important; family: roles of women in; gender

World Hakka Evangelical Association, 94
worldview
　Christian, 99
　Western, 99
　of the younger generation, 131
worship
　definition of, 8
　of ancestors. *See* ancestor practices
　Christian. *See* Christian worship
　of Guangong. *See under* gods: worshiped
　of Guanyin. *See under* gods: worshiped
　of the heaven god (Tiangong). *See under* gods: worshiped
　of hungry ghosts. *See* hungry ghosts
　of idols. *See* idols
　of land god (*tudigong*). *See under* gods: worshiped
　of Mazu. *See under* gods: worshiped
　translation issues regarding related English and Chinese words, 7–8
　of *yiminye*. See *yiminye*
Wu Ruicheng, 78, 80–81, 87, 89–91, 93–95
Wu Xueming, 60

Xia Zhongjian, 78, 80–81, 85, 252
Xu Wenxiong, 58–60

Yang Changzhen, 60
Yang, Kuo-shu, 108, 111
Yang, Li-shou, 65–68
Yang, Philip Q., 21–22
Yang, Wenshan, 82, 85–86
yiminye, 71, 152

Zelinsky, Wilbur, 49
Zeng Zhengzhong, 78, 80–81, 87, 89–95
Zheng Lianming, 78

www.ingramcontent.com/pod-product-compliance
Lightning Source LLC
Chambersburg PA
CBHW052147300426
44115CB00011B/1550